THE MASK OF SANITY

THE MASK OF SANITY

HERVEY CLECKLEY, M.D.

Clinical Professor of Psychiatry, Emeritus,
Medical College of Georgia, Augusta, Ga.;
author of *The Caricature of Love* and of
The Three Faces of Eve
(with Corbett H. Thigpen)

A PLUME BOOK
NEW AMERICAN LIBRARY
MOSBY
TIMES MIRROR
NEW YORK AND SCARBOROUGH, ONTARIO

Publisher: Thomas A. Manning
Assistant editor: Nancy L. Mullins
Production: Barbara Merritt

MOSBY MEDICAL LIBRARY

The ideas, procedures, and suggestions contained in this book are not intended as a substitute for consulting with your physician. All matters regarding your health require medical supervision.

This is a revised edition of a book published by The C.V. Mosby Company under the same title

NAL books are available at quantity discounts when used to promote products or services. For information please write to Premium Marketing Division, The New American Library, Inc. 1633 Broadway, New York, New York 10019.

PLUME TRADEMARK REG. U.S. PAT. OFF. AND FOREIGN COUNTRIES
REGISTERED TRADEMARK—MARCA REGISTRADA
HECHO EN FORGE VILLAGE, MASS., U.S.A.

SIGNET, SIGNET CLASSICS, MENTOR, PLUME, MERIDIAN and NAL BOOKS are published by The New American Library, Inc., 1633 Broadway, New York, New York 10019, in Canada, by The New American Library of Canada, Limited, 81 Mack Avenue, Scarborough, Ontario M1L 1M8

Library of Congress Cataloging in Publication Data

Cleckley, Hervey Milton, 1903-
The mask of sanity.
"A Plume book."
1. Sociopathic personality. I. Title.
RC555.C5 1982 616.85'82 82-2124
ISBN 0-452-25341-1 AACR2

5 6 7 8 9 02/A/235
Printed in the United States of America

To L. M. C.

From chaos shaped, the Bios grows. In bone
And viscus broods the Id. And who can say
Whence Eros comes? Or chart his troubled way?
Nor bearded sage, nor science, yet has shown
How truth or love, when met, is straightly known;
Some phrases singing in our dust today
Have taunted logic through man's Odyssey:
Yet, strangely, man sometimes will find his own.
And even man has felt the arcane flow
Whence brims unchanged the very Attic wine,
Where lives that mute and death eclipsing glow
That held the Lacedaemonian battle line:
And this, I think, may make what man is choose
The doom of joy he knows he can but lose.

Preface

The first edition of this book was based primarily on experience with adult male psychopaths hospitalized in a closed institution. Though a great many other psychopaths had come to my attention, most of the patients who were observed over years and from whom emerged the basic concepts were from this group. During the following years a much more diverse group became available. Female patients, adolescents, people who had never been admitted to a psychiatric hospital, all in large numbers, became available for study and afforded an opportunity to observe the disorder in a very wide range of variety and of degree.

This additional clinical experience, helpful comment in the reviews of the first edition, enlightening discussion with colleagues, and an improved acquaintance with the literature all contributed to modify concepts.

Since the first edition of this book revisions of the nomenclature have been made by the American Psychiatric Association. Like most psychiatrists I continue to think of the people who are the subject of this book as *psychopaths* and will most often refer to them by this familiar term. *Sociopath* and *antisocial personality* will sometimes appear, used as a synonym to designate patients with this specific pattern of disorder.

Although I spared no effort to make it plain that I did not have an effective therapy to offer, the earlier editions of this book led to contact with psychopaths of every type and from almost every section of the United States and Canada. Interest in the problem was almost never manifested by the patients themselves. The interest was desperate, however, among families, parents, wives, husbands, brothers, who had struggled long and helplessly with a major disaster for which they found not only no cure and no social, medical, or legal facility for handling, but also no full or frank recognition that a reality so obvious existed.

Telephone calls from Chicago, Denver, Boston, and The West Indies and letters from Miami and Vancouver have convinced me that the psychopath is no rarity in any North American community but that his problem is, by what seems to be an almost universal conspiracy of evasion, ignored by those therapeutic forces in the human group which, reacting to what is biologically or socially morbid, have sensibly provided courts, operating rooms, tuberculosis sanatoriums, prisons, fire departments, psychiatric hospitals, police forces, and homes for the orphaned, the ill, the psychotic, and the infirm. The measures taken by the community to deal with illness, crime, failure, contagion are, one might say, often far from perfect. It cannot, however, be said, except about the problems of the psychopath, that no measure at all is taken, that nothing exists specifically designed to meet a major and obvious pathologic situation. Communications from physicians, sociologists, psychologists, students, and others from Europe, some from countries behind the Iron Curtain, and also from India, Australia, and other distant parts of the world continue to arrive. One interesting, stimulating, and deeply appreciated comment came from a physician stationed in Antarctica. These communications convince me that the psychopath presents an important and challenging enigma for which no adequate solution has yet been found.

Although still in the unspectacular and perforce modest position of one who can offer neither a cure nor a well-established explanation, I am encouraged by ever-increasing evidence that few medical or social problems have ever so richly deserved and urgently demanded a hearing. It is still my conviction that this particular problem, in a practical sense, has had no hearing.

Although I still have no effective treatment to offer for the psychopath, it has encouraged me to feel that this book has, perhaps, served a useful purpose in making clearer to the families of these patients the grave problems with which they must deal. Apparently many psychiatrists, and many other physicians, have over the years advised relatives of psychopaths to read *The Mask of Sanity.* The response of these relatives has given me deep satisfaction and has helped me to feel that efforts to pursue this study are not in vain. Although we may still be far from the goal of offering a cure, perhaps something has already been done to focus general interest on the problem and to promote awareness of its tremendous importance. This must be accomplished, I believe, before any organized attempt can be made by society to deal adequately, or even cogently, with the psychopath. Even now, forty-one years after the first edition of this book was published, I often receive several letters a week from wives, parents, brothers, or other kinsmen of psychopaths. Most of these letters help me to feel that this book has at least enabled many people to see more clearly and realistically the nature of the problem with which they have had to deal blindly and in a strange and almost unique confusion. These correspondents often tell me that this book has been of great value in helping them understand better the disorder of a husband, wife, child, or sibling and plan more realistically and effectively to deal with situations heretofore entirely unpredictable and incomprehensible. I am most grateful for these generous and gracious expressions of approval.

It is a privilege to thank friends, colleagues, and others who have given me help and encouragement in formulating my concepts and in preparing material for this book.

It could not have been written without the constant assistance of my wife, Louise Cleckley, who devoted many months of her time over the years not only to the routine of typing and proofreading but to the mutual effort of shaping the essential concepts to be presented into articulate form. Her notable contributions included stimulus, encouragement, and a wisely critical presence during the conative and affective fluctuations apparently inescapable in such a task. They were given in such quality as to be acknowledged as genuine psychotherapy.

Dr. Corbett H. Thigpen, my medical associate of many years, has played a major part in the development and the revision of this work. His observations and his thought, available to me during innumerable pleasant and stimulating hours of discussion, have assisted and profoundly influenced my own conclusions. Without his limitless generosity in relieving me over long periods of heavy and urgent responsibilities in teaching and in clinical activity, it would have been impossible for this volume to be written. My debt to him in this, and my gratitude, I can acknowledge but cannot fittingly express.

For similar assistance I am also grateful to my other medical colleagues, Dr. B. F. Moss,

Dr. Jere Chambers, and Dr. Seaborn S. McGarity, Jr. Aid in clarifying several important points was given me also by John Creson and by Wayne Thigpen. In the preparation of the fourth edition Cornelia C. Fulghum's generous and effective efforts were indispensable. It is a pleasure also to express appreciation to Marilyn York, Linda Tingle, Patricia Lilly, and Patricia Satcher, secretaries who very kindly and effectively aided me on many occasions, and to my daughter, Mary Cleckley Creson, whose support has been constant and of inestimable value.

The long-delayed appearance of this edition of *The Mask of Sanity* would not have been possible except for the generous and superb contribution of Louise Thigpen. Her efforts in assisting me to organize scattered items of material, to formulate and present more effectively concepts still unclear in the script, will be held in memory by me, with admiration and with deep gratitude. Her work in typing difficult copy against deadlines and her sagacity in steering me clear of equivocations, and of blunders under pressure, were extraordinary and indeed beyond the call of duty. Her part in this revision of *The Mask of Sanity* I acknowledge and value as a genuine and gracious collaboration.

Hervey Cleckley

Introduction

The present volume grew out of an old conviction which increased during several years while I sat at staff meetings in a large neuropsychiatric hospital. Many hundreds of such cases as those presented here were studied and discussed. The diversity of opinion among different psychiatrists concerning the status of these patients never grew less. Little agreement was found as to what was actually the matter with them. No satisfactory means of dealing with them was presented by any psychiatric authority, and meanwhile their status in the eyes of the law usually made it impossible to treat them at all. They continued, however, to constitute a most grave and a constant problem to the hospital and to the community.

On assuming full-time teaching duties at the University of Georgia School of Medicine, I found these patients similarly prevalent in the wards of the general hospital, in the outpatient neuropsychiatric clinic, and in consultation work with the various practitioners of the community and with the hospital staff. The overwhelming difficulty of finding facilities for their treatment has been no less urgent than the yet unanswered question of what measures to use in treatment. How to inform their relatives, the courts which handle them, the physicians who try to treat them, of the nature of their disorder has been no small problem. No definite or consistent attitude on the part of psychiatric authorities could be adduced in explanation; no useful legal precedent at all could be invoked, and no institutions found in which help might be sought by the community.

Contents

section one · Introduction

chapter 1 · An outline of the problem

SANITY—A PROTEAN CONCEPT

A millionaire notable for his eccentricity had an older and better-balanced brother who, on numerous fitting occasions, exercised strong persuasion to bring him under psychiatric care. On receiving word that this wiser brother had been deserted immediately after the nuptial night by a famous lady of the theatre (on whom he had just settled a large fortune) and that the bride, furthermore, had, during the brief pseudoconnubial episode, remained stubbornly encased in tights, the younger hastened to dispatch this succinct and unanswerable telegram:

WHO'S LOONEY NOW?

This, at any rate, is the story. I do not offer to answer for its authenticity. It may, however, be taken not precisely as an example but at least as a somewhat flippant and arresting commentary on the confusion that still exists concerning *sanity.* Although most patients suffering from one of the classified types of mental disorder are promptly recognized by the psychiatrist, many of them being even to the layman plainly deranged, there remains a large body of people who, everyone will admit, are by no means adapted for normal life in the community and who, yet, have no official standing in the ranks of the insane. The word *insane,* of course, is not a medical term. It is employed here because to many people it conveys a more practical meaning than the medical term *psychotic.* Although the medical term with its greater vagueness presents a fairer idea of the present conception of severe mental disorder, the legal term better implies the criteria by which the personalities under discussion are judged in the courts.

Many of these people, legally judged as competent, are more dangerous to themselves and to others than are some patients whose psychiatric disability will necessitate their spending their entire lives in the state hospital. Though certified automatically as *sane* by the verbal definitions of law and of medicine, their behavior demonstrates an irrationality and incompetence that are gross and obvious.

Material to distinguish from our subject

These people to whom I mean to call specific attention are not the borderline cases in whom the characteristics of some familiar mental disorder are only partially developed and the picture as a whole is still questionable. Many such cases exist, of course, and they are sometimes puzzling even to the experienced psychiatrist. Certain people, as everyone knows, may for many years show to a certain degree the reactions of schizophrenia (dementia praecox) of manic-depressive psychosis, or a paranoia without being sufficiently disabled or so generally irrational as to be recognized as psychotic. Many patients suffering from incipient disorders of this sort or from dementia paralytica, cerebral arteriosclerosis, and other organic conditions pass through a preliminary phase during which their thought and behavior are to a certain degree characteristic of the psychosis, while for the time being they remain able to function satisfactorily in the community.

Some people in the early stage of these familiar clinical disorders behave, on the whole, with what is regarded as mental competency, while showing, from time to time, symptoms typical of the psychosis toward which they are progressing. After the disability has at last become openly manifest, enough episodes of deviated conduct can often be noted in retrospect to make the observer wonder why the subject was not long ago recognized as psychotic. It would, however, sometimes be not only difficult but unfair to pronounce a person totally disabled while most of his conduct remains acceptable. Do we not, as a matter of fact, have to admit that all of us behave at times with something short of complete rationality and good judgment?

• • •

I recall a highly respected businessman who, after years of outstanding commercial success, began to send telegrams to the White House ordering the President to dispatch the Atlantic Fleet to Madagascar and to execute Roman Catholics. There was at this time no question, of course, about his disability. A careful study revealed that for several years he had occasionally made fantastic statements, displayed extraordinary behavior (for instance, once putting the lighted end of a cigar to his stenographer's neck by way of greeting), and squandered thousands of dollars buying up stamp collections, worthless atticfuls of old furniture, and sets of encyclopedias by the dozen. None of these purchases had he put to any particular use. When finally discovered to be incompetent from illness, an investigation of his status showed that he had thrown away the better part of a million dollars. For months he had been maintaining 138 bird dogs scattered over the countryside, forty-two horses, and fourteen women, to none of whom he resorted for the several types of pleasure in which such dependents sometimes play a part.

Aside from persons in the early stages of progressive illness, one finds throughout the nation, and probably over the world, a horde of citizens who stoutly maintain beliefs regarded as absurd and contrary to fact by society as a whole. Often these people indulge in conduct that to others seems unquestionably irrational.

For example, the daily newspapers continue to report current gatherings in many states where hundreds of people handle poisonous snakes, earnestly insisting that they are carrying out God's will.* Death from snakebite among these zealous worshippers does not apparently dampen their ardor. Small children, too young to arrive spontaneously

*"And these signs shall follow them that believe; in my name they shall cast out devils; they shall speak with new tongues; they shall . . . take up serpents and if they drink any deadly thing it shall not hurt them"—[Mark 16:17-18] .

at similar conclusions concerning the relationships between faith and venom, are not spared by their parents this intimate contact with the rattler and the copperhead.

It is, perhaps, not remarkable that prophets continually predict the end of the world, giving precise and authoritative details of what so far has proved no less fanciful than the delusions of patients confined in psychiatric hospitals. That scores and sometimes hundred or even thousands of followers accept these prophecies might give the thoughtful more cause to wonder. Newspaper clippings and magazine articles before the writer at this moment describe numerous examples of such behavior.

In a small Georgia town twenty earnest disciples sit up with a pious lady who has convinced them that midnight will bring the millenium. An elderly clergyman in California, whose more numerous followers are likewise disappointed when the designated moment passes uneventfully, explains that there is no fault with his divine vision but only some minor error of calculation which arose from differences between the Biblical and the modern calendars. During the last century an even more vehement leader had thousands of people, in New England and in other states, out on the hillsides expecting to be caught up to glory as dawn broke. Indeed, conviction was so great that at sunrise many leaped from cliffs, roofs, and silos, one zealot having tied turkey wings to his arms the better to provide for flight. Those who had hoped to ascend found gravity unchanged, the earth still solid, and the inevitable contact jarring.

Few, if any, who prophesy on the grounds of mystic insight or special revelation come to conclusions more extraordinary than those reached by some who profess, and often firmly believe, they are working within the methods of science. A notable example is furnished by Wilhelm Reich, who is listed in *American Men of Science* and whose earlier work in psychopathology is regarded by many as valuable. Textbooks of high scientific standing still refer to his discoveries in this field.

It is indeed startling when such a person as this announces the discovery of "orgone," a substance that, it is claimed, has much to do with sexual orgasm (as well as the blueness of the sky) and that can be accumulated in boxes lined with metal. Those who sit within the boxes are said to benefit in many marvelous ways. According to the *Journal of the American Medical Association,* the accumulation of this (to others) nonexistent material is by Reich and his followers promoted as a method for curing cancer. A report of the Council of the American Medical Association lists the orgone accumulator with various quack nostrums under "Frauds and Fables." The presence of any such material as orgone impresses the physician as no less imaginary than its alleged therapeutic effects. The nature of such conclusions and the methods of arriving at them are scarcely more astonishing than the credulity of highly educated and intellectual people who are reported to give them earnest consideration.

During the 1940s crowds estimated as containing 25,000 or more persons, some of them having travelled halfway across the United States, stood in the rain night after night to watch a 9-year-old boy in New York City who claimed to have seen a vision which he described as "an angel's head with butterfly wings."

A clergyman of the Church of England during World War II confirmed as a supernatural omen of good the reported appearance of a luminous cross in the sky near Ipswich. In our own generation men of profound learning have expressed literal belief in witchcraft and approved the efforts of those who, following the Biblical injunction, put thousands to death for this activity.

These headlines from a daily newspaper deserve consideration:

NOW IN MENTAL HOSPITAL,

ACCUSED OF TREASON, HELD INSANE,

EZRA POUND GIVEN TOP POETRY PRIZE

My interest in this news does not indicate that I hold it to be impossible for a person with a serious psychiatric disorder sometimes to write good poetry or to achieve other worthwhile attainments.

The headlines nevertheless reflect a bewildering conflict of evaluation in which some of the paradoxical elements strongly suggest absurdity. They also bring to mind what sometimes seems to be a rapt predilection of small but influential cults of *intellectuals* or *esthetes* for what is generally regarded as perverse, dispirited, or distastefully unintelligible. The award of a Nobel Prize in literature to André Gide, who in his work fervently and openly insists that pederasty is the superior and preferable way of life for adolescent boys, furnishes a memorable example of such judgments. Renowned critics and some professors in our best universities reverently acclaim as the superlative expression of genius James Joyce's *Finnegan's Wake,* a 628-page collection of erudite gibberish indistinguishable to most people from the familiar word salad produced by hebephrenic patients on the back wards of any state hospital.

Let us illustrate briefly with the initial page from this remarkable volume:

> riverrun, past Eve and Adam's, from swerve of shore to bend of bay, brings us by a commodius vicus of recirculation back to Howth Castle and Environs.
>
> Sir Tristram, violer d'amores, fr'over the short sea, had passencore rearrived from North Armorica on this side the scraggy isthmus of Europe Minor to wielderfight his penisolate war: nor had topsawyer's rocks by the stream Oconee exaggerated themselse to Laurens County's gorgios while they went doublin their mumper all the time: nor avoice from afire bellowsed mishe mishe to tauftauf thuartpeatrick: not yet, though venissoon after, had a kidscad buttened a bland old isaac: not yet, though all's fair in vanessy, were sosie sesthers wroth with twone nathandjoe. Rot a peck of pa's malt had Jhem or Shen brewed by arclight and rory end to the regginbrow was to be seen ringsome on the aquaface.
>
> The fall (bababadalgharaghtakamminarronnkonnbronntonnerronntuonnthunntrovarrhounawnskawntoohoohoordenenthurnuk!) of a once wallstrait oldparr is retaled early in bed and later on life down through all christian minstrelsy. The great fall of the offwall entailed at such short notice the pftjschute of Finnegan, erse solid man, that the humptyhillhead of humself prumptly sends an unquiring one well to the west in quest of his tumptytumtoes: and their upturnpikepointandplace is at the knock out in the park where oranges have been laid to rust upon the green since devlinsfirst loved livvy.

The adventurous reader will, I promise, find any of the other 627 pages equally illuminating. It is not for me to say dogmatically that *Finnegan's Wake* is a volume devoid of meaning. Nor could I with certainty make such a pronouncement about the chaotic verbal productions of the patient on the back ward of an old time state hospital.

Ezra Pound's continued eminence as a poet and the almost worshipful admiration with which some scholars acclaim *Finnegan's Wake* are likely to evoke wonder from the man of ordinary tastes and reactions if he gives these matters serious consideration.

Graduates of our universities and successful businessmen join others to contribute testimonials announcing the prevention of hydrophobia and the healing of cancer, diphtheria, tuberculosis, wens, and broken legs, as well as the renting of rooms and the raising of salaries, by groups who reportedly work through "the formless, omnipresent God-substance" and by other metaphysical methods. One group publishes several magazines which are eagerly read in almost every town in the United States. Nearly 200 centers are listed where "prosperity bank drills" and respiratory rituals are advocated. Leaders solemnly write, "the physical body radiates an energy that can at times be seen as a light or aura surrounding the physical, especially about the heads of those who think much about Spirit."

The following are typical testimonial letters, and these are but three among many hundreds:

> I wrote to you somewhat over a week ago asking for your prayers. My trouble was appendicitis, and it seemed that an operation was unavoidable. However, I had faith in the indwelling, healing Christ and decided to get in touch with you. Well, as you might expect, the healing that has taken place borders on the so-called miraculous. I spent an hour each day alone with God, and I claimed my rightful inheritance as a child of God. Naturally the adverse condition had to disappear with the advent of the powerful flow of Christ-Life consciously directed towards this illness.

• • •

> You will be interested to know that just about the time when my prosperity-bank period was up I went to work in a new position, which not only pays a substantially higher salary but . . . [etc.] . I should probably not have had sufficient faith and courage to trust Him had it not been for the Truth literature.

• • •

> Thank you for your beautiful and effective ministry. I have had five big demonstrations of prosperity since I had this particular prosperity bank. Last week brought final settlement of a debt owed me for about seven years.

Not a few citizens of our country read, apparently with conviction, material such as that published by the director of the Institute of Mental Physics, who is announced as the reincarnation of a Tibetan Lama. This leader reports, furthermore, that he has witnessed an eastern sage grow an orange tree from his palm and, on another occasion, die and rise in a new body, leaving the old one behind. Many other equally improbable feats of thaumaturgy are described in eye-witness accounts.

The casual observer has been known to dismiss what many call superstition as the fruit of ignorance. Nevertheless, beliefs and practices of this sort are far from rare among the most learned in all generations. A fairly recent ambassador to the United States, generally recognized as a distinguished scholar, died (according to the press) under the care of a practitioner of Christian Science.

Even a doctor of medicine has written a book in which he attests to the cure of acute inflammatory diseases and other disorders by similar methods. But let him speak directly:

> At another time I examined a girl upon whom I had operated for recurrent mastoiditis. At the time of my examination she was showing definite signs of another

> attack. . . . Absent treatments stopped her trouble in two days. To one who had never seen anything of the kind before, the rapidity with which the inflammation disappeared would have seemed almost a piece of magic.
>
> • • •
>
> A third case is that of a woman who carried a bad heart for years. About a year ago she experienced an acute attack accompanied by pain, nausea, and bloating caused by gas. Her daughter telephoned to a practitioner of spiritual healing and explained the trouble to her. The reply was that an immediate treatment would be given. In ten minutes the trouble was gone, and there has been no serious recurrence since.

The more one considers such convictions and the sort of people who hold them, the more impressive becomes the old saying attributed to Artemus Ward and indicating that our troubles arise not so much from ignorance as from knowing so much that is not so. Hundreds of other examples like those mentioned are available to demonstrate that many persons of high ability and superior education sincerely cherish beliefs that seem to have little more real support from fact or reason than the ordinary textbook delusion. Such beliefs are held as persistently by respected persons and influential groups, despite evidence to the contrary, as by psychotic patients who are segregated in hospitals.

Let it be understood that I am not advancing an opinion that those who are persuaded by prophets that the world will end next Thursday or that those who appeal to faith healers to protect a child from the effects of meningitis should be pronounced as clinically psychotic and forcibly committed to hospitals. Despite the similarity between the way such beliefs are adopted and the way a schizoid or paranoid patient arrives at his delusions, and despite the similar lack of evidence for considering either true, people such as those now under discussion are usually capable of leading useful lives in harmony with the community and sometimes of benefit to society. Few things, in my opinion, are more basic than the necessity for people to allow each other freedom to believe or not to believe, however sacred, or however false, different creeds may be held by different groups.

Convictions that the world is flat, that one must not begin a job on Friday, or that Mr. Jerry Falwell of the Moral Majority is omnipotent are apparently held by some in reverent identity with the deepest religious attitudes of which they are capable. In this basic sense, each man's religion, as contrasted with the dogma or illusion in which he may frame it, his basic attitude and emotional response to whatever meaning and purpose he has been able to find in his living, deserves respect and consideration. The Methodist, the Mormon, and the Catholic, as well as the man who cannot accept any literal creed as a final statement of these issues, can honor and value, in a fundamentally religious sense, the valid reverence and the ultimate subjective aims of a good Mohammedan. This is possible without the ability to share his pleasant convictions about the likelihood of houris in paradise.

TRADITIONS THAT OBSCURE OUR SUBJECT

In raising general questions about personality disorder, we have briefly considered (1) persons suffering from illnesses that progress to major mental disability and (2) the numerous citizens of our nation, many of them able and well educated, who hold beliefs generally regarded as unsupported by evidence and considered by many as irrational or even fantastic. Aside from these groups and aside from all types of patients recognized as psychotic, there remains for our consideration a large body of people who are incapable of leading normal lives and whose behavior causes great distress in every community.

This group, plainly marked off from the psychotic by current psychiatric standards, does not find a categorical haven among the psychoneurotic, who are distinguished by many medical characteristics from the people to be discussed in this volume. They are also distinguished practically by their ability to adjust without major difficulties in the social group.

Who, then, are these relatively unclassified people? And what is the nature of their disorder? The pages that follow will be devoted to an attempt to answer these questions. The answers are not easy to formulate. The very name by which such patients are informally referred to in mental hospitals or elsewhere among psychiatrists is in itself confusing. Every physician is familiar with the term *psychopath,* by which these people are most commonly designated. Despite the plain etymologic inference of a *sick mind* or of *mental sickness,* this term is ordinarily used to indicate those who are considered free from psychosis and even from psychoneurosis. The definitions of psychopath found in medical dictionaries are not consistent nor do they regularly accord with the ordinary psychiatric use of this word.*

In a 1952 revision of the psychiatric nomenclature the term *psychopathic personality*was officially replaced by *sociopathic personality.* Subsequently the informal term, *sociopath,* was often used along with the older and more familiar *psychopath* to designate a large group of seriously disabled people, listed with other dissimilar groups under the heading *personality disorder.* Still another change in the official terminology was made in 1968 when the designation *sociopathic personality* was replaced by *personality disorder, antisocial type.* In the 1980 edition of the *Diagnostic and Statistical Manual of Mental Disorder, III* of the American Psychiatric Association, the designation has been changed slightly to *antisocial personality disorder.* In referring to these people now formally classified by the term *antisocial personality disorder,* I shall continue to use also the more familiar and apparently more durable term, *psychopath.* The diagnostic category, *personality disorder,* officially includes a wide variety of maladjusted people who cannot by the criteria of psychiatry be classed with the psychotic, the psychoneurotic, or the mentally defective. Until fairly recent years it was by no means uncommon for the report of a detailed psychiatric examination made on a patient in a state or federal institution to end with this diagnostic conclusion:

---

*Stedman's Medical Dictionary (1972): "Psychopath: The subject of a psychoneurosis. One who is of apparently sound mind in the ordinary affairs of life but who is dominated by some abnormal sexual, criminal or passional instinct."

Dorland's Illustrated Medical Dictionary (1974): "Psychopath: a person who has an antisocial personality. *sexual* p., an individual whose sexual behavior is manifestly antisocial and criminal."

Blakiston's New Gould Medical Dictionary (1949) gives: "A morally irresponsible person: one who continually comes in conflict with accepted behavior and the law."

Curran and Mallinson (1944) say: "The only conclusion that seems warrantable is that some time or other and by some reputable authority the term psychopathic personality has been used to designate every conceivable type of abnormal character."

1. No nervous or mental disease
2. Psychopathic personality

Traditionally the psychopath (antisocial personality) has been placed in general diagnostic categories containing many other disorders, deviations, abnormalities or deficiencies, most of which have little or no resemblance to his actual condition. From the category *personality disorder,* as last defined in 1968, a number of these dissimilar and apparently unrelated psychiatric conditions have been removed. It is not likely, however, that all the confusion promoted by the older classifications will subside promptly.

In the early decades of our century a large group of abnormalities, mental deficiency, various brain and body malformations and developmental defects, sexual perversions, delinquent behavior patterns, and chronically mild schizoid disorders, were all classed as *constitutional psychopathic inferiority.* After the ordinary mental defectives and most of the cases with demonstrable brain damage or developmental anomalies were distinguished, a considerable residue of diverse conditions remained under the old classification.

As time passed and psychiatric study continued, an increasing number of observers felt that the term *constitutional* was scarcely justified for some of the several disorders listed in the categories just mentioned. Eventually the term was officially discarded in our country and *psychopathic personality* was adopted, not only for the type of patient to be discussed in this volume but for a good many others easily distinguished from him in life but only with difficulty in the nomenclature.

Some time after the period during which it was generally assumed, by the physician as well as by the clergyman, that abnormal behavior resulted from devil possession or the influence of witches, it became customary to ascribe all or nearly all mental disorder to bad heredity. Even in the early part of the present century this practice was popular. Before relatively recent developments in psychopathology and before any real attempt had been made to understand the meaning and purpose of symptomatology, the invocation of inborn deficiency or "hereditary taint" was, it would seem, grasped largely for the want of any other hypothesis.

Another factor contributing to the popularity of belief in hereditary causation lies, perhaps, in the fact that families of patients in state hospitals were investigated and all deviations recorded. Most of these histories revealed aberrant behavior, if not in a parent or grandparent, at least in some great uncle or distant cousin. It is surprising that some investigators gave such little consideration to the fact that few men stopped on the street could account for all relatives and antecedents without also disclosing one or more kinsmen whose behavior would attract psychiatric attention.* This is not to say that there is no reasonable likelihood of inborn deficiencies playing a part, perhaps a major part, in the development of the psychopath. It is to say that one is not justified in assuming such factors until real evidence of them is produced. If such evidence is produced, these factors must be weighed along with all others for which there may be evidence and not glibly assumed to be a full and final explanation.

In recent years a contrary tendency has become prominent in psychiatry, a tendency

*The ease with which defective heredity may be found in any case in which one looks for it is well known. A study published in 1937 revealed that 57 percent of a group of normal people showed a positive family history of "neuropathic taint."

to make, on the basis of symbolism and theoretical postulates, sweeping and unverifiable assumptions and to insist that these prove the cause of obscure personality disorders to lie in specific infantile, or even intrauterine, experiences. This practice has become exceedingly popular and has, in my opinion, led to many fanciful and absurd pseudoscientific explanations of the psychopath and of other psychiatric problems. Let us bear in mind that the currently prevalent psychodynamic theories are of such a nature that they can be glibly used to convince oneself of the truth of virtually any assumption, however implausible, that one might make about what is in the unconscious but what is never brought to consciousness or otherwise demonstrated. Let us not mistake these easy and unsupported assumptions for actual evidence.

After many years of work in psychiatry as a member of the staff in a closed hospital devoted to the treatment of mental disorders, and after many other years in charge of the psychiatric service in a general hospital, I believe that these curious people referred to as sociopaths or psychopaths, in the vernacular of the ward and the staff room, offer a field of study in personality disorder more baffling and more fascinating than any other. The present work has been attempted because of an ever-growing conviction that this type of disorder is far less clearly understood than either the well-defined psychoses or the neuroses and that this lack of understanding is, furthermore, not sufficiently recognized and admitted. Although I do not pretend to achieve a final explanation of so grave and perplexing a problem, it is hoped that a frank and detailed discussion may, at least, draw attention to the magnitude of the problem.

The chief aim of this study is to bring before psychiatrists a few of these cases, typical of hundreds more, who have proved so interesting to the writer, so difficult to interpret by the customary standards of psychiatry, and all but impossible to deal with or to treat satisfactorily in the face of prevalent medicolegal viewpoints. Many of these cases have been classified consistently as psychopaths by not one but a number of expert observers, usually by several staffs of psychiatrists, and nearly always with unanimity. Others are so similar and so typical that few, if any, experts could find grounds to question their status. It is my belief, however, that this diagnosis, as it is authoritatively defined and as it is generally understood, fails to do justice to the kind of patients considered here.

It is hoped that such a presentation may be of interest to physicians in general practice and, perhaps, to medical students, as well as to those whose work is confined more specifically to personality disorders. It is, indeed, the physician in general practice who will most often be called on by society to interpret the behavior of such patients as these and to advise about their treatment and their disposition.

These people, whom I shall usually call psychopaths for want of a better word, are, as a matter of fact, the problem of juries, courts, relatives, the police, and the general public no less than of the psychiatrist. Referring to such patients, Henderson says:

> It is often much against his better judgment that the judge sentences a man whose conduct on the face of it indicates the action of an unsound mind to serve a term of imprisonment. But he is almost forced to do so because, according to our present statutes governing commitment, the doctor may not feel that he is justified in certifying the individual as suitable for care and treatment in a mental hospital.

It is important that the average physician at least be aware that there is such a problem. According to the traditional standards of psychiatry, such patients are not eligible for admission to state hospitals for the psychotic or to the numerous hospitals of the same type maintained by the federal government for veterans of the armed services. They are classed as sane and competent and, theoretically at least, are held responsible for their conduct. Because they are so classed, none of the measures used to protect other psychiatric patients (and their families and the community) can be applied to bring them under any sort of treatment or restriction, even when they show themselves dangerously disordered. By many psychiatrists they have in a technical sense been considered to be without nervous or mental disease. There are many arguments that can be brought forward in support of these beliefs, particularly if one adheres strictly to the traditional and currently accepted definitions of psychiatry and minimizes or evades what is demonstrated by the patient's behavior.

It is difficult, however, for society to hold these people to account for their damaging conduct or to apply any control that will prevent its continuing. Those who commit serious crimes have a history that any clever lawyer can exploit in such a way as to make them appear to the average jury the victims of such madness as would make Bedlam itself tame by comparison. Under such circumstances they often escape the legal consequences of their acts, are sent to mental hospitals where they prove to be "sane," and are released. On the other hand, when their relatives and their neighbors seek relief or protection from them and take action to have them committed to psychiatric hospitals, they, not wanting to be restricted, are able to convince the courts that they are as competent as any man.

It is pertinent here to remind ourselves of the considerable change that has occurred during recent centuries in the legal attitude toward antisocial conduct and punishment. Formerly, all who broke the laws were considered fit subjects for trial, and penalties were inflicted without regard to questions of responsibility or competency. As Karl Menninger, among others, has emphatically pointed out, not only were the irrational considered fully culpable, but also young children and idiots. It has also been said that at an earlier date, animals and even articles of furniture, trees, and stones were brought to trial, fantastic as it seems to us now, and sentenced to legal penalties.

Today the murderer who hears what he believes is God's voice telling him to kill is not, as a rule, considered legally responsible for his crime. He is likely to be committed to a psychiatric hospital for the protection of society and for his own best interest, but not as a punishment. This legal attitude has become so axiomatic, so familiar to the man on the streets, that it is well for us to remember it is relatively new.

Since publication of the earlier editions of this book much more drastic changes have been called for and, to some degree, have occurred in popular and even in legal attitudes toward serious antisocial activity. Some of the demands made in behalf of what is often called permissiveness are based on false assumptions, often on truly absurd assumptions. Among these, apparently, is the relatively popular conviction that those who perpetrate heinous and brutal crimes should not really be blamed or, at the most, not be blamed greatly, or seriously punished. Another assumption is that psychiatry has discovered an effective means of curing even the most vicious criminals, and that they should not be sentenced to prisons but regularly sent to psychiatric hospitals. This concept is indeed flattering to psychiatry in view of our record with its woeful lack of evidence that we possess any means of this sort whatsoever.

Popular among some groups who consider themselves progressive is the belief that society instead of the criminal should be held responsible for the unprovoked murders, brutal rapes, and other outrages that blight our civilization. Another factor that sometimes seems to play a part in the doctrine of permissiveness is the popular psychiatric theory that crimes are often carried out in order to obtain punishment for unconscious feelings of guilt weighing on the tender conscience of the criminal. Referring to a sane man convicted of murdering, in cold blood and without provocation, eight young women some years ago, one psychiatrist was quoted as expressing the conviction that this murderer should be regarded as being just as free from guilt as any of his victims.

We might also bear in mind that once only obvious irrationality was regarded as personality disorder, as disability. Medically we recognize the fact that many less obvious disorders are more serious and incapacitating than those with gross superficial manifestations that can be readily demonstrated. In our attempts to appraise the psychopath and his disorder, it will be helpful to bear these facts in mind and not to forget that our present medicolegal criteria are based on knowledge that is far from complete.

These people called psychopaths present a problem which must be better understood by lawyers, social workers, schoolteachers, and by the general public if any satisfactory way of dealing with them is to be worked out. Before this understanding can come, the general body of physicians to whom the laity turn for advice must themselves have a clear picture of the situation. Much of the difficulty that mental institutions have in their relations with the psychopath springs from a lack of awareness in the public that he exists. The law in its practical application provides no means whereby the community can adequately protect itself from such people. And no satisfactory facilities can be found for their treatment. It is with these thoughts especially in mind that I seek to present the material of this book in such a manner that the average physician who treats few frankly psychotic patients may see that our subject lies in his own field scarcely less than in the field of psychiatry. After all, psychiatry, though still a specialty, can no longer be regarded as circumscribed within the general scope of medicine.

In nearly all the standard textbooks of psychiatry the psychopath is mentioned. Several recent textbooks have indeed made definite efforts to stress for the student the challenging and paradoxical features of our subject. Often, however, tucked away at the end of a large volume, an obscure chapter is found containing a few pages or paragraphs devoted to these strange people who take so much attention of the medical staffs in psychiatric hospitals and whose behavior, it is here maintained, probably causes more unhappiness and more perplexity to the public than all other mentally disordered patients combined. From some textbooks the medical student is likely to arrive at a conclusion that the psychopath is an unimportant figure, probably seldom encountered even in a psychiatric practice. Nor will he be led to believe that this type of disorder is particularly interesting. Not only is the chapter on psychopathic personalities often short and sometimes vague or halfhearted, but even this until fairly recently was nearly always involved with personality types or disorders that bear little or no resemblance to that with which we are now concerned. Although it is true that these other conditions were for many decades officially placed in the same category with the one discussed here, which I believe is a clinical entity, it is hard to see how any student unfamiliar with the latter could profit by encountering it vaguely placed in a company of assorted deficiencies and aberrations that are by no means basically similar.

It is my earnest conviction that, traditionally confused with a fairly heterogeneous group under a loose and variously understood term, a type of patient exists who could, without exaggeration, still be called the *forgotten man of psychiatry.* If this patient can be presented as he has appeared so clearly during years of observation, if some idea can be given of his ubiquity, and, above all, if interest can be promoted in further study of his peculiar status among other human beings, I shall be abundantly satisfied. It is difficult to contemplate the enigma that he provokes without attempting to find some explanation, speculative though the attempt may be. My efforts to explain or interpret are, however, tentative and secondary to the real purpose of this volume, which is to call attention to what may be observed about our subject.

NOT AS SINGLE SPIES BUT IN BATTALIONS

An attempt to determine the incidence of this disorder in the population as a whole is opposed by serious difficulties. The vagueness of officially accepted criteria for diagnosis and the extreme variation of degree in such maladjustment constitute primary obstacles. Statistics from most psychiatric hospitals are necessarily misleading, since the psychopath is not technically eligible for admission and only those who behave in such an extremely abnormal manner as to appear orthodoxly psychotic (that is to say, as suffering from another and very different disorder) appear in the records. If the traditional legal and medical rules were regularly followed, statistics from state hospitals and from the federal psychiatric institutions would show no psychopaths at all. Let it also be noted that these institutions contain a vast majority of the patients hospitalized in the United States for mental disorder. Most statistical studies therefore cannot be regarded as even remotely suggesting the prevalence of this disability in the population.

These facts notwithstanding, it is still impressive to note what the records of a typical psychiatric institution revealed during twenty-nine months shortly before 1941. During this period 857 new patients were admitted to one federal hospital, where a staff of ten psychiatrists, including myself, classified them after careful examination and study. Of this group, 102 received the primary diagnosis of psychopathic personality, being considered free of any other mental disorder that could account for the difficulties that led to their admission. This group, comprising nearly one-eighth of all those admitted, indicates that the disorder is far from rare. The records also show 134 other patients classified under *alcoholism* or *drug addiction,* many of whom I believe were fundamentally like those diagnosed as psychopaths, the addiction and other complications being secondary. If even one-half of these are considered as psychopaths, we arrive at a figure of 169, or almost one-fifth of the total.

These statistics from one psychiatric institution cannot, of course, be taken as proof that the disorder is so prevalent everywhere. One must not overlook the fact, however, that each of these patients was accepted despite rules specifically classifying him as ineligible and often as a result of conduct so abnormal or so difficult to cope with that he was considered a grave emergency. Another factor worth mentioning is the psychopath's almost uniform unwillingness to apply, like other ill people, for hospitalization or for any other medical service. The survey at least suggests that these patients are common and that they constitute a serious problem in the average community and a major issue in psychiatry.

I have been forced to the conviction that this particular behavior pattern is found among one's fellowmen far more frequently than might be surmised from reading the literature. If the nature of the disorder in question defines itself throughout the course of this work with sufficient sharpness and clarity to be recognizable as a pathologic entity, little doubt will remain that it presents a sociologic and psychiatric problem second to none.

The man who develops influenza or who breaks his arm nearly always thinks at once of calling his doctor. The unconscious victim of a head injury is promptly taken by his family, by his friends, or, lacking these, by casual bystanders to a hospital where medical attention is given. Persons who develop anxiety, phobia, or psychosomatic manifestations are likely to seek aid from a physician. Even those who demur and delay since they fear they will be called weak or silly because of symptoms commonly classed as psychoneurotic can be, and usually are, persuaded by their families after varying periods of reluctance to ask for help.

Children, of course, often seek to avoid both the pediatrician and the dentist, despite the advice of parents. But the parent seldom fails, when need of treatment is a serious matter, in getting the child, with or without his willingness, into the hands of the doctor. Many patients ill with the major personality disorders we classify as psychoses do not voluntarily seek treatment. Some do not recognize any such need and may bitterly oppose, sometimes by violent combat, all efforts to send them to psychiatric hospitals. Such patients, however, are well recognized. Medical facilities and legal instrumentalities exist for handling the problem, and institutions are provided to accept such patients and hold them, if necessary against their own volition, so long as it is advisable for the patient's welfare or for the protection of others.

When we consider on the other hand these antisocial or psychopathic personalities, we find not one in one hundred who spontaneously goes to his physician to seek help. If relatives, alarmed by his disastrous conduct, recognize that treatment, or at least supervision, is an urgent need, they meet enormous obstacles. The public institutions to which they would turn for the care of a schizophrenic or a manic patient present closed doors. If they are sufficiently wealthy, they often consider a private psychiatric hospital. It should also be noted here that such private hospitals are necessarily expensive and that perhaps not more than 2 or 3 percent of our population can afford such care for prolonged periods. No matter how wealthy his family may be, the psychopath, unlike all other serious psychiatric cases, can refuse to go to any hospital or to accept any other treatment or restraint. His refusal is regularly upheld by our courts of law, and grounds for this are consistent with the official appraisal of his condition by psychiatry.

Nearly always he does refuse and successfully oppose the efforts of his relatives to have him cared for. It is seldom that a psychopath accepts hospitalization or even outpatient treatment unless some strong means of coercion happens to be available. The threat of cutting off his financial support, of bringing legal action against him for forgery or theft, or of allowing him to remain in jail may move him to visit a physician's office or possibly to enter a hospital. Subsequent events often demonstrate that he is acting not seriously and with the understanding he professes but for the purpose of evasion, whether he himself realizes this or not. He usually breaks off treatment as soon as the evasion has been accomplished.

Since medical institutions traditionally refuse to accept the psychopath as a patient and since he does not voluntarily, except in rare instances, seek medical aid, it might be surmised that prison populations would furnish statistics useful in estimating the prevalence of his disorder. It is true that a considerable proportion of prison inmates show indications of such a disorder. It is also true that only a small proportion of typical psychopaths are likely to be found in penal institutions, since the typical psychopath, as will be brought out in subsequent pages, is not likely to commit major crimes that result in long prison terms. He is also distinguished by his ability to escape ordinary legal punishments and restraints. Though he regularly makes trouble for society, as well as for himself, and frequently is handled by the police, his characteristic behavior does not usually include committing felonies which would bring about permanent or adequate restriction of his activities. He is often arrested, perhaps 100 times or more. But he nearly always regains his freedom and returns to his old patterns of maladjustment.

Although the incidence of this disorder is at present impossible to establish statistically or even to estimate accurately, I am willing to express the opinion that it is exceedingly high. On the basis of experience in psychiatric outpatient clinics and with psychiatric problems of private patients and in the community (as contrasted with committed patients), it does not seem an exaggeration to estimate the number of people seriously disabled by the disorder now listed under the term *antisocial personality* as greater than the number disabled by any recognized psychosis except schizophrenia. So far as I know, there are no specific provisions made in any public institution for dealing with even one psychopath.

METHOD OF PRESENTATION

Before attempting to define or describe the psychopath (antisocial personality), to contrast him with other types of psychiatric patients, or to make any attempt to explain him, I would like to present some specimens of the group for consideration.

This procedure will be in accord with the principles of science in method at least, since, as Karl Pearson pointed out in *The Grammar of Science,* this method always consists of three steps:

1. The observation and recording of facts
2. The grouping of these facts with proper correlation and with proper distinction from other facts
3. The effort to devise some summarizing or, if possible, explanatory statement which will enable one to grasp conveniently their significance

Long ago, keeping these steps clearly in mind, Bernard Hart gave an account of personality disorder in *The Psychology of Insanity* that has, perhaps, never been surpassed for clarity and usefulness. Psychopathology has not been a static field, and many new concepts have arisen which make Hart's presentation in some respects archaic and unrepresentative of viewpoints prevalent today in psychiatry. This point notwithstanding, the method followed by Hart remains an example of how the problems of personality disorder can be approached with maximal practicality with minimal risks of mistaking hypothesis for proof or of falling into the schismatic polemics that, scarcely less than among medieval theologians, have confused issues and impeded common understanding in psychiatry. Without claims to comparable success in the effort to follow Hart's method, I acknowledge the debt owed one who set so excellent an example in the early years of this century.

The most satisfactory way in which such clinical material could be presented is, in my opinion, as a series of full-length biographic studies, preferably of several hundred pages each, written by one who has full access to the life of each subject. Only when the concrete details of environment are laid, as, for instance, in an honest and discerning novel, can the significance of behavior be well appreciated. Certainly no brief case summary and probably no orthodox psychiatric history can succeed in portraying the character and the behavior of these people as they appear day after day and year after year in actual life.

It is not enough to set down that a certain patient stole his brother's watch or that another got drunk in a poolroom while his incipient bride waited at the altar. To get the *feel* of the person whose behavior shows disorder, it is necessary to feel something of his surroundings. The psychopath's symptoms have for a long time been regarded as primarily sociopathic. It is true that all, or nearly all, psychiatric disorder is in an important sense sociopathic, in that it adversely affects interpersonal relations. In most other disorders the manifestations of illness can, however, be more readily demonstrated in the isolated patient in the setting of a clinical examination. In contrast, it is all but impossible to demonstrate any of the fundamental symptoms in the psychopath under similar circumstances. The substance of the problem, real as it is in life, disappears, or at least escapes our specialized means of perception, when the patient is removed from the milieu in which he is to function.

All that surrounds and has ever surrounded the schizophrenic or the man with severe obsessive illness is, of course, important to us if we seek to understand why these people became disabled. Lacking all information except what might be gained from either of these patients (with whom one is, let us say, confined in an oxygen chamber on the moon), the observer will, nevertheless, have little trouble in discerning that there is disorder and in discovering a good deal about the general nature of the disorder.

Aside from questions of cause and effect, we have little opportunity even to realize the existence of the subject we must deal with unless the psychopath can be followed as he departs from the (essentially in vitro) situation of physician's office or hospital and takes up his activities in the community on a real (and socially in vivo) status.

It is with such convictions in mind that we shall often include detail of the environment, perhaps digress to the patient's husband or parents, report glimpses of the patient through the eyes of a lay observer, and at times attempt, from what material is available, a tentative reconstruction of situations that can be experienced adequately only at firsthand. It is regrettable that so much detail of this sort is difficult and often impossible to obtain. Without adequate knowledge of his specific surroundings in the community, there is no way for more than the insubstantial image of his being, like the picture projected from a lantern slide, to reach awareness. The real clinical entity is approachable only in the unstatic, actual process of the patient's life as he takes his specific course as a personal and sociologic unit.

The disorder can be demonstrated only when the patient's activity meshes with the problems of ordinary living. It cannot be even remotely apprehended if we do not pay particular attention to his responses in those interpersonal relations which to a normal man are the most profound.

If no schizophrenic had ever spoken, we would probably have little realization of what we understand (incomplete as this is) of auditory hallucinations. The schizophrenic can, by his verbal communication, give us some useful clues in our efforts to approach many of his problems. Little or nothing of this sort that is reliable can, by ordinary psychiatric examination, be obtained from the psychopath. Only when we observe him not through his speech but as he seeks his aims in behavior and demonstrates his disability in interaction with the social group can we begin to feel how genuine is his disorder. Studying the psychopath almost entirely in the orthodox clinical setting in which patients ordinarily appear is like examining the schizophrenic with our ears so muffled that his reiterated and quite honest claims of hearing voices of the dead talking to him from the sun and from his intestines fail to reach our perception.

If another analogy be permitted, let us say that a pair of copper wires carrying 2,000 volts of electricity, when we look at them, smell them, listen to them, or even touch them separately (while thoroughly insulated from the ground), may give no evidence of being in any respect different from other strands of copper. Let us, however, connect them to a motor (or have someone seize both of them at once) and we find out facts not to be perceived otherwise. The unmistakable evidence of electricity appears only when the circuit is made. So, too, the features that are most important in the behavior of the psychopath do not adequately emerge when this behavior is relatively isolated. The qualities of the psychopath become manifest only when he is connected into the circuits of full social life.

The sort of presentation our problem requires is, of course, impossible. However, in an effort to give at least a vivid glimpse of the material under consideration, I have made use of a somewhat different form of report than that customarily offered.

The impersonal and necessarily abstracted picture of these psychopaths in a purely clinical setting fails to show them as they appear in flesh and blood and in the process of living. In the restricted and arbitrary range of activities afforded by hospital life, their tendencies cannot be so truly and vividly demonstrated as in the larger world. To know them adequately, one must try to see them not merely with the physician's calm and relatively detached eye but also with the eye of the ordinary man on the streets, whom they confound and amaze. We must concern ourselves not only with their measurable intelligence, their symptomatology (or, rather, lack of symptomatology) in ordinary psychiatric terms, but also with the impression they make as total organisms in action among others and in all the nuances and complexities of deeply personal and specifically affective relationships. To see them properly in such a light, we must follow them from the wards out into the marketplace, the saloon, and the brothel, to the fireside, to church, and to their work.

In attempting this, however incompletely and inadequately, it is perhaps desirable for us not to trade our naiveté at once for the experienced clinician's discriminating viewpoint. Let us first watch them in their full conduct as human beings, not neglecting even the impression they make on Tom, Dick, and Harry, before trying to frame them in a scheme of psychopathology.

The terms I shall use to describe them may often imply that they are blamed for what they do or suggest an attitude of distaste or mockery for some of their behavior. Most psychiatrists regard such patients, unlike those suffering from ordinary psychoses, as legally competent and responsible for their misconduct and their difficulties. The faulty reactions in living that these patients show are indeed difficult to describe without sometimes using terms that come more readily to moralists or sociologists or laymen than to psychiatrists. The customary psychiatric terminology does not, I believe, offer a range of concepts into which we can fit these people successfully.

With other patients whose disorder is frankly recognized, we can, by our impersonal and specifically medical language, communicate fairly well to each other what we have observed. Some aspects of the psychopath that elude such language may be reflected, however imperfectly, in the simplest accounts of direct impression by those who have been closest to him and have felt the impact of his anomalous reactions. For these reasons, then, and with apology, reference may be made to some actions as outlandish, foolish, fantastic, buffoonish.

The chief aim of this book is to help, in however small a way, to bring patients with this type of disorder into clearer focus so that psychiatric efforts to deal with their problems can eventually be implemented. It has of course been necessary and in every way desirable to eliminate all details that might lead to the personal identification of any patient whose disorder has been studied and recorded. All patients referred to have been carefully shielded from recognition. It is nevertheless true that the psychopath engages in behavior so unlike that of others and so typical of his disorder that no act can be reported of a patient from Oregon seen ten years ago without strongly suggesting similar acts by hundreds of psychopaths carried out in dozens of communities last Saturday night. I can only express regret to the scores of people whose sons, brothers, husbands, or daughters I have never seen or heard of but who have, no doubt, reproduced many or perhaps all of the symptoms discussed in this volume. This disorder is so common that no one need feel that any specific act of a psychopath is likely to be distinguishable from acts carried out by hundreds of others.

In discussing the possible influence of environment on the development of this disability, I hope I will not promote unjustified regret or remorse in any parent. Hundreds of times fathers and mothers have discussed their fear that some error or inadequacy on their part caused a child to become a psychopath. Most parents of such patients personally studied impress me as having been conscientious and often very kind and discerning people. As will be brought out later, I do not believe obvious mistreatment or any simple egregious parental errors can justifiably be held as the regular cause of a child's developing this complex disorder. All parents, no doubt, make great as well as small mistakes in their role as parents. It has seemed at times that the very points about which some mothers and fathers feel most uneasiness are the opposite of those so regretted by others and assumed to be the crucial mistakes that have contributed to the maladjustment of a child. Less than in most other kinds of psychiatric disorder has it seemed to me that one could find and point out as causal influences gross failures on the part of the parents which people of ordinary wisdom and good will might have readily avoided.

During recent years it has become popular to blame parents in glib and sweeping terms for all, or nearly all, of the misconduct or inadequacy of their children. It has also become popular to insist that society and not the one who commits the crime should be held responsible for murder, rape, and armed robbery. Sometimes these claims are made without any appeal to evidence at all but merely by repetition of the familiar cliché. Some psychiatrists have even attempted to account for antisocial behavior by assuming that the parents unconsciously want their sons or daughters to commit criminal or immoral acts and that the progeny carry out these wishes while remaining unconscious of their motives. These conclusions, like many others that have been drawn in the attempt to give fundamental and *dynamic* explanations of things still unknown, rest chiefly on theoretical assumptions—assumptions made on the basis of analogy or arbitrarily interpreted symbolism about what is in the unconscious but what is never brought forth into consciousness or otherwise submitted or demonstrated. This, I maintain, does not constitute genuine evidence as it is known to science, law, or common sense. I hope that the great numbers of conscientious and honorable parents who to my knowledge have struggled courageously over the years, despite grief and frustration, to rehabilitate their sons and daughters (and to make restitution in their behalf to society) will not be led by such fanciful explanations to blame themselves unjustly.

Cruvant and Yochelson have expressed the opinion that strong and inappropriate negative attitudes toward psychopaths are commonly aroused in psychiatrists who attempt to deal with them as patients. It is scarcely surprising if such reactions tend to occur, when one considers all the disappointments and the frustrations involved in treatment and the repeatedly demonstrated irresponsibility and callousness of these patients.

When there is an opportunity to follow the career of a typical psychopath, his pattern of behavior appears specific—something not to be confused with the life of an ordinary purposeful criminal or of a cold opportunist who, in pursuit of selfish ends, merely disregards ethical considerations and the rights of others.

This pattern, I believe, differs no less distinctly than the specific and idiomatic thought and verbal expressions of schizophrenia differ from those of the mentally defective and from other psychiatric conditions. Never in faults of logical reasoning, or in verbal confusion or technical delusion, but rather in the sharper reality of behavior, the psychopath seems often to produce something as strange and as obviously pathologic as the following statement taken from the letter of a patient with schizophrenia:

> Financial service senses worries of 35 whirlpools below sound 1846, 45, 44, A.D. Augusta City treasur, Richmond County treasur, United States Treaur of Mississippi River flood area. Gentlemen will you come to . . . and idenafy none minastrative body that receives the life generated by fourth patented generative below sound. Further arrange financial credit for same. Would like two bedrooms at up town Hotel and convenient to roof garden. Until you gentlemen decide further what my occupation is you may as well announce me as comforting 35 whirlpools below sound. May you gentlemen have gray eyes and thick bones as the flat sense minastrated are very valuable in idenafying me.

Even such a relatively simple bit of word salad stands out at once as indicative of profound and specific disorder within the writer. As in the words of the schizophrenic, so in the behavior of the psychopath there seems to work a positive knack for producing situations that can be accounted for only in terms of a psychiatric condition that is unique.

section two · The material

chapter 2 · The disorder in full clinical manifestations

MAX

This patient first came to my attention years ago while I was serving my turn as officer of the day in a Veterans Administration psychiatric institution. His wife telephoned the hospital for assistance, stating that Max had slipped away from her and had begun to make trouble again. With considerable urgency and apparent distress she explained that she was bringing him to be admitted as a patient and begged that a car with attendants be sent at once to her aid.

He was found in the custody of the police, against whom he had made some resistance but much more vocal uproar. The resistance actually was only a show consisting for the most part of dramatically aggressive gestures made while he was too securely held to fight and extravagant boasts of his physical prowess and savage temper. His general demeanor in this episode suggested the familiar picture of small boys, held fast by peacemakers, who wax ever more eloquently militant as the possibilities of actual conflict diminish.

He came quietly with the attendants and on arriving at the admission ward was alert, self-assured, and boastful. Extolling his own mettle as a prizefighter, as a salesman, and as general good fellow, he was nevertheless friendly and even flattering toward the examining physician and the hospital.

He was far from what could be called drunk. In fact, it would be stretching a point to say he was "under the influence." He had been drinking, it is true, but he knew well what he was doing, and only by an impracticable flight of fancy could one attribute his behavior primarily to liquor.

At the admitting ward of the hospital, accompanying papers promptly revealed that the patient's desire for treatment arose in consequence of some checks which he had forged in Spartanburg, South Carolina. He had been arrested and convicted, but an agreement was reached whereby, instead of being sent to jail, he might come to the hospital for psychiatric treatment.

His wife, his attorney, and representatives of a veterans' organization pointed out that he had frequently been in hospitals for the treatment of mental disorder and maintained that he was not responsible for his misconduct.

He seemed pleased to be at the hospital and was expansive and cordial but a little haughty despite his well-maintained air of camaraderie. Although a small man, only 5 feet, 6 inches tall, he made a rather striking impression. His glance was fresh and arresting. His movements were quick, and he had an air of liveliness vagueley suggestive of a chipmunk. Though preposterously boastful, he did not show any indications of a psychosis.

The hospital records showed that he had been a patient eight years previously for a period of two months. During this time of study he showed no evidence of a psychosis or a psychoneurosis and was discharged with a diagnosis of psychopathic personality. He was found to have tertiary syphilis, but neurologic examination and spinal fluid studies showed no evidence of neurosyphilis.

Though at first cooperative and agreeable on this previous admission, he soon became restless and expressed dissatisfaction with the hospital. He was granted parole, but on his first pass into town he got into an altercation in which words were more prominent than blows and was held by the police for disturbing the peace.

After losing parole, he became constantly unruly in petty ways, often insulted the nurses and attendants, and several times egged on mildly psychotic patients to fight each other or to resist the personnel on the ward. On being questioned about this conduct by physicians, he glibly denied all and showed little concern at being accused. Since he was not considered as suffering from a real nervous or mental disorder and since it was difficult to keep him on any ward except the closely supervised one among actively disturbed patients, he was discharged.

Records show that he sought hospitalization on other occasions after having been fined a half-dozen or more times for brawling on the streets and for petty frauds. There is every reason to believe, from the evidence of careful reports by the Red Cross and by social service workers, that when his troubles with the civil authorities became too discomforting he sought the shelter of a psychiatric hospital.

Several months previously he had spent six weeks at a Veterans Administration hospital in Maryland after getting into similar trouble with the police in Wilmington, Delaware. He complained at the time of having spells during which he lost his temper and attacked people, often, according to his story, with disastrous results, since, again according to his story, he had at one time been featherweight boxing champion of England.

According to the psychiatric history at the Maryland hospital, he had, in describing these spells, mentioned some points that would suggest epilepsy. As soon as he came to the hospital and was relieved of responsibility for the trouble he had made, the so-called spells ceased. His description of them varied. Sometimes, when particularly expansive, he boasted of superconvulsions lasting as long as ten hours, during which he made windowpanes rattle and shook slats from the bed. After being in the hospital for several weeks and apparently beginning to grow bored, his talk of spells died down and he seemed to lose interest in the subject. He was discharged after the staff had agreed that the alleged seizures were entirely spurious and the patient himself had all but admitted it. The diagnosis of psychopathic personality was made.

Between his first visit to the present hospital and his recent return, he had been in five other psychiatric institutions, each time following conflicts with the law or pressing difficulties with private persons. In all the records accumulated during these examinations and investigations, no authentic symptom of an orthodox mental disorder is noted. True enough, there are statements by wives and other interested parties about spells and opinions by the laity, such as the following which was quoted by his attorney on one occasion to shield him from the consequences of theft:

> I had occasion to be in Dayton, Ohio, recently and talked to the people running the . . . Loan Company at . . . Street, having stopped there for about an hour between trains en route for Chicago. I was informed by these gentlemen that he had wheels in his head.

Statements such as the foregoing, opinions that he is "undoubtedly goofy," that he does not behave like a man in his proper senses, abound in the ponderous stack of letters, medical histories, social service reports, records of court trials, and other materials that have accumulated in this man's wake. One who reads his strange and prolix story and, even more, one who knows the hero personally is only too ready to fall into the vernacular and agree. Nevertheless, it was equally true on reviewing his record at the time of his new admission that no symptom impressing a psychiatrist had been mainfested and that many groups of psychiatrists had, after careful study, continued to find him free of psychosis or psychoneurosis, in other words, sane and responsible for his conduct and even without the mitigating circumstance of a milder mental illness.

Once during this period he had been sent to prison in a southern state for forgeries a little more ambitious than his routine practice. At the instigation of his second and legal wife, who consistently flew to his aid (despite her chagrin at the patient's having meanwhile consummated two bigamous marriages), well-meaning officers of a veterans' organization became interested and took up the cudgels.

Wearying sharply of prison, the patient had for some time been talking on all occasions about a blow on the head that he had sustained while in service. This alleged incident, though absent from his military records, had cropped up frequently but not regularly during his hospitalizations. Sometimes the blow, which he had sustained accidentally from the butt of a gun that a companion was breaching, had merely left him dizzy for a moment. Again it had knocked him unconscious for a short period and necessitated several days' rest in his tent.

Max now became more specific about his wartime injury and explained that he had suffered a severe concussion, lying out stark and unconscious for some eight or nine hours. Attorneys pointed out his many periods of treatment in psychiatric hospitals. The governor soon agreed to parole him into the custody of a federal hospital in Mississippi.

During his present sojourn in the hospital he was for several weeks happily adjusted on the admission ward, busy doing small favors for the physician, congenial with all the personnel, and helpful and kindly toward psychotic patients. He was alert, quick-witted, nimble with his hands, and entirely free from delusions, hallucinations, or any of the broader personality changes associated with the ordinary psychoses. He was by no means "nervous," even in the lay sense, and showed no emotional instability or signs of ungovernable impulse. Rather than an excess of anxiety, he showed the reverse, apparently finding little or nothing in his present situation or in all his past difficulties to cause worry or uneasiness.

As the time passed, however, he began to grow restive. He became somewhat condescending toward the physician, frequently referring to himself as a man of superior education and culture and boasting that he had studied for years at Heidelberg.

Shortly before the time set for him to come before the staff, he demanded his discharge. This was denied. He now became involved in frequent altercations with attendants and sometimes fought desultorily with other patients. These fights always started over trifles, and Max's egotism and fractiousness raised the issue. He never attacked others suddenly or incomprehensibly as might a psychotic person motivated by delusions or prompted by hallucinations. The causes of his quarrels were readily understandable and were usually found to be similar to those which move such types as the familiar schoolboy bully. Usually his adversaries were patients also disposed to quarrel. No signs of towering rage or even of impulses too strong to be controlled by a very meager desire to refrain appeared.

He always took care not to challenge an antagonist who might get the upper hand. During this period he talked much of his past glories as a pugilist, describing himself as former featherweight champion of all the army camps in the United States. The desire to show off appeared to be a strong motive behind many of his fights. As will be brought out later, he was indeed a skillful boxer. These stories were not delusion but the exaggeration and falsifying, sometimes unconscious or half-conscious, that are often seen in sane people and sometimes even in those who are able, intelligent, and highly successful.

Max was often caught sowing the seeds of discontent among other patients whom he encouraged to break rules, to oppose attendants, and to demand discharges. He made small thefts from time to time. This trend culminated in his kicking out an iron grill during the night and leaving the hospital. He took with him two psychotic patients, and numerous others testified that he had tried to persuade them to leave also.

The next afternoon he was returned to the hospital by the police after being arrested in the midst of a brawl that he had caused by cheating at a game of chance in a dive. He had taken a few beers but was shrewd, alert, and well in command of his body and his faculties.

He now insisted on his discharge from the hospital against advice and was brought before the medical staff. The diagnosis of psychopathic personality was again made. In his demands to be released, he arrogantly maintained that he had been pardoned outright by the governor of the state that had imprisoned him, pointed out vehemently that he was sound in mind and body, and expressed strong indignation at being confined unjustly in what he referred to as a nut house. It was then pointed out to him that he was not pardoned but merely paroled, and he was told that if discharged at present he would be returned to the penitentiary.

Here his wrath began to subside at once and marvelously. Hastily, but with some subtlety, his tone changed, and he began to find points in common with the advice he had been receiving from the staff. He left the room in a cordial frame of mind, tossing friendly and fairly clever quips back at the physicians, nearly all of whom he had known during some of his many admissions to various hospitals.

About ten days later he was pardoned outright by the governor and almost immediately took legal action which got him discharged against medical advice.

Many similar adventures had occupied his time prior to the recent admission. Some of these had resulted in his being sent, as in the episode just cited, to psychiatric hospitals from which he promptly obtained his release by legal action. Others had led him to jail and to the police station dozens of times for charges not sufficiently serious for him to utilize the expedient of psychiatric hospitalization as a means of escape.

A series of troubles had led to his reaching the hospital on this last occasion. As mentioned previously, he had many years ago divorced his first wife and remarried. The second legal spouse continued to play an important part in his career. As the proprietress or madame of a local brothel generally conceded to be the most orderly and, perhaps in a limited sense, the most respectable institution of its sort in the city, she was constantly embarrassed by the actions of her husband. Though enjoying a good part of the revenue from this ever-lucrative business, Max troubled himself little to maintain the dignity of the house.

In fact, it seemed that he went out of his way to complicate matters for his wife. If not through his daily and nightly brawls or uproars in various grogshops, dance halls, or juke joints, then by putting slugs into slot machines or serving as fence in some petty thieving racket, he brought the police in search of him down on the "house of joy" that maintained him.

Though satisfactory understandings were said to exist between this institution and the law, policemen suddenly appearing at the door and trooping through the hallways proved anything but conducive to that sense of security and dignity Mrs. ________ had long and justly boasted for her house.

Especially after a few drinks Max also liked to go about the house bragging to clients and to entertainers alike of his prowess in various lines, intruding on parties still at the "downstairs stage" of the night's activities, minding everybody's business, and inevitably turning the conversation to his superiorities. Most of the time he was quite amiable in this role—a cordial, but an all too cordial, host under circumstances in which people are usually concerned more with definite and perhaps pressing aims of their own than with the glowing reminiscenses of another. Occasionally when crossed, he became threatening even with clients and, though open strife was usually avoided, hot, wild words and strenuous scenes sometimes followed, with Max exulting in the aftermath by pacing up and down the corridors of the house, shadowboxing, cursing, crying out his pugilistic titles and victories, and challenging all comers.

No one realized better than his wife, a woman of experience and good judgment in such matters, what an unhappy effect these antics had on her clientele quietly seeking pleasure behind doors before which Max roared and paraded. Naturally she sought to silence him and to lead him off to the quarters they shared. Usually, however, her appearance served merely as a focus for his ire, and the tumult she sought to quell redoubled through her efforts. More than once under such circumstances he pursued her into her room, the wrangle having moved on to open violence, and there beat her to his heart's content. Mrs. ________, a tall and heavy person, gave a casual impression of being twice as large as Max. Furthermore, she was a woman of considerable strength. She often fought back vigorously, and, though she seldom succeeded in landing a telling blow that would discourage her marital opponent, her resistance made the fight much more lively and greatly augmented the uproar of thuds, slaps, crashes, oaths, grunts, and honest yells of pain.

Over several years this connubial life had been interrupted frequently by Max's departure, which he usually took in heat after quarrels such as those just described. Often he left voluntarily with obscene curses at his wife on his lips. Sometimes she called the police after he had covered her with minor bruises and abrasions from his practiced fists and had him forcibly ousted. Over the years he spent perhaps two-thirds of his time away, going from city to city and living by his wits, which are sharp indeed. When caught in his minor frauds, which he practiced not only on the public but also on those associated with him in his ventures, he quickly left town. Or, if retreat was not quick enough, he spent a few days in jail, from which he soon obtained release by telling of his imaginary head injury, of his "spells," or of anything else that occurred to his fertile mind as a means to make people believe he was incompetent because of "shell shock." When his situation turned out to be more serious, he telegraphed or telephoned his wife, who at once flew to his aid, usually with some little money at her disposal.

He covered the entire eastern seaboard on these trips and made several expeditions into the Midwest. For a few weeks in Nevada he lived well off of money he milked from slot machines by some ingenious device or contraption or maneuver. His inventions of this type are numerous and highly practical. He could, perhaps, make an excellent living indefinitely off such takings if he did not, when drinking, and often when sober, boast too widely of his cleverness or otherwise bring himself to the attention of the police.

It has been mentioned that earlier in his career, but after his second marriage, he had been wedded to other women bigamously. His wife learned of these episodes, and legal action was taken by the deceived women. From these minor troubles he was extricated by his shrewdness, the aid of his wife, and the power of his familiar tactics of claiming incompetency and irresponsibility.

This gambit of moves seems to have gained rather than lost effectiveness by repetition. It has become virtually a joker in the deck, or rather up the sleeve, and it has never failed him yet. One cannot but wonder if the juries, the courts, and other authorities are not overwhelmed by precedent and, seeing that his grounds for impunity have been upheld so often in the past, fail to challenge them adequately. Precedent is, of course, freely admitted to weigh heavily in law. On the other hand, these nonmedical observers seem to weigh seriously the plain facts of the patient's conduct when they decide that he is not a normal man, whatever term psychiatrists may use to designate him.

The immediate cause of Max's return to the hospital on this occasion was indirectly connected with a third bigamous marriage which he had recently made while off on one of his tours from connubial security. With his new partner he tried his hand again at forgery on a somewhat larger scale than usual. He prospered for a while and, flushed with prosperity and bravado, brought his new bigamous partner home with him on a visit to the brothel where his legal wife was struggling to restore standards which had suffered during his presence.

As might well be imagined, quarreling broke out at once between the two wives. Max, still in character, did nothing to pour oil on these sorely troubled waters. In fact, his every move seemed designed to whip up the already lively doings to a crescendo. The dispute culminated in a vigorous and vociferous set-to during which both women were pretty thoroughly mauled, furniture was broken, and the brothel all but wrecked. Max's most important personal contribution to the fray was a broken jaw for his legal wife, the madame of the house.

It is interesting here to note that, despite his continual brawling with both men and women over so many years while drinking or while quite sober and despite his ferocious threats of violence and his pretty genuine ability as a pugilist, no serious bodily harm had before this come to anyone at his hands. I believe that the substantial injury was unintentional, an act of thoughtless exuberance committed in the heat of a situation eminently and subtly designed to bring out high enthusiasm in such a man as our hero.

Having succeeded in bringing off a scene that even in his career stands out as a little masterpiece, he took the bigamous partner and fled back to the nearby city where his forgeries were in progress. Almost on his arrival detection met him, and hard on its heels came prosecution from home in consequence of the jaw breaking. To these difficulties charges for his latest bigamy were added. As such disasters began to accumulate about Max, his legal wife, finally aroused, decided for the moment to lend her influence to the punitive forces.

In the court action that followed, the present, and third, bigamous wife received an adequate sentence to the state penitentiary, and for a while Max's own fortune seemed none too bright. Wrought upon by his protestations, however, and perhaps influenced as well by the disappearance of her rival from the scene, his old protector, the legal wife, was won over and began to work with her husband. Soon matters were arranged for him to escape the ordinary consequences of his deeds and be sent again to a psychiatric hospital. His last admission, with which this account began, was the result.

Safe in the familiar harbor of a psychiatric hospital, he was for a week or more friendly, cooperative, and apparently content. He was at all times shrewd, somewhat witty on low levels of humor, and entirely free from ideas or behavior suggesting any recognized psychosis.

He became very friendly with me during this period and talked entertainingly and with enthusiasm about his many adventures. He denied all misconduct on his part but admitted that he had often been in trouble because of his wife and others. It was not the denial of a man who is eager to show himself innocent but the casual tossing aside of matters considered irrelevant or bothersome to discuss. After briefly laughing off all accusations, he at once shifted the subject to his many triumphs and attainments.

Telling of his early life in Vienna, his birthplace, he spoke of his excellent scholarship in the schools, of his preeminence at sports, and of the splendid figure in general he had cut as a youth in that gay and urbane city. In none of these statements did he lay in details such as might be expected of a man developing a delusional trend. No psychiatrist, and few laymen for that matter, would have had the least difficulty in recognizing all this as "tall talk" designed to deceive the listener and to put the talker in a good light. All the patient's reactions showed that he himself was far from being taken in.

His birth and upbringing in Vienna coincide with the facts as obtained from his army records. His alleged experiences at Heidelberg are recorded many times on his own testimony. He described himself as a distinguished student in that honorable university, referring to Kant and Schopenhauer and several of the Greek philosopers as special subjects of his study. He spoke also of a deep interest in Shakespeare during his student days and sought to give the idea that he was celebrated among his fellows for his knowledge of the Bard.

The shrewdness and agility of his mind were prettily demonstrated in these references to the picturesque and traditional gaieties of student life, and to the works of the philosophers and poets. No less vividly and convincingly did he reveal an utter lack of real acquaintance with any of the subjects in which he boasted himself learned.

He knew the names of a half-dozen Shakespearean plays, several catchpenny lines familiar to the man on the streets, a scattering of great names among the philosophers. He was totally ignorant not only of the systems of thought for which these philosophers are famous but also even of superficial and general facts about their lives and times that any person, however unintellectual, could not fail to remember if he ever had the interest to read of such matters. Of Shakespeare he knew practically nothing beyond the titles that rolled eloquently from his tongue and a few vague and jumbled conceptions that have crept into the ideologies of bootblacks, peasants, and gamins the world over.

Furthermore, he had no interest, as contrasted with knowledge, in any matter that could be called philosophic or poetic. He liked to rattle off his little round of fragmentary quotations, the connections and the connotations of which he realized only in the most superficial sense, to contribute a few pat and shallow saws of his own believed by him to be highly original, iconoclastic, and profound, to boast generally of his wisdom, and then to go on to descriptions of his other attainments and experiences.

To my surprise, he was several times taken by psychiatrists who studied him briefly and by social service workers as a man of some intellectual stature. His story of study at Heidelberg, though usually discounted, was, if the implication of the psychiatric histories is correctly read, sometimes taken as true or probably true.

Although my actual contact with Heidelberg is superficial enough, I had no difficulty in demonstrating in the patient a plain lack of acquaintance with the ways of life there. The general plan of study and the physical setup of the university, matters that would be familiar to anyone who had been an undergraduate there, however briefly and disinterestedly, were unknown to Max. He showed that he might have passed through the town and that he had heard and still clearly remembered gossip and legend from the streets of Vienna about the university and its customs, but he had no more real understanding of it than a shrewd but unlettered cockney would have of Cambridge.

This phase of his examination provided, in my opinion, a striking example of the ambiguity inherent in our word *intelligence.* Here was a man of exceptional acumen. His versatile devices of defraud, his mechanical inventions to overcome safeguards which ordinarily protect slot machines and other depositories of cash, and his shrewd practical reasoning in the many difficulties of his career demonstrate beyond question the accuracy, quickness, and subtlety of his practical thinking. His memory is unusually sound; his cleverness at manipulating bits of information so as to appear learned is exceptional. He is not a man to be taken in by the scheming of others, though he himself takes in many. One can truthfully say about him that he is "bright as a dollar," "smart as a whip," that "his mind is like a steel trap."

His ability to plan and execute schemes to provide money for himself, to escape legal consequences, and to give, when desirable, the impression that he is, in the ordinary sense, mentally deranged, could be matched by few, if any, people whom I have known. In such thinking he not only shows objective ingenuity but also remarkable knowledge of other people and their reactions (of *psychology* in the popular sense) at certain levels, or, rather, in certain modes of personality reaction. He stands out for the swiftness and accuracy of his thinking at solving puzzles and at playing checkers. At any sort of contest based on a matching of wits he is unlikely to come off second best.

To consider his intelligence (or should one say wisdom?) from another viewpoint, from that of the ordinary man's idea of what is good sense about working out a successful plan of life on a long-term basis, only the story of his career can speak adequately. Be it noted that the result of his conduct brings trouble not only to others but almost as regularly to himself.

To take still another point of view and consider him on a basis of those values somewhat vaguely implied by "intellectuality," "culture," or, in everyday speech, by "depth of mind," we find an appalling deficiency. These concepts in which meaning or emotional significance are considered along with the mechanically rational, if applied to this man, measure him as very small or very defective. He appears not only ignorant in such modes of function but stupid as well. He is unfamiliar with the primary facts or data of what might be called personal values and is altogether incapable of understanding such matters. It is impossible for him to take even a slight interest in the tragedy or joy or the striving of humanity as presented in serious literature or art. He is also indifferent to all these matters in life itself. Beauty and ugliness, except in a very superficial sense, goodness, evil, love, horror, and humor have no actual meaning, no power to move him.

He is, furthermore, lacking in the ability to see that others are moved. It is as though he were blind, despite his sharp intelligence, to this aspect of human existence. It cannot be explained to him because there is nothing in his orbit of awareness that can bridge the gap with comparison. He can repeat the words and say glibly that he understands, and there is no way for him to realize that he does not understand.

But let us return to the patient's conduct. He talked at length of his ability as a fencer, maintaining that he was the best swordsman, or one of the best, at Heidelberg during his student days and was also well known and feared in Vienna. He spoke of the championship he had won at boxing while in the army, boasting often of a belt which he still possessed symbolizing this achievement. On hearing that I had had a slight experience in amateur boxing, he offered to demonstrate his skill and to teach me some points. Ostentatiously he insisted that I stand up and, pulling his punches, went through a number of sequences. He did this several times, always choosing a place on the ward where he could be observed by a large group of patients and attendants. He gave every indication of being a practiced boxer. This is borne out also by army records, which indicate that he won some small prize as champion of his battalion or regiment.

Even before his presentation at the staff meeting, he again became dissatisfied, making complaints against the nurses and attendants, demanding special foods and privileges, bullying other patients, and inciting them to make trouble. At staff meeting the diagnosis of psychopathic personality was reaffirmed.

On failing to get his discharge at once, he became even more fretful and unruly and threatened to break out of the hospital. It became difficult to care for him on the ward for well-adjusted patients in which he had been placed, so he was transferred to the closely supervised ward, where he found himself surrounded by actively disturbed and egregiously psychotic companions.

He complained at once of this to his wife, who came to the hospital authorities in tears and with angry protestations, saying that it was an outrage to put her husband with all those *crazy* men who were violent and combative and who might hurt him. Earlier on the ward she had made the same protest to an attendant, who had saltily remarked on the inconsistency of such worries about a husband so well known for his boasts of might and ferocity and pugilistic skill. She made the matter so sharp an issue that Max, after promising to cooperate, was moved to a quieter ward.

Now, for a short while, he was more agreeably disposed. Boastfully he told me that he was, in addition to all his other parts, an artist of remarkable ability. He asked to be given a loaf of bread, stating that he would mold from it creations of great beauty and worth. On getting the bread, he broke off a large chunk, placed it in his mouth, and began to chew it assiduously, apparently relishing the confusion of his observers. After proceeding for a length of time and with thoroughness that once would have met with favor from advocates of the now almost forgotten cult of Fletcherism, he at last disgorged the mess from his mouth and with considerable dexterity set about modeling it into the figure of a cross. Soon a human form was added in the customary representation. Rosettes, intertwining leaves, garlands, and an elaborate pedestal followed. The mixture of saliva and chewed bread rapidly hardened.

He now requested a pass to go into town, saying that he must obtain shellac and appropriate paints to complete his creation. He made it plain that he was molding this statuette for me, and it was clear that he regarded it as a most flattering favor. Since it was judged unwise to send him out alone, he was allowed to go in company of an attendant. He returned with his materials but also with the strong odor of whiskey on his breath.

The whiskey had been obtained in this manner: Pleading a call of nature which, judging by his frantic tone and impressive grimaces, the attendant deemed urgent, he hurriedly sequestered himself in a toilet. After waiting for what seemed like a most liberal interval, the attendant went to inquire into the delay. On receiving no response, he forced the door only to find that Max had made his escape through a small window near the top of the room, a feat that would have been extremely difficult for an ordinary man.

Guided by a happy instinct, the attendant hurried to a nearby dive where whiskey was sold and surprised our hero in the midst of his second or third potation. He was drinking to his own cleverness at outwitting the attendant and in loud, imperious tones commanded all present to drink with him and at his expense.

The attendant found him insolent and intractable at first but, with strong moral support from the proprietor and others, led him out after settling charges for drinks to all, which Max had grandly assumed without a cent in his pockets.

For the rest of the day he was surly and idle except for his efforts to promote quarrels, but on the morrow, extolling again his virtuosity as a sculptor, he settled down and finished his gift to me. It was indeed an uncommon production. The chewed bread had become as hard as baked clay. The whole piece was very skillfully and ingeniously shaped, dry, firm, and as neatly finished as if done by a machine. It was, furthermore, one of the most extravagant, florid, and unprepossessing articles that has ever met my glance. Max presented it with mixed pride and condescension, with an air of triumph and expectancy that seemed to demand expressions of wonder and gratitude beyond reach of the ordinary man. I did my best but felt none too satisfied with my efforts.

Max now asked for daily bread and for a room to be set apart as an atelier where he proposed to work regularly and without distracting influences. In the hope that this activity would keep him out of trouble, all his requests were granted. He immediately demanded full parole also but, when it was not obtained, agreed to wait a short while for it.

For a week he worked steadily, his mouth crammed with the doughy mass, his jaws chewing deliberately, his hands nimbly shaping spewed-out hunks of the mess into various neatly finished and exact, but always garish, forms. His coloring of the flowers and garlands and imitation jewels, vivid red, pale purple, sickly pink, always struck a high level of the tawdry blended with the pretentious. The most gaudy atrocities of the dime store must give ground before such art.

He sent messages to the medical director of the hospital, to the supervisor of attendants and the chief nurse, and to many others whom he felt it well to ingratiate that objets d'art awaited them in his studio. He was visited by these people and by various prominent ladies of the city interested in welfare work and active in helping disabled veterans. To most of these he made presentations as well as moving speeches about his misfortunes, his gifts, and his ambitions. His demands for parole now became more vehement. Many influential citizens begged that he be given this chance to rehabilitate himself. As a matter of fact, he had been reasonably cooperative while at his new work. Parole was granted.

The police brought him back after a few hours. His left hand showed a painful laceration, the result of a severe bite inflicted in retreat by a barroom opponent who had resorted to this vaguely Parthian maneuver after finding Max's pugilistic skill too great to cope with in the ordinary manner. He showed some evidence of drink but was by no means sodden. Nor did he in any way give the impression of a man sufficiently influenced by liquor to have his judgment appreciably altered or any violent and extraordinary impulses released. In contrast with some of the other patients discussed here, Max, though a ready drinker, never or very rarely drank to the point of confusion. There is no record in all the saga of his being brought in senseless from the highways or fields. At the worst he could scarcely be classed as more than a moderate drinker.

He made no excuses for violating his parole but blamed others in full for the trouble he had started and felt grossly misused by the man he had attacked, by the police, and by the hospital that revoked his parole.

His wife at once pled for restoration of his parole, and a number of other influences supported her. Max reiterated the familiar argument: why deny liberty to a man classed as sane? Parole was restored after a week. Surprisingly, Max got through two days without difficulty, but on the third, burst into the office of the supervisor of attendants and vehemently demanded that a former attendant, dismissed for incompetence, be reinstated at once. He had brought this man with him into the office. Inspired by a couple of highballs but by no means drunk, he thundered and swaggered, threatening to use political influences to have the supervisor discharged if all his demands were not met forthwith. He named various political powers which he boasted that he could command. These influences, he very truly pointed out, had lent themselves to his efforts to get out of jail and out of hospitals in the past. He insisted, furthermore, that certain other attendants whom he disliked be discharged. Storming and cursing and threatening, he was removed to a closed ward.

Somewhat disgruntled, he ceased his modeling in postprandial bread and sulked, irritable and aggressive, among his psychotic companions. Soon, however, he became more agreeable and after a few days came swaggering into my office to display a new product of his ingenuity. Borrowing a dollar bill and a pair of scissors, he cut out five rectangles of plain paper identical in size and shape with the bill and poised himself with a faintly prestidigitatorial air.

"Watch this," he boasted.

As he cut up his models of the bank note and manipulated the pieces, he called for paste to be brought. Then, after a shrewd and tricky rearrangement, he pasted together his fragments.

"Count them," he ordered in the grand manner.

Not five but six paper models lay on the table, all plainly patched, but all defying the ordinary eye to detect any appreciable loss of substance.

Within a week his wife, after haunting the hospital and begging for his parole, insisting that she needed him at home, that she was in want, succeeded in taking him out in her custody. Late that night local policemen brought him back. After giving his wife what might be called an average beating, he had caused considerable uproar at a bar and fled to another dive where, after trying to get loans from a few idlers, he boasted and quarreled until the police intervened.

He remained then on a closed ward for about a week. After this time, legal charges against him having been dropped, he demanded release against medical advice. Since he was sane and competent in the eyes of law and science, he was discharged.

Two months later local newspapers carried small headlines calling attention to his being taken by federal agents after a protracted investigation in Texas. For weeks patched-up five-, ten-, and twenty-dollar bills circulated in several Texas cities, and Max, decked in flashy finery, drove about in his own car, and splurged lavishly on food, drink, and women. The surprising volume of mutilated notes at last caused comment and finally suspicion. After skillful and persistent efforts, the federal agents finally worked out the puzzle and brought it to Max's feet.

My colleagues and I felt that perhaps our acquaintance with Max had ended. Federal justice is widely regarded as less relenting and less distractible than municipal and state justice. For most lawbreakers this may, indeed, be true. Max's old ploy, however, had not lost its charm. Some months later he was in a psychiatric hospital and shortly afterward at large.

His career continued. The records show that once, while under a five-year sentence to a state penitentiary, he stressed his former syphilitic infection and boasted so vehemently in his old style that a physician who saw him in prison made a diagnosis of dementia paralytica. No neurologic or serologic findings supported this opinion, which was offered by a general practitioner after one interview. This was enough to start the familiar cycle of prison-to-hospital-to-freedom.

Once again, when anxious for shelter, he boasted that he could communicate with ancestors who had died thousands of years ago. His wife joined in and claimed that he had seen monkeys and baboons chasing him. At a general hospital a tentative diagnosis of schizophrenia was offered. Back at another psychiatric hospital he showed no evidence of an orthodox psychosis and after a short time got his discharge.

Again when pressed by a court verdict, he claimed amnesia for a period of two years, during which he had been active at defrauding. A suspicion of hysteria was expressed by some physicians. At the psychiatric hospital he stuck for a while to this story of amnesia, but, his vanity being aroused, he recalled in detail all his experiences. It was plain from his manner that he had not suffered from any true amnesia, and he no longer took pains to make anyone believe that he had.

A few years later he was again brought to the hospital. This time his wife insisted that his beatings were too much to bear and stated that he had threatened to kill her with an axe, explaining that he could do so with impunity since he was a mentally disabled veteran and that, as she well knew, he had always succeeded in escaping the consequences of any crime. She soon recovered from her fears and asked for his parole. At the insistence of both man and wife, he was discharged after a few weeks.

Be it noted that despite his vigorous threats such as the one just mentioned, Max seldom, if ever, tried with deliberate intention to do anyone serious physical injury. This fact has especial weight in view of his boasted and pretty satisfactorily demonstrated immunity from penal consequences. In important respects he appears to differ fundamentally from those who are regularly or often inclined toward major violence or murder. In his innumerable conflicts with the law he has appeared usually in the role of petty bully, perpetrator of frauds, sharper, con man, swindler, thief, and peace-disturbing braggart.

Some months later I, with other phychiatrists, testified at court when efforts were being made to have Max committed by law as "insane." Several citizens whom he had defrauded and seriously troubled in other ways, finding that he was not vulnerable to fines or sentences in the municipal courts, hoped to obtain relief and protection by getting him into a psychiatric hospital.

The psychiatrists could not avoid admitting that he showed no evidence of anything that is officially classed as a psychosis. Despite some sort of misgivings, I had to agree. Yet it seemed plain that this man, though free from all technical signs of psychosis, was far less capable of leading a sane, or satisfactory, or acceptable life, less safe or suitable to be at large in any civilized community, than many, perhaps than most, in whom psychosis can be readily demonstrated and universally accepted as unquestionable. Was there any means I could suggest by which he might through existing laws and institutions be more adequately controlled and kept from destructive folly? Or by which the community might be better protected from his persistent antisocial activities? As I groped without avail for an answer, the sense of futility became truly oppressive. Max, neat and well groomed, insouciant, witty, alert, and splendidly rational, rose, beaming, to hear again the verdict of freedom.

TOM

This young man, 21 years of age, does not look at all like a criminal type or a shifty delinquent. In fact, he stands out in remarkable contrast to the kind of patient suggested by such a term as *constitutional inferiority.* He does not fit satisfactorily into the sort of picture that emerges from early descriptions of people generally inadequate and often showing physical "stigmata of degeneracy" or ordinary defectiveness.

Tom looks and is in robust physical health. His manner and appearance are pleasing. In his face a prospective employer would be likely to see strong indications of character as well as high incentive and ability. He is well informed, alert, and entirely at ease, exhibiting a confidence in himself that the observer is likely to consider amply justified. This does not look like the sort of man who will fail or flounder about in the tasks of life but like someone incompatible with all such thoughts.

There is nothing to suggest that he is putting on a bold front or trying to adopt any attitude or manner that will be misleading. Though he knows the examiner has evidence of his almost incredible career, he gives such an impression that it seems for the moment likely he will be able to explain it all away. In his own mind he has evidently brushed aside so satisfactorily such matters as those to be mentioned that others, also, caught up in the magic of his equanimity, almost share his invulnerable disregard.

Tom has so plainly escaped the ordinary and, one would think, the inevitable consequences of his experience that, in a sort of contagion, his interviewer is also affected. The effect is to make it seem more plausible to accept the whole detailed reality of a life as dream or illusion than believe that this man could so regard it were it otherwise. With indisputable evidence that a human being has been run over and dismembered by a series of freight trains and that the bodily remnants have subsequently been put through a sausage grinder, any investigator will have definite and vivid preconceptions of what he will behold. The evidence itself bleaches, suddenly and automatically, at the sight of the intact victim, whole, smiling, immaculate, unscarred, without a scratch. What happened to the anatomic unit in this allusion scarcely seems more drastic than what, as a social unit, the patient before me had experienced.

This poised young man's immediate problem was serious but not monumental. His family and legal authorities were in hope that if some psychiatric disorder could be discovered in him, he might escape a jail sentence for stealing. Despite many years of disappointment, the family still sought some remedy, some treatment or handling, that might bring about favorable changes in the patient's behavior. Those concerned with the legal aspects of the immediate problem had dealt with this man often in the past and saw in his conduct indications of something more than, and something different from, an ordinary or sane antisocial scheme of existence. His high intelligence made it difficult for them to account for what he did on that basis.

Evidence of his maladjustment became distinct in childhood. He appeared to be a reliable and manly fellow but could never be counted upon to keep at any task or to give a straight account of any situation. He was frequently truant from school. No advice or persuasion influenced him in his acts, despite his excellent response in all discussions. Though he was generously provided for, he stole some of his father's chickens from time to time, selling them at stores downtown. Pieces of table silver would be missed. These were sometimes recovered from those to whom he had sold them for a pittance or swapped them for odds and ends which seemed to hold no particular interest or value for him. He resented and seemed eager to avoid punishment, but no modification in his behavior resulted from it. He did not seem wild or particularly impulsive, a victim of high temper or uncontrollable drives. There was nothing to indicate he was subject to unusually strong temptations, lured by definite plans for high adventure and exciting revolt.

Often when truant from high school classes, Tom wandered more or less aimlessly, sometimes shooting at a farmer's chickens, setting fire to a rural privy around the outskirts of town, or perhaps loitering about a cigar store or a poolroom, reading the comics, throwing rocks at squirrels in a park, perpetrating small thefts or swindles. He often charged things in stores to his father and stole small items, cigarettes, candy, cigars, which he sometimes gave away freely to slight acquaintances or other idlers he encountered. Though many wasteful, inopportune, and punishable deeds were correctly attributed to him, these apparently were only a small fraction of his actual achievement along this line.

He lied so plausibly and with such utter equanimity, devised such ingenious alibis, or simply denied all responsibility with such convincing appearances of candor that for many years his real career was poorly estimated. Among typical exploits with which he is credited stand these: prankish defecation into the stringed intricacies of the school piano, removal from his uncle's automobile of a carburetor for which he got 75 cents, and selling of his father's overcoat to a passing buyer of scrap materials.

Though he often fell in with groups or small gangs, he never for long identified himself with others in a common cause. In the more outlandish and serious outcroppings of group mischief he sometimes played a prominent role. With several others he broke into a summer cottage on a nearby lake, stole a few articles, overturned all the furniture, and threw rugs, dishes, etc., out of the window. He and a few more teenage boys on another expedition smashed headlights and windshields on several automobiles, punctured a number of tires, and rolled one car down a slope, leaving it slightly battered and bogged in a ditch.

At 14 or 15 years of age, having learned to drive, Tom began to steal automobiles with some regularity. Often his intention seemed less that of theft than of heedless misappropriation. A neighbor or friend of the family, going to the garage or to where the car was parked outside an office building, would find it missing. Sometimes the patient would leave the stolen vehicle within a few blocks or miles of the owner, sometimes out on the road where the gasoline had given out. After he had tried to sell a stolen car, his father consulted advisers and, on the theory that he might have some specific craving for automobiles, bought one for him as a therapeutic measure. On one occasion while out driving Tom deliberately parked his own car and, leaving it, stole an inferior model which he left slightly damaged on the outskirts of a village some miles away.

Meanwhile, Tom continued to forge his father's name to small checks and to steal change, pocketknives, and textbooks at school. Occasionally, on the pretext of ownership, he would sell a dog or a calf belonging to some member of the community. His youth made long terms of imprisonment seem inappropriate, it being felt that this might confirm him in a criminal career or teach him additional and more malignant antisocial techniques. He was ineligible for the state hospital.

Private physicians, scoutmasters, and social workers were consulted. They talked and worked with him, but to no avail. Listing the deeds for which he became ever more notable does not give an adequate picture of the situation. He did not every day or every week bring attention to himself by major acts of mischief or destructiveness. He was usually polite, often considerate in small, appealing ways, and always seemed to have learned his lesson after detection and punishment. He was clever and learned easily. During intervals in which his attendance was regular, he impressed his teachers as outstanding in ability. Some charm and apparent modesty, as well as his very convincing way of seeming sincere and to have taken resolutions that would count, kept not only the parents but all who encountered him clinging to hope. Teachers, scoutmasters, the school principal, etc., recognized that in some very important respects he differed from the ordinary bad or wayward youth and made special efforts to help him and to give him new opportunities to reform or readjust.

When he drove a stolen automobile across a state line, he came in contact with federal authorities. In view of his youth and the wonderful impression he made, he was put on probation. Soon afterward he took another automobile and again left it in the adjoining state. It was a very obvious situation. The consequences could not have been entirely overlooked by a person of his excellent shrewdness. He admitted that the considerable risks of getting caught had occurred to him but felt he had a chance to avoid detection and would take it. No unusual and powerful motive or any special aim could be brought out as an explanation.

Tom was sent to a federal institution in a distant state where a well-organized program of rehabilitation and guidance was available. He soon impressed authorities at this place with his attitude and in the way he discussed his past mistakes and plans for a different future. He seemed to merit parole status precociously and this was awarded him. It was not long before he began stealing again and thereby lost his freedom.

The impression he made during confinement was so promising that he was pardoned before the expiration of the regular term, and he came home confident, buoyant, apparently matured and thoroughly rehabilitated. Considerable work had been done with him at the institution, and he seemed to respond well to psychiatric measures. He found employment in a drydock at a nearby port and talked modestly but convincingly of the course he would now follow, expressing aims and plans few could greatly improve.

His employers found him at first energetic, bright, and apparently enthusiastic about the work. Soon evidence of inexplicable irresponsibility emerged and accumulated. Sometimes he missed several days and brought simple but convincing excuses of illness. As the occasions multiplied, explanations so detailed and elaborate were made that it seemed only facts could have produced them. Later he sometimes left the job, stayed away for hours, and gave no account of his behavior except to say that he did not feel like working at the time.

There seemed to be no cause for dissatisfaction, no discernible change in his attitude toward the work. When he chose to apply himself, he did better than most. It was plain to the employers that this promising young man was not merely lazy or, in an ordinary way, fretfully restless.

The theft of an automobile brought Tom to jail again. He expressed remorse over his mistake, talked so well, and seemed so genuinely and appropriately motivated and determined that his father, by making heavy financial settlements, secured his release. After a number of relatively petty but annoying activities, another theft made it necessary for his family to intervene.

Reliable information indicates that he has been arrested and imprisoned approximately fifty or sixty times. It is estimated that he would have been put in jails or police stations for short or long periods of detention on approximately 150 other occasions if his family had not made good his small thefts and damages and paid fines for him.

Sometimes he was arrested for fomenting brawls in low resorts, for initiating fights, or for such high-handed and disturbing behavior as to constitute public nuisance. Though not a very regular drinker or one who characteristically drank to sodden confusion or stupefaction, he often exhibited unsociable and unprepossessing manners and conduct after taking even a few beers or highballs. In one juke joint imbroglio he is credited with having struck a fellow reveler on the head with a piece of iron. No serious injuries resulted, although great uproar and spectacular commotion prevailed. Under similar circumstances he was once in, or on the fringes of, an altercation in which gunplay occurred and another man received a minor flesh wound. Meanwhile, he continued to forge his father's name to checks, often insisted on sleeping through breakfast, obtained loans through ingenious misrepresentations, and ran up debts which he simply ignored.

Tom's mother had for some years suffered special anxiety and distress because of his unannounced absences. After kissing her good-bye and saying he was going downtown for a soft drink or to a movie, he might not appear for several days or even for a couple of weeks. Instead of his returning, a long-distance telephone call might in the middle of the night arouse the father, who would be entreated to come at once to nearby or distant places where the son had encountered unpleasant complications or, perhaps, restraint by the police.

He expressed particularly heavy penitence for all the worry and sleepless nights he had caused his mother, maintaining that he loved her dearly and that nothing about his life so displeased him as having given her even a moment's distress. He spoke as if with feeling about the patience, generosity, and understanding of his father and seemed to believe the filial bond was unusually fine and satisfactory.

Recently an elderly friend of the family who was in town on business learned something of the situation. This man, whose experience in dealing with other people and their problems was considerable (and very successful), undertook the task of helping the patient. Though he had heard a good deal about past exploits, he could not but feel hopeful after his first talk. A little later he took the patient with him on an automobile ride, feeling that in this way he could bring the problem to full discussion by a more natural, informal approach.

The conversation, once begun, developed amazingly. The younger man not only promised to behave from now on in an exemplary fashion but analyzed and discussed his past in such a way that the older found there was little that could be added. Despite his interest and his experience in such matters, he had seldom, if ever, encountered a more plausible interpretation of human mistakes and social confusion, of how distortion of aims and maladjustment develop out of the complicated influences and situations of modern living. Even more than the pertinent presentation of cause and effect and the cogent steps proposed for solution, the young man's appearance of sincerity in all these realizations impressed the older counselor. He spoke as the wisest and most contrite of men would speak and seemed to have a more detailed and deeper understanding of his entire situation than even the most sagacious observer could reach.

The patient talked not only of what he would avoid but discussed plans for work and recreation, for development and progressive maturation. Tom emphasized how his irregular hours and unforeseen absences had kept his parents much of the time not sure whether he was dead or alive. Before the ride was over, the judicious counselor was encouraged and deeply optimistic. In addition, he was so impressed by points this young man had brought out and by his apparent earnestness and resolution that he felt himself wiser from the experience. Moved and stimulated, he admitted that he had obtained new and valuable viewpoints on life and deeper seriousness. He had been stimulated to review his own patterns of behavior and to seek a better and more progressive plan of self-expression. In this frame of mind he bade the patient good night, letting him out of the car at the front gate of the parents' home.

The patient did not even enter the house. After going in the gate, he walked through the grounds, went out by a back entrance, and was not heard from that night. He was not, in fact, heard from for a week. News then came of his being in jail again at a nearby town where he had forged, stolen trifles, run up debts, and carried out other behavior familiar to all who knew him.

This young man apparently has never formed any substantial attachment for another person. Sexually he has been desultorily promiscuous under a wide variety of circumstances. A year or two earlier he had married a girl who had achieved considerable local recognition as a prostitute and as one whose fee was moderate. He had previously shared her offerings during an evening (on a commercial basis) with friends or with brief acquaintances among whom he found himself. He soon left the bride and never showed signs of shame or chagrin about the character of the woman he had married or of any responsibility toward her.

During World War II Tom maintained over some months an offhand relationship with the wife of a man in combat overseas. When in town he ate at her house, sometimes slept there with her, but was as heedless of her and her feelings as of his parents. She apparently suffered some anxiety when, after making plans and promises to do something special with her, he disappeared and she heard nothing from him until he called her from another city (reversing the charges) to chat casually and sometimes to speak eloquent words of endearment. Sometimes he took precautions to deceive her about his sporadic sex relations with other women; sometimes he forgot or did not bother.

On returning from his trips during World War II, he sometimes told interesting stories of having been for a time in the navy, narrating with vivid and lifelike plausibility action in which he had participated and which led to the destruction of a German submarine off Jamaica or the pursuit of a raiding warship off the coast of Greenland. Again he would talk at length about his experiences transporting airplanes from Miami to Havana or accidents leading to hospitalization and operation and diverse adventures with nurses, other patients, interns, etc. Once, during a stag-party discussion of venereal disease, he even fabricated an account of having caught one or more of these unenviable maladies and enlightened his listeners about treatments he had received, drugs, dosage, and complications.

None of these fraudulent stories had a real element of delusion. When really caught in the lie about any of them and confronted with definite proof, he often laughed and passed it off as a sort of joke.

After these events and many others similar in general but differing in detail, Tom seemed modestly pleased with himself, effortlessly confident of the future. He gave the impression of a young man fresh and unhardened, in no respect brutalized or worn by his past experiences. He also seemed a poised fellow, one who would make his decisions not in hotheaded haste but calmly, whether these were prompted by immediate whim or by intentions he had much time to entertain.

GEORGE

This man was 33 years of age at the time I first saw him and admitted him to a psychiatric hospital. He stated that his trouble was nervousness but could give no definite idea of what he meant by this word. He was remarkably self-composed, showed no indication of restlessness or anxiety, and could not mention anything that he worried about. He went on to state that his alleged nervousness was caused by shell shock during the war. He then proceeded to elaborate on this in an outlandish story describing himself as being cast twenty feet into the air by a shell, landing in his descent astride some iron pipes, and lying totally unconscious for sixty days, during all of which he hovered between life and death.

A physical examination showed George without any evidence of injury or illness. In fact, he was a remarkably strong and active man, 6 feet tall and 170 pounds in weight. Later, in an athletic meet held on the hospital grounds, he showed himself an exceptional sprinter and broadjumper, surpassing many able competitors ten years younger than himself in these events. Prolonged observation and psychiatric study brought out no sign or suggestion of a psychosis or a psychoneurosis. Despite his original complaint of nervousness, he was at all times calm and without the slightest evidence of abnormal anxiety. He ate and slept well, did not complain of any worries, and was free of phobias, compulsions, conversion reactions, tics, and all other ordinary neurotic manifestations.

Records of this man's career show that he has been confined in various mental hospitals approximately half the time since he became of age. In addition to periods ranging from a few weeks to six months at federal institutions in Texas, Tennessee, Mississippi, Georgia, and Florida, he was also frequently sent by the government to private psychiatric hospitals and invalids' homes. Between these experiences he spent a good part of his time in the local county jail or in other jails at Birmingham, Montgomery, Mobile, and other towns that he visited. He was taken in sometimes for drunkenness and disorderly conduct, at other times for writing bad checks, petty theft, reckless driving of automobiles, obtaining money under false pretenses, snatching the purse from a prostitute, taking possession of a house whose owners were off on vacation, and similar actions. Extravagant but insincere threats to harm his wife and four children made after taking a few drinks and lunacy charges also accounted for a dozen or so arrests.

During all the observation at various hospitals mentioned, as well as at a state mental hospital where George also spent a short time, no technical evidence of a psychosis or a psychoneurosis was mentioned. His wife and friends have repeatedly persuaded local authorities to consider him as mentally deranged and to have him sent to hospitals rather than let him face the various charges brought against him from time to time.

On other occasions, when he was refused admission by hospitals where physicians had already studied him more than once and declared him sane, competent, and not in need of psychiatric treatment, friends and relatives have had him arrested, have prevailed upon local doctors to sign statements that he is deranged and dangerous, and have brought pressure to bear so that hospitals, in the light in which the case was presented, had not choice but to readmit him.

The doctors involved in such procedures, country practitioners for the most part, never mention technical evidence that would indicate a psychosis or a psychoneurosis as they are described in the textbooks. Such statements as these are typical:

> Something is decidedly wrong mentally. I don't think I have ever come in contact with a man as unreliable as he is. He worries everybody that has fooled with him until they hate him. The County authorities are tired of boarding him as he is not a criminal. (*Family physician*)
>
> Everybody who comes in contact with him agrees that he should be confined permanently . . . very unreliable as to his word of honor. (*County physician*)

A physician who owns a private hospital located at a town nearby, in explaining his refusal to accept the patient again, ends by saying "we do not cater to his class."

He is described as frequently drinking whiskey to excess and as sometimes taking Veronal, Luminal, Amytal, and bromides to ease himself in the aftermath of a spree. Although there is no record of alcoholic hallucinations, many bizarre and notable actions are described when the patient has had something to drink.

On a cold February day he rushed, fully clothed, down to the creek and sprang in. After thrashing about, yelling and cursing to no purpose and creating a senseless commotion, he swam back to land without difficulty. One fine spring evening he is said to have run entirely naked through the streets of the town. He once sat up all night under the house striking matches aimlessly.

Generally believed reports indicate that late one night he, with several drinking companions, succeeded in releasing a half-tamed bear from the cage in which it was kept at a filling station to attract trade. A good deal of fright, some civic uproar, and hasty precautionary measures ensued. Assiduous and painstaking effort by a number of local volunteers led to the bear's relatively uneventful return to his cage. According to available information, the bear was not terribly dangerous but sufficiently so to make a man of anything like ordinary responsibility sharply restrain all impulses to loose him on the outskirts of an unprepared community. The patient denied having been a party to this exploit, but the evidence against him is strong.

In view of this man's failure to make any effort to conduct himself sensibly through so many years, there is no wonder that many are found to say that he is of unsound mind. He has done no work except for occasional periods when for a week or ten days he would show considerable promise in such occupations as automobile salesman or clerk in a grocery store. It was not long before he proceeded, in the language of an elderly uncle often called on to deal with these problems, to "launch himself on another pot-valiant and fatuous rigadoon."

After studies of his case were completed, and on the basis of his cooperative and technically sane behavior he was given parole privileges. He promised, of course, not to drink or to break any other rule of good conduct and expressed many fine intentions positively and reassuringly. Six days later he staggered into his ward and attempted to go to bed without being noticed by the attendant. On being found so plainly "in his cups," he raged petulantly, first denied any contact with stimulants, and finally, with indignation, admitted having taken one-half glass of beer. His eyes were bloodshot, he could scarcely stand, and he spoke in wild, boastful, almost unintelligible accents. A bottle of cheap whiskey was discovered hidden under his mattress.

According to the custom of the hospital, George was now confined to a closed ward where his superficial sanity stood out arrestingly from the delusional babbling and the blank-faced, staring inertia of his psychotic fellows. He was always intelligent and agreeable, frequently pointing out the obvious inconsistency of his being confined among "insane" people. Pleading important business downtown, he was, after three weeks, given a pass to go out in the care of a hospital attendant for a few hours. He returned in good condition, but when night came on, he refused to go to bed, cursed, and spat at the nurse who tried to advise him. His breath reeked of raw liquor, and a search disclosed a half-empty pint bottle in his pocket. The attendant who took him to town denied having allowed him to purchase whiskey and could only surmise in astonishment that the patient must have slipped off for a moment and obtained the bottle while pretending to go to the toilet.

A few weeks after this incident the patient's wife came to town and asked to take him out on a pass, agreeing to assume full responsibility. When she returned him to the hospital, it was evident that he had drunk liberally, and the wife confessed herself as having been unable to deal with him.

The next day a man living near the hospital advised that he had fired a revolver at the patient on being alarmed by his behavior. George, after loitering about the premises boisterous and vaguely threatening, began to fumble at a window as if trying to force his way in. The shot had not been aimed at George but only in his general direction in order to frighten him. This end was satisfactorily achieved, for at the report he made off in a clatter of undignified haste.

About a month later, on strong promises of good behavior, George was again given parole. Within a few days he climbed over the fence and rented an automobile. After racing in this for a while about the road to no special purpose, he wrecked it in the city streets and was taken to jail.

This cycle of events was repeated several more times. The man was obviously not where he belonged when confined on a closed ward with extremely psychotic patients of the ordinary type. Just as plainly he showed himself unable to remain on an open ward with mildly psychotic patients who succeeded in adapting themselves to a life of limited freedom. Finally, on being kept under close supervision for several weeks following a senseless and troublesome spree, he demanded his discharge in a well-written letter emphasizing his sanity and the inappropriateness of his hospitalization. He was released accordingly.

Six months later he was sent back to the hospital from the local jail, where he had been confined after striking a man with a shovel. He had, as was his wont, been drinking but showed little evidence of being affected by alcohol. The other man was walking peacefully by when our patient engaged him in a dispute about possession of the pavement. "Flown with insolence and [perhaps] with wine," he found the other's conciliatory attitude not to his taste, waxed more overbearing, and ended by felling his presumed adversary with a deft blow. He did not on this occasion seem to lose control of himself like a man in a genuine rage who might have struck blow after blow. His deed seemed prompted more by fractiousness and impulses to show off than by violent passion.

His application for admission was at first refused by the hospital, since only patients suffering from mental disorder in the commonly accepted sense are eligible. His wife and influential friends thereupon invoked higher authorities, who arranged for him to be taken. This time he was again found to be free from all symptoms of recognized mental disorder, and his condition was classified in the following terms: (1) *no nervous or mental disease* and (2) *psychopathic personality.* He did not complain of nervousness as he had at the time of his first admission but instead insisted that he was a sane and well man and demanded full privileges to come and go as he pleased, saying that the authorities who arranged for him to come to the hospital had promised him this.

It was plain that George regarded the hospital simply as an expedient by which he might escape the legal consequences of his behavior. After being kept for a few weeks on a closed ward, he was allowed to go out on the grounds alone with the understanding that after a few days he would be discharged as sane and competent. He could not, however, keep out of trouble. On the third day of his freedom he was seen by the guard driving at high speed through the gate in a car belonging to one of the physicians. Chase was offered, and after a lively race he was overtaken about fifteen miles from the hospital, having battered in a fender and broken a headlight of the car on the way.

It is hardly necessary to point out that this man had repeatedly been instructed in the rules to be observed while on parole, that he knew the driving of an automobile by a patient in this hospital to be a serious violation of his trust, not to speak of the theft, or the unauthorized borrowing he proclaimed it to be. When finally caught, he appeared as sane as before, showing no evidence of any episodic loss of his usual reasoning power. He had not been drinking when he took the automobile and, of course, the pursuit was too hot for him to obtain liquor while in flight, though in view of his previously demonstrated ingenuity and dispatch in fulfilling this want, it would scarcely have been surprising to find him properly raddled.

On his return to the hospital, he did not show the slightest sign of remorse over having taken possession of and having succeeded in damaging the car belonging to a physician who had always been particularly kind to him. The owner's willingness to free him from responsibility for his deed he took as a matter of course, expressing neither gratitude nor satisfaction. In fact, he dismissed the whole matter as insignificant, and his prevailing attitude was that of a man generally ill used. Some weeks later he was sent home.

About six months afterward his wife telegraphed the hospital that she could no longer cope with her husband, whom she described as being still in such folly as that already recounted. He did not, however, arrive by the train he boarded. It was subsequently learned that he got off along the way, obtained a few drinks, and made a clamorous nuisance of himself in the station until the police came to cut short his activities.

A little later he was readmitted following a series of misadventures in no way different from those already mentioned but including a period in the state mental hospital. He was alert and rational and just as he had always been before, except for the presence of a urethral discharge of gonococcic origin. He gave a false account of his activities, saying that he had been working on a farm and had been in no trouble at all. The records showed that he had not turned his hand to make an honest dollar since he left and that a week had seldom passed without his buffoonish or antisocial activities arousing consternation in the neighborhood and bringing him to the attention of the police.

He was freely communicative and scarcely waited for encouragement to give an explanation of how he came by his gonorrhea. The records show that after causing some commotion in town by maudlin or threatening outbursts on the streets and silly, pompous threats about harming his wife, he had been brought in, bedraggled and disconsolate, from a ditch where he lay and confined to jail.

The jail, George said, was crowded, and the jailor, who knew him to be a good fellow, placed him in a cell on the women's section of the building. The bars of his cell were about six inches apart and so, according to his story, he was separated from and yet provocatively close to the women prisoners. These, his neighbors, were seven girls ranging from 14 to 20 years of age and awaiting transportation to the women's reformatory.

He said that at night, when the lights were out, these girls would disrobe and, coming to the bars, would entice him, calling him "pretty boy" and "country boy" and otherwise teasing and challenging him until he began to indulge in sexual intercourse with them between the bars in order to make them leave him alone. He says that he continued this practice with each of them every night during the rest of his sojourn there, the transactions taking place always in the dark and through the separating barrier. From one or all of these women he says he caught the gonorrhea which now troubled him.

He appeared to be proud of this story, which, however, is probably no more accurate than his stories of exemplary behavior and hard work or his frequently expressed intentions to conduct himself like a sensible person. Prolonged observation of the patient in the hospital showed him to be more prone to drift about street corners and bars, to indulge in petty gambling or theft, to cadge and impose on chance acquaintances, or to raise some puerile and futile clamor than to seek intercourse with one woman, much less with many.

Since this last admission his story has been the same as before. On recovering from gonorrhea, he was, after being found sane and competent, given freedom of the grounds. He soon left without permission and was found in the hands of the police. Back again on a closed ward he was dissatisfied and with irrefutable arguments pointed out the incongruity of his being assigned to a place among men content to sit all day in silence staring blankly at nothing or who murmured incessantly that their heads were full of gold, radium, and diamonds, that they had no stomachs or intestines, that the Masons were playing on their sexual organs by radio, that they were sickened by the odor of the bells.

It was here, however, that George had to be kept, a perfectly clear-minded person, neat, polite, and quick witted, in striking contrast to his fellows, whose lips moved inarticulately as they responded to hallucinatory voices and some of whom urinated and defecated on themselves, sought to eat dead roaches, etc.

This was not, of course, an ideal environment for him. He was therefore sent back to the parole ward time after time, only to prove himself unadaptable after periods ranging from a few days to a few weeks. When put on the closed ward among better adjusted patients with schizophrenia or dementia paralytica, men who worked on a farm detail or at woodwork, he took advantage of his situation and escaped. During much of his time in the hospital it has therefore been necessary to keep him among the actively disturbed, badly deteriorated patients where supervision is complete and possibilities of escape are limited.

When last heard from, he was again hospitalized. Opportunities are continually offered him to improve his situation. From time to time parole is restored, and occasionally his wife takes him home on furlough. Always, however, he causes trouble for himself and others for no discernible purpose.

The last news of him was that he violated his parole by leaving the hospital. After sustaining himself by his customary activities for a week or ten days and staying clear of the police he again came to grief. With the aim evidently of stealing a hen or a few fryers or perhaps to evade pursuit, he slipped into a farmer's chicken house. Having brought along a bottle and perhaps being delayed by needs to avoid detection, he drank injudiciously. Next morning he was found in the coop, where he had apparently wallowed and groped through the night. Called by the farmer, attendants brought him to the hospital. Here on a closed ward we find him, among helpless, irrational people and subject to the strict control and attention required for those who cannot direct themselves.

Though he left school after completing the eighth grade, he writes letters that would do credit to a college graduate. In these he insists on having his freedom, stating that his difficulties in the past have been minor and that he is ready and thoroughly able to settle down to an exemplary life. He often stresses the fact that his wife and children need his protection and support. His family history is entirely negative. Parents and grandparents were hard-working, sober folk, liked and respected in the little rural community in which the present generation lives. One sister and three brothers are leading normal lives there today.

FRANK

The following letter was received by an influential senator in Washington and referred by him to the hospital:

Dear Sir:

It is with regret that I find it necessary to seek consideration from higher authority but I have been confined in the Veterans Administration Hospital at ________, ________ for two years.

During my period of incarceration here I have tried in every available way to cooperate with the officials, but it seems an impossibility to get any consideration from them toward gaining my freedom.

I was placed here on the recommendation of my sister because she thought I was a drug addict, and she has written some pretty nasty things against me to the officials here.

I can prove to the satisfaction of all concerned that I am not a confirmed drug addict or habitual user of any form of drug sufficiently to warrant continuous confinement. I am not a criminal, nor had I the slightest minor charge of any description against me at the time I came here. The Staff here has rated me less than 10 percent disabled and discontinued all government compensation; therefore, I believe you will agree with me that any man with a less than 10 percent disability could not possess a physical or mental disorder sufficient to prevent his having his freedom and making his own livelihood.

I am not even allowed parole privileges of the grounds as a great many of the patients here are. Some are continually violating institutional rules and still retain their parole privileges undisciplined.

I have two children, who need my support and as long as I am kept incarcerated I can't assist them in any way for I have no means other than my labor to support them.

I hereby humbly request you to intercede in my behalf and demand these officials here to grant my release in order that I may be able to support my children to the best of my ability as is every man's duty.

There are quite a few men in these institutions that are nothing short of impositions on the government and taxpayers of the United States. They, the same as myself, are perfectly capable mentally and physically to support themselves and should be forced to do so.

I have begged for parole, trial visit, or any other means to prove myself self-sustaining, but the authorities here seem to take my plea as a joke and make a lot of promises that they have no intention of putting into action.

I will gladly submit to any physical or mental examination you may deem necessary to assist you in obtaining my release from this place.

I pray that you will give my earnest request your immediate consideration.

Please be assured that I hold no malice toward any of the officials here or elsewhere but my only objective in writing you is to gain my freedom and support my children.

Please let me hear from you personally,

Yours very respectfully,

Frank ________

The writer of this letter has behind him a formidable record of misadventure.

Detailed knowledge of Frank's early life is not available beyond the following facts. The son of a rustic blacksmith, he was raised in a small hamlet near the mountains of north Georgia. So far as can be learned, no members of his family suffered from nervous or mental disease or made themselves objectionable in the community. He completed the fifth grade in school, where he was considered by no means a dull boy, though often truant. Many of the hours he was supposed to have spent in school or working at some necessary chore for his family he is reported to have idled away in loitering about a local millpond drowning goats and doing other senseless or uninviting deeds of mischief.

While still legally a minor, Frank forged his father's name to a false statement about his age and enlisted in the National Guard. He was given vocational training by the government after his discharge from the army. He tried several courses but made no serious effort to complete any of them. In his community he soon made himself a problem, sometimes drinking to excess, often behaving in a rowdy and threatening manner, and contracting to buy small businesses, filling stations, and farms but never living up to his agreements.

Local ex-servicemen, believing that he took morphine and that treatment might help his maladjustment (commonly referred to as nervousness), had him sent to a psychiatric hospital. He remained for a month, then returned to continue in his old ways.

Now began a series of hospitalizations which extends to the present time. He would be sent first to one place, then to another. He has been treated in state hospitals, in federal hospitals, and in private institutions at the expense of the government. All told, he has been admitted no less than nineteen times to strictly mental hospitals maintained for the purpose of treating psychotic people. Sometimes he remained only three or four weeks; sometimes six or even eighteen months. Over the years his periods of hospitalization have grown slightly longer and his intervals outside shorter. He has never, during the course of fifteen years, been free longer than a few months. While not under the care of psychiatrists he has received considerable attention from the police. His jail sentences number seven at the present writing, including a term of nine months in the Leavenworth Penitentiary (where he was sent for forging a prescription for morphine) but not counting a score or more of overnight or weekend stops in police stations.

Despite these preoccupations, Frank has found time to marry and have four children and to become ordained as a minister in a small religious sect noted for vigorous evangelical fervor. His marital relations have been most unsatisfactory during the interludes when he was free to be with the family. His wife reports that he curses her and fights with her, and it is well established that he seizes any money that is available, rents automobiles, and drives aimlessly about the countryside, often drinking to excess and, according to some reports, occasionally taking morphine.

At times he has seemed proud of his ecclesiastical title, referring to himself as a pastor and assuming unctuous and haughty airs. He has not, however, occupied himself with whatever ministerial duties he was supposed to fulfill any more consistently than with other work.

His friends have obtained many positions for him. He is shrewd, neat in appearance, and an excellent talker. He makes a good impression at first but always shirks his responsibility to such an extent that it is impossible to retain him.

A few years ago he was given a place at a gas station and seemed, surprisingly, to show considerable interest in his work for several days. It was then discovered that he had been drawing off all the gasoline he could and taking it to a nearby town where he sold it and bought morphine from dope peddlers, most of which he, in turn, sold at a tremendous profit to local addicts.

He has been consistently arrogant and aggressive toward his neighbors and acquaintances, usually over triffling matters. After taking a few drinks, he has often threatened others, claimed things that were not his own, and made such a nuisance of himself that local police would be called to deal with him.

He is boastful and histrionic, more eloquently and aggressively so with a few highballs, and much given to temper tantrums. He frequently threatens to kill himself over some petty vexation and once offered a pistol to his wife, urging her grandiloquently to shoot him. He has never made an attempt, however, to harm himself, though his opportunities have been unlimited.

He has been reported as having convulsive seizures. These developed when he was refused special attention by physicians and seemed, according to their descriptions, plainly and consciously designed toward obtaining various ends. This manifestation has also been noted when he was confined to jail and wanted to be sent to a mental hospital in order to escape charges that had been brought against him. These so-called seizures have been observed several times in this hospital by competent psychiatrists. They did not in any way suggest epilepsy nor were they convincing as possible reactions of true hysteria. The patient is unquestionably conscious and shows that he is behaving intentionally in this way to gain a recognized end. Unlike a conversion phenomenon, the purpose does not appear to be concealed from his conscious awareness.

Though occasionally confused after heavy drinking (perhaps with the addition of drugs), he has at all other times been entirely rational, alert, shrewd, and free from delusions and hallucinations.

Early in Frank's career his disturbance was diagnosed on several occasions as hysteria, sometimes as both psychopathic personality and hysteria. Once he was given a diagnosis of psychopathic personality with psychotic episodes. There was not, however, any evidence of behavior or symptoms different from what he has shown on other occasions. There is reason to suspect that the real and pressing need to keep this patient hospitalized may have played an important part in his being so classified. The genuinely irrational and incompetent behavior, no doubt, supports the use of such a term as *psychosis,* despite the lack of any additional symptoms.

The irrational behavior that has characterized him is not based on a delusional system or on any loss of the good reasoning ability he shows on examination. Some of his most turbulent misconduct has, of course, been exhibited while he was intoxicated. At such times he naturally lacked his customary shrewdness and alertness. However, this cannot conscientiously be called a psychotic episode beyond and above his well-known inadequacy but rather the manifestation of inebriety. I do not mean to say that this man is normal but only that he has none of the recognized types of mental disorder, episodic or constant. If his drunken and wayward episodes are to be termed psychotic, then it would seem that his state at other times might also be termed psychotic, since it is in his shrewd, technically sane condition that he decides to add the picturesque touches of intoxication which he well knows will bring him to the attention of the police.

At this hospital, at the state hospitals, and at the other institutions to which Frank was sent in recent years he has been considered a sane man without psychotic episodes. The symptomatic diagnoses of drug addiction and chronic alcoholism have been added.

During all these years he has shown no evidence of deterioration or regression, and at 38 years of age was the same clever, alert person he was described as being twenty years previously. Unlike nearly all real morphine addicts, he does not show ordinary withdrawal symptoms or other signs of physical illness and acute distress when, after being admitted to the hospital, he is deprived of opportunities to obtain the drug.

If the reports that he takes morphine have any factual basis, such use must be sporadic. There is little or no evidence that effects of the drug have regularly played any major role in his behavior. It appears that his chief connection with drugs has been through his part in peddling them.

His career in the hospital has been marked by frequent paroles, which are always terminated by his failing to return, returning drunk, or being taken up by the police for petty theft, swindling, or futile and unprovoked disorder. Though ingratiating and outwardly cooperative when he is trying to obtain parole or discharge, he constantly schemes to escape or, surreptitiously, to call upon high authorities to have him released. Once, while helping attendants on the disturbed ward, he succeeded in turning hot water into a tub in which a psychotic patient lay in a continuous bath. He did not try to injure the man seriously, but merely to hurt him a little as a joke. This is a fair example of the inane, humorless mischief that underlies the pretentious front assumed by this former pastor.

Despite his medicolegal status, which, of course, is technically regarded as constituting sanity, those interested in finding some practical way to protect him and his family and to cope with the ever-accumulating problems succeeded on one occasion in having him committed by the court. Those close to the situation evidently found in his behavior reasons for action more compelling than the abstract criteria that stood in the way of such a step. After being held in the hospital for several months, despite his reiterated demands for discharge against medical advice, he called in an attorney.

Frank had in the past always found no difficulty in leaving when it suited his purpose or his whim. In view of his well-demonstrated inability to live in freedom, he was now, by means of the legal commitment, kept against his wishes in order to spare his family, the community, and himself the hardships he had brought about before and was sure to bring about again. The attorney for the government, in attempting to resist habeas corpus proceedings, found himself in a familiar dilemma, as the following quotations from his letter show:

> It is evident that the medical staff at the hospital are using the term *insane* to convey the meaning of the medical definition of the word rather than the legal definition. In other words, the thought back of the use of the word appears to me to be that it is the opinion of neuropsychiatrists that this man is not suffering from a mental disease as physicians understand the term, that he does not have a psychosis. It does appear, however, that it is their opinion that the state of his mind due to drug addiction and also manifested by his past antisocial behavior is such as to warrant the conclusions that he is incompetent and that he should receive treatment in a hospital for the cure of nervous and mental diseases. To say, however, that he is incompetent but not insane presents a rather inconsistent picture with which to go into court. We may be confronted with such a question as why he needs to be in a hospital for the care of nervous and mental diseases if he has no nervous or mental disease.
>
> I am inclined to think that the terms *insanity* and *incompetency* so far as their

> legal significance is concerned are used interchangeably and that the important point to be considered, whether you call a man insane or merely admit that he is incompetent, is whether the person is incapable of administering his personal estate in the normal manner of a prudent man and whether there is definite evidence of a more or less prolonged departure from normal behavior as compared with the standards of the community, such as dissipation of funds, unwise purchases, and utter lack of appreciation of values.
>
> Because of the fact that I anticipate some difficulty in trying to show that the man is incompetent but not insane, I would appreciate an expression of your views on the matter. It occurs to me also that a man ought to be confined who is a menace to others and likely to do harm to others, even though his mental condition may be due in part to inadequate mental development and in part to the use of drugs. He may be just as dangerous to himself or to others as a person suffering from a mental disease and who, according to the purely medical definition of insanity, would be pronounced insane.

Of course, it might be asked why these people are not let out of the mental hospitals and left to the police. If they are considered responsible for their misdeeds, let them be punished. This, as a matter of fact, is what the average psychiatric hospital is nearly always forced to do, whatever its physicians may think of the wisdom and practicality of such a procedure. These men are studied, found free of recognized mental disorder which might make them unaware of what they are doing, and are sent back out into the world. They are arrested not once but many times. Most of them seldom commit such serious crimes that they are kept out of circulation in penal institutions for long periods. Only rarely can they be kept for more than a few days. They do not follow any purposive criminal life. They make a nuisance of themselves to the community as a whole and often tragically wreck the lives of those close to them, and all to no discernible end. The police and the courts tire of them. Through various influences they are forced back on the mental hospitals where they take legal action to regain their freedom, only to begin the process again.

If, as stated in the quotations previously cited, it would be difficult to prove this man incompetent but not insane, it would be far more difficult, by existing definitions of psychiatry, to prove him insane. His perfectly rational (superficial) behavior under scrutiny, his freedom from delusions, his shrewdness, his alertness, and his convincing plan for a normal, useful life, in short, his plain sanity as this is ordinarily understood, make it all but impossible for a judge or a jury to call him insane. Psychiatrists familiar with his long record of senseless behavior are able to see more reason to do so than could be brought out before a court in terms of abstract criteria by which the decision is determined. But according to the accepted standards of psychiatry, his diagnosis carries with it an official and automatic endorsement of the patient as sane and competent. No matter how strongly impressed by real and practical evidence to the contrary, all physicians testifying in such a case must admit that the official technicalities approve this paradox.

Having won his case in court, the patient was released against medical advice. Frank did not go home but remained in the city where he at once claimed the attention of the police. On being released after a few days in jail, he took a room at the best hotel and annoyed other guests by various tactics such as trying to borrow money, sponge on them for a meal, or sell them something useless or nonexistent. He became at times loudly boastful or rowdy and eventually fell on the floor drunk. He refused to pay for his room and resisted the management's attempts to remove him.

He sought loans under bold-faced pretenses, ran up debts without regard to the possibilities of payment, and telephoned and wrote to his family, threatening suicide unless his demands for money were promptly met. There are indications that he was not inactive during this period in old devices of petty thievery, shortchanging, and various types of fraud, sharp practice, and connivance that exist, more or less, on the fringe of organized but illegal racketeering found in any city.

Nothing, however, could be pinned on him by the law that led to his being effectively controlled. In all issues of this sort that arose he had his record as a patient once legally committed and often confined to psychiatric institutions. This record was, in his ingenious hands, of considerable value as insurance against penal restraint.

After several arrests the police began to call on the hospital to relieve them of their problems with this man. They were told that nothing could be done, since he had been legally removed and the hospital was enjoined by the court not to hold him. Soon afterward the police and various local people began to seek advice on how to deal with him from the attorney who had liberated this man.

The patient himself soon joined in, coming repeatedly to the attorney's office or his house, sometimes drunk and always unreasonable, to shout about the injustices of the world, borrow money, evade threatening penalities, and to demand diverse preposterous services. The veteran had promised to pay the attorney's bill with bonus money, but now it appeared that this money had already been squandered. Hoping to collect his fee and, no doubt, from humanitarian impulses, the attorney sought to keep in touch with his client. Those with whom he had run up bills and floated little loans joined others swindled or defrauded in small matters and took up their problems with the patient's legal representative. Soon the incessant complaints from annoyed people, the client's own nagging or uproarious invasions upon him at all hours, and the constant queries of the police drove him to seek relief. The patient being again in jail, the attorney persuaded him to agree to return to the hospital voluntarily and pled with the physician in charge to take him back, confessing himself at fault ever to have released such a scourge on the community and on himself.

Arrangements were made for readmission. The patient arrived in custody of a policeman. He was still somewhat stimulated from a recent intoxication but, though overbearing and pompous, showed no signs of real drunkenness nor of an officially recognized psychosis.

Frank took a high-handed manner, swaggered about, and finally refused to come back into the hospital, saying that he had no mental disease and that he preferred to return to jail where he would soon be released to carry out important business plans and social activities. He enjoyed the incident, played up his role dramatically, and took a peremptory and haughty tone with everyone.

He soon obtained his freedom, but some weeks later after running up big debts, giving several more bad checks, and participating in a series of senseless, bawdy escapades, he was finally returned to the hospital. Three months later he again obtained his discharge on a writ of habeas corpus but not through the same attorney. The story in its broad essentials was repeated.

Since his last admission, following the exploits just mentioned, he has been true to form. After varying periods on a closed ward, parole has been given; he has lost it repeatedly and gone back among "demented" and helpless groups with whom he is, to say the least, not at home. He has continued at all times free from the technical stigmata of psychosis, remaining crafty, intelligent, and superficially cooperative while trying to gain his ends.

Frank takes advantage of every opportunity to make trouble in the hospital and is rather restless and extremely dissatisfied. He sends frequent letters to women in town to whom he regards himself as paying court. These are written in a neat hand, well spelled, and well expressed and are much better letters than would be expected from a man of his education. They are marked with self-righteousness, extreme egotism, trite sentimentality, and monumental falsehood. His tone is that of a lover who regards his own passion as very high and rare.

"Only God knows," he writes, "why I wasn't left over there among the poppies with my heroic buddies," falsely describing himself as a captain in charge of 272 men. "My wife never understood me!" he complains in the same letter. What does he expect of her? The question invites meditation.

ANNA

There was nothing spectacular about her, but when she came into the office you felt that she merited the attention she at once obtained. She was, you could say without straining a point, rather good looking, but she was not nearly so good looking as most women would have to be to make a comparable impression. She spoke in the crisp, fluttery cadence of the British, consistently sounding her "r's" and "ing's" and regularly saying "been" as they do in London. For a girl born and raised in Georgia, such speaking could suggest affectation. Yet it was the very opposite of this quality that contributed a great deal to the pleasing effect she invariably produced on those who met her. *Naive* has so many inapplicable connotations it is hardly the word to use in reference to this urbane and gracious presence, yet it is difficult to think of our first meeting without that very word coming to mind, with its overtones of freshness, artlessness, and candor.

She had passed her fortieth birthday some months before. Neither her face nor her figure had lost anything worth mentioning. Despite her composure, she gave a distinct impression of energy and playful spontaneity, an impression of vivid youth. In response to ordinary questions about her activities and interests she spoke of tennis, riding, and reading. More specific inquiry brought out opinions on Hamlet's essential conflict, comparison between the music of Brahms and the music of Shostakovitch, an impressive criticism of Schopenhauer's views on women, and several pertinent references to *The Brothers Karamazov.* She expressed opinions on current affairs that seemed to make excellent sense and talked with wit about the cyclic changes in feminine clothes and the implications of atomic physics for the future. What she had to say was particularly interesting, and she said it in just the opposite of all those many ways of talking that people call making conversation.

As discussion progressed, the picture of a rather remarkable woman became more and more distinct. Here was evidence of high intelligence and of considerable learning without discernible bookishness or consciousness of being "an intellectual." Her manner suggested wide interest, fresh and contagious enthusiasms, and a taste for living that reached out toward all healthy experience. Having a cup of coffee with her or weeding a garden would somehow take on a special quality of fun and delightfulness. Something about her over and beyond her looks prompted the estimate that she would be very likely to elicit romantic impulses, strong sensual inclinations, from most men who encountered her. Here, it seemed, was natural taste without a shadow of posed estheticism, urbanity without blunting of response to the simplest of joys, integrity and good ethical sense with the very opposite of everything that could be called priggish or smug. She showed nothing to suggest she meant to give such an impression or that she had any thought as to how she seemed.

Even with a detailed record of Anna's career clearly in mind, it was difficult indeed not to come to a conclusion that all the well-authenticated facts of that record should be ignored, since they were so thoroughly contradicted by the obvious character of this appealing woman. The banal but nevertheless insistent thought that such a psychiatric history must apply to some other person was hard to dismiss. Prior to this interview a great deal of trustworthy information had been made available to me. Anna's mother and father had given her story at length. A reliable psychiatrist in whose small private hospital she had been treated on numerous occasions furnished not only an ordinary history but many details from his firsthand experience with her over the previous twenty years. Her family physician had grown up in the same community with the patient and, through his personal acquaintance with her and her associates since childhood, had access to a remarkable amount of unusual information. He, as well as another medical practitioner who was also a relative, gave further details. Other sources of fact and opinion lay in several patients treated in the past whose relations with Anna at various periods of her life were significant. In the course of treatment, material had emerged in these other cases that rounded out her history and afforded additional means to evaluate her own reactions in interpersonal relations.

It is too much of a story to tell in a chapter or in a single book. And, no matter how told, it could not be believed except by those who have already had experience over years with such patterns of behavior. Familiarity with a temporary cross section of such a life (as, for instance, during a single period of hospitalization), plus a generalized account of what preceded, would almost surely convince any psychiatrist of the diagnosis, but this would probably fail to give him the challenging sense of wonder, the awe that arises from a contemplation of the accumulated detail in its specific essence.

Her family first became aware that Anna had serious problems through the discovery of a boys' club in the local high school which, if not exactly founded in her honor, had at least been organized about her as the central figure. Comprised of ten or twelve members in their early teens, a secret society in a sense, the group, like many Greek letter fraternities, had special phrases, symbolic signs, and countersigns. Encountering each other at the soda fountain or passing in the school corridor, two boys might slowly flex the fingers of their hands (so as to suggest a rounded aperture, possibly), leaving their arms dangling as if to veil slightly from alien observers a mystic communication.

Amid the chattering of groups over their chocolate shakes or hamburgers, certain phrases were thrown out stamped with idiom by the tone of voice and a special knowing quality in the accompanying glance. Small talk proceeded along lines common to pubertal groups. Baseball scores were predicted, and estimates were voiced as to whether or not a certain girl would neck or pet or perhaps do a French kiss on the third date. The occasional gestures and the allusive words provoked curiosity among the uninitiated without actually revealing the secret content. Numerous small groups of boys, sometimes only three or four, sometimes more, banded by a common interest in cars, sports, a secret shack in the woods where they met to gamble, or in some other affair, often reserved for themselves a peculiar connotation in bits of familiar language or devised codes of slang, verbal, digital, and postural, to transmit among the elect understandings of special recognitions best reserved from the surrounding masses.

First and fundamentally, the comprehension of the entire adult world was glibly evaded by this communication system. In mixed gatherings, allusions could be made, say to a half bottle of cheap liquor stored weeks ago in a hollow tree near the riverbank. This often evoked an arcane deviltry through which the girls could be teased but in which they could not fully mingle. Groping among confused and paradoxical concepts of virility, some boys could find stimulus (or protectiveness) in neologisms and fresh innuendos pertaining to the act of excretion and its subtle relationships to insult, sexuality, and infinite defilement.

Like dozens of other small, spontaneously forming and dissolving fraternities centered around interests that ranged from baseball to techniques of mutual masturbation, the group whose special interest lay in Anna did not for a while attract undue or sustained scrutiny from the adult world. The club had come into being after a discussion among several boys not particularly well acquainted with one another. Their talk had veered desultorily from literal accounts of what they had done to certain girls to playful variations on the theme of personal insult by the versatile (and at times fantastic) use of strongly obscene words.

As every junior high school boy knows, this argot of double-talk can bring a stimulus of exaggeration into the simplest statement and at the same time literally indicate matters so grotesquely perverse that they probably lie beyond biologic experience. Though at times seized upon to express actual rage or contempt, even the most objectionable formulations are oftener used in amiable or even affectionate badinage and horseplay. The actual nouns and verbs, chiefly those of four letters (occasionally those of three or five), denote parts of the body involved in excretion and the genital organs of man and woman, and eliminative and sexual activities. Mingled in a sort of sewer slang, seasoned with an abnormal, even obsessive, interest in feces, weirdly sadistic, rounded out with participial references to olfactory and other sensory outrages, this unprintable language is worn so smooth by continuous repetition among pubertal boys that even its more literal meaning often bypasses their awareness.

In calling this language unprintable I am not uncognizant of the fact that there is not one of the forbidden words that has not occasionally appeared in books and that all of them can be seen scrawled on the walls of toilets. These words, however, in isolation or in different contexts, cannot even hint at the terrible significance so obvious in the context of speech into which they are woven. Though some attention has, of course, been given by psychiatry to what is now being mentioned, it is an area that deserves further study. The material is so highly charged that even in medical or in any other technical writing it cannot be handled freely. The actual discussion that led to the beginning of the club to which we are giving attention cannot be presented to the reader.

It is, of course, for one thing not directly accessible to me in full detail, although there is sufficient information to reconstruct a reliable approximation in concrete terms. The nature of Anna's behavior and experience in her relationship to the club can scarcely be conveyed by a generalization. From what material is available about this specific incident and with the aid of confirmatory detail gathered from the review of many similar situations, let us, as best we can (tentatively, but with sufficient evidence to give confidence that the approximation is in substance valid) attempt to reconstruct a little of the scene. A few typical fragments may be helpful.

The boys had been hanging around together at a spot near the riverbank where they sometimes fished, talking in the sort of bull session that often arose.

> "Butch, you sure ----ed me up on that algebra assignment last night."
>
> "Aw ---- Jack, you ----ed yourself, you damn old horse's ---. Just because the prof wouldn't suck up all that bull ---- you tried to hand him, don't give me that kind of ----. The prof just up and ----ed on you. That's all there is to it. He ----ed on you good. Right in your eye."
>
> "---- ----- to Prof. Blank! Why that ---- half ---sted ----sucker almost ------ed me out of a pass on the last test."
>
> Another boy diverted this trend of conversation by claiming he got a piece of ---- from the woman who washed dishes at the Greek's hot dog stand, boasting that it was plenty good ----, and cost only fifty cents.
>
> "---- on that old ----." Butch commented disparagingly. "If you put a croker sack over her head I might give two bits for it."
>
> "Reason old Butch talks so finicky is because he can't even get up a ----! Betcha a hundred dollars if all the ---- in the world was sprawled right there in front of him that ---- ------- couldn't even raise a ----!"
>
> "You dirty ------ --- you," Butch answered, slightly irritated, "You're talking about your -----self. Everything you say goes back on yourself." Apparently feeling this was a little lame, he added quickly, "Bet old Jack ain't ever even ----ed off in his pants!"
>
> "Maybe all he's done is just to ---- in 'em," Bill commented merrily. "Bet that's what old Butch would do if a girl had no better sense than to let him think she'd let him ---- her."
>
> Turning now from this exchange of compliments, the boys offered bits of information and speculation about several girls with whom all had some acquaintance.
>
> "I understand Sue White's begun to put out a little ----," Bill said. "---- no!" Butch disagreed. "Sure would like to get myself a little of that ----. But Sue's a nice girl."
>
> "Pete Green says he finger ----ed old fat ---ed Rita. . . . " Pausing a moment, he continued listlessly, "Can't think of her last name. You know who I mean. Lives in the big house next to Sam Beech's uncle."
>
> "Wouldn't be surprised," Butch agreed. "I dry ----ed her myself the second time I ever got her alone. On the other hand, you can't believe anything that damn mother ----ing --- ---- Green says," Butch added.
>
> Feeling his enmity to Pete Green, who, a month or two ago, had made him back down with the threat of "slapping the living ----" out of him, Butch continued in unspoken thought. *Damn that Pete Green! If that ---- ---- ever tries to cross me up again I'll tell him I'll ---- his ---- mother up the --- ---- with a two by four and then ---- in his ---- face! That would shut him up, maybe!* Pete had intimidated Butch several times in the past. He knew he wouldn't dare to provoke a fight by talking to Pete in any such way, but it eased his feelings a little to think about it.

> "Tell you what I'd like to try," Bill admitted, after a moment of silence, "is some of that ---- Anna Blank packs. Every day in biology class I keep thinking I'll take a shot at it . . . but somehow with a girl like that. . . . I just don't know. . . . " Bill could not quite express what made him cautious. It was not only that her father and mother were rich and prominent and powerful in the community and her older brother strong enough to beat him half to death if anything, even about a try, was found out. It was more than that. Most of the girls you did these things to were sort of *from the other side of the tracks.* But by no means all of them were. You could get away with it lots of times with ones supposed to be real nice. Lots of goofy fellows still thought some of them *were* nice, Bill realized in an inexpressible wave of superiority and vague elation. Some poor damn ---- ----s would even marry them some day.

The sort of thin, ruthless exuberance that glowed in the boy screened an underlying stratum of personal insecurity probably common to all mankind and sometimes particularly disturbing at this age. He did not try to account for the triumphant feeling or to ask if it sprang chiefly from ideas of debasing the female or, perhaps even more, from the scornfully superior position to the other male he thus attained in fantasy. Thoughts of this sort did not enter Bill's consciousness, but factors influenced his feeling which, if he had understood them, might have produced such thoughts. By no means given to violence in action, this boy would not have inflicted physical injury on another. In imagination, as in cartoons, all sorts of fatalities occur without anyone really getting hurt.

> Still musing on Anna, Bill continued. "She sure is built, that girl! She's built just like a brick ---- house."
>
> Butch and Jack, who had been looking slyly at each other, gave a low whistle almost simultaneously. Then they began to interchange a sort of chuckling that was half laughter and half teasing, designed to provoke curiosity in their companion. After a while Bill was told how easy it was to get ---- from Anna. Each of the other boys gave a detailed account of his own experiences, including one success by Jack in the storage room at school. These experiences were quite recent and until now had not been widely discussed by either Butch or Jack.

Each had, in fact, been surprised and, though this was not admitted, also shocked to discover that Anna was not a "nice girl." A confused disillusionment no doubt played some part in their present emphasis on the opposite evaluation of this girl who had, rather typically, represented the "sacred" (sexless) female in their thoughts. The fear of so honoring a female who turned out to be this other sort of thing loomed as a threat to one's own manhood. The untouchable priestess, once disclosed as an impostor, must be thoroughly defiled. Thus man sometimes seeks protection from confusion through which he himself risks the defilement of personally enshrining one who will make his virility (honor) the laughingstock of the group.

Fortified by this enlightenment, Bill partook of Anna's favors soon afterward. The boys found a special pleasure in talking together about their achievements. Soon a friend of these three was told about their source of pleasure, then another friend, and still another. At first each boy had gone alone, but as time passed it became more practical for several to visit Anna together. An appointment would be made by one of those interested. Anna, under the pretext of taking a walk or going to visit a friend would, without detection, make her way to a building situated on the other side of the large garden behind her house. Now used as a storehouse and garage, the building was originally a stable, and its former hayloft afforded reasonable privacy. The boys, by coming from another street through a hedge back of the garage, could make their way unnoticed to the rendezvous. Safe opportunities, though fairly frequent, were limited because the chauffeur was sometimes in the garage. There were also days when the gardener worked nearby, or, rarely, Anna's brother might be there exercising with barbells and other gymnastic equipment he kept in another part of the building. This, no doubt, was a factor in the group's choice of coming together, particularly as its membership expanded. Of even more importance, perhaps, was a specific satisfaction found by some in entering upon the venture together. The closely shared experience seemed to enhance the pleasures of club conversation when they gathered later to talk over what happened.

In the morning it was customary for the captain of the baseball team, the chairman of the debating club, and others interested in extracurricular activities occasionally to announce plans for meetings of their various groups. One morning, in response to a dare by other club members, Jack came forward and in a bold voice called out: "At the beginning of lunch hour there'll be a meeting of the *Animal Crackers* in Room 49." There was a scatter of giggling and some random speculation on the part of a few teachers, but no official inquiry about the club was made and no adult thought of any play on Anna's name or caught improper innuendos.

The existence of the club and their daughter's undesirable situation was finally brought to the attention of Anna's parents through its effect on another person.

Among the older boys who had been attracted by Anna was one who had apparently turned to her in the utmost seriousness. All accessible information indicates that this boy fell in love with Anna not by a trivial attraction but with all the vividness and lifeshaking stir that the first complete and genuine experience of this sort can bring to an earnest young man almost ready for college. The younger girl, suddenly having become mature in body, loomed like something never seen before upon his awareness. There is reason to believe that he was determined to marry her and resolved to be scrupulously faithful through all the years he must wait for this. There is nothing to suggest he did not seek her with strongly passionate physical desire, but apparently his idealization of her and fear of arousing even further impulses, which it would have been for him a desecration to fulfill under these conditions, caused him to treat her, if not like an untouchable goddess, at least with extraordinary restraint. Anna, it seems, behaved in such a way that he was sure she reciprocated his feelings not only in kind but also in degree.

Reports as to how he discovered the relations of Anna with the club are somewhat conflicting. It is almost impossible to believe that fortune was so unkind as to have him blunder upon an actual meeting of this group with the customary activities in progress. So it is said to have happened. At any rate, he received enlightenment in such a convincing way that the impact was sudden and trenchant.

In his immediately subsequent state, rumored to be a "nervous breakdown" at the time, his family physician, after considerable difficulty, seems to have obtained some idea of what he had experienced. Being a relative of Anna's mother and a boldly conscientious man, he felt that the situation demanded attention and disclosed something of it to her parents.

Insofar as the complicated and seldom obvious attitudes that enter into the administration of parental authority and guidance on such an occasion can be evaluated, it seems that this girl's father and mother avoided the typical mistakes that might have been made. Neither attempted to conceal the humiliation and distress brought upon them by such conduct. After adequate frankness about their reaction to the conduct itself, they tried to avoid rubbing it in by moralizing reiteration. A decision was made for Anna to be sent at once to a fine boarding school in a distant state. Apparently feeling that the daughter could not fail to be critically traumatized by realizations that withered them with pain and shame, Anna's mother and father tried, as some people are able to do after losing eyesight or a first child, to accept what has happened without evasion but nevertheless to turn with all resolution available to what is ahead and not to stir what is tragic or hideous, but now past and unmodifiable. There does not seem to have been gross error in glossing over what had taken place or minimizing the possible consequences. Both parents tried to support Anna by emphasizing opportunities in the future and by their knowledge that in the process of growing up it is not uncommon for people to make mistakes that in the adult world would be fatal.

Anna's apparent reactions were such as to enable all the family to be entirely sincere in showing her their continued confidence, their respect, and their love. In choosing a fine private school with high academic standards, she seemed to be showing her serious intentions about the future. Her keen interest in choosing clothes, her care in getting exactly the right sort of curtains for the dormitory room might have suggested to some almost too easy and quick a recovery from the fell blow she was thought to have suffered, but at the time this seemed instead a fit and appealing veil of insouciance that she bravely, if not almost heroically, pulled about her to conceal with stoic and patrician grace the terrible trauma her spirit had sustained. Even in the short period of time before she left for the East, the outwardly blithe air that Anna displayed when she joked and laughed with friends who came by (her ability to seem blandly preoccupied in getting the new rock records and those popular designer jeans that the shop was expecting any day now) provoked fleeting but ominous thoughts in the family that such poise, considering the full circumstances, might be a little excessive.

Excellent reports on Anna came for several months from the distant school. She was doing well in her studies and already she had won a place on the swimming team. She seemed also to have found herself almost at once in the warm affection of teachers and students. One teacher, in a letter to her mother, spoke of Anna's "unusual promise in English" and of her "surprising maturity of outlook." Anna's own letters, though few, were warm with expression of devotion that seemed to follow the inimitable idiom of sincerity.

In these letters she sometimes mentioned her conviction that she knew of no way to express her gratitude except to show by her own conduct that she did deserve the trust her mother and father had shown in her and the support of their love and understanding. No happiness could mean more than that she would find in making them feel they could be proud of her again.

Such letters were building up in these parents an encouragement they sorely needed and offering (as an anodyne for their anguish and humiliation) increasing hope that as parents they had not, perhaps, failed their daughter utterly. Meanwhile, reports began to come from the school which seriously disquieted them.

Anna had apparently broken a number of rules, most of them involving minor issues, it is true. She had twice been caught smoking with several other girls; she had four times stayed out considerably beyond hours; she had cut several classes;

she had spoken disrespectfully to a teacher. But, after all, such misdemeanors often indicate a healthy sort of growing up, and her parents were anxious to avoid forcing Anna into rigid propriety as compensation for her terrible error.

A final decision was reached that Anna could not be kept at school when a good many more serious symptoms came to light. Several petty thieveries (at first assumed to be absentminded borrowings), flagrant but ingenious cheating in laboratory work, calm lies about matters that were accepted as points of honor—all of this added up to make her expulsion imperative.

At the half-dozen or more subsequent schools attended by Anna she often seemed to have changed, and for varying periods her family's hope was high. Her behavior at each place fell into similar but not identical patterns. Like the persisting theme in a complicated work of music, her actions took diverse courses but came always to an identical point, which for her was failure. A Brahms concerto may spread and range, with woodwinds at one phase carrying the movement and, a little later, the violins manifesting something of another sort or the piano (as if in reply to the orchestra) weaving a fresh subject into the manifold skein; so through her history appeared episodes of variety and genuine novelty, all contributing to a design of impressive versatility but leading to an inevitable conclusion.

Once or twice Anna completed the entire year, but nearly always each new institution found itself unable to handle her after a few months. Sometimes she worked steadily during the summer and easily completed courses she had missed in her numerous shiftings about. Perhaps on the basis of an excellent performance on the entrance examination, she gained admission to a distinguished college for women and, after being expelled, briefly attended a smaller college and two state universities. On other occasions she undertook training in business school, in hospitals (nursing, x-ray technician) and in social work. She often expressed spontaneously a lively interest in this or that career and worked out her plans with good judgment, but, after widely varying periods during which she applied herself, she regularly ended by quitting voluntarily or being dismissed.

When Anna sought some new job with which to occupy herself or sought to enter some course of training, she seemed to have no hesitation in giving as references those who had no choice except to describe her as entirely unreliable and unfit for what she planned. Sometimes the reason for her failures seemed not to lie so much in antisocial or spectacularly improper acts as in other maladaptations.

Among the almost limitless accumulation of incidents that loom in a retrospective glance at her career, only a few can be given here, and these in the utmost brevity.

From one prep school she was dismissed though standing high in her classes after it was proved she had placed a half-dozen or more rubber condoms so that these useful items would become unmistakably evident when several couples seated themselves on the two sofas that flanked the fireplace. Here, almost directly under chaperoning eyes, the younger pupils not yet given permission to go out with their boyfriends had circumspect dates on certain evenings. No sudden scurrying of mice could have evoked more hearty squeals or such quick explosive male laughter than the magiclike appearance of these unmistakable objects, some neatly rolled, others generously stuffed. Had only one or perhaps even two of the condoms emerged inconspicuously into view as the soft cushions shifted with the seating of couples, it might have been possible for an alert girl, or perhaps even for one of the self-conscious and preoccupied boys, to cover it and hide it away before general attention was aroused. Anna, it seems, had given some thought to this. Perhaps with time and retelling, some exaggeration has colored the event. It is said that an elastic band was set to snap one condom boldly forth and that others were placed so they would slip down from under the antimacassars. At any rate, Anna made certain of a conspicuous display. Struck almost witless by the appearance of such an object in her lap (whence it had dropped from the top of the sofa), one girl released the initial squeal. Such uproar ensued automatically that hastening chaperones missed little of the scene.

On numerous occasions Anna made difficulties for herself by driving off in cars that belonged to teachers or other school employees. Only once, or possibly twice, during her teens does it appear she had serious intentions of stealing the car for permanent possession. On the other hand, there were periods when she frequently stole underwear, stockings, and ornaments (usually inexpensive costume pieces or club pins) from other students and even from those in authority.

While at the university, for a time she fell into the sporadic practice of relieving her dates of small amounts of cash she discovered in their pockets during heavy petting. Under such circumstances she also, but more rarely, took a pocketknife or a bunch of keys. At one finishing school where personal dignity among the faculty was emphasized, she is said to have lost her place as a student by neatly lettering on the door of the office of the sedate Latin instructress a concise advertisement.

Hot p__________ available here—cheap!

After making good grades in a well-known college and having been in no serious trouble for several months, she began lying in bed too late to attend her early classes. Interviews with the college physician, and eventually with a psychiatrist, followed. After several warnings and probationary measures, and just in time to avoid expulsion, she began to attend all classes again.

During an interval in which she had no further trouble with the faculty, Anna alienated and outraged several girls in the dormitory with whom she had been very friendly. After a few bottles of beer which the group had shared, she entered the rooms occupied by two of these friends and, in their absence, urinated on several evening dresses which they highly valued. (After the act she refolded the dresses neatly and put them back, sodden and malodorous, in the drawers.) It was a number of days before evidence emerged that unmistakably connected Anna with this deed.

Observations that in themselves were highly suggestive but not final proof were for a while withheld by those who could not bring themselves to believe Anna capable of such behavior. She easily denied such a possibility to several who spoke with her separately in the hope of finding facts that would exonerate her. She also fabricated evidence to establish her innocence so calmly and so freely that it carried almost axiomatic conviction. On being confronted with plain proof from several sources, she was able to smile off the affair and dismiss it as a whimsical prank. Some felt it was their responsibility as a group to report this incident, but so much was brought out in Anna's behalf that all finally agreed to let the affair go no further.

Merely tabulating these and many other details of Anna's behavior tends to suggest rather easily formulated motivations. With a more complete story these appear less likely. If a good many of the stealing incidents are isolated, some would no doubt be inclined to interpret them as ordinary compulsive reactions. On the other hand, personal contact with her does not give the impression of an underlying anxiety or of any strong drive against which she struggles or which she would like to reject. In addition to taking things for which she has little or no need (and which might symbolize some ordinary unconscious aim), she also steals in response to a real though mild desire to possess or for convenience.* With a more inclusive view of her activities the thefts become more difficult to account for satisfactorily by the specific and familiar theories of compulsion. They, like so many of her other symptoms, seem part of a different and far less circumscribed psychopathology.

Concentrating on the long record of her outlandish sexual promiscuity (some of which will soon be given), the most naive observer would perhaps think of "nymphomania" or at least of very powerful erotic drives. Others might surmise that she is and has always been a frigid (or partially frigid) woman who finds stimulation but never orgasm and who is driven more or less consciously to all sorts of indiscretions in a never-ending quest. Neither of these hypotheses seems to account for Anna's behavior when one becomes familiar with more evidence pertaining to her inner experiences.

Anyone's real inner experience is, of course, difficult to arrive at even by conjecture and perhaps impossible to establish by proof. And because Anna is so accomplished in devising falsehoods on any subject and in making them so convincing, her own statements can hardly be taken as necessarily true. There seems, indeed, but one way (and this one obviously not permissible) to discover directly a woman's physical reactions to intercourse; and even then she can, it is said by some, often be misleading if she so wishes. Despite these difficulties, a rather convincing impression emerges that Anna's sexual problem is very different and far more complicated than anything that has been mentioned.

It seems likely that she has frequently experienced the physiologic reactions of orgasm but that these reactions have been a minor factor in her behavior pattern. Sometimes, while having technically satisfactory relations with a husband, she would continue intercourse with other men who, it seems, failed entirely to arouse or to gratify her in the usual sense. As a matter of fact, while living with the husband who, more regularly than any other man she can recall, made her "respond," she initiated and continued relations with several other men. From some of these she neither particularly wanted nor ever received pleasure that could be called sensual or romantic.

Although such conclusions are necessarily speculative (as they are, indeed, about any patient) and not scientifically verifiable, it seems most probable that this woman has somewhat less than ordinary conscious sexual motivation and that the most significant feature of her sexual experience is that, despite frequent mechanical responses, it has meant so little to her. The localized sensory reaction has not been greatly valued nor has it seemed to play a dominant role in directing her conduct. Anatomic intimacy with men has never been associated with interpersonal relationships of any consequence or duration. Important as this fact may be (granting that our estimate is in some measure correct), it still does not offer a circumscribed area in which a final explanation for Anna's career can be readily drawn. In every other aspect of social experience also this woman has similarly failed to develop any sort of relationship with another human being that seemed to have much meaning for her or, to put it another way, that could influence her to any consistent, obviously purposive behavior.

---

*See p. 147 for further discussion of these points, particularly of the contrast between "compulsive" and "impulsive" symptoms.

It is true indeed that this casual or "cheap" use of physical sexuality often appears to be a confused sort of vengeful or self-destructive response to hurt and rejection or to misleading essential concepts of "male" and "female." The pattern followed sometimes suggests that such behavior may represent (with varying degrees of awareness in the subject) a "throwing of oneself away." It may at the same time seem to return a hurt and symbolize a protest too profound and too complicated for words.* Anna's sexual behavior and her generalized self-destructiveness (at social and personal levels) might be interpreted on such a basis. Let us remember, however, that such an interpretation is speculative. Let us refrain from projecting items of psychiatric theory into Anna's unconscious and from assuming that they constitute evidence of emotional reactions in infancy that have shaped her subsequent course and by which we can confidently explain her career. Perhaps, some might say, serious and subtle traumatic events unknown to herself and others, even during the first year of her life or later, planted the seeds of a profound (unconscious) conflict which she has been forced to act out in this malignant pattern. No real evidence of this, however, has emerged in the study of her case.

We may also consider the possibility that such a person as Anna might be born with a subtle and specific biologic defect. Perhaps, despite a high capacity for intelligence and charm, something necessary for wisdom or for sincere and major human feelings was left out or incomplete in her development. Capacities very different and much simpler are incomplete in the person born with color blindness or with a spastic deficiency in the motor system. Such biologic deficiencies are not necessarily hereditary. Let us assume that a defect in development may leave such a person as Anna without the capacity to attain deep loyalty or genuine love or to adequately recognize and react to the major goals and values of human life. The lack of major satisfactions and aspirations and the freedom from serious scruples or remorse might leave such a person free to act out any whim of folly or rebellion and offer some explanation for such a career as Anna's.

At 40 years of age, during our first interview, Anna absentmindedly checked the preliminary information blank to indicate her status as divorced. She spontaneously changed the pencil mark to show that she was married. As a matter of fact, Anna's current marriage had lasted a good many years. It is true her husband was such in name only, but he served a practical purpose. The couple had not seen each other or otherwise communicated since shortly after the nuptials, but the legal existence of this union deterred Anna in one aspect of her behavior that had formerly given considerable trouble to her family and their attorneys.

Before her last wedding and over a long period, she had fallen into the habit of marrying on an impulse apparently as trivial as what might lead another woman to buy a new dress. With one man after another she casually completed the legal ceremonies and entered into this monumental contract, the groom being now an adventurous taxi driver, now an opportunistic bar companion, or, again, a delinquent idler she encountered in her social work.

The succession of divorces and the repeated financial settlements demanded by vagrants and petty rascals she had on several occasions espoused threatened the family resources. In contrast with some other cases of similar illness, Anna's marriage series was halted by the prospect of legal bigamy.

*See Chapter 5, A case showing circumscribed behavior disorder.

The husbands of this series were not (or certainly not usually) men who took the bride very seriously. This cannot be said of her earlier husbands, two of whom were distinguished and wealthy men and, according to the evidence, genuinely and deeply in love with Anna. With one of these, an architect of international repute, she lived for a while in England. To him and almost simultaneously to his wayward brother Anna is said to have given gonorrhea which, as the first year of marriage drew to a close, she inadvertently picked up from a sycophantic interior decorator, a person, according to report, more active homosexually than otherwise.

I entertain some skepticism about the details of this episode. Such an extravagant and perfectly timed series of events scarcely seems possible. Though usually ready to deny anything inconsistent with chaste and honorable behavior, this patient has in other moods seemed to relish adding fanciful touches to the already spectacular reality. Her promiscuity has, however, been so lavish that coincidences almost impossible in a hundred other lives combined hardly seem unlikely in hers. There is little doubt that she was sufficiently unfaithful for this or something equally bizarre to have befallen the husband.

On being detected in activities that would produce fear, shame, or consternation in others, this patient often showed simple insouciance. Once at college she did so well for so long that hope returned to her family. Apparently she had found herself at last. After a succession of excellent reports, one showing failures in four subjects appeared. Anna was called on long-distance telephone by her father, who wanted to lose no time in trying to find some remedy for the trouble.

Her easy, happy laughter relieved him deeply, even before she had time to go on and explain the mistake that had been made in the dean's office. She had just heard of it but had not realized the rather comical error had been transmitted to any report that reached him and her mother. Actually she had not realized it was quite time for these reports to be mailed out. She had been, you see, pretty busy—but "mighty happy," too. Warmed within and deeply reassured, he left the telephone completely at ease.

Within a few days, sure enough, there came official acknowledgment of the mistake. The grades of another girl had been confused with those of his daughter. The true report was even better than those excellent ones which had been coming regularly now for months. The dean's signed name and the official school paper and forms would have dispelled any suspicions of fraud had suspicions arisen. Anna's tone and manner when she spoke over the telephone were such, however, that no doubt at all seemed justified.

Soon truly disturbing information came from the school. Not only was Anna failing dismally in all studies, but serious misconduct had brought the question of her expulsion to a crucial point. Wiring his daughter that he was taking the first train, the father also instructed her to make appointments for him with the college authorities.

On arriving he found that no appointments had been made. He was entirely unexpected. He was surprised, furthermore, to find that Anna had left for the weekend, after convincing the house mother that she had parental permission to visit an imaginary aunt. Apparently she typed letters and forged signatures to bring off this deception with cleverness comparable to that employed in getting the school stationery and report forms and successfully utilizing these to send false reports to her family.

On her return after the weekend she seemed surprised to find her father still there and at first expressed vexation with him. He never learned just what misadventures befell his daughter, who had apparently roamed about in a large city nearby. She took all the discussion of her recent acts with equanimity, apologized for her mistakes, and admitted that it was quite inexpedient to bring off such deceptions when it was apparent to her they would certainly and promptly be discovered. She said she did not know precisely why she had acted in such a plainly injudicious way, but she never seemed curious or really concerned about the possibility of discovering a reason for the behavior.

What would have happened to this patient had it not been for the extraordinarily ample estate of her family and for their persistent care? One can only speculate. We need not here estimate how many times she was released from jails in widely scattered cities by their efforts, how many times she was hospitalized, how many beginnings with psychotherapy were made by various experts. It is interesting to note that Anna, unlike so many whose conduct closely resembles hers in other respects, seems never to have committed a major felony or tried to do serious physical injury to another.

It is true that she was badly beaten up in some sort of night spot brawl in St. Louis. On this occasion several of her ribs were fractured and a lung was punctured; her brother, who flew to her aid from Baltimore, thought at first her injuries would prove fatal. Though occasionally, when drinking, she has taken an active part in slapping or hair-pulling incidents, she has shown little inclination to attack. In similar episodes she rarely initiated gross vocal disputes or was vulgarly aggressive with words. Calmness seemed more characteristic of her than high temper, although it is recorded that in her teens she was expelled from one academy for publicly telling off a school authority in a speech vehemently and versatilely obscene and closing with references anything but flattering to the state of his "third leg."

Many of these incidents, which in isolation appear spectacular, occurred while Anna passed in the community as a reliable, conforming, and extraordinarily attractive woman. Much of the time she seemed poised, polite, and a paragon of happy behavior. For a while during her early twenties she taught a Sunday school class. Her teachings were ethically admirable and she gave a strong impression of sincerity. She often worked for a month or more at a time, efficiently and with what seemed pleasure, at the Red Cross and in other welfare activities. Most who knew her casually in these endeavors would have been genuinely astonished to learn that she had any serious personality problem.

Once while hospitalized for a week or ten days, she left the almost universal impression of being a delightful patient. Courteous, composed, undemanding, and cheerful, she took discomforts and minor pains in a way that elicited admiration. During this brief period, in which a benign nodule was surgically removed from her breast, she casually accepted cunnilingual attentions from a female attendant (apparently a true lesbian) and also sought to entice an intern. In these enticements she went so far as to get the fly of his trousers open before accepting his determination to refrain.

Occasionally during her early thirties, but also a few times since, Anna engaged in a pastime known in some circles as *gangbanging.* There were minor variations of procedure. Usually drinks with five or six men, whom she might pick up in one of the less inviting honky-tonks or night spots about town, constituted the first phase. Later the group rode out into the country and all her companions had sexual relations with her, each taking his turn. On such an exploit, argument once arose about whether or not she had stolen a cigarette lighter belonging to an escort, and the group, uniting against her, threw Anna into a creek and then drove off, leaving her to walk home.

This patient spent a good deal of time reading. In contrast to many psychopaths who readily claim all sorts of entirely imaginary learning, she showed considerable familiarity with literature of many sorts. She seemed to read Shakespearean plays, the major Russian novels, pulp magazines, and comic books with about the same degree of interest. Her factual knowledge about what she had read seemed good, though it must be admitted she often falsified with assurance when questions led her into unknown areas.

She played complicated music on the piano with fine technical skill and spent a good deal of time doing so. She had an accurate acquaintance with current scales of intellectual and esthetic fashion and could probably have avoided offense even to the most snide of editors of the most avant-garde of little magazines. How she reacted to such matters in the innermost and final chamber of her being can only be surmised. My impression is that *King Lear* and *True Confessions* elicited responses in no fundamental way different.

There is little I can offer in explanation for the biologic enigma I trust is apparent. Despite abundant time to approach the patient directly, unusually rich detail furnished by others, and even the rare chance of treating psychiatrically more than one other upon whose life her own had impinged traumatically (and, so it would almost seem, of seeing her through more than one set of eyes), despite all this, I cannot reveal the forces that patterned her. I have opinions, but opinions are not facts.

Without claiming there is anything demonstrable or profoundly explanatory in such an appraisal, I would give these impressions. It is unlikely that she experienced (in what can reasonably be called ordinary awareness) much of the emotion that we associate with the various deeds she has carried out. In both quantity and quality her emotions, I believe, have regularly fallen short of the affect we almost automatically assume must prompt, accompany, or follow such actions as hers. Though appearances of emotion were sometimes impressive in Anna, it seems probable that these were chiefly facsimiles of actual feeling, an automatic and undesigned mimicry. Though she had vexations and minor satisfactions and though she could at times get mad and could be a little fond of people, Anna never really seems to have meant much harm to others or to herself.

One of the physicians who had often treated her expressed his bewilderment about how real seemed her disregard of what was obvious, how strangely she escaped the subjective consequences of her experiences. Taking a phrase from the Russian novel about prostitution, *Yama,* to embody his reaction, he said, "All the horror is in just this—that there is no horror."

A thoughtful and now elderly member of her family whose advice her parents and one of her early husbands had often sought was particularly impressed with what he described as an unbelievable but somehow authentic innocence that Anna never seemed to lose. Experiences that would harden an ordinary person conspicuously or ensure a conscious cynicism, mordant and profound, seem to fall lightly on her spirit, to leave her surprisingly serene. The person just mentioned, after more than two decades of concern with her problems, finds even more surprising than all the unfortunate acts combined, Anna's thoughtless assumption that she is to be trusted in all matters, that her behavior has been essentially honorable and ladylike, and the fact that her self-respect is apparently bright and unblemished.

CHESTER

On his first admission to the closed ward of a psychiatric hospital, Chester, 24 years of age, was friendly and alert. His freedom from anything that would suggest an ordinary psychosis was immediately noticeable. He explained to the examiner that he did not suffer from any nervous or mental disorder and emphasized the statement that no question of such a condition had ever come up in his case. He said that he came to the hospital for further examination of a serious injury to his ankle which he sustained while in the army and for which he hoped to get a pension.

When told frankly that, according to accompanying reports, he had been admitted because of persistent antisocial and irresponsible behavior, spectacular alcoholic episodes, and extreme maladjustment, he affected considerable surprise and insisted that some mistake had been made. In fact, his surprise seemed real.

It was pointed out to him that unquestionable evidence from his parents, relatives, and friends, as well as from a social service report, established the fact that he had been stealing, defrauding others, and making a boisterous nuisance of himself when drunk since he was 16 years of age.

It was brought to his attention that he had been expelled from a military school for gross and inveterate misconduct, had been confined in jail a dozen times recently for similar reasons, and had been supported and protected by his father, who spent a good part of his time getting this son out of the troubles which he made for himself and others almost daily. The patient appeared very much astonished at such reports, denied everything, and, in a convincing fashion, dismissed the question of all personal difficulties and maladjustment as little short of preposterous.

After careful observation in the hospital for a month, no evidence of delusions, hallucinations, or any other sign of what is regarded as a psychosis could be discovered. Chester was presented before a medical staff of ten psychiatrists who unanimously considered him sane and competent and made the diagnosis of psychopathic personality. He was kept in the hospital on pretexts and out of common sense because of his long history of extreme maladjustment.

He was at all times alert and usually cooperative, reacted with a very natural dislike to being on a closed ward, and continually asked for a discharge, insisting that he was entirely sane and improperly hospitalized.

On being granted parole of the grounds, he promptly left without permission and went home. At the insistence of his father he was granted a furlough status. Within a few days he had insolently suggested sexual intercourse to a respectable woman, committed several inconsequential thefts, and sold for $5.50 a good rug taken from his parents' home. After having a few drinks, he is reported to have cursed and further expressed his contempt by spitting on the foot of a great uncle who encountered him on the street and politely engaged him in conversation. Later that afternoon he talked eloquently to a half-dozen or so bystanders in the park about patriotism, honor, God, and the true meaning of morality.

Meanwhile, he had cashed several small checks on a nonexistent bank account and, posing as the emissary of a respected cousin (whose husband was cashier in a local bank), obtained $20.00 which he convinced an old friend of the family was needed to settle a small obligation that had arisen after banking hours.

When drinking, he usually became rowdy. He made no effort whatsoever to find employment and roamed about the town or countryside, often sleeping in the woods and fields. His father and brothers had no choice but to seek him out in the byways and hedges and bring him in, often laboring strenuously at this task far into the night. He was often found dirty, disheveled, and alone. Toward his family he was sullen and carping, his reactions those of petty irritation. He complained constantly that his father meddled with him and at times ascribed all his troubles to this interference. Finding it impossible to supervise such a person, even with the frequent assistance of local police, who obligingly locked him up in jail for a day or two during his worst episodes, the father soon sent him back to the hospital.

On arrival, he was manifestly vexed and seemed at a loss to understand his situation. "I can't see why they don't let me alone. I don't bother anybody. Why can't I go about my business like any other man?" These and similar remarks he repeated many times in tones showing well the dissatisfaction that any normal man would feel on being, without cause or reason, deprived of his liberty.

Before returning to the hospital Chester had complained bitterly to his father, stating that he would kill himself rather than come. The father recognized this threat of suicide as insincere but typical of the somewhat dramatic airs often assumed by the patient. Except for past experience with such threats, it would have been natural to think desperation would be consistent with his intensely strong distaste for restraint of any sort.

He was kept now on a closed ward, from which he repeatedly schemed to escape, once stealing keys from an attendant and several times fomenting plots among other patients. After two weeks he succeeded in his efforts and soon appeared at home (fifty miles from the hospital) in a magnificent state of boisterous intoxication. He continued at home in complete idleness except for some enterprising petty thefts, long speeches about the need of increased virtue in women (delivered in local poolrooms), several brawls arising from his being caught cheating at dice, some bold-faced begging, and numerous maneuvers to obtain money illegally, including forgery.

Despite peaceful intervals of a week or more, he continued to demonstrate an irresponsibility so utter that one is taxed to describe it. After several additional experiences in jail he was brought back to the hospital by his father, who confessed himself at his wit's end.

During psychiatric examinations the patient again denied that he had caused any trouble or done anything that would justify his being brought to the hospital. He admitted having taken a few drinks and tried to conclude some wise business deals but still insisted that he never drank much or ever behaved irresponsibly or in such a way as to cause trouble.

He glibly dismissed all the massive accumulation of detail concerning his lack of responsibility, his failure to show normal interests in life, his indifference to the serious trouble he gave relatives and friends, and the purposeless folly that had consumed all his efforts for years. The adroitness with which he denied everything and the brisk, facile manner in which he excused himself and glossed over his record made it clear that his mind was free of any seriousness whatsoever in regard to his past and of any real intention to behave more sensibly in the future. One thing only in this man impressed his examiners as having some emotional weight. This was his vivid chagrin at being confined and his persistent, restless longing to be free.

Many attempts were made to make him realize that he could stay out of the hospital only by avoiding inappropriate conduct and acts plainly damaging or embarrassing to others and by conducting himself so as not to be an unbearable burden on his family and the community. He admitted that he did not really enjoy or have any particular reason for doing as he did, and reports substantiate this, representing him as a sullen, glum fellow in bars and poolrooms, a man without convivial gaiety or other signs of stimulation, apparently more unhappy in his efforts to celebrate than in his usual state.

I am convinced that this man obtains no delight at all from whiskey, that whatever may be his purpose in drinking, it does not result in the attainment of pleasure. Every effort was futile to make him see what was so obvious, that he had brought his troubles on himself, and that only by staying sober could he retain his freedom. He absolutely refused to face any fact and slipped nimbly from reality to the world of his evasions.

A few weeks later, because of a death in his family, he was allowed to go home in custody of his father. He immediately got out of the house and slipped off to a nearby town, where he drank himself into a state of maudlin intoxication, made a nuisance of himself in several public houses, engaged in minor street brawls, and wandered cursing and muttering aimlessly through the streets until found by his relatives.

At the funeral the next day, having skillfully obtained more whiskey, Chester appeared at first poised and sober. Signs of drunkenness, however, soon appeared, and the patient proceeded to make a shocking and memorable impression. Vomiting and defecating while in the aisle of the church contributed to this effect. As an elder brother was attempting to expedite his departure with minimum conspicuousness, these momentary and incomplete reactions took place.

The father sent him back to the hospital as soon as arrangements could be made. Although the patient could not have been unaware that his father had informed the hospital of his conduct and explained the circumstances under which he returned, he said with the greatest assurance on arriving that he had voluntarily come back before expiration of his furlough, merely for the day and in order to have the furlough extended. He insisted that his conduct at home had been above reproach and demanded parole privileges until arrangements were made for him to leave the hospital. At this time he was entirely free from all effects of alcohol.

This man is the son of a rather prosperous farmer and merchant. His home is in a Southern town of ten thousand inhabitants. His father, though not highly educated, is a successful, sensible man and genuinely respected in the community. Of his three siblings, a sister is married and in good circumstances, one brother is a physician, and the other is a lawyer. All are successful and seem well adapted to their environment.

The patient was raised in the same environment with his sister and brothers, but from early youth, unlike the other children, he showed some signs of his present inadaptability. He learned rather easily in school and successfully completed his studies each year until he reached the sixth grade. His truancy then became so pronounced that he could not be kept in school any longer. On being sent to a strict military school, he proved intractable and was expelled after a few weeks. Though remarkably lazy and unpersevering, he showed at this time what appeared to be a slight interest and an astonishing talent in tinkering with radios. His parents, who throughout his whole life have shown exceptional patience and gone to no little expense and trouble with him, sent him to New York to study radio work. He was very eager to go and urged this plan on the family. His older brother, the physician, was Chief of Staff in a New York hospital at the time and agreed to keep in touch with him and try to exercise any necessary supervision.

From the very beginning it became apparent that the venture was useless. Chester could not be induced to attend classes. He showed no interest whatsoever in his work or in anything else, lying about his room much of the time and going out alone on adventures without much purpose or content—on missions to borrow a dollar through solemn-faced fraud or, by cheating or some sort of chicanery, to pick up a little extra change or to beat the game by getting a free ride on the bus or the subway and, perhaps, to climax the day by slipping out of a restaurant without paying for his meal. His brother, after earnest and persistent efforts to persuade him to take advantage of his opportunities, had to give up and send him home.

Many other efforts have been made to help this young man find some place in normal life. Various positions have been found for him, but he always refuses to maintain the slightest interest in any work.

The ordinary pleasures of mankind seem to have as little charm for him as work. Though he has had sexual relations with prostitutes and other available girls, he never formed a real attachment for any. Even casual physical encounters with women claim his interest far less than sporadic bouts of solitary drunken torpor in remote cotton fields or aimless hours spent idling about uninspiring hamburger stands and poolrooms. When at 22 years of age he ran off to enlist in the army, his father did not try to interfere, hoping the discipline of that life would stabilize him.

Since the incidents just mentioned, he has on several other occasions obtained parole and violated it promptly by carrying out various antisocial acts which seemed to have no definite purpose, no conceivable explanation in terms of human impulse. He has also succeeded again in escaping from closed wards. On getting out, he always repeats his former conduct. Sometimes he has remained cooperative for a month or more, abiding by the rules of his ward, helping attendants with their work, assisting and directing frankly psychotic patients. During such periods he would talk frequently with his physician, discussing his plans for the future, maintaining that he fully realized drinking or stealing or not taking life seriously enough was his trouble and declaring that he would never act so unwisely again.

He appeared to be a sane, quick-witted young man with good judgment and reasonably earnest intentions. So convincing was the impression he made that time after time the various physicians who had charge of his case would decide that parole was advisable despite his history. Within a few hours or sometimes a few days he would appear at his home in a wretched state, land in jail because of unacceptable behavior, take an automobile and get caught, or, lacking opportunity for something more active to do, get himself too drunk to leave town and fall into the hands of the local police.

On one occasion, several days after being returned by his family from such an escapade, Chester came to me smiling and at ease. He spoke briefly of his plans for the future and insisted on having parole at once. In support of this request he sought to make the point that he had proved himself trustworthy and reliable under all circumstances. Looking me squarely in the face, he asserted with modest firmness, "You know that I'm *a man of my word.*" He repeated this statement several times and spoke most intelligently and convincingly in his own behalf. When asked how he pretended to be a man of his word after breaking it so many times, so flagrantly, and so recently, he showed no sign of being confounded.

His memory was of course clear, and he accurately recognized all the circumstances under which he had given his word not to leave the hospital, to steal, to forge, or to drink whiskey, as well as his invariably and prompt violations of every promise. He seemed to seek in the phrase *a man of his word,* which he uttered in tones of quiet pride and assurance, some magical charm that would irrationally persuade me to trust him. Indeed, he himself appeared to be well convinced by his statement. On seeing this man for the first time, one would have read into him a fair degree of sincerity and conviction. To me he seemed rather to be activated by a mimicry of these things, an insubstantial shadow of emotion which the patient, knowing nothing else, confused in his own mind with what he assumed other people felt when they used such a tone. Having never in his whole life, so far as I could find in examining him, looked a fact of this sort in the face, he was untroubled by even the hardest, sharpest contrast between fact and falsehood and stood free to indulge, with a kind of automatic imitation sincerity, in any fantasy he chose.

During his repeated hospitalizations his case was reviewed many times. No evidence of a psychosis in the commonly accepted sense of the word was found in his past record or in his current behavior or thought. At each presentation before the medical staff every member has agreed that he is "sane and competent" and that he should be classified under the term *psychopathic personality.* He is bright rather than dull, and his reasoning powers on all general matters and on test questions are average or better than average.

Here, then, is a man whose measurable intelligence is not at fault, whose extrinsic situation is normal, and who is entirely free from the delusions and other mental disorders of the recognized psychoses. His environment is favorable, and his opportunities, past and present, insofar as they can be estimated, appear better than the average. He is not visibly indifferent or emotionally isolated in the ordinary sense of those words, but, in sharp contrast to the schizophrenic or the deteriorated patient with organic brain disease, he reacts with a very natural antipathy to his situation when confined. Several of the psychiatrists who observed him have expressed the belief that he detests being in the hospital more than any man they ever saw there.

Why, then, does he always take these active steps to get himself back in confinement just as soon as he gets away? It has been clearly demonstrated to him that he will have to spend most of his life in confinement as long as he persists in his present ways. The opinion held by some physicians is that such people as this patient are merely spoiled, that they would behave more sensibly if not pampered, and that if promptly confined to jail or left in whatever other difficulties they bring down on their own heads, they would finally control themselves. I believe that consistent, prompt, and regular punishment for unacceptable conduct is of great value in treating most people who persist in flagrant misbehavior, delinquency, or crime. I believe it is usually of far more value than any form of dynamic psychotherapy. In this patient, however, it proved quite ineffectual. No ordinary punishment could be much more severe than confinement on a closed ward is to this particular man. He has had it thoroughly explained to him that he will remain here until he can adapt himself to normal life outside. He not only gives up everything that other people seek but also, because of confinement, he sacrifices the chance to follow the inappropriate patterns of behavior into which he falls almost at once when left to his own devices.

Whatever strange goals or pseudogoals there may be to prompt and shape his reactions as a member of the community, these too, it seems, fail to motivate him sufficiently, fail to induce decisions and acts that would give him the freedom to pursue them. It has been demonstrated to Chester repeatedly, in the hardest aspects of the concrete, that his characteristic acts put him back in a situation he finds particularly disagreeable. This does not produce the slightest modification in his behavior.

If we attempt to interpret his antisocial conduct as a rebellious manifestation, a symbolic protest against customs, principles, people, and institutions that he will not accept, we might presume he would take more pains to avoid the interruption of his efforts along this line. If there is unconscious need for him to make trouble in the community and to achieve heroic stature as a general nuisance, his steps to fulfill this need seem peculiarly illogical. They promptly result in the termination of his action. Arguments for such motivation in more effective criminal careers and in circumscribed patterns of delinquency seem more plausible than in such a case as this. If loitering, theft, swindling, "disgracing himself," running up debts, and social sabotage in general are his goals, the pursuit of these he must give up when he comes under close supervision on the closed ward.

Is he seeking, then, not to fulfill these goals but to frustrate the impulses to fulfill them? Or is he seeking punishment as something even more desirable than the perverse goals surmised above? The claim of such motivational schemes has been advanced. Perhaps some patients who show more interest in their predicaments may reveal hidden attitudes, old wounds or grudges, or forgotten but distorting influences that suggest such an interpretation.

From this patient, however, none of the many psychiatrists who dealt with him could obtain any underlying material to confirm such speculations. As hypotheses about his disorder, such interpretations impress me as having very little plausibility. It might be assumed that if deep penetration of his personality and adequate exploration of his innermost life could be achieved, substantial evidence of cause and effect would emerge in some convincing explanation. It seems likely, however, that a valid explanation would prove to be one far more complex than anything just suggested. An important clinical feature of his disorder seemed, nevertheless, to lie in the specific and obdurate difficulty in finding out anything at all about less superficial attitudes or real inner purposes and meanings.

In closing the summary of this case, let the point be emphasized again that this man does not seem driven by hot temptations to his injudicious deeds. What he does when free fails to give him much pleasure. Chester is in no way like a man who sacrifices all the ordinary satisfactions of life for some enthralling sin which will later bring him to ruin. The well-known human motives that sometimes lead a respected and successful business man to lose fortune and family in his pursuit of an illicitly loved woman or some other transitory but enticing joy are not discernible in this case.

> My candle burns at both ends;
> It will not last the night;
> But ah, my foes, and, oh, my friends—
> It gives a lovely light.
>
> *Edna St. Vincent Millay*
> "A Few Figs from Thistles"

Such a scheme of life, whatever might be said for its final wisdom, has no apparent place in this patient's maladjustment. The allegory of Faust selling his soul to the Devil in order to quench a thirst for rarer joys than this life holds is absurdly inappropriate.

It is most difficult to believe that Chester is reacting to powerful drives that *force* or *compel* him into obviously disastrous actions. On the contrary, everything about him suggests a drifting approach, a casual and weak impulse, a halfhearted whim rather than an explosive release of passion in the forbidden deed. Instead of a pathologic intensity of drive, there seems to be a pathologic general devaluation of life, a complex deficiency, confusion, or malfunction in what chooses aims and directs impulse.

Nothing that he expresses or that can be observed about him suggests a great stress or inner conflict in which strong opposing forces clash and from which emerges deep instinctual gratification as he makes off with a stolen car, thoroughly cleans out an opponent by fraud in crap shooting, saddles his father with a heavy debt, or drains his bottle and brawlingly defies the police. Nor is there anything yet detected about him that suggests true relief of inner tension as he reacts to society's restraints and retaliations. If these are his fundamental mechanisms, they are so deeply concealed that they show no surface or subsurface repercussion of emotion that suggests in the least their nature or their existence.

JOE

Joe came in the custody of two friends to apply for admission to the hospital. He had with him commitment papers showing that he had at his own request been declared incompetent.

Joe was alert and intelligent and conducted himself in a manner that suggested a person of poise, good judgment, and firm resolution. He was anything but the sort of figure that might come to mind in thinking of a patient sent for admission to such an institution.

He frankly admitted that he was not insane in the ordinary sense of the word and therefore was not eligible according to the letter of the law for admission into a hospital of this sort. He urged, however, that he be accepted, stating that for the last sixteen or seventeen years he had been drinking to great and foolish excess in periodic sprees. He seemed to be remarkably frank and straightforward, admitting that he had made an unholy mess of his life and caused misery untold for his wife, his parents, and his friends. At times he became much depressed, he said, when ruminating over the magnitude of his failure. He appeared earnest in his strongly expressed determination to pull himself together and make a fresh start.

A rather unusual and impressive sincerity seemed to distinguish this man from some with similar histories of psychopathic drinking and psychopathic failure. He did not promise to become a new man. He admitted that he knew it would be most difficult for him to change his ways and seemed to realize that his many collapses in the past after similar good intentions told against his present chances.

Records that accompanied him gave the information that three years previously Joe had attempted suicide by severing veins in both arms. Definite scars were visible four or five inches above the wrists. Since he had not played up this phase of his case, his statement that he had really tried to kill himself was particularly convincing. Though patients officially not psychotic and considered responsible for their own troubles and misdeeds are not technically eligible, it was decided to take this man.

His history of a suicide attempt furnished plausible grounds for calling his case an emergency, and his apparently desperate intention of escaping from the pattern of his past folly promised that treatment in a mental hospital might give him a chance to gain insight and forge new resolution, which he would need in starting over again.

During the month of psychiatric study and constant observation that preceded diagnosis before the staff, this man proved to be a model patient. He was cheerful, convivial, alert, and energetic. He asked for work and at once made himself useful, checking out laundry, typing various lists, helping psychotic patients, and performing many other duties. Quick, accurate, and reliable, he seemed to take a real pleasure in all work that he could get and actually accomplished much more than an average man could.

He was at all times in perfect contact, reasonable, optimistic, and plainly intelligent. During examinations he told his story with a remarkable appearance of frankness and insight.

"I suppose, Doctor, I am still a child emotionally," he admitted in explanation of the fifteen years during which he threw away many valuable positions, lost his wife, and went repeatedly to sanatoriums that offer drinking cures and to mental hospitals. He seemed to realize that his conduct was extremely irrational and without reward, agreeing that he had been quite unhappy nearly all the time and a source of grief and despair to others.

Drinking, Joe said, was not in his opinion the cause of his trouble but merely a symptom of some obscure flaw in his makeup. This defect he found it hard to define or describe, although he spoke very intelligently and almost, it might be said, profoundly. He distinguished between his own case and the various psychoses, maintaining that he was entirely sane but admitting that, though sane, he had behaved more foolishly than a bona fide "lunatic," and for no purpose.

He mentioned the writings of Freud, Jung, Bleuler, and William A. White and showed familiarity with psychiatric terminology that is unusual for a layman, as well as a surprisingly good acquaintance with the literature.

"I suppose I must be a constitutional psychopath," he concluded after describing his many opportunities, his many confident resolutions to adjust, and his inevitable, quick failures.

As in so many cases of this sort, drinking, being a tangible and superficial activity, is often stressed by the family and the patient as if it were the major source of difficulty. Being at a loss to account for antisocial and self-damaging acts in terms of real purpose, it is customary for them to decide that these must have been carried out because some drinks had been taken. I do not share such a belief. This patient, like a good many others, was more inclined to discuss drinking than his more essential difficulties, so this at first was the chief topic.

"But why do you drink?" he was asked. "Why do you let yourself take the first drink, when you realize by now to what it will lead?" It was hard to say, he admitted. He felt he had not for many years obtained pleasure from the effects of whiskey. Even if there had been some extraordinary pleasure in drinking, he felt sure this would not have been worth even a small part of the price he had paid.

Perhaps habit was a factor, Joe suggested; perhaps he was emotionally conditioned to repeat this disastrous step, no matter how plainly reason warned him against it. He spoke of possible forces within his mind that might seek failure, unconscious tendencies to defeat himself. Desire to escape from the difficulties and failures of life, he felt, might influence him to seek intoxication. On the other hand, he believed the failure and difficulties would not occur if he did not drink. He was confident that drunkenness led to the many disastrous actions he had taken.

Joe emphasized his belief in a vicious cycle of sequences, the drink causing him to get in grave difficulty, to lose what he most wanted, and then his subsequent disappointments causing him to seek refuge in drink. Though some casual influence may lie in this, it is apparently secondary and superficial. When in extremely advantageous positions, in situations he described as ideal, without provocation or known purpose, he often acted in such a way as to lose all that he said he found desirable and to make failure inevitable and spectacular.

On being asked if he really found life worthwhile, if a normal life offered anything to him, he quickly answered that it did. He appeared frank in affirming that there was in him a strong and persistent will to succeed, an urge to get at the satisfactions of existence which most people choose in preference to the sort of career he had known with its almost fantastic and presumably frustrating reverses and maladjustments.

As Joe discussed the possibility that impulses unrecognized by him might play a part in his way of life, he seemed like one with an almost Socratic respect for the depth and extent of the unknowable. It was entirely possible, he maintained, that he might be deceiving himself. Perhaps, he admitted, there were tendencies within, whose presence he did not suspect. As he continued, he spontaneously questioned his essential sincerity but in such a way as to make him seem even more sincere than heretofore.

This man's apparent insight, freedom from evasiveness, and willingness to admit himself responsible for his misfortunes are, it might be said, inconsistent with his history, which is typically that of a psychopath. In my opinion, however, none of these qualities, which appeared to be so highly developed in him, are real. It is perhaps more accurate to say that, whatever reality there may be in these qualities, it is not integrated into the person's functioning. It does not emerge objectively in the acuality of behavior.

In time, his insight comes to seem but a mimicry of insight. He uses the words that one who understood would use, but they do not have a corresponding meaning. He speaks with every evidence of conviction and sincerity, but when one studies him over a period of time, it becomes apparent finally that he is merely going through the motions, that he is not actually living the feelings he describes so well. His evasiveness, of almost Dostoevskian complexity, consists in an openness which is actually no openness at all. He freely gives up discrediting information about his weakness and his failures and appears to take them with ardent seriousness, to understand them, to regret them to the bottom of his heart, and to intend to learn and profit by them. But all the while he is, for the most part, merely using the words, the gestures, and the expressions without entering into the feeling and the understanding. We find ourselves dealing not so much with a genius at acting but with a person who, in the most important matters, has no capacity of distinguishing between what is acting and what is not.

Joe is not really facing facts now but only acting in charade in which he faces imitation facts. He says he is responsible for his failures and seems to accept this responsibility honestly and to have normal regret for the pain he has caused others, but in studying him it becomes apparent that the regret is something quite different from what we have presumed he was talking about and that he is able to act as if it were profound only because he is utterly unaware of what real and serious regret is—because he does not experience real and serious emotions.

It is difficult to describe this impression without implying that the patient's reactions are being identified with deliberate fraud or with hypocrisy in its ordinary meaning. There is, however, a fundamental difference. Psychopaths notoriously deceive and falsify, with strict awareness of the intention and about any sort of situation.

Voluntary and quite conscious decisions to lie occur and are carried out in discussing the points on which we attempt to estimate insight and the genuineness of emotions, desire, grief, remorse, love. In addition to such factors, however, we encounter misleading reports of another sort.

In all probability, Joe was often accurately describing his reactions insofar as he could. Something left out of his experience made it impossible for him to see that the words he used did not refer to such emotional actualities as they would in another. One might say this constitutes a kind of strange and paradoxical sincerity, something a little like the report of a color-blind man (without knowledge of his defect) who after investigation swears conscientiously that the horizon is gray, though it actually blazes with all colors of the sunset.

Such a comparison is, however, full of implications that may mislead us. It can also be said that this particular patient, when it suits his purposes, does not hesitate to falsify with full deliberation.

In time a typical glibness about the major social disasters of his life reveals itself, and one sees that this man has a sort of pride in the spectacular capers he has cut. He admits that he is to blame for his wife's having had to divorce him because of periods of desertion and gross, repetitive, and almost publicly transacted acts of infidelity. Even now, while full of expressed intentions to change his ways, he shows no genuine concern for the fate of this former wife and little or none for his children. He admits his childishness, his failures in every undertaking, and his flagrant lack of consideration for others. He admits some dozen or two arrests in the last year and a half for causing disorder in public and for unacceptable conduct while drinking. But he is very solemn in assuming that he is a *man of honor* in the most unqualified sense, despite what he confesses as his faults. He states that he will not break his word and that he has never committed an act against anyone else for which he should have been arrested. He admits that the alleged suicide attempt was a pure fraud and that he had made a false statement about it in order to get into the hospital. He had cut his arms only to frighten his wife and parents and to create a dramatic scene in order to gain his ends with them. He describes his exploit in detail, admitting its extreme childishness. He remembers that he took care to pull over a chair and to fall with a great thud and clatter so that he would attract sudden attention and become at once the center of an exciting scene.

This, for the sort of man he is known to be, is admitting a great deal. But he at once insists that he has always been a man of his word, ignoring the many incidents in his history to the contrary. He leaves out many well-established facts that would not fit in with the picture he now means to give of himself, as a man who has done many foolish and unpardonable things but who is still a "gentleman" fundamentally. He always insists that the many women with whom he has had relations were those who would obviously excite romantic feelings, though this is by no means true. He says repeatedly that sexual relations are no pleasure to him unless he gives the woman pleasure too, but one can see that this is an opinion he has picked up from reading and that it has nothing to do with the reality of his life. Actually his experiences with women have been casual, incomplete, and of so little real significance to him that he has been known to drink himself into a state of impotence rather than continue even the primary physical exercises of the relationship. Later he says that no woman among the many with whom he has had intercourse ever afforded anything of serious significance to him; but he feels that this is rather to his credit as a romantic lover. "I am in love with love!" he concludes tritely.

Joe speaks of his misadventures with what would pass for admirable humor, and this would have been real humor had there been a contrasting seriousness in his understanding to give it meaning. But his light touch in dealing with his own faults and his own follies loses significance when it becomes apparent that for him there is no tragic reality against which it is maintained.

At 38 years of age, he is athletic, well groomed, and rather handsome. The story of his life as he gives it is in most of the outer facts identical with the story as given in social service reports and by his friends.

Joe's father was a prominent man in one of the largest cities in Alabama. High ambitions were entertained for this son, and he was given every educational opportunity. He feels that his mother had puritanical ideals of life and wished him to live according to them. He admits that he made no attempt to suppress his natural inclinations and says that he enjoyed sexual intercourse frequently since he was about 13 years of age. He was unusually bright in school and made rapid progress despite interruptions caused by pneumonia. He was sent to a celebrated preparatory school in the East where he did well in his studies and achieved athletic prominence in football and tennis.

He then entered the state university but after two years transferred to Virginia Military Institute. Before graduating he enlisted in the army. He was later discharged with the rank of corporal. He then entered law school at the state university and after three years graduated with high distinction, being named valedictorian for his class.

Joe had already begun to show irresponsibility, often walking out of class capriciously and ignoring serious duties as well as matters on which his own welfare depended. He had also on isolated occasions begun to show the tendency to behave outlandishly when he drank. He was very capable and successful in the practice of law when he gave his attention to it, but he soon lost interest and neglected his work. His father was, however, able to cover most of his deficiencies and keep him in an appearance of success. He often entertained big ideas but did little to put them into practice. He constantly made excuses and was full of high-sounding promises, few of which he made any attempt to fulfill.

The patient himself accounts for his loss of interest in law as resulting from an idealistic outlook. He states that he entered his profession with the assumption that actual justice was the criterion of legal decisions; finding this to be far from true, he had little patience left for the law.

He was at this time settling down to serious drinking, as he expresses it. As a matter of fact, his essential untrustworthiness and his tendency to squander his resources and throw his responsibilities upon others stand out in his behavior while not drinking at all, although in his own account of his career he tends to cloak his more important aspects of maladjustment under the explanation of alcoholic influence.

Joe became interested in running for city council, threw himself with great energy into the race, and after a shrewd and active campaign was elected. According to the social service reports, most of his drinking was done alone, even at this time when he was in his early twenties. On occasions when he drank in company, he often misbehaved in most extraordinary and distressing ways.

Once when a guest at a formal dance held in a small town fifty miles away from his home, he threw a large crowd of respectable people into extreme consternation. After taking some drinks, he walked out on the dance floor, cut in on an attractive young lady, and joined with the crowd as it gave itself up to the disco beat.

Stopping brazenly in a semisecluded corner of the dancing area, Joe drew sudden attention from the astonished eyes of a hundred dancing couples, and from the band. These at first found it difficult to credit their perceptions or to act as they watched him jerk his partner's dress up over her head, set himself to work divesting her of her undergarments, and, despite her struggles and screams, commence on the first steps toward an attempt at sexual intercourse in these inauspicious surroundings. A tumult ensued. He was snatched from his victim and removed from the dance floor at once. Only the energetic intervention of his friends saved him from violence.

A year later he married. The wedding was delayed because Joe, about a month before the announced date, ran off with another girl, the respectable daughter of a professor in the university. He hid out with this partner in a cheap hotel to avoid pursuit by her parents but eventually, after many highly embarrassing and unseemly episodes, went off into maudlin or uproarious drunkenness and finally stupor, leaving his partner in illicit love to her own devices.

Joe's marriage was from the first a failure. He neglected his wife, lay out for days in drinking sprees, wandered off and spent the night in low dives, and availed himself of every opportunity to have casual intercourse with other women.

He made little pretense now of working, neglecting even his position on the city council which had cost him some shrewd planning and considerable effort to obtain. According to the opinion of those who know him, he was not interested in the position itself, that is to say, in anything he might accomplish thereby, but only in the petty fame it might bring him. He enjoyed stepping into various roles in which he played the big shot.

Joe's father, who is a very influential man, some time later got him appointed judge of a local court. This position paid an excellent salary and required only about an hour of work daily. This, however, was too much. He would not attend even to the barest minimum of his duties, refused to go to his office, wandered on pseudoadventures in distant cities without making any provision for his responsibilities to be met, often without letting his family know he was going or informing them of his whereabouts. Despite the zeal of friends and relatives to make good his deficiencies, he lost this very valuable position.

His father bought him a house, leaving it encumbered with a small mortgage in order to stimulate the patient to use his funds constructively and free himself from his obligation. Although receiving an ample income to make these payments, he made no effort to do so but instead, as his father later discovered, took out another large mortgage and squandered this money as well as his income.

There seemed little incentive or definite purpose in the actions through which he destroyed his opportunities and squandered his and his parents' resources. One can discern no strong recognizable temptation, no formulated course of living, good or evil, for which be abandoned what others find so desirable.

Although his father supplied Joe's wife and children (he has two daughters) with money and continued to give him opportunities to make an easy living at law, he worked little or not at all and spent his time getting in and out of police stations, going time after time to hospitals where he remained for a few weeks or a month, only to return and take up at once his former practices.

After several years of such living he was sent to a federal psychiatric hospital in Mississippi for study and treatment. Nothing to suggest a psychosis or a psychoneurosis could be found. He showed himself to be highly intelligent and energetic but inclined to be domineering, especially toward his father, whom he would not allow to come on the ward and visit him. After five weeks he left against medical advice. He was classed as a case of psychopathic personality.

Three months later Joe set off in his car, sober and apparently enthusiastic about the prospect of his vacation, to join his wife and children who were spending a few weeks at a summer resort in the Tennessee mountains. On the way he picked up another woman, then after they had a few drinks together apparently lost interest in her. Stopping in a small town in northern Alabama, he left his companion in the car, making some excuse, and went to a railroad station, throwing away the keys to his car on the way in a gesture of careless bravado. At the station he stood before a timetable, closed his eyes, and put down his finger at random. Noting that he had by chance fallen on Tulsa, he bought a ticket and, bringing along a good supply of whiskey, left without more ado for that city.

Nothing was heard from him for several weeks. Leading the life of a bum or city tramp who lives by his wits, he was active at panhandling, petty fraud, and other schemes and tricks to pick up small sums. He fell more than once into the hands of the police. Always disarming and impressive, he cleverly talked himself out of the usual consequences.

At length an acquaintance of Joe's family ran across him in Texas and notified his father, who sent him funds at once by telegraph so that he could come home. Instead, he bought more whiskey and continued his rambles, drinking sometimes with chance acquaintances he found in bars, occasionally drinking alone, and staggering about uninviting sections of town or out into the countryside.

After going to Minneapolis, he wandered on an odd impulse into the tent where a celebrated evangelist was exhorting sinners. One of the evangelist's assistants happened on him and urged him to accept salvation and join the troupe. Although an unbeliever, he was attracted by the idea and, with a great show of enthusiasm, announced his intentions of devoting his life to the work.

Professing a lusty rebirth, he attached himself to the evangelist and went on to Chicago, where he was active and successful in bringing in the penitent and getting them out on the sawdust trail. He also showed himself extremely able and for a while industrious in running a mission where vagrants were fed. He told utterly false but dramatic and convincing stories of his life to the religious workers and seemed like one remarkably suited to his new calling.

Joe continued at these activities for several weeks, not drinking and enjoying himself fairly well. He maintains that he never entertained any serious belief in the doctrine of the evangelist or experienced any sensations of penitence or sanctity. "I just sold myself somehow on the idea of doing it," he says with a broad smile.

Meeting a red-haired girl, his thoughts inclined in another direction. Leaving the evangelist's party, he put up with her at a hotel where he briefly enjoyed her charms, then abandoned her as casually as he had begun the relationship.

For a while now he turned to alcohol, taking no interest in anything and summoning only enough energy to get the bottle and drink himself back to snoring oblivion. Shortly afterward he returned home, made a few brief gestures at working, but chiefly idled and drifted.

He continued in this fashion for a year, keeping his wife in misery and perplexity and his father active by day and night in efforts to get him out of jail and to whip up some interest in him to make a new start. Occasionally he spoke seriously of having obtained a new outlook and worked for a few weeks or a month, always showing excellent ability and succeeding with ease in all he attempted. No matter how bright were his prospects, he soon threw them up and went on another round of idle wanderings, self-defeating and apparently boring antisocial routines, or on mirthless and unhappy drinking bouts.

Finally Joe's wife divorced him and went to live with his father, who assumed full obligation for her support and that of the children, treating her with the greatest kindness and consideration.

Some time later the patient's father sent him to New York for another of his fresh starts. He had for years professed an interest in writing and during his sober interludes had turned his hand occasionally to journalism. In New York he worked for several weeks and evidently was headed for some success, having already had a few articles accepted, one by a magazine of wide circulation.

Idle drifting among dull and delinquent groups, vagrancy, and sporadic drunkenness now intervened. He soon ceased all efforts to write and led very much the sort of life typical of men who have no opportunities left and (lacking an alternative) exist about large cities, lost to interest and incentive, in states often referred to as *being in the gutter.* Sometimes brawls in barrooms and quarrels about cheating in games of chance brought him into contact with the police. For several months he wandered in the slums of the city, often being brought in by the police or taken to Bellevue and other hospitals for brief periods of treatment.

On returning home, Joe's career began all over again at the point on which he had left off and continued until his present admission to this hospital. Though always cooperative, he was anxious to go before the staff for diagnosis as soon as possible, since he would only then become eligible for parole. Tactful and not obviously demanding, he did not at first press his requests but, after several delays had occurred, sent the following lines to the physician in charge of his case:

Request is respectfully made
By R __________ number 6-7-3-0
That his humble case may be laid
Before a busy medico.

Patient seldom hears the voices,*
Never waxes vitriolic;
Quite discerning in his choices
For a chronic alcoholic.

Quiet and cooperative,
He is no wise sadistic;
Records have it that his native
Instincts are all altruistic

A suicidal tendency
Is foreign to his credo,
Due to the marked ascendancy
Of exhibitionistic ego.

---

*This reference to hearing voices is, of course, made in jest. He has never experienced hallucinations.

Voluntarily committed,
The patient can stand the gaff
If only he were permitted
Presentation to the Staff.

Patient does not wish a discharge
From this psychopathic knoll;
He has no urge to roam at large,
But he would like to have parole.

And so, if it is convenient,
Your call is respectfully urged;
Hoping that you will be lenient
When my rye psychosis is purged.

There is little need to give in detail the record of his failures to adjust to these new responsibilities. His behavior was virtually the same as that already described in such patients while on parole status in psychiatric institutions in a similar situation. It was clear to him that freedom would be curtailed if irresponsible or antisocial actions occurred.

No matter how often he was brought in by police or hospital attendants or confined at the station for unacceptable behavior, always, in requesting restoration of parole, he seemed to have complete confidence in himself and to feel sure that others would feel likewise. His superficial charm, plausible explanations, and apparent sincerity enlisted the support of all who met him.

During his various periods on parole he met many women, some of whom he convinced he was being treated with incredible injustice at the hospital. Several intelligent and attractive women, persuaded that he was not understood, began to visit the hospital and intercede with authorities there whenever restriction of his privileges became necessary.

Even female employees of the hospital were not immune to his charm and found it difficult to believe he was anything but a wonderful and trustworthy fellow whose only difficulties arose from poor judgment or unfair attitudes on the part of his family or the physicians. Some of the nurses whose past experience with similar problems and direct observation of this subject would, one might think, make it impossible for them not to recognize his serious disorder seemed for a while inclined to believe that such an impressive man as this simply could not continue in failures so futile.

At the weekly dances held for patients he intrigued and delighted large numbers of feminine visitors. Some of these devoted themselves to his cause, quickly convinced that sufficient sympathy and full demonstration of faith in his inherent manliness would resolve his difficulties.

At Joe's suggestion some of these admirers wrote to officials of veterans' organizations and even to congressmen in Washington, insisting on special intervention in the case. On many occasions the patient violated the terms of his parole, returning several hours late from passes after being with some of these kind and zealous women who had become increasingly determined to mother him or perhaps to save him by more frankly exciting methods.

Despite all these efforts in his behalf, his behavior became worse and consequently his periods of parole briefer and less frequent. He soon demanded his discharge. His family emphasized the great and needless difficulties that would result and urged, in the name of common sense, that he not be released. Since the commitment furnished legal authorization, the medical staff kept him despite his protests.

At the suggestion of the chief of staff, who had consistently reacted to Joe's failures with extraordinary patience, steps were taken that would lead to his soon regaining parole privileges. Just before these steps were completed, communications arrived from Washington citing bitter complaints about the hospital, quoting vicious and startling accusations against this patient's particular advocate, the chief of staff, who, in the opinion of many, had often gone too far in trying to meet his demands.

The patient had written to government officials, employing his cleverness, learning, and ingenuity in such a way as to make some people in high authority suspect that the most fantastic and implausible injustice had been done him. He had, furthermore, so used his father's standing in his home community and so manipulated the great respect in which his father was held that he evoked an extraordinary reaction. Some in Washington were so stirred and misled by his tactics that they apparently acted under the impression that the father's testimony supported that of the son.

When questioned about this surprising attack directed chiefly against the most lenient of all his physicians, Joe, supercilious and a little arrogant, insisted on skipping these subterfuges and getting down to brass tacks about the restoration of his parole. There seemed to be no sense of shame or dismay in this role or at having nothing at all to back up the serious charges he had made.

After being granted parole again, he so conducted himself that the police put him behind bars and notified the hospital of this fact. Shortly afterward he attempted to escape. The attempt was made soon after he had given his word, with all describable aspects of sincerity and with a clear demonstration that he fully understood his commitments and agreed to abide by them.

He became more and more difficult to deal with by the rules and procedures of a hospital set up for the ordinary type of psychotic patient. After a trying period for himself and his physicians, he called in an attorney. By legal procedures that followed the approved technicalities, he obtained his wishes.

Less than a week after Joe's departure from the hospital he returned in such a state that anyone could tell he needed shelter and assistance. At the outer gate of the hospital grounds he demanded that he be admitted. The physician on duty interviewed him and explained that legal steps had been taken which made it impossible for the hospital to readmit him. He begged and argued and brought forth the most cogent and practical and pertinent of reasons why he should be under supervision and treatment. The physician who talked with him agreed with all he said. But despite this agreement and common understanding, there was no means by which Joe could be taken back.

MILT

An incomplete account of this patient will be offered. His behavior and his apparent subjective reactions differ little from those of the patients already presented. He serves, however, as an example of the psychopath who resorts to no alcoholic beverage. Although drinking is sometimes prominent in a superficial appraisal of the clinical picture, nonalcoholic psychopaths are not so rare as the preceding accounts might lead one to believe. Since many observers still tend to explain such patients' essential difficulties as being caused by drinking and in legal matters stress is put upon this factor, it is, perhaps, worthwhile to consider this case.

At 19 years of age, Milt was admitted to a general hospital for psychiatric study. His mother and other relatives who had brought him from his home in a neighboring state expressed the greatest perplexity about his condition. The behavior that had resulted in his hospitalization became prominent about two years previously, but he was described as being sporadically unreliable and unresponsive since the early teens.

The patient's family were people of considerable means and had for many generations been prominent and highly respected in a city of approximately 100,000 inhabitants. His male antecedents had been judges, bank presidents, distinguished physicians, and brokers. The women on both sides of his family were almost uniformly charming and responsible members of the community. Four years prior to Milt's admission to the hospital his father's business failed, and in the consequent readjustment it was revealed that the father had disposed of large funds illegally. The family was able, however, to make arrangements that prevented serious legal action, and the father became established in another business. Except for this episode the father's career does not show any evidence of unusual or serious antisocial behavior. Nothing at all in the father's activities can be found that would suggest the kind of behavior so prominent in the son. However indefensible the misappropriation of funds may be, it is an action based on motives that anyone can understand, though one may not approve of it. Sufficient income still existed for the family to live well. The patient's older brother, an older sister, and one younger brother were all regarded as normal and attractive young people. The two older siblings had finished college successfully.

The first thing that caused the parents worry was the patient's apparent failure to take anything seriously. Milt often became involved in adolescent pranks, but, unlike his playmates, he did not profit by his mistakes. If he, with other boys, destroyed property during the celebration after a high school football victory, he seemed unable to realize his responsibility for the damage. His verbal apologies were magnificent, and he seemed in discussion to understand fully that he had been in the wrong. But he would soon repeat the same deed and, if apprehended, would express his regret with the same charming politeness but apparently without any awareness that the continued repetitions robbed his promises of conviction.

Milt's mother describes him as having become callous, saying that there seemed to be no way in which she could arouse any actual response. He agreed readily when rebuked, so readily, in fact, that the mother finally began to feel that the meaning of her words did not touch him.

An incident during the previous year illustrates this young man's specific indifference to stimuli accepted as basic by the ordinary person. His mother, who had just returned from the hospital after major surgery, found it necessary to attend personally to an urgent matter of business. Our patient graciously volunteered to drive her on this mission in the family's car.

On the whole he had been thoughtful and attentive to her during the illness, and she had tried to grasp some shreds of encouragement from his apparent attitude on which to build hope again that favorable changes lay ahead. She had recovered sufficiently to sit up and to walk about a little, but the surgeon had strongly prohibited any major physical exertion.

It was necessary to cross a long bridge over a river at the edge of town to reach their destination, and both the patient and his mother were vexed when the car stopped near the center of this bridge, leaving them inconveniently isolated. Milt, who was rather expert in such matters, soon found the cause of the trouble. A fuse had blown out. There being no extra fuse on hand and relatively little traffic at this hour, he offered to walk to a garage less than a half mile distant and bring back the simple article needed. Darkness was falling, and it was difficult to estimate when another car might pass which could be utilized to expedite the trip to the garage. Most drivers crossed this bridge at high speed, and there might be difficulty in flagging anyone down as darkness increased.

Bidding his mother an affectionate good-bye, Milt cheered her with the assurance that he would be back in less than fifteen minutes. Someone at the garage, he pointed out, would be glad to drive him back, so she would be left alone hardly more than a moment.

After a half hour uneasiness developed in the mother as she waited and wondered about the possibilities of an accident having befallen her son. An occasional car racing across the bridge prompted dreadful speculations about hit-and-run drivers and the much publicized dangers of mutilation and death on the highways. When an hour had passed, Milt's mother, perhaps more susceptible to stress than ordinary because of her recent operation, became desperate.

Her own situation was far from pleasant. The business she had to transact was important, and she had not regained sufficient strength to put up easily with this complication. Forbidden to walk any considerable distance, she found herself unhappily marooned in a spot where it was not unnatural for a woman left alone for an indefinite time to think of unpleasant possibilities, including robbery or personal molestation.

Her increasing worry about her son diverted her from preoccupation with her personal safety but finally brought her to a point little short of panic. After waiting about an hour, she got out, stood in the middle of the bridge, and at length succeeded in signaling a motorist who drove her home.

Almost frantic, she telephoned two hospitals to inquire at the emergency room about injured persons recently brought in from the road. She had already sent her younger son with a neighbor who offered assistance by car to inquire at the garage where Milt had told her he would get the needed fuse and to search that neighborhood. Before this expedition returned, Milt himself appeared.

He had, he explained, procured the fuse, started the car, and driven on home. During the next hour he by turns showed vexation at his mother for not having waited until he so belatedly got back and a bland immunity to any recognition that he had behaved irresponsibly or inconsiderately.

Milt had begun his trip to the garage with commendable haste. Shortly after leaving the bridge, he passed a tobacco shop. Noting that the afternoon's football scores were being posted on a blackboard, he lingered for ten or fifteen minutes to check results.

During this interval he recalled that a girl he knew lived a half block down a side street in this neighborhood and decided to drop in on her for a moment. She greeted him cordially, and he spent approximately an hour in her company. There is no evidence that any sudden sexual urge or any other strongly tempting impulse diverted our patient. He had no special liking for the girl, and no attempt was made to gain even the mildest erotic favor.

Milt chatted with the girl amiably but desultorily about trifling matters. His departure followed the arrival of her date for the evening, whose rights to her company he acknowledged after a pleasant exchange of courtesies by bidding them good-bye and going on his way.

It is interesting to note that this conduct did not result from absentmindedness, from specific amnesia or confusion, or from some attraction so enthralling or distracting as to delay or divert a person from even a mildly serious mission. He was quite aware all through the episode of his mother waiting on the bridge and seems to have been free from any grudge or other impulse that would influence him deliberately to offend her or cause her hardship. Missing from his realization, apparently, was the evaluation of her emotional reactions that would in another have outweighed a whim so petty as that which in Milt gained easy ascendancy.

During his third year at high school he began to practice truancy, one or more times a week not going to school at all but hanging around poolrooms, going to the movies, or aimlessly wandering in the streets and parks. His absences were, of course, reported, and, as he could not have failed to foresee, became known each time to his parents. He often began by denying, simply and with the most thorough appearance of innocence, all charges of truancy. After the charges had been obviously demonstrated as true, he gave ingenious excuses. As these episodes continued, his excuses became more easily recognized as absurd or impossible. He always expressed regret, usually admitted himself at fault, and never failed to make convincing promises that the truancy would never recur. Efforts were made by various relatives, by physicians, and by scoutmasters to find out why the boy behaved as he did. He did not show a particular interest in any hobby or in any dissipation. All were at a loss in trying to discover what could possibly be his motivation. He was apparently frank with those who tried to investigate his reactions, seldom became sulky or evasive, and never showed anything that looked like genuine embarrassment or a realization that he had been caught in a lie. He always stated that he understood the necessity of attending school regularly and seemed from what he had to say about it actually to understand this better than the average boy of his years.

Meanwhile, he mixed freely with his contemporaries, attended dances, and played football. Sometimes he failed to attend football practice, deciding instead to loll about his room. He was, however, quite energetic when he chose to bestir himself. His ability was regarded as high by all his teachers, though his academic standing suffered from the gross neglect with which he treated his studies.

Not only his parents but also the two older siblings noted that he began to show less interest in companions of his own social status and to seek the company of boys and girls who were regarded by his friends as beneath him in taste and intelligence. Although many of his new associates were of questionable moral standing, they are described as being depressing or boring rather than actively depraved. He did not appear to be particularly driven by sexual urges for which he might be seeking fulfillment with these girls who were his so-called social inferiors. He did occasionally have intercourse but probably no more often than other boys of his age and class.

Now and then he failed to return to his home during the night, choosing to stay with some of his new acquaintances. He was never reported drunk and apparently did not use alcohol at all. When questioned about his absence, he usually made glib excuses. When his stories were broken down, he often showed pique and seemed to feel that he was being unjustly bothered. Sometimes he would admit his inconsiderateness with what seemed strong sincerity. But a week later his parents would pace the floor, telephone dozens of his acquaintances, and spend a miserable night of anxiety, only to see him appear the next day with some casual explanation.

Once after he had remained away for two full nights, the police were called. He was picked up at a dive where slot machines and other gambling devices furnished amusement to mill workers and rustics from the surrounding countryside. He had previously driven over to a nearby city with a casual acquaintance who had gone there in the course of his duties as a traveling salesman. The fact that he had not taken the trouble to inform his mother of his intentions seemed to him a trifle in comparison with what he indignantly regarded as the meddling of his family in asking the police to look for him.

He showed little regard for the convenience or the property of others, sometimes misappropriating things that he apparently did not mean to keep or sell but that he put to his own use without ordinary regard for the trouble inflicted on relatives, friends, or strangers. An example will illustrate.

Noting that a family in the neighborhood was on vacation, he tampered with the wiring of their car until he arranged connections by which he could start the motor without a key. Driving off to the house of a slightly younger friend, he explained that an uncle had given him the car and that he was leaving on a pleasure trip to New York. Another fellow, he said, who had planned to go with him had to give up the trip at the last moment. Our patient suggested that the friend come along.

Everything indicated that the situation was as represented. There was casual mention of details that suggested ample financial provision for all needs. Making hasty arrangements and telling his family of the fine opportunity, the friend joined in the expedition.

Our patient showed no signs of haste or uneasiness, and the other boy's parents later regarded it as almost inconceivable that he could have been so self-assured under the circumstances.

Both travellers were surprised when they ran out of gasoline seventy or eighty miles away from town. The fuel gauge was out of order and had given misleading information.

The boy who had been persuaded to come along soon got other surprises. It became apparent that Milt had only a few dollars on him and was expecting his guest to contribute most of the expense for gas. Suspecting a good deal now about the situation, the friend refused to give over what he had and decided not to go on.

Making his way to the nearest telephone, our patient called his family by long distance (reversing the charges) and told them of being stranded in this lonely spot, that he lacked sufficient funds to get back, and that he needed them to come for him at once.

Milt had apparently hoped to get some money from his companion at the beginning, then to sponge or panhandle along the way, to beat the bill at restaurants and filling stations, perhaps to get additional cash from time to time by playing slot machines or gambling in night spots or by misrepresentations or petty swindling. He thought, too, that, if it became necessary, he could sell the spare tire, a new spotlight, the radio, or other accessories from the car. The patient intended, it seems, not to dispose of the car itself but to return it surreptitiously after it had served his purpose.

It is interesting to contrast the ingenuity in some features of his plan with the injudiciousness of the general scheme. The talk of going all the way to New York with which he beguiled his companion probably represented a vague hope (if lucky breaks occurred), but the unlikelihood of getting that far did not deter the patient in his actions.

Apparently Milt said to himself, "Well, if we don't make it all the way to New York, at least we'll have a good trip and see a lot of other places nearer at hand."

His parents, who had been deeply worried over his unexplained absence, drove through a hard rainstorm in haste and arrived exhausted and considerably upset. Milt was calm and full of ingenious explanations. His father arranged for the misappropriated automobile to be returned to its owner. The patient seemed not to understand why everyone got so upset and "nagged at him" about what had happened.

He did not seem to be prompted by strong yearning for adventure or any obvious, formulated, or purposeful criminal bent. Though he frequently stole small sums of money from his family, he did not engage in robbery or any regular and understandable misdemeanors while out on these jaunts.

He was at this stage sent off to a strict school in Virginia where discipline was stressed more than studies. After many misadventures he graduated satisfactorily. During his time at the preparatory school he showed no real or serious formulation of an aim and no encouraging tendency to change. When at home during vacations he continued his old practices. His family often sought to find out if he misunderstood or resented anything in their treatment of him. He was offered more freedom, a larger allowance, and other inducements to be more cooperative and considerate. He accepted these proposals but always continued to steal money from his mother's purse, to pawn objects from his home, or to go off for a day or two with the family car, sometimes damaging it or leaving it without gas.

After graduating from school he entered a well-known military college in the East. For a year his progress in his studies was uneven. He was plainly bright, but he sometimes failed to attend an examination or to appear at drill. Occasionally he disappeared for longer periods. He gave various and very shrewd accounts of illness at home and of other emergencies. Since the college specialized in reshaping headstrong youths, unusual efforts were made to keep him despite his many irresponsible and absurd capers. He consistently cheated and lied but when rebuked denied all charges with astonishing suaveness and aplomb.

Shortly before his admission to the hospital he had been expelled, during his second year, from the military college. The events that led to the expulsion were typical of the psychopath. After a long series of irresponsible and often dishonest acts Milt went downtown without permission when the cadet corps was assembling for a formal drill in celebration of the visit of a high military authority. He remained away all that afternoon and night but returned the next day, quite casual, and gave glib but hollow excuses for his absence. He had not been drinking and he knew perfectly well that he would have to face serious disciplinary action on his return. He was not a forgetful or absentminded person but appeared to be quite deliberate in his failures.

Shortly after this and while confined to barracks Milt slipped away again and deliberately started a rumor that he had married a local prostitute. This story came to the school authorities and was for a time believed to be true. Later it was proved false, the patient having thought it a good joke to spread the report. While action on these matters was pending, he slipped out of his quarters again against the college regulations. Two other cadets, responsible in the matter, had to report him. He at once denied their report, though the facts were plain and plainly showed him in falsehood. His family was informed that it had become impossible to persuade anyone to room with him and that the student body could not put up any further with him.

Milt arrived home apparently well pleased with himself. He admitted that he was sorry to leave college, for which he had voluntarily expressed a desire and to which he had never objected. He quickly placed all the blame for his expulsion on others and seemed to feel that nothing more should be said of it. What explanation he gave his parents centered about points of honor and principles which he let them know it was not modest or quite proper to speak of frankly and fully. He meant to promote the belief that he had, out of respect to the stoic traditions of honor in the school, sacrificed himself to protect another. There was not the slightest thread of truth in the skein of lies and false implications he built up about this, but it very naturally appealed to his parents.

Examination at the hospital showed a splendid figure of a young man slightly over 6 feet tall, weighing 180 pounds, and free from any sign of physical illness. Milt was neatly and becomingly dressed, distinguished in manner, alert, and intelligent. Although his politeness was unfailing, it was plain that he thought the psychiatric examination a bore. He confessed that he held it as nothing short of ridiculous for his parents to consider that there was any possibility of his having a personality disorder. He showed no interest in efforts to approach whatever emotional factors might lie behind his maladjustment and apparently was incapable of realizing that he had shown signs of maladjustment. His technical reasoning powers were excellent.

All the information about his past was discussed. Milt made many ingenious excuses, and if too much undeniable evidence was presented for him to persist in them, he dismissed the point. He would, in response to leading questions, state at times that phases of his situation seemed serious, but it was plain that he was not moved. No evidence of any substantial affective relation with his family, with girls, or with friends could be elicited. In discussing his expulsion from college, he maintained that he had been a victim of the military code of honor, allowing himself to be sacrificed instead of denying the report of the other cadets, which he calmly maintained was a falsehood.

"It had to be me or those boys. They were seniors, and it would have been harder on them than on me to be sent down."

A few days before entering the hospital he had been arrested for speeding after taking the family car without permission. He was given a summons but neglected to appear at court the next morning. The police found him and brought him to the station, where he telephoned his parents and indignantly demanded that they come at once and have him released. Hoping that the night in jail might be helpful, they refused to do so, carefully explaining their reasons. On being released, he showed plainly that he felt he had been seriously misused but condescendingly offered a cool forgiveness. Milt had no excuse for not answering his summons except to say that he had overslept. He had, however, been on the streets for several hours when the police arrested him at about noon.

This patient showed no sign at all of an ordinary psychosis. He was self-possessed, shrewd, and entirely calm except for a superficially polite impatience to be gone from the hospital.

Milt was told frankly that everything indicated a serious condition and one that demanded his attention and his major efforts. He was bored with all efforts to approach him but agreed to undertake a detailed plan that was worked out. It was plain that he had no idea of doing so. On leaving the hospital, he continued exactly as he had been doing before.

GREGORY

I first saw this patient when he was 13 years old. He was referred for study and treatment by a psychiatrist who had already tried to deal with his problems for several years and who had shown great personal interest in his complicated situation. Gregory came to me from the detention center in a large southern city where he had been confined after setting fire to the local cathedral. Though he did not succeed in causing serious damage to the cathedral, the exploit was considered daring and precocious for a boy of his age. Before he was controlled by confinement in the detention center he set another fire in a large apartment building that caused substantial damage.

About a month before the fire-setting episodes Gregory was expelled from school for "stealing and destructiveness." Several months before this he had been in the juvenile court and confined in the detention center for setting fires, stealing, and wandering off from home and staying away sometimes for several days without any word to his parents. These early acts of fire setting gave some of the doctors who examined Gregory at this time the impression that he might be suffering from a circumscribed form of character disorder or a compulsive disorder, perhaps from the condition sometimes called pyromania. Such a disorder would drive the patient specifically to set fires and burn down buildings. His subsequent history does not confirm this interpretation. Though Gregory continued to carry out various destructive and antisocial activities, he did not, so far as we can determine, ever set another building on fire. On the other hand his exploits grew ever more versatile.

From Gregory's medical history a few items recorded during this period by parents, doctors, social workers, friends of the family, and relatives seem worthy of our attention:

> During last year caught robbing parking meters. . . . His sisters say "he's a perfect gentleman at home." . . . Now in detention center. . . . Often stayed away from home for days. . . . Recently stole money on several occasions, also a bicycle. . . . Any remorse shown by this boy is staged. . . . Tells lies freely and convincingly. . . . Seems to have no understanding of the meaning of his deeds. . . . Inveterate stealing. . . . Superficial expressions of affection to mother but these apparently have little reality. . . . Mother says patient was a problem since he began to walk. . . . Seemed sweet and loving. . . . Roamed off. . . . Now stays away for days at a time. . . . Mother drives about for hours searching for him. . . . Shows no real remorse. . . . I wish to add that he seems to hurt those who extend themselves to help him. . . . I have had to learn to beware of Gregory when he has brought me gifts.

Unlike some of the other patients we have discussed, whose gross maladjustment was first noticed as alarming during adolescence, Gregory presented many problems even in the very early years of his life. His parents report that he was extremely uncooperative in toilet training, and that soon after he learned to walk adequately, serious difficulties arose through his "roaming and wandering away." In order to curb this tendency and his destructiveness, he was, on the advice of his pediatrician, a few times tied to his bed. He circumvented this effort to control him by pleading a need to go to the bathroom, where he got possession of his father's razor, concealed it, and used it to cut the restraints when they were reapplied. The account given by his family includes these items:

> At a very early age he dragged a gun into the room in an apparent attempt to shoot me [his mother] . . . . He pulled the trigger but luckily the bullet didn't get into

> the firing chamber. My God, if he had done that he would have had it to live down all his life. . . . Hour after hour we would try to discipline him but it was no use. . . . The boy would always succeed in getting another chance. . . . But he has always been so lovable. . . . He would set up an atmosphere of peace and goodness and then sneak off. . . . If caught, he would be appropriately very, very sorry and then everybody would offer him forgiveness and another chance. . . . After he began school he kept roaming off and was often gone for several hours or several days. . . . He would steal money, buy candy with it, and give the candy away.

One of the physicians who treated Gregory prior to his adolescence felt that a hyperkinesic disorder might be playing an important part in his trouble and that he would probably settle down when 14 or 15 years old and make a normal adjustment. Another physician felt that his basic disorder might be thalamic epilepsy, chiefly on the basis of an electroencephalogram report that now in retrospect does not seem definitely indicative of this or of any other organic disorder.

A psychoanalytically oriented psychiatrist who worked very hard and long with Gregory felt convinced that "he does not have a basic psychopathic structure" and that "his so-called delinquent acts," were related to emotional trauma in very early life. From the psychiatrist's report let us note these opinions:

> He should be seen at this office at least three times a week for psychotherapy and should also be seen at the ____________ Foster Home by a parole officer or counsellor four or five times a day at regular and spaced hours. I do not feel that there is any danger in releasing this boy from the detention center to the community provided we, step by step, give him increasing degrees of freedom.

This psychiatrist succeeded in getting Gregory released from the detention center where he had been placed for repeatedly robbing parking meters and for persistent truancy. The therapist repeatedly expressed strong confidence that the boy would respond to treatment and become satisfactorily adjusted. His sponsorship of Gregory led the school from which he had been expelled to take him back for another chance.

In addition to giving prolonged and concentrated psychotherapy, this psychiatrist took great pains in trying to modify various environmental factors. His efforts along this line included having Gregory come as a guest into his own home to mingle there with his own children. Gregory at this stage of his life, and also later, could at times give a remarkably convincing impression of having changed profoundly and of having gained crucial insight. It is, perhaps, not remarkable that his psychiatrist kept renewing his hopes of success. He seems truly to have gone beyond the ordinary call of medical duty in his almost heroic efforts to rehabilitate Gregory. Despite these efforts and those of many other psychiatrists, psychologists, social workers, teachers, clergymen, and others, Gregory continued in his destructive, irresponsible, and antisocial patterns of behavior.

When I next saw Gregory he was 25 years old. He had been sent from prison by the court for additional psychiatric study and for advice about what steps should be taken next. The judge apparently shared some of my bewilderment about this man's career and about what might be done to prevent, or to minimize, a persistent repetition of what had for so long been going on.

This time Gregory had stolen a police squad car, driven about in it for a while, with no particular end in view, and, carelessly, run it into a ditch, causing some damage. In view of his many unpleasant encounters with the police through arrest and his many attempts to escape from them, it seems strange, indeed, that he should choose this particular automobile to steal, and that he would steal it through a mere impulse to ride around and while away the time.

In addition to this latest felony, the records show that Gregory's maladjustment and his antisocial activities had continued unabated over the years. Perhaps it is worthwhile to note a few additional items from his more recent medical records:

> Whenever he'd get a job he'd steal or just quit. . . . All this began early in life and now when he's almost 25 it still goes on. . . . Stealing cars. . . . Always makes a good impression and people trust him but he always betrays the trust. . . . Has been sent to state hospital many times. . . . Usually they won't keep him but a few weeks. . . . Once state hospital kept him almost a year. . . . According to Mother, doctors at state hospital say that he is normal, "nothing wrong with him." . . . Once he seemed to be doing well for three or four months but then old troubles began again. . . . Stole sister's auto and impersonated a naval officer. . . . Gets in fights from time to time. . . . Drinks sometimes but apparently liquor plays little part in his behavior. . . . Sometimes, when arrested, claims that liquor is responsible (not himself) and that the man who sold him liquor should be punished, not himself. . . . Cruelly mistreats younger brother (now 14 years old).

It is remarkable indeed how often this man has been released by prisons and by psychiatric institutions and gone free to continue in a self-destructive and criminal career. At times he has worked regularly and apparently adapted himself to the demands of normal life for several weeks and occasionally for several months. A few years before I last saw Gregory in connection with his stealing the police car he eloped from the state hospital where he had been sent as an alternative to prison. He went to Atlanta, where he impressed a stranger so favorably that he was given a job in this man's service station. Soon the man and also his wife and children were so charmed by Gregory and so impressed by his account of his misfortunes that they took him in to live with them and would not accept any pay for board and lodgings. He worked regularly at this job and apparently kept out of trouble for several months. Everyone considered him a trustworthy and delightful person and felt strong inclinations to help him in any way possible. This episode of Gregory's career was terminated when he stole several hundred dollars from his benefactors and disappeared. Valuable pieces of the family silver were also missing. After squandering the money on a lavish weekend in Miami, he apparently settled down to work in a small Florida town and kept out of trouble for four or five weeks. Neither his family nor the people in Atlanta who had befriended him knew where he was or whether he was living or dead, until news came out of his being arrested again in Florida.

This man has several times made suicidal gestures by lightly cutting the skin at his wrists. These cuts or scratches were always done with caution and with due concern for his safety. Such acts were carried out, apparently, to gain some material end, to insure that he be sent to a psychiatric hospital as mentally ill instead of to prison, or to evade some other unpleasant consequence.

Once when pursued by the police he climbed onto the high catwalk of a bridge over a tidal river and threatened, if pursuit continued, to throw himself down from a height of over 200 feet to a dramatic death. This proved to be an empty threat.

When the patient was in the hospital he described this episode for me eloquently and in lavish detail. He claimed, however, that he was considering suicide because of a girl he dearly loved. He spoke of himself as adoring and cherishing this girl so much that he felt he should kill himself because he had once taken advantage of her love for him to have sexual relations with her. According to Gregory, in this spectacularly pious and puritanical vein, he had, in a way, desecrated her according to the high standards of his spiritual affinity. So, though eager to marry her, he felt he should heroically redeem himself by death. He represented himself as still engaged to this girl, as loving her beyond measure, and as looking forward with vivid anticipation to their marriage.

Within a day or two of this discussion of his romantic love and deathless devotion he took up with a female patient in the hospital and tried to persuade her to marry him. He also tried to seduce her despite the close supervision and restrictions of the hospital. With the appearance of great seriousness he told me about the very special feeling he had developed for this new woman and how she had brought him tremendous, deep insight and a sort of spiritual redemption that would enable him to avoid all trouble in the future. He said that he now hoped to get parole and move to Augusta where he could marry this recently encountered woman and work regularly to support her and take care of her every need. A few days later he expressed quite different ideas and seemed to have lost all interest in the matrimonial plans so recently made with the female patient.

Gregory has shown attention to a number of women and, so far as can be learned, has probably had sexual relations with a good many of them. There is no indication that he ever developed any personal attachment to any of them, despite many claims of high and chivalric love, such as those just mentioned.

During Gregory's last time in the hospital under my care I was particularly impressed by several points about his attitude that made me wonder again about the psychopath's specific lack of insight.

He repeatedly emphasized the point that he *needed help* and had turned to us at the hospital to join him in his effort to get to the bottom of his trouble and straighten himself out. His repetition of this plea about how much he needed help brought a comment from one of the attendants in the hospital to whom he had repeatedly boasted of the many clever deeds by which he had gained his own ends illegally. The attendant said, "He keeps talking about how he needs help, but I don't think he needed all that help to do the things that brought him here."

Gregory had never sought psychiatric help except when it seemed that it might facilitate his escaping prison, enable him to avoid some other penalty, or to achieve some selfishly desired aim.

During our interviews Gregory repeatedly expressed the strong conviction that it would be shockingly inappropriate for him to be sent to the state prison and forced to serve his term there.

"Why, that place is full of criminals, people hardened in crime," he said, as if in a spectacular unawareness that he, himself, had committed more crimes than most of the inmates now held there. "That's not the proper place for me. . . . No telling what might happen to me there among people of that sort."

His repeated and emphatic statements about how he needed help and how earnestly he sought this help seemed ever more plainly to indicate that he called out for psychiatric intervention only because he looked on it as something to keep him out of the state prison. Over and over during various discussions he returned to the subject of the state prison and emphasized with great conviction, "That's certainly not the right place for me."

Gregory's utter lack of understanding (or should one say his refusal to recognize?) why it might be considered just and appropriate for him to go to the state prison for committing crimes similar to those committed by others confined there well illustrates a major point that I think often distinguishes the psychopath from other people who carry out criminal acts. Other criminals do not, of course, want to go to prison, and often protest against it. But they do not seem to have this strange conviction that they are, or should be, somehow exempt from prisons that were made to control people who commit the very crimes of which they themselves have been convicted.

Recently I saw a 19-year-old who had served time at several youth detention centers and later at a typical penal institution. He had been convicted again of a major offense, and there was every reason to believe that he was due to go back to the prison. Blandly and confidently, he expressed the conviction that he should instead be paroled and allowed to go back to college and get a degree. When the question of his being sent back to prison was raised, he scornfully dismissed the idea in these words: "Why that wouldn't do any good. I've already been *there* and you see what happened later. Anybody ought to realize that's *not* the place for me. It wouldn't help a bit."

I am not likely soon to forget the all but sublime insouciance with which this young man bypassed all considerations of personal responsibility for having continued in crime after serving time in prison. The only fault that he seemed to feel really deserved critical appraisal was that the institution had failed to keep him from carrying out his own deliberate felonies after he was released from its control. Though he did not actually suggest that legal action be taken against the penal institution or the court that had sent him to it, he seemed to feel vindicated in a strange way, to feel that the blame or shortcoming had all been satisfactorily allocated to other people or to institutions that had unreasonably interfered with his natural rights.

This 19-year-old seen such a short time ago seemed to echo Gregory, himself, perfectly in this respect, to reflect Gregory's precise attitude and the attitude of other psychopaths who have impressed me as showing this astonishing and specific lack of insight.

Gregory, according to my last news of him, has continued in the old familiar patterns. Perhaps the repeated evasion of ordinary penalties through commitment to psychiatric hospitals or through intervention by his family contributed to the assumption in Gregory, and in so many others like him, that he deserves an immunity or a relative immunity from the law. I think, however, that the roots of this attitude lie deeper, probably in the core of the psychopath's essential abnormality—perhaps in a lack of emotional components essential to real understanding.

In my report to the psychiatrist through whom the court referred Gregory to me I find these conclusions:

> It would be impossible to describe adequately this young man's career without writing hundreds of pages. His repeated antisocial acts and the triviality of his apparent motivation as well as his inability to learn by experience to make a better adjustment and avoid serious trouble that can be readily foreseen, all make me feel that he is a classic example of psychopathic personality. I think it very likely that he will continue to behave as he has behaved in the past, and I do not know of any psychiatric treatment that is likely to influence this behavior appreciably or to help him make a better adjustment.

Gregory, like all psychopaths whom I have seen, apparently knows in a verbal sense the distinctions between right and wrong, and he can express convincingly good intentions for the future and formulate excellent plans for a wise, happy, and socially acceptable life. I do not, however, believe that this indicates at all that he will follow such plans and alter his past pattern of maladjustment.

As you know, I am very much interested in patients of this sort and feel that they are the least understood of all psychiatric patients. I also feel that unlike other psychiatric patients there is no specific provision made by society for handling them adequately or dealing logically with the problems they create.

I appreciate so very much your letting me see him and am sorry I cannot be more hopeful about his prognosis.

STANLEY

During the summer of 1972 a small item of news appeared in many of our daily newspapers over the country. It was an item that immediately engaged my attention. Over the two short columns was printed this arresting headline:

YOUNG MAN INDUCES FIVE TEEN-AGE GIRLS TO SHAVE THEIR HEADS

The report, as I remember it, did not go into much detail about this unusual event or give an adequate account of the young man's methods of persuasion, of his motives, or of just what impulses might have prompted the five girls to take such an unusual and, one might even say, such an unnatural step. Among my first thoughts on this accomplishment was that Stanley must surely have been the man who brought it about. Who in the entire world but Stanley would have thought up such an exploit? Who else would have had the inclination to carry it out? Though the news report did not actually identify Stanley as the man involved, it brought back many memories of when I was trying to deal with him and some of the complicated and unusual problems his behavior kept creating for those concerned with him, and for himself.

Like a number of other patients presented in this book, Stanley repeatedly showed evidence of superior abilities and demonstrated over and over that he could succeed in studies, in business, in impressing and attracting other people, and in virtually anything he might choose to undertake. And, similarly, he lost, or seemed to throw away, with no sign of adequate motivation, everything he gained, and especially the things that he claimed meant most of all to him. Unlike some of the other patients discussed, Stanley had not yet, when I last had news of him, served long terms in prison for felonies. Aside from his more spectacular illegal activities, he would probably have spent a considerable time in confinement because of his persistence in writing bad checks had it not been for the intervention and the heavy financial sacrifices of his parents. He did not hesitate to write a check, whether or not there were funds to cover it, whenever he felt he would like to have additional money to squander on some caprice. Even when he was active at work and making far more than enough money for his needs, he blithely continued in this practice. It had been necessary also for his family to shield him from the usual consequences of many and various other types of illegal and irresponsible behavior that would otherwise have led to imprisonment. These statements appear in a letter from his mother:

> We don't have the money to pay these bills off. And we don't have the money to keep paying big hospital bills, but something has got to be done with him. . . . So, I don't know what we're going to do. . . . We are willing to go *the last mile* to do what we can for him financially and with your help. . . . If he would just *stop charging* he would not have to worry about finances. . . . He is arrogant and mean to me, his mother . . . hateful to his little sister, and fussy to everyone with whom he comes in contact. . . . Please help us. . . . Get him straightened out. . . . We do love him with all our hearts and we both cry and don't sleep . . . over his problems. We will do whatever you advise. . . . We *love this boy* with all our hearts and it is just killing us. . . . All the things he does.

Typical of his behavior in high school is an incident that occurred while he was making excellent grades and holding positions of leadership. With no notice or indirect indication of restlessness, Stanley suddenly vanished from the scene. He failed one day to appear at classes and did not show up at home that night. After he had been gone for over two weeks, a period of great anxiety for his parents, who had no way of knowing whether he was living or dead, the police finally discovered him working successfully in a large department store in Knoxville, Tennessee, approximately 150 miles away. He seemed quite unconcerned with the ordeal to which he had subjected his parents. At college, and also during recent years, he has often run up long-distance telephone bills, sometimes charging calls amounting to hundreds of dollars to his parents. He has also run up similar bills charging to various other telephones, some listed in the names of friends of the family, others in the names of strangers who were truly astonished to find themselves heavily billed for numerous calls to distant cities.

During his first year at the university he was accused by a girl he had recently met of getting her pregnant after solemn promises of matrimony. Before this trouble was settled by his family, at considerable expense, a similar accusation was made by another girl in a different state. Later that year, during the summer vacation he took a sudden notion to return for a brief visit to the university. To set out without delay on the trip of approximately 100 miles he casually stole a truck that happened to be at hand. It was heavily loaded with dairy products. State police pursued him, and in the chase he turned over the truck, wrecking it and injuring a companion he had persuaded to go along with him. The damages, including hospital bills, cost his family several thousand dollars.

Despite his many antisocial and irresponsible acts in the past, Stanley seemed at times to settle down. On a number of these occasions his parents thought that he had at last attained maturity and decided finally to use his abilities consistently in a constructive pattern of living. In his mother's record we find this item:

> Was for many months in high school active and well behaved in boy scouts. . . . For a while during last trimester of second year at college took major role in organizing and leading group to promote *Christian Life on the Campus*. . . . Planned big programs, made fine speeches, led in all the various activities.

While still in college, he showed his excellent persuasive abilities during one summer vacation selling Bibles down in the Cajun country near the Gulf of Mexico. During this time he was living with his first wife, who eventually had to leave him because of his tyrannical demands and his predilection for beating her up severely at the slightest provocation. It is difficult to imagine conduct of this sort in one who ordinarily gives the impression of a well-bred and considerate gentleman. The evidence is strong, however, to support his first wife's claims. There is also evidence that indicates he would lock the doors and force her to stay when she sought to escape violence by returning to the protection of her parents. Sometimes officers of the law had to be called by neighbors to obtain her release from his extreme abuse.

In discussing the first wife's accusations of such conduct as this, Stanley usually brushed them aside as a typically feminine and somewhat ridiculous exaggeration of some minor disagreement. When confronted with undeniable evidence to the contrary, he admitted having taken mild physical measures to influence her, saying that he "just couldn't stand her screaming and bawling." This habit of hers, he said, made him lose his temper. When it was emphasized to him that her weeping and outcries did not precede the beatings but occurred only after the beatings began, he showed very little response. Apparently he felt that this crucial point was not sufficiently important to argue about and seemed to dismiss it without further thought as something virtually irrelevant, or at most a trifle.

Chiefly because of this physical maltreatment, the first wife left him on many occasions. When with her and when separated, he easily obtained employment, usually as a salesman. While he worked, his income was ample for any ordinary needs. During one period of prosperity he was very successful selling small computers for household use. He later added as a sideline the enthusiastic promotion and sale of waterbeds shortly after these were introduced and hailed as a stimulating erotic innovation. His profits from these enterprises were for a while spectacular until he lost both jobs through a combination of neglect and irresponsible conduct. On many other occasions he worked with what seemed to be real enthusiasm for periods of varying lengths. Then, without any particular reason, he would give up an excellent job at which he was distinguishing himself. On other occasions he would have to leave the valuable position to flee from prosecution for some legal offense.

Even while his first wife was living with him and his income was ample, he usually ran up heavy debts. When his mistreatment would force his wife to leave him or when he would capriciously stop work, he often celebrated the occasion by a special splurge of unnecessary expenditures. Sometimes he would go out merrily and buy on credit several expensive suits and ample supplies of new shoes, shirts, and neckties. On one such occasion he impulsively bought a motorcycle which he never got around to using. Despite the fact that his parents have been faithful and active in succoring him and have often been hard pressed in making restitution in his behalf, it remains difficult to see how he has been able to continue for so long on so heedless and hazardous a course. Notes made by his mother concerning one such episode follow:

> Charged clothes for $650 one store in Atlanta.
> Charged clothes for $400 one store in Greenville.
> Charged clothes for $350 one store in Charlotte.
> Charged clothes for $135 one store in Spartanburg.
> Charged a ring in a jewelry store for $110.
> Charged more clothes.
> Charged two waterbeds for $750.
> Gave about twenty-five bad checks, some of which his father made good. The others are here and there and the law has some of them.

Over the years Stanley has proved himself a master at misrepresentation in situations where the truth would cause him difficulty or put him in a bad light. He has also been scarcely less active and ingenious in the fabrication of elaborate lies that seem to have had little or no chance of helping him gain any material objective. Though his mother is living and has been active in trying to deliver Stanley from the various troubles into which he plunges, he convinced his first wife that she had died during his second year in high school. He often discussed with his wife during the first years of their marriage his emotional reactions to this alleged loss and sometimes dwelt at length on complex but purely imaginary problems that it brought into his life. He succeeded in making her believe also that his father's present wife (his actual mother) was not only his stepmother, but also the identical twin sister of the mother who gave him birth. On at least one occasion he told a psychiatrist that when he was about 10 years old his mother frequently had adulterous relations in his presence with various men. When the plausibility of this claim was questioned, Stanley explained, or seemed to feel that he explained, by saying, "It was because she *knew* she could trust me with anything."

While separated from his wife for a period of several months, he went for a short time with a divorcee not long out of her teens, who will here be designated as Marilyn. During this brief courtship he convinced her that though he had once been married, his wife and also his 2-year-old son had died. Actually they were at the time living in another state with the wife's parents. Though not working at the time and in very heavy debt, he picked out and ordered for Marilyn a diamond engagement ring. His mother in her notes makes this comment:

> He went to a jewelry store and had the man order a $6,000 ring—a diamond for a girl—he is still married to Margaret—this was for a Marilyn. His father and I had never heard of her. It just happened that I went into the jewelry store to return something for him and I was told about the diamond. I cancelled it, of course.

At their first encounter, or soon after, he convinced Marilyn that he was deeply in love with her and had every intention of marrying her. She had no way of knowing that these intentions, if they ever existed, had greatly changed (or that Stanley's wife was still living) until he came to her with what must have been one of the strangest, most surprising, and most inappropriate proposals ever made by man to woman. He requested and persistently urged Marilyn to write a letter to his wife and in it explain to her that Stanley's love for her (the wife) was strong and genuine and to implore her to accept and welcome him back without further delay. I have inexpressible respect for this young man's powers of persuasion and have often marvelled at his accomplishments in getting people, sometimes the most unlikely people, enlisted in working with him to bring about his various and sometimes incompatible or absurd aims. Despite these extraordinary powers, Marilyn could not be induced to take the role that he tried to press upon her. Though extremely shrewd in many ways, Stanley, in discussing this matter, seemed to show some peculiar limitation of awareness, some defect in sensibility, of a nature I cannot describe or clearly imagine. This often led him into gross errors of judgment that even very stupid people would readily see and easily avoid.

The reactions Marilyn must have had to the unusual role he proposed and urged upon her invite many questions. Putting further speculation about these reactions aside for the moment, I asked Stanley if he did not think it might have seriously damaged the cause he sought to further if Marilyn had written the letter to intercede for him. Surely, I thought, it would occur to Stanley that such a letter from the other woman would point out and emphasize his sexual infidelity during the separation.

"Oh, no," said Stanley, in tones of strong and almost indignant conviction. "My wife *knows* I'd never be unfaithful to her."

He then went into some detail about her unassailable confidence in his sexual loyalty. "Why," he said as if in real pride, "I promised her that if I *ever* did that with another woman, I'd let *her* know about it right away."

I then brought up the point that he had given me plainly to understand that he and Marilyn had been indulging in sexual relations freely and regularly up to the time when he made his request for her intercession. Stanley seemed in no way dismayed. "But my wife," he said confidently, "she doesn't know about *that.*"

In this discussion I thought at moments I sensed some points about Stanley's inner being that I could never formulate adequately, even to myself. I did not, of course, find it remarkable that such a man as he would be unfaithful to his wife or that he made and broke promises of the sort just mentioned. Something in his attitude seemed to give fleeting and very imperfect hints of a difference far within that distinguished him in a very special way from the usual or ordinary human being who is unscrupulous and unconcerned about veracity or honor. When Stanley said, "My wife *knows* I'd never be unfaithful," there was in his tone what seemed to be the very essence of truth and sincerity. There was pride in his voice that seemed rooted in this essence. Could it be that for the moment he lost awareness that he was lying? Perhaps even awareness of what truth is? If so, I think this oversight might have occurred because to him it mattered so little. Whether his sworn fidelity was real or not was apparently no more than an academic question empty of substance. The only tangible issue was whether or not it contributed toward gaining his ends. Whether the fidelity existed or his oath had been honored was, for Stanley, a matter that could interest only a sophist who concerned himself not with actualities, but with mere verbalistic capers. With Stanley's attention focused on the real and important issue, this bit of irrelevant sophistry may not have edged its way clearly into his awareness.

Though Stanley's parents sought treatment and help for him from psychiatrists and other doctors and from counsellors of various sorts, he himself seemed to feel no need of this and only responded by brief simulations of cooperation in order to escape some unpleasant consequence or to gain some egocentric end. On two or three occasions he voluntarily entered psychiatric hospitals, apparently to impress his wife by making her think he had at last realized he needed help and meant to change some of his ways. These visits were brief and fruitless and seemed plainly designed to manipulate domestic situations or to elicit new financial aid from his parents.

It is interesting to note that excessive drinking has not been a discernible factor in this young man's career. Nor is there evidence to indicate that his behavior has been significantly influenced by marijuana, amphetamines, LSD, heroin, or the other drugs that have been so popular among those of his age group. His many notable and sometimes puzzling exploits were apparently decided upon and carried off on his own, without extraneous stimulation or chemical aid. In high school, and in college during the late 1960's, he was often thrown with and sometimes almost surrounded by groups of young people who went about in ragged blue jeans, with unkempt beards and long dirty hair that seemed to offer a standing invitation to lice. With many of these young men it was considered stylish and desirable to leave out their shirttails and, on formal occasions, sometimes to come barefooted. Among these could be found many who thought of themselves as radical activists defying the "establishment" and its laws, moral codes, and conventions. In contrast, Stanley wore traditional clothes and remained clean-shaven with neatly trimmed auburn hair. He seemed to have no special interest in changing or challenging society or in promoting rebellion. Verbally he expressed allegiance to law and order and regularly identified himself with traditional virtues.

Let us note briefly a few examples of Stanley's typical power to convince and to persuade. A year or two before his second wife had to leave him he had no difficulty in getting a young woman to turn over to him all her savings, which she had accumulated by steady work over years and which she had been carefully guarding to give her two young children some measure of security. She had clear knowledge of Stanley's repeatedly demonstrated financial irresponsibility and, one would think, almost certain knowledge of what would happen to her savings. More recently he succeeded in arranging for admission to the hospital of a young woman with whom he had been living for a few weeks. She was legally married to another man but had left his bed and board. Stanley was able somehow to convince the ordinarily strict and uncompromising authorities in charge of admission to this hospital that insurance his employer carried on him would cover this woman in the same way as if she were indeed his wife. She did not claim his name as her own or attempt to falsify otherwise her name and status. When she was dismissed, the hospital was left with a large unpaid account that is almost certain to withstand even the most heroic efforts at collection.

On another occasion Stanley escaped the consequences of a felony charge by serenely posing as an undercover agent working with the authorities against organized pushers in the hard drug traffic. This ruse apparently worked well enough for him to avoid arrest and to leave the state and eventually to take further intricate steps to escape the legal consequences that would almost surely have been disastrous to the ordinary man.

His unusual ability to make conviction spring to life and continue to flourish against adversity, and even obvious contradiction, emerges again in a somewhat different area. An attractive and sensitive young woman whose early years had been extremely unhappy and, perhaps, had given her a far greater than ordinary need for genuine and unstinted love, seemed to find at last in Stanley what she had sought above all else in life. She was separated from her husband and for a long time had been loved dearly by another man who apparently offered her everything in his life without qualification or demand for ordinary reciprocation. Stanley grossly mistreated this appealing sexual partner, who continued to live with him despite gross and flaunted infidelity, severe and repeated beatings, and other unprovoked outrages. In attempting to explain why she continued with him despite real fear that he might kill her, she said that somehow he made her feel genuinely loved for the first time in her entire life.

This statement seemed at first to suggest that Stanley might possess remarkable physical prowess and skill at sexual relations. It also might suggest that his partner was masochistic and actually found some perverse satisfaction from being mistreated. Continuing study of her reactions and her attitude gave increasing, and finally convincing, evidence that in neither of these possibilities lay a likely explanation of her loyalty. The more she discussed their physical activities in sexual relations, the more Stanley's performance seemed unimaginative and his abilities at best ordinary. What she thought he offered her was not primarily physical. It was, I believe, precisely what he was almost infinitely incapable of offering, even in a small degree, but what he apparently simulated with complete success, casually and without effort. It was, she repeatedly said, the way he made her feel personally valued and cherished, deeply and truly loved, rather than a remarkable sensuously erotic experience that bound her to him. One can but marvel that Stanley, and only Stanley, of all the men she had known, could give her this invincible impression of sincerity in personal love and make it convincing time after time despite the repeated and trenchantly disillusioning contradictions demonstrated so vividly and so painfully, and sometimes brutally, by his conduct.

During another period of marital separation, this time from his second wife, Stanley carried out an exploit worthy of our attention. After a brief sexual adventure with another attractive young woman, Yvette, he apparently tired of her and turned his attentions to Sally, one of her friends from a nearby town. She, too, was responsive, and everything seemed to indicate a serious and progressive love affair. This new relationship, however, was abruptly terminated by a sudden trip to Europe that Stanley decided to make for reasons that he never made convincing, or even quite clear, to me.

Though varying somewhat from time to time in his account of this venture, Stanley has nearly always included most of these items. He claims to have learned from Sally that Yvette was about to leave the country, that she was planning to spend some time in Brussels, and later in other parts of Europe. Stanley says that on hearing this he called Yvette's home and was told that Yvette was not there. He nevertheless persisted in seeking all sorts of information about her trip, apparently making a nuisance of himself and pressing her father repeatedly for information on points the father felt were not properly a matter of Stanley's concern. The father finally hung up, and afterward neither parent would talk with Stanley on the telephone. They had apparently been unhappy about Yvette's former association with him and did not want it to be renewed.

Stanley sought out Sally again. According to his story, Sally now told him that Yvette had a chronic infirmity that required medication regularly and that she had left for Brussels with the wrong drug. Stanley insisted that Sally also informed him that Yvette would die if she kept taking this other medicine instead of that which was prescribed and appropriate. She did not, he maintains, know Yvette's address beyond the fact that she was thought to be somewhere in Brussels. This, briefly, is Stanley's usual explanation for his impromptu and, in some respects, astonishing flight by jet plane to Europe.

When asked why he did not get word to Yvette by some simpler means, such as having Sally notify her family, he does not give a really adequate explanation. He repeatedly emphasizes his sense of mission, the urgency of his task, and his determination to fulfill it. He also fills in details of action and adventure on the way to Brussels and while there in such a way as to conceal, or at least almost magically blur, the deficiencies that leave the account of his maneuvers so far from convincing.

His relations with Yvette had, on his part, never been serious. Even these relatively casual relations had for a considerable time been broken off. He was no longer regarded as a suitor and probably not even regarded now as a friend, so it seemed pertinent to wonder and to ask why he should so emphatically seize his role as the appointed one to plunge into such an extravagant undertaking on her behalf.

"Why," Stanley answered promptly, and in his best tones of knight-errantry, "I'd have done that for anybody."

It is beyond my power to describe the glibness or convey what I believe to be the lack of substance and reality, the emptiness of real human feeling, in these fine words that came to him so readily.

It has not been possible for me to obtain any evidence to support Stanley's claim that he was convinced that Yvette was in danger, or that she had actually gone to Brussels, or that any mistake had been made about any medication she might be taking. Few things seem to me much more implausible than that Stanley ever cared deeply for Yvette even during the time he was seeing her. Nothing suggests that he maintained a serious interest in her welfare after he had lost touch with her and at the time he departed for Europe.

His parents had no warning of his intentions. From notes about Stanley by his mother, I quote:

> We knew he still owed $4900 on the trailer his wife and child were living in . . . plus $700 for just junk we didn't know about. . . . He'd changed jobs five times that year. . . . And his wife had left him nine times. . . . But he gave a lot more bad checks. . . . He then wrote one for $859 and flew to Brussels, Belgium. He just wrote the check and took off.

Stanley talks freely about his apparently unanticipated and suddenly contrived trip to Europe. He maintains that within approximately twenty-four hours he packed luggage, made financial arrangements, flew to New York, obtained a passport, got emergency clearance on matters such as vaccination and other medical technicalities, communicated with the State Department in Washington to explain his mission and enlist aid, found a seat on the first jet to Europe that would get him to Paris (and so in close reach of Brussels), and was well on his way across the Atlantic. To various questions about how he moved so fast and expedited so many matters that ordinarily make for delay, he has ready and enthusiastic, though not always convincing, answers.

His parents confirm the story that he moved with marvelous dispatch. They also report a flood of bad checks that throw light on how he took care of the heavy initial expenses of the flight. Most energetic, ingenious, and experienced travellers, even if in urgent haste, would, I dare say, have needed at least a week to complete such arrangements. And they would have needed actual money—and a good deal of it! One gets the impression that Stanley sliced through the ordinarily paralyzing masses of bureaucratic technicalities and red tape with ease and celerity suggestive of Alexander the Great when confronted by the Gordian knot.

In expediting transactions and in manipulating people for this exploit, Stanley must have been at his best. The implausible story about Yvette having carried with her the wrong medicine and its alleged threat of danger to her life must have taken on lyrical notes in his telling. His success in carrying out such a trip indicates that at times he must have made his presentation irresistibly convincing. It seems not unlikely, however, that at other times, Stanley may have used other ruses and employed additional schemes to gain his ends. I have often wondered whether Sally or anyone else told Stanley that Yvette had gone off unwittingly with improper medication and that she was in any sort of danger, or whether he thought up this story entirely on his own and used it to account for a sudden, dramatic and irresponsible jet flight to Europe prompted by impulses having nothing whatsoever to do with Yvette.

According to his parents, Stanley had been in very serious and unusually pressing trouble several times during the months before his unforeseen trip to Europe. He had more than once suddenly left one state and fled to another, giving no information to family or friends of his new address. Perhaps he was again seeking to escape prosecution for some criminal deed or evade the threat of dangerous measures by some person or group whom he had given reason to seek retaliation.

On the other hand, it must be remembered that Stanley has often carried out various extremely injudicious projects, suddenly and with no apparent regard for the consequences, and without any discernible goal that could, in terms of ordinary human motivation, account for his conduct. After such behavior he has on a number of previous occasions invented implausible pretexts for his conduct similar in some respects to the story of Yvette.

Among Stanley's most striking features has been the tendency to spring heedlessly into action at the behest of what often seems little more than idle whims. Neither the threat of danger nor the likelihood of other serious consequences has seemed to check him. Penniless and faced with legal action for deeds that would ordinarily lead to years of confinement in prison, he has been known to celebrate by buying a half-dozen expensive and superfluous suits and two new cars, and then, to complete the job, by forging some additional checks to pay for a vacation trip to some plush resort in another section of the country.

His parents first learned that Stanley was abroad through a telephone call from the American embassy in Belgium. In his mother's notes appears this item:

> When they told my husband Stanley was in Brussels, Belgium, he keeled over with a heart attack and I had to call an ambulance and send him to a hospital in Charlotte. He was nearly dead on arrival.

A few days later his mother wrote:

> Now today, we have had fourteen long-distance telephone calls from North Carolina, South Carolina, and from government agencies in Washington requesting his whereabouts. I am about to go crazy from people calling up about him.

Stanley himself gives a vivid account of much excitement and of spectacular adventures in Brussels. He tells of riding all around the city in cars with newspaper men and with police agents. He dwells on the publicity he obtained, saying that his picture and also that of Yvette appeared on the front pages of newspapers in Brussels. He says that he had taken an old picture of her with him and that the press cooperated in his efforts to find her by printing it along with reports of his gallant efforts to find her and save her. He also reports that, through people at the American embassy, radio broadcasts gave an account of his mission and called on the public for aid in his endeavor. There is little doubt that Stanley gives a romanticized and at times perhaps a fantastic account of the stir he made in Europe. He speaks not only of headlines on the front pages of the Brussels newspapers but claims also that articles appeared in English in a Paris edition of a New York paper.

He becomes enthusiastic in discussing his arrival in Brussels, his appeals to the press, and his work with members of the American embassy and various diplomatic and civic agencies which he claims cooperated with him in his alleged romantic mission of mercy.

If he obtained even a fraction of the notoriety he reports, this might have contributed to his being able to cash bad checks and to obtain other financial aid from various agencies abroad. There seems little doubt that he grossly exaggerates and indulges in fantastic lies as he recounts his adventures, but there is reason to believe he attracted enough attention with the publicity he gained to persuade first class hotels and restaurants to honor his checks and enable him to live for a while in high style while he pursued his course as a dedicated man on a desperate mission of mercy.

There is every reason to believe that he stayed at the finest hotels, entertained at very expensive restaurants, and attracted much favorable attention. Apparently the public attention he attracted played a part in enabling him to establish credit and cash checks in ways not possible to most travellers. He boasted that he met and made friends with "at least 100 Americans" while in Brussels. Apparently he succeeded for a while in endowing his proclaimed role not only with plausibility but with heroic and romantic aspects.

His relations with newspapermen and with diplomatic agencies abroad led to many transatlantic calls to his parents and, for a while, to the parents of Yvette. The confusion and emotional stress of these calls and the ever-accumulating bad checks written before Stanley left kept his parents under extreme anxiety. The heart attack sustained by his father proved to be temporarily disabling but not so serious as it first appeared.

Stanley admitted that he never found Yvette. From the best information available to me now it seems probable that she was not in Brussels at the time, perhaps not in Belgium. If Stanley learned of this even before he left the United States, I hardly think it would have stopped him once he had worked up momentum to launch himself in the impulsive exploit. Here he seemed to find a role that highly elated him in some peculiarly egoistic fashion. In it he seemed to find a satisfaction somewhat similar to but greater than the satisfaction apparently given him by some of his other less elaborate lies and posings and his sprees of squandering money that he did not possess. The more I learned of Stanley, the more I thought it likely that he perhaps lost track of Yvette as a real person and clung to her name as something on which to focus and use as an expedient to further his self-centered and irresponsible transatlantic prank. Some idle or uninformed remark might well have served as a spark to set off his fancy and his impulse to play a truly spectacular role. No serious consideration of the consequences would be likely to check the acceleration as Stanley let himself go.

Though several years after the event Stanley can still give a remarkable account of his sudden jet flight to Europe and his adventures in Brussels, there is a great deal that in retrospect makes it difficult to see how even he could have convinced so many people of so many implausible things. The newspaper accounts and pictures (some of which his parents still retain) establish the fact beyond question that Stanley got to Brussels and that he must have attracted a great deal of attention. Telephone calls from newspapermen and from people connected with the American embassy, his parents report, confirm this and indicate that Stanley must have created a remarkable stir and a great deal of confusion. His own report, which can hardly be counted upon as accurate or trustworthy, pictures him as being hailed and feted in Brussels in a style and on a scale almost comparable to the welcome Charles Lindbergh received in New York after his historic solo first airplane flight across the Atlantic ocean.

This account of Stanley began with headlines from a newspaper. It seems to me appropriate to close the report with another small item of news that appeared in 1975 in a local paper:

> "PREACHER" BLESSES AUGUSTAN'S WALLET, COLLECTS $175 FEE
>
> An agreeable young man who identified himself as a "preacher" blessed an Augusta man's wallet Tuesday and collected a $175 fee, Augusta Police said.
>
> The preacher, dressed in a black suit and hat, with black-string tie, showed up at the door of John Doe, 1436 Maple Street, early Tuesday afternoon, police said.
>
> According to reports Doe and the helpfully concerned cleric prayed together. The preacher then asked if he could bless Doe's wallet.
>
> Doe told police he found $175 missing from the wallet after the preacher left.

Neither this item nor the first identifies Stanley as the protagonist. Both, however, reflect something of his all but inimitable qualities and skills and convey to anyone who has known him a vivid sense of his presence.

chapter 3 · Incomplete manifestations or suggestions of the disorder

The voice is Jacob's voice, but the hands are the hands of Esau.
—GENESIS 27:22

DEGREES OF DISGUISE IN ESSENTIAL PATHOLOGY

The cases already reported are only a few among many hundreds whom I have observed. All of these people, when their records over the years are considered, strike one as remarkably similar. If the story of each could be told in detail, it is believed that the similarity would become more plain to any reader. It is the contention of the present argument that this personality disorder shapes and hardens into the outlines of a very definite clinical entity or reaction type, into a pattern of disorder quite as recognizable and as real as any listed in psychiatric nomenclature. When a large number of such patients are considered carefully, the vagueness with which they are often regarded lessens and the type emerges certainly not less sharp than that type on which is based the concept of schizophrenia. But vague as the concept of schizophrenia remains and various as its manifestations are, the schizophrenic, when recognized, is promptly called a patient with mental illness and treated as such. The psychopath, however, continues to be treated as a petty criminal at one moment, as a mentally ill person at the next, and again as a well and normal human being—all without the slightest change in his condition having occurred. I do not have any dogmatic advice as to a final or even a satisfactory way of successfully rehabilitating these psychopaths but believe that it is important for some consistent attitude to be reached.

In the hope of letting major features of the clinical picture emerge more clearly, the following case reports are added. The persons already described are regarded as typical examples showing the disorder in its distinct clinical manifestations of disability. Many of them are plainly unsuited for life in any community; some are as thoroughly incapacitated, in my opinion, as most patients with unmistakable schizophrenic psychosis. Whether this is to be regarded as a more or less willful contrariness or as a sickness like schizophrenia, in which the patient is to be protected and looked after, may for the moment be put aside.

In the reports that follow, an effort has been made to present persons who are able to make some sort of adjustment in life and who may perhaps be regarded as less severely incapacitated, and in varying degrees. These patients are offered as examples showing, in some respects, indications of the same disorder seen in the others. In them, however, it may be regarded as milder or more limited. The psychopathologic process, the deviation (or the arrest), is, as with the others, a process affecting basic personal reactions; but here it has not altogether dominated the scene. It has not crowded ordinary successful functioning in the outer aspects of work and social relations entirely out of the picture.

Some of these patients I believe are definitely psychopaths but in a milder degree, just as a patient still living satisfactorily in a community may be clearly a schizophrenic but nevertheless able to maintain himself outside the shelter of a psychiatric hospital. Others might not deserve to be called psychopaths but seem to show strong, even if not consistent, tendencies and inner reactions characteristic of the group. They might be compared to the plain and complete manifestations of the psychopath as the schizoid personality might be compared to the schizophrenic patient who is obviously psychotic. An example will perhaps make this comparison more concrete.

Some years ago I was consulted by a man 32 years of age whose only complaint was of a general listlessness which he had noticed for about a year. He was a tall, rather slender person, slightly brittle in manner, and gave a definite impression of being not very much worried about his complaint. He lived with his parents in a small town where he made an excellent salary as a machinist in a large mill. He enjoyed the title of engineer, though he had no formal education beyond that obtained in a rural high school. Examination soon brought out the fact that he had never had sexual relations with a woman. He had, however, made the attempt not once but many times, the first attempt being twelve years ago. He succeeded in having erections, but premature ejaculation always occurred and he failed entirely to effect an entrance.

This situation, which most young men would find extremely distressing, he spoke about very casually. Questions concerning his attitudes toward love and women brought rather stereotyped answers. He denied ever having scruples about fornication. To him it was evidently neither good nor bad. His attempts to practice were, it would seem, made with a vague idea of doing what was the custom. He professed to be concerned in overcoming his inability to perform intercourse and showed no embarrassment and little reticence about sexual questions but gave a strong impression of having only the shallowest interest. His entire emotional life seemed perfunctory and without warmth. Nothing in his experience could be elicited that brought forth any vividness or enthusiasm. He said that he was at present going with a girl whom he would like to marry, but his attitude toward her seemed without any tangible desire or eager anticipation. At times he gave a stilted, incongruous little laugh that sounded almost exactly like the manneristic laugh so familiar in actual schizophrenics. No delusions or hallucinations could be brought out. He had been leading an outwardly successful life and was a fairly conscientious and reliable member of society.

The man just mentioned could certainly not be called legally incompetent at present. Nor would he, by most psychiatrists, be classed as a case of schizophrenia, with all the practical implications of being adjudged psychotic. He is mentioned in order to compare him with the patient who is psychotic and who is frankly schizophrenic.

As an example of the developed schizophrenic, let us consider a former patient of mine who often sat for hours in a corner staring vacantly into space, his lips moving and silly, grimacing smiles flitting across his face. Sometimes this man would not answer questions, apparently not even hearing them, so absorbed was he in subjective contemplation. Again he would grin glassily and wink his eye or occasionally speak with passion about strange machinery in a distant city which enemies whom he referred to merely as "they" were using to inject queer colors into his thoughts and sometimes to make him ejaculate. This man at times suddenly attacked others. It was eminently necessary to keep him on a closed ward and under close supervision.

In some of the cases to be presented such a comparison probably would not be justified. Some patients might more accurately be thought of as showing scattered indications of such a disorder, suggestions of a disturbance central in nature but well contained within an outer capsule of successful behavior much deeper that the merely logical and theoretical rationality of the fully disabled psychopath. In those who consistently support themselves and pass regularly as acceptable members of the social group, we can only be astonished at the difference between such technical outer adjustment and the indications of deeper pathologic features so similar to those found in the complete manifestation of the disorder.

There are many patients who show relatively circumscribed antisocial behavior or temporary episodes of gross, general delinquency, who have, I feel, much less in common with the obvious psychopath than those who make a better outward impression but who consistently show signs of inner subjective reactions typical of the clinically disabled patient.

These patients with temporary or circumscribed maladjustment or self-defeating behavior will be referred to later at greater length.* They are mentioned here to distinguish them not only from the fully manifested psychopath but also from those who, over the years, show more subtle indications of widespread and intractable defect or deviation in essential personal reactions and subjective evaluations.

The psychopathologic process, or state, which I believe is seriously disabling the patients already presented may be regarded as affecting in part and in varying degree those yet to be discussed. It may now be added that I believe that in these personalities designated as partially or inwardly affected, a very deep-seated disorder often exists. The true difference between them and the psychopaths who continually go to jails or to psychiatric hospitals is that they keep up a far better and more consistent outward appearance of being normal. This outward appearance may include business or professional careers that continue in a sense successful, and which are truly successful when measured by financial reward or by the casual observer's opinion of real accomplishment. It must be remembered that even the most severely and obviously disabled psychopath presents a technical appearance of sanity, often one of high intellectual capacities, and not infrequently succeeds in business or professional activities for short periods, sometimes for considerable periods.

I maintain, however, that the actual but concealed pathology in some of the patients now to be described is in a deeper sense also far-reaching and profound. Although they occasionally appear on casual inspection as successful members of the community, as able lawyers, executives, or physicians, they do not, it seems, succeed in the sense of finding satisfaction or fulfillment in their accomplishments. Nor do they, when the full story is known, appear to find this in any other ordinary activity. By ordinary activity we do not need to postulate what is considered moral or decent by the average man but may include any type of asocial, or even criminal, activity so long as its motivation

*See Chapter 5, A case showing circumscribed behavior disorder.

can be translated into terms of ordinary human striving, selfish or unselfish.

The chief difference between the patients already discussed and some of those to be mentioned lies perhaps in whether the mask or facade of psychobiologic health is extended into superficial material success. I believe that the relative state of this outward appearance is not necessarily consistent with the degree to which the person is really affected by the essential disorder. An analogy is at hand if we compare the catatonic schizophrenic, with his obvious psychosis, to the impressively intelligent paranoid patient who outwardly is much more normal and may even appear better adjusted than the average person. The catatonic schizophrenic is more likely to recover and, despite his appearance, is often less seriously disordered than the paranoiac.

It becomes difficult to imagine how much of the sham and hollowness which cynical commentators have immemorially pointed out in life may come from contact in serious issues with persons affected in some degree by the disorder we are trying to describe. The fake poet who really feels little; the painter who, despite his loftiness, had his eye chiefly on the lucrative fad of his day; the fashionable clergyman who, despite his burning eloquence or his lively castigation of the devil, is primarily concerned with his advancement; the flirt who can readily awaken love but cannot feel love or recognize its absence; parents who, despite smooth convictions that they have only the child's welfare at heart, actually reject him except as it suits their own petty or selfish aims: all these types, so familiar in literature and in anybody's experience, may be as they are because of a slight affliction with the personality disorder now under discussion. I believe it probable that many persons outwardly imposing yet actually of insignificant emotional import really are so affected.

Let us not, however, attempt to explain all pretense and all fraud on this basis. There are many other psychopathologic reactions besides the one with which we are now concerned. And some of these, too, are capable of producing such results. Let us be especially chary about assuming this limitation in our enemies or our neighbors. The mechanisms of reaction formation, projection, rationalization, and many other distorting influences work in all of us at the behest of envy, pique, or prejudice. It is not easy to estimate correctly the degree of our neighbor's sincerity, the worth of an artist's production, or the clergyman's real motive.

Some of the episodes or symptoms mentioned in the brief sketches that follow may represent less profound inner disturbance than anything properly belonging with that of the real psychopath. Many of the acts might in isolation occur in the lives of people who at length achieve excellent adjustment not only externally but also within themselves. The material to follow is offered not primarily for the purpose of making a diagnosis of psychopathic personality but in illustration of features that specifically characterize the psychopath and that may, against a background of better general adjustment, emerge in sharper clarity. What can be learned from fantasy or dream in the normal person, from prejudice or many socially admired forms of self-renunciation, has been of value in psychiatric efforts to understand schizophrenia and other grave personality disorders. Many of the characteristics and reactions seen in extreme exaggeration among the psychotic appear sometimes to be utilized by those of great talent and excellent psychiatric status in the successful pursuit of valuable personal and social aims. It is unlikely that the specific reactions of the psychopath can be directly utilized for important positive accomplishment. It is believed, however, that many persons in bewilderment and frustration temporarily fall into similar reactions and eventually, finding better means of adaptation, profit from what has been learned through the pathologic experiences.

The following accounts are given, then, for what light they may reflect on the serious clinical disorder manifested in the previous cases.

THE PSYCHOPATH AS BUSINESSMAN

No attempt will be made to give a detailed history of this man. Suffice it to say that the incidents mentioned are not isolated experiences in the general life pattern but rather expressions of a motif that persistently recurs to interrupt the outward serenity.

He is now 50 years of age, and he has gone on to achieve considerable business success, being an equal partner in a wholesale grocery concern. As a businessman there is much to be said for him. Except for his periodic sprees, he works industriously. He has contributed foresight and ability to the business, whereas his partner has contributed the stability necessary to keep things going when he is out of action.

He is pleasant and affable during his normal phases, which make up the greater part of his time. One gets the impression, however, that ordinary life is not very full or rich, that strange gods are ever calling him, and that the call is far dearer to his heart than anything else. He is, perhaps, like a man who through necessity has given himself over to foreign ways for most of his hours and who goes on fairly patiently but without spontaneity until the time when he can throw it all aside for a while and go wholeheartedly at what he finds really to his taste.

These recesses are sometimes taken at intervals of a week; occasionally several months go by without one. They sometimes last merely a few days, sometimes a week or more.

He does not drink in groups with men and women whom he meets in the ordinary course of his life. It would never occur to him to have a cocktail party or to serve drinks to friends in his own house. Apparently he can see no point in what might be called ordinary or normal drinking, in the sense, say, of taking several highballs to be warm and lively, to talk more gaily to pretty women and cut a finer figure in their eyes, to be more playful, to throw aside the routine problems of the day, and to express oneself a little more vividly.

If he drinks at all, it is to reach a state of roaring folly and perhaps to continue until he may fall limp. He frequently goes out of the city and, in some hotel of dubious standing, gathers a few coarse companions and begins to pour liquor into himself. His associates are usually uninteresting drifters or vagrants ready to accept any handout. Sometimes obvious psychopaths are included. Often whores are called into the room where this noisy group of fat, middle-aged men are already staggering about, sweaty in their undershirts or lying out half stupefied across the beds or on the floors.

The women are stripped or encouraged to strip themselves, and among those men still able to flounder about a great clamor arises. The women are chased about and fumbled over. Intercourse is accomplished by the more energetic ones, not in the privacy ordinarily considered desirable but in the presence of all and often on beds across which a more sodden member of the group lies snoring.

Men and women stumble about, the men pouring more and more whiskey into themselves, the women usually drinking little but occasionally picking their senseless companions' pockets. Daylight often finds a few of this jolly brotherhood still wobbling feebly or crawling about the room in search of more liquor.

During the next day some pull themselves together and depart, others remain drinking and cursing through the morning and afternoon. Consciousness and power to speak or sit erect come and go through the hours. During these more lucid intervals some find what they take as exceeding delight in sitting, naked and unsteady, on the edge of an untidy bed, staring at a companion, smiling inanely, and, in slurred, mushy tones, repeating for thirty minutes or more: "You old son of a bitch. You old son of a bitch, Jack. You old son of a bitch, you."

After such exploits the subject of our discussion returns home feeling pretty ill but apparently refreshed spiritually for his other kind of life. At times his sprees will take the classic form already described, which consists in having someone drive him out into the woods where he drinks to semiconsciousness and, after lying out for a satisfactory period, allows the person to drive him home.

Usually these extravaganzas take place without attracting general attention, but occasionally exuberance carries the play beyond its early secluded setting and the public is treated to puzzling displays. Returning from several days of ordinary lying out and still boisterous and maudlin by turns, this executive, disappointed in his wife's failure to greet him with proper enthusiasm, took a few more pulls from the bottle. Feeling suddenly much misused and sorry for himself, he rushed out on the lawn and began to bewail in thunderous tones the general injustice of his situation.

Since the time was high noon on Independence Day, he soon drew a fair-sized audience. Stimulated by this, he rushed to the dog's kennel and fumbled with the brass-studded collar of his big Doberman pinscher, who, patient-eyed, watched his frantic master. Gaining possession of the collar, he placed it around his own neck and, with the leash flying behind, set off at a lively pace through the neighborhood. Attempting to bark like a dog as he went and shaking his collar, he succeeded in conveying his conviction to the public. Not only was he, so to speak, "in the dog house" (in his wife's disfavor), but in vigorous canine outcries he registered his protest.

Trotting over the well-kept lawns and about the gardens, he was observed by many acquaintances who lived near him in this fashionable section of the city. Occasionally, in bursts of zeal, he practiced or mimicked the dog's well-known ritual in which eliminative and gregarious impulses blend. By the time he drew near the outskirts of town, he had a retinue of small boys in his wake. Realizing now that it was Independence Day, he led them to a small store where fireworks were sold and, roaring with wordy generosity, bought for them dozens of Roman candles, firecrackers, and skyrockets.

For a while his irrelevant shouts merged with the hissing and popping of fireworks but, becoming always more aggressive and purposeless, his efforts to direct his companions began to vex them. With the well-known callousness of small boys where mischief is concerned, they hit upon the idea that it would be more fun to direct their Roman candle barrages at or close about this comical stranger and to chase him.

As the skyrockets began to whiz by his wobbling head and the fiery balls from Roman candles began to play about his vicinity, he blundered into flight. With the shouting, joyous band behind, he made a zigzag progress which finally led him to the house of a friend.

This man has never been admitted to a psychiatric hospital. He has often spent a few days in general hospitals while sobering up and occasionally a week or more in retreats which advertise their success in *curing the liquor habit.*

For perhaps 80 or 90 percent of his existence he has been a prosperous and respected member of his community and outwardly is not unlike other men of the same position.

THE PSYCHOPATH AS SCIENTIST

The limitations of space allow only a few highlights to be thrown on this man's interesting career. In his late twenties he was already a doctor of philosophy and the co-author of several creditable papers on subjects in the general field of physics.

Although delayed by truancy and alcoholic escapades for a year in obtaining his degree, he always showed noteworthy ability in a technical sense so long as he applied himself. Now and then he was disabled for several days or a week, during which times he drank enough to remain semiconscious or climbed into trees, from which he hurled noisy defiance at his friends and later at policemen who attempted to get him down. He drank chiefly alone and sometimes urinated in bureau drawers or his own or his roommate's shoes, and indulged in other pranks of the same caliber.

Having obtained his degree, he had little difficulty in securing a satisfactory post on the faculty of a state university. He did not, however, enter upon these duties. Having taken up residence with an aunt in the university town several weeks before the beginning of classes, he at once proceeded to drink on weekends and to haunt public houses of unsavory reputation.

One night a few days before the formal beginning of the academic year he made himself particularly disagreeable to his companions, who consisted of two prostitutes and a local derelict. In a mood of great irritability and arrogance he quit this group and joined another woman of the streets with whom he had frequently consorted but in whom he had never shown any special interest. During the next hour he drank little but spent his energy ridiculing and slandering his acquaintances in town, the faculty of the university, and particularly his aunt, who was his only local relative. At about 3 o'clock in the morning he astonished all present by announcing in imperious tones that he and his present companion would straightway join themselves in holy matrimony. Before leaving with such company as he could gather, he took pains to telephone his aunt and insist peremptorily that she attend the nuptials.

One may be left to imagine the consternation and confusion of the elderly and very circumspect lady as she sought first to understand and then to counsel her nephew.

On arriving at the residence of a justice of the peace, the aunt and friends whom she had brought left nothing undone in efforts to dissuade our subject from proceeding. In desperation they pointed out not only the defects of character so plain in the prospective bride but also her considerable age, her poorly made false teeth, and her unprepossessingly dyed hair. With oaths, obscenity, and a very artificial show of gaiety, the bridegroom waved aside these objections and fulfilled his aims.

The next day he condescendingly allowed his aunt to begin efforts to annul the marriage, but, while expressing his approval, he took very little active part. When earnestly questioned about his motivation, he casually averred that the whole affair was meant as a joke.

"But on whom is this joke?" an elderly friend of the family asked with some asperity.

"Why, on me, I suppose," confessed the disinterested bridegroom, laughing with what appeared to be a calmness and lack of concern almost incredible under the circumstances. He never showed any signs of serious worry or of shame, although he glibly confessed to being in the wrong. The affair became widely known, and authorities in the university succeeded in obtaining their new instructor's resignation before he actually took up his duties.

He promptly abandoned the woman he had married, and his family made some settlement with her. After a financially successful year as a car salesman, in which he got into trouble somewhat less frequently than usual, he decided to return to the academic world.

He obtained several other good positions in universities, where his work was fitful but promising. His personal life soon became so spectacularly designed to embarrass the institution that he had to be dropped. One of these positions he lost, after several minor efforts of the same sort, by the following bit of conduct.

After becoming drunk and conspicuously turbulent in his quarters, where efforts were being made to nurse him and to cajole him back to an appearance of what might be called sanity, he disappeared and could not be located for several days.

The authorities at the college remained in a state of considerable anxiety about his fate. This was terminated by a telephone call made by a local veterinarian to the professor in whose department our subject worked. The professor, a person of authentic and altogether unstudied dignity and a scholar of national importance, was probably the last man on earth whom a normal youth would desire to rouse out of bed at midnight and treat to a display of absurdity. Humor of no lesser order than his dignity characterized him. Though peaceful, unaggressive, and tolerant as a man can be, some deep subjective poise enabled him when prodded sufficiently to utter a quiet and ironic rebuke fit to unfrock a bishop.

The veterinarian informed this considerable personage that his missing research fellow was at present in the dog hospital and had insisted that this news be delivered to no other than himself, and at once. The bland, laconic lines of the professor's face subtly hardened. Pausing as he reached for his socks, he swore inaudibly.

On arriving at the dog hospital, he found his younger colleague sprawled in a large cage or cubicle used to house ailing Great Danes or St. Bernards. The young man at once yelled to the professor, announcing in glee that prophecies by the latter about his *going to the dogs* were now amply fulfilled—so what of it! His clamorous outcries rose above the din of barking dogs, who, aroused by the presence of so unusual a kennel-mate, gave voice vigorously and in unison.

The veterinarian explained that his new patient had come in some urgency and insisted on going to where the convalescent dogs were kept. Somewhat bewildered, but thinking perhaps that his visitor had good reason to inquire into the condition of some canine acquaintance, he promptly brought him to the kennels. The strange young man at once climbed into his present berth, defied the veterinarian to remove him, sang, shouted, cursed, and finally insisted that his superior be called.

Finally agreeing to come out, he remained generally obstreperous and at once began to blame a grave and gentle older colleague for his plight. The latter, who had been sincerely interested in trying to keep this promising young man from destroying himself, had, he said, set him off on the present spree by offering him a bottle of beer at lunch several days previously.

Despite many apparently self-imposed and purposeless obstacles in his career, he continues to obtain positions, sometimes keeping them as long as a year. His family is called upon to see him through difficulties when they arise, and he continues to speak of those who assist him as if he considered them in a large measure responsible for his troubles.

THE PSYCHOPATH AS PHYSICIAN

When first seen by me, he was still in his early forties. From the country town in which he was practicing medicine an inquiry came concerning his professional ability. Everyone regarded him as a brilliant man. His patients loved him, and while he was working regularly, his collections were more than adequate. It was often impossible to find him, for now and then, in the classic manner, he lay out in third-rate hotel rooms or in the fields semiconscious until he could be found and coaxed back home.

This was tolerantly accepted as one of his idiosyncrasies by the rustic folk he attended. It was inconvenient, but like drought and the boll weevil, what the devil could one do about it? The community, in which not only social drinking but even card playing and dances were generally regarded as devices of Satan, intuitively sensed that Doc's doings had little or nothing in common with the proscribed gaieties or frivolities. Although a man known to drink for pleasure and even a woman who smoked cigarettes might have been ostracized, local deacons and town gossips made no concerted attack on the doctor.

The inquiry about his ability mentioned previously was prompted by the following incident.

A patient whom he had been attending off and on for several weeks had noticed that he occasionally seemed glassy-eyed and slightly irrelevant. Neither she nor her family, however, was prepared for such a bedside manner as was his on the last visit.

When the door was opened for the doctor, he swung in unsteadily with it, hanging desperately to the knob, which he apparently hesitated to relinquish. Breathing hard, he muttered inaudibly for a moment, winked inanely at three children who had withdrawn to a corner, gave several short, piercing cheers, and slipped to the floor. Retaining his instrument bag in one hand, he began, still prone, to crawl toward his patient's room. Switching his body from side to side, he made slow but spectacular progress, hesitating every few yards to give a series of hoarse, emphatic grunts or barks. This pantomime was taken by the family to represent an alligator slipping through a bog. In this manner he reached the bedside of the patient.

This man's history shows a great succession of purposeless follies dating from early manhood. He lost several valuable hospital appointments by lying out sodden or by bursting in on serious occasions with nonsensical uproar. He was once forced to relinquish a promising private practice because of the scandal and indignation that followed an escapade in a whorehouse where he had often lain out disconsolately for days at a time.

Accompanied by a friend who was also feeling some influence of drink, he swaggered into this favorite retreat and bellowed confidently for women. Congenially disposed in one room, the party of four called for drinks. For an hour or more only the crash of glasses, scattered oaths, and occasional thuds were heard. Then suddenly an earnest, piercing scream brought the proprietress and her servants racing into the chamber. One of the prostitutes lay prostrate, clasping a towel to her breast, yelling in agony. Through her wails and sobs she accused the subject of this report of having, in his injudicious blunderings, bitten off her nipple. An examination by those present showed that this unhappy dismemberment had, in fact, taken place. Although both men had at the moment been in bed with her, the entertainer had no doubt as to which one had done her the injury.

Feeling ran strong for a while, but, by paying a large sum of money as recompense for the professional disability and personal damage he had inflicted, the doctor avoided open prosecution. Before a settlement had been made, the guilty man attempted to persuade his companion to assume responsibility for the deed. It would be less serious for the other man, he argued, since his own prominence and professional standing made him a more vulnerable target for damaging courtroom dramatics and for slander. His companion, however, declined this opportunity for self-sacrifice with great firmness.

Less spectacular performances include locking himself in a hotel room alone where he would drink to stupefaction, arouse the management, break furniture, telephone his wife that he had decided to kill himself, drink more, and remain until taken by police or friends who broke open the door.

He also contributed vividly to the liveliness of a dance some years ago. His older brother, whom he was visiting in a New England town and who was an officer in a country club where the dance was in progress, remonstrated with him, urging him to leave because his loud and disorderly behavior, having already attracted unfavorable attention, was now beginning to cause consternation. Whooping in indignation, he at once grappled with his elder on the porch of the club where they stood.

The orchestra having stopped for intermission, a large number of ladies and gentlemen were strolling on the terrace below. Attracted by frantic outcries, reiterated curses, and the sound of scuffling above, these bystanders looked up to see the two brothers whirling dizzily in combat. The younger man, his strength finally prevailing, got the older against the banister and seemed about to throw him over. As observers ran to quell the tumult, our subject, having in his position of vantage breath to spare for oratory, caused the golf course to echo with his threats and insults.

"You bastard! You goddamned ________ bastard! You son of a bitch! I'll kill you, bastard and son of a bitch that you are!" he yelled, pushing his brother back farther over the banister as the echoes returned his violent words. One wonders whether the brother was observant enough at the moment to note the two-edged nature of the term with which he was being so loudly reviled. Rescuers soon interrupted the performance. Our subject could very probably have thrown his brother over before they came, but his intention apparently was to make a scene rather than to inflict serious injury.

After one of his longest periods of regular work and apparently satisfactory adjustment, which lasted nearly a year, he attended the meeting of a regional medical society in a large city, where an exploit brought him to the notice of local newspapers.

> FOUND DRUNK ON HIGH ALTAR OF ST. PHILIP'S CHURCH
>
> A man listed as Dr. ________ ________ of ________ was arrested yesterday morning and charged with burglary when he was found asleep on the altar of St. Philip's Church. Officer J. G. Coates who made the arrest said that a painter engaged in painting St. Philip's dome found the door to the church open this morning and called him. Investigation revealed the man asleep on the altar. The officer quoted Dr. ________ as saying that someone else had been with him but that he could not remember who. The doctor seemed to be eminently rational but could give no adequate reason for his inopportune presence in such a place. While a charge of burglary had been placed, according to records at police barracks, a complete examination of the church property revealed the fact that nothing was missing.

He proved to the satisfaction of the authorities that he had entered the church with no intention of stealing or doing any other damage. I am indeed strongly convinced that this contention was correct. Finding a man in so preposterous a situation, the newspaper reporters had mistakenly, but understandably, assumed that some motive such as burglary must, of plain necessity, be responsible for his presence. What his purpose really was, we must admit, is difficult to explain in terms of ordinary human strivings.

He often swears off drinking and expresses the intention of devoting himself to constructive and regular occupation but, despite all the serious troubles that his conduct has brought him, he actually continues as before.

THE PSYCHOPATH AS PSYCHIATRIST

In the group who show some fundamental characteristics of the typical psychopath but who make a good or fair superficial adjustment in society are sometimes found people who hold responsible positions. Lawyers, business executives, physicians, and engineers who show highly suggestive features of the disorder have been personally observed. Perhaps one would think that the psychiatrist, with good opportunity to observe the psychopath, would eschew all his ways. I believe, however, that a glimpse can be given of characteristics of the psychopath in such a person.

Let us first direct our attention to him many years ago when, as an author of some papers on psychiatric subjects, he attracted the interest of several inexperienced young physicians then at the beginning of their careers. The articles, it is true, were marred by grammatical errors and vulgarities in English a little disillusioning in view of the suave and pretentious style attempted by the author. At the time, however, they impressed this little group of naive admirers as having all the originality that the author so willingly allowed others to impute to them, and, as a matter of fact, implied not too subtly himself in every line of his work.

When seen later at a small medical meeting at which no experienced psychiatrists were present, this author seemed very grand indeed. The actual ideas expressed in his paper were, to be fair, culled from the primers of psychiatry and psychology, but he had an authoritative way of making them seem entirely his own, and marvelous, too. Despite his cool and somewhat commanding air, he succeeded in giving an impression of deep modesty. Everything seemed to accentuate his relative youth which, in turn, hinted of precociousness and of great promise. The effect he had on his audience, most of whom were general practitioners from small towns, was tremendous. An opportunity to meet this splendid figure of a psychiatrist and to sit at his feet during the rest of the evening was avidly welcomed by several of his new admirers.

Dr. ———, though still in his middle thirties, enjoyed a wide and enviable reputation in a section of the country where psychiatrists were at the time almost unknown. After some work at hospitals in a distant state where he was born, he had come and set up as a specialist in his present habitat. He soon obtained a small institution in which he began to direct treatment of psychiatric patients. Reports indicate that it flourished and expanded greatly.

It was generally agreed that his learning and ability were chiefly responsible for his rapid rise to local prominence. Ephemeral rumors hinted that the idolized Dr. ——— made a practice of treating by expensive and doubtful procedures any patient of means whom he could obtain for as long as the money lasted and of then dismissing him or sending him promptly to a state hospital. It was also heard that with female patients he sometimes suggested, or even insisted on, activities (as therapy) that are specifically proscribed in the Hippocratic oath. But what physician has not had similar things said about him? The impressive bearing of the man and his reiterated and rather eloquent appeals for higher scientific consecration on the part of his colleagues snuffed out these feeble stirrings of adverse criticism, which were almost universally ascribed to jealousy.

The lion of the evening seemed to put himself out in being gracious to his young admirers who were indeed nobodies on the fringe of the wonderful field that he seemed to dominate. His good fellowship was so hearty and yet so suave that one could scarcely bring himself to see the faint underlying note of condescension.

The privilege of driving this relatively great personage out to a country place where hospitality beckoned was seized by one of the young physicians. In the car an attempt was made to turn the conversation to psychiatric questions that Dr. ——— had raised in his papers. He made a few stilted replies but soon drifted from the subject into talk that was hardly more than pompous gossip. His companion, fearing that such a learned man might be talking down to spare him the embarrassment of incomprehension, kept returning to psychiatry, trying to make it plain that no such embarrassment would discount the pleasure of hearing the master. Soon the replies of this alleged master left the young man in serious doubt not only as to the great one's knowledge, but even as to his interest in the subject.

Dr. ———, in his more popular talks and articles, as well as occasionally in those directed toward rural medical groups, often gave psychiatric interpretations of literature and art. One of his more recent efforts in this line touched briefly but ambitiously on the works of Marcel Proust. Being then in the middle of an earnest pilgrimage among the psychopathologic wonders of *Remembrance of Things Past,* the fledgling psychiatrist, perhaps hoping to make a good impression but also eager for enlightenment, ventured a question on this subject.

The master at this time was calm and alert, but his remarks were so beside the point that his disciple wavered. Dr. ——— was perfectly self-assured, in fact politely pontifical, but the more he talked the clearer it became that he had not read the book at all. It finally became equally clear that even Proust's name was unfamiliar, and the disquieting suspicion dawned on his admirer that he had never encountered it except in the excerpt from some review which he had apparently come upon and used. He had not been sufficiently interested in what he plagiarized even to retain the name and was now imputing it to some imaginary Viennese psychiatrist. He followed this pretension only for a moment, however, and only as a stepping stone to banalities with which he was familiar and about which he spoke with such deliberation and assurance that they almost seemed marvelous. Never in all this persiflage did he show the least sign of confusion or timidity. Apparently he felt that he had kept intact his impressive front. Even at this stage of the acquaintanceship it was hard to avoid suspicion that any important distinction between such a front and more substantial things was not in the orbit of his awareness.

With some remark about putting aside these grave and ponderous subjects, he sang a few lines of a surprisingly obscene ditty, clapped his companion on the back, and suggested with gusto: "When their social doings are over, let's you and I go get us a couple of good frisky women!"

Despite the conviviality implicit in this remark (and no less in his tone), in some way hard to describe he still maintained the attitude of one who means to insist on his distinct superiority even while for a moment generously waiving certain restrictions of caste and allowing his companion a more respectable footing. It was only a quasi equality that he offered, however—an indulgence such as an adult might allow a child who on some special occasion is permitted to sit up and play that he is grown. The friendship he seemed to offer was at best a condescending one.

His discourse during the rest of the drive, especially after he had stopped on the way for "a couple of quick ones," was coarse and humorless. It seemed impossible to strike a sincere idea from him on any subject.

At the host's place a merry but entirely civilized company was found drinking, singing around the piano, or talking enthusiastically in small groups. The singing was in key, and the talking was not loose or aimless. For the most part the gathering was composed of people who, though lively, had some interest in general ideas as contrasted with the trivia of daily life, and a few slowly ingested drinks brought out humorous and interesting conversation. The house was not very large or the furnishing spectacular, but the place, like the men and women present, gave a strong impression to the newcomer that he was in orderly surroundings, among people of dignity and good will.

A young, very good-looking married woman who had an amateur but genuine interest in psychiatric questions and who meant to be polite to the distinguished stranger began talking to him with enthusiasm. He soon led her off into another room. A moment later, on passing through this room, one of the young physicians was hailed by a feminine voice and, responding, found the two in a nook, the lady pulling herself away from the doctor with some effort but with equanimity. It was plain that his crudely aggressive overtures were not welcome to her, and she urged the other man, who was an old friend, to join them on the davenport. Apparently trying to start a conversation, she asked the celebrity about psychoanalysis, a subject on which he sometimes expounded to lay gatherings in such a way as to give the erroneous impression that he was a qualified analyst.

"If I could get you out in a car I'd psychoanalyze you right now," he muttered, low but loud enough to be overheard, accompanying his words with a confident leer. The savant had evidently misread the spirit of the party. The lady rose, smiled quickly at her other companion as if to say she knew a disagreeable fellow when she saw one, and quietly rejoined a group.

Dr. ______ now expressed the desire for straight liquor, making strong, derogatory remarks about cocktails and those who drank them. Ordering his former disciple to come, he strode toward the kitchen. The former disciple, by this time feeling heavily responsible for the master, made haste to follow.

In the kitchen Dr. ______ began to order the servants about in profane and petulant fashion. He had gulped one or two small whiskeys when several men wandered in looking for ice. One of these, an eager intern, expressed interest in the important investigative work that Dr. ______ had begun now, in loud, boastful tones, to announce himself engaged in.

"If you want a job there, son, just lemme know," he thundered. Swaggering about, he made an all-embracing gesture. "At the ______ Institute I'm *it.* I'm the big cheese, I tell you." No one saw fit to dispute these claims.

He began then a tirade on the subject of his executive ability, his scientific standing, his knowledge of the stock market, his sexual power, and his political influence. Having delivered himself of this, he pushed his audience aside and sauntered back into the sitting room. There he recognized an old acquaintance, a physician who had formerly been on the resident staff with him at some hospital but in an inferior capacity. This man, a newcomer, was talking with the hostess in the midst of a small group of men and women.

"Why you old son of a bitch!" Dr. ______ shouted. "Come over here and set your goddamned a-- in this chair and talk to your chief."

It was no time for vacillation. The newcomer and the young physician who had accompanied Dr. ______ to the party caught each other's eye and quickly hurried the celebrity to the door. He pulled back at first but soon came along satisfactorily as both companions sought so earnestly to cajole him that the words of each were lost to the other. Turning to his companions just as the door was gained, he shouted:

"Whores, did you say?"

On the way to his hotel he began to protest. He was by no means confused from drink.

"Be goddamned if I go there! What kind of dirty bastards are you anyway?"

He became insistent—even defiant—about going where he could obtain women. The new member of the party, who had seen him through many episodes and who, to the other escort's relief, kindly assumed charge of the case, advised that he be humored.

Dr. ______ himself, through an effervescence of obscene threats, muttered directions to the driver. Expecting to find an ordinary whorehouse, both of his companions were surprised to arrive at a large outdoor pavilion where an orderly dance was going on. Before a definite decision could be reached about what to do, Dr. ______ was out of the car.

"Luke! Luke!" he yelled imperiously.

A pleasant-looking man appeared.

"You've got to get us a good piece of t--- and get it quick, boy!" he ordered. "We'll wait here and watch 'em dance by."

The man called Luke, so far as could be learned, was under serious obligations to Dr. ______ and apparently meant to obey him. He confided that he had stood by his friend and benefactor in many such sprees in this town. Luke had pleasant manners and was not drinking.

"God, that's one!" the savant muttered. "What an ---! Can you get that slut out here, Luke?" He was far enough away not to be overheard by the dancers. Luke smiled and shook his head. "There's one!" the doctor commented again with enthusiasm. "She's rutting! That one's rutting! I can tell it." His subsequent remarks can hardly be suggested even in writing on a medical subject.

His two companions left him now in custody of Luke with instructions that he be brought back to the car when this was possible without violence. Luke had asked not to be left with sole responsibility.

Some time later the doctor returned. It was difficult to judge whether or not he had gained all the satisfaction he sought. He made it plain that he had found a companion, but despite his boastful garrulousness did not give the final details of the encounter. In view of his windy frankness, this caused doubt as to how far he had succeeded in his aims. Beyond question he had made considerable progress. He announced this much loudly, holding up a finger, sniffing it as he did so, and making a comment of such ingenious distastefulness that even his brother physicians blenched with revulsion. The new disciple could not but ruminate about what appraisals of woman and of human relationships, what attitudes toward basic goals, prevailed beneath this successful man's ordinarily impressive exterior.

On the road back to his hotel he cursed truculently at other cars. He came in willingly. While going up on the elevator, he pinched the buttocks of the girl who ran it, apparently oblivious of several passengers. There was no gaiety or human touch in these actions, only a sullen, derogatory aggressiveness. He uttered vague challenges and threats emphasizing his combative prowess and his readiness to fight anyone who might take issue with him on any question.

On entering his room, he immediately made for a whiskey bottle and began calling raucously for ice. He became loud and offensive when his companions sought to excuse themselves, banged the table with his fists, and offered grandiosely to fight and to fight at once. He was a tall, powerful man and by no means too drunk to put on a lively and embarrassing scene if crossed.

He cursed the bellboy, who had arrived meanwhile, with such foul oaths it was incredible that he took them. Pouring himself a quick drink, he called for careful attention from his companions.

Had he told them about his children? No. They must see pictures of them. He began to praise them extravagantly, to extol his love for them in sickening terms of pathos, or pseudopathos. He spoke of his plans for their future. His entire manner began to change, and it was plain that he had determined notions about keeping all his children what he called *pure.* A surprisingly moralistic aspect of this psychiatrist began to appear. Cheap expressions of sentimentality fairly gushed from him. In a loosely emotional strain he recited rhymes by Edgar A. Guest about the little ones. Then he momentarily broke down and blubbered. Tears ran down his cheeks.

The bellboy had brought ice, and Dr. ________ insisted on pouring out drinks, swaggering about now in his earlier manner. When his companions insisted on leaving, he promptly announced that he would accompany them. He could not be persuaded to go to bed and quickly became overbearing when persuasion continued. Though he had, of course, taken a good deal of whiskey, he seemed to know perfectly what he was doing. In fact, he did not really seem drunk in the ordinary sense of the word. Both of his companions felt that this was not a person irresponsible for the moment who must be protected and prevented from doing things he would regret. On the contrary, one was strongly impressed that this was the man himself.

Going down on the elevator, he renewed his practices on the polite girl who operated it, becoming so annoying to her that his companions had to interfere. He called a taxi and insisted that all proceed at once to a whorehouse. Having had enough experience for one night in trying to be their brother's keeper, his companions were obdurate. He drove off, cursing them viciously as disgraceful specimens of humanity and making derogatory remarks about their virility.

"What's the matter with him?" asked the younger.

"Just a queer fellow that way," replied the one who knew him well. "He's cool and calculating, a good executive, and a rather pleasant man superficially during the week, though always a little arrogant. Even when on the job he's not to be trusted. Every time he gets a chance, he does just about what you've seen him do tonight. He keeps under wraps of outer dignity at the hospital, and he's careful not to take them off under circumstances that would cause him to get in serious trouble. He passes as a great gentleman in polite but unsophisticated circles at home. But the cloak must be very uncomfortable. Almost every weekend he makes an opportunity to get it off, and he's always then just the man you saw tonight."

"But won't his reputation suffer from what he did tonight?"

"Probably not. He is a long way from home. Since the town is small, he evidently assumed that all the people he was thrown with tonight were country bumpkins who don't count for much and who would be overawed by him. He judges people only by superficial appearances of wealth and power, and he is seldom impressed except by gaudy display. He kept up a good front at the medical meeting. He is exceedingly shrewd, in a shallow sense, about where and when he behaves naturally. At home he often goes off into swamps with groups of men far beneath him in his own estimation and who are apparently flattered to be chosen. The trips are ostensibly to catch catfish or, in the winter, to shoot ducks; but actually it's merely to get rowdily drunk, boast and shout inanely, and sprawl about on the ground or in muddy boats around the camp. He wasn't drunk tonight. Out in the swamp he often passes through this obscene, blustering phase in an hour or two and reaches the sodden state that one might suspect is his goal.

"Sometimes he wants women. It doesn't matter what women or under what circumstances. Some of the people who know him say that he prefers low, unprepossessing partners, but it has always seemed to me that there was no preference at all, and I've seen him often. A beautiful woman means no more to him than an imbecilic harlot, but on the other hand, the harlot means no more than the beautiful woman.

"Sometimes when the idea of sex is stirring him he gets too drunk to make much of his opportunities. I'll never forget one incident. It was about daybreak down in the swamps where we'd been fishing. He'd gone out on a sexual mission pretty drunk. We found him at a whitewashed shack. It was time to leave for home, so another fellow and I rolled him off a fat illiterate washerwoman. She must have weighed two hundred pounds!

" 'Sakes, Boss,' she muttered, 'he's far gone dis time. Ain't done nuthin' yet!' It was my last fishing trip with him."

The next morning with fresh sunlight streaming into the hotel, the youngest member of the group, having finished breakfast, met Dr. ______ in the lobby. He was emerging from a telephone booth. Tall, self-assured, clear-eyed, neat as a dandy, and fashionably dressed, he looked the fine figure of a man.

He spoke affably. With a disarming, boyish smile he made some reference to the previous evening. His polite expressions and poised tone made clear the implication that it had been a pleasant occasion and had cemented friendships. The inconspicuous trace of condescension first noted on meeting him was now more obvious, but this somehow tended to make his cordiality seem more precious. He was as sober as a man can be and showed no signs of *hangover.* Indeed, as his other companion of the night had said, he must have been drinking very moderately.

The former admirer of Dr. ______, who was an old friend of the lady whom the doctor had offered to "psychoanalyze" in a parked car the night before, stopped at her house later in the day to say good-bye before leaving the city.

"Come in. I must speak to you," she said. There was some indignation in her tone but more mischief and merriment.

"What about your friend, the famous psychoanalyst?" she said, relishing, in all friendliness, the other's discomfiture. She was a person of some sophistication and poise. Being also pretty, vital, and desirable to men, she knew well how to take care of herself in ordinary company. She had been married for several years and gave a strong impression of being happy and in love with her husband.

"Well," she continued, "I must tell you. You are interested in queer people."

"Early this morning the cook came and woke me up. 'It's the telephone,' she said. 'Damn the telephone, Lou!' I told her. 'Don't you know I was up till all hours last night?' 'Yes'm,' she answered, 'but the gentleman says you'll speak with *him,* and it's important business.'

"I picked up the phone.

" 'Good morning, Mary' said an unfamiliar, self-assured, masculine voice. I was wondering who it could be—knowing me well enough to use my first name and still so pompous. Then, just as I recognized the voice:

"Mary, this is Doctor ______.' From his tone you'd have judged he thought I ought to sing for joy!

" 'Yes indeed,' I said. He then baldly suggested that I make a date with him for this afternoon. He'd come out for me at 4 P.M. or, better still, he suggested, I could meet him at a drugstore downtown.

"Really, there was something so superior about him, a sort of indescribably cool insolence, or I don't know what . . . about his manner, I mean . . . and after last night! . . . not just the proposition itself . . . that I fairly turned white with rage.

"I wanted so much to blast him with scorn that I was at a loss for words. When you get that mad it's easy to lose your head. The calm and effective expression of indignation by which ladies in Victorian novels squelched 'insults' is hard to put into the idiom of today. Trying not to make myself unnecessarily ridiculous, but trusting the reply would register as final, I said, 'Is that so? *Sorry,* but I'm afraid I'll have to forego that pleasure.'

"He then insisted, not like a lover or even like one who's making any decent pretense of being a lover, but coolly, almost arrogantly. I must have succeeded in making myself a little clearer by this time, for he resigned himself about this afternoon. But I wasn't done with him.

"He then began to say that he would be back in this city soon, probably every now and then. He'd like to see me on some of these occasions. He'd call me when he came. No, perhaps it would be better if he dropped me a note and let me know when he'd be here. Then I could call *him! I* was getting so vexed that I scarcely caught the implication that he didn't want to telephone and find George here.

"For a moment I couldn't answer. Then I suddenly remembered the way he announced himself: 'Mary, this is *Doctor* ________!' The overwhelming effrontery of the whole farce came over me. It was too much! 'Mary, this is *Doctor* ________!' That priceless ass calling me by my first name and referring to himself as 'Doctor ________!' And under such circumstances! Why, he probably pictured us having our little bout of 'love' in the same strain. 'You're so lovely, Mary, do let me take off your pants!' 'Oh, Doctor ________ (blushing), you're so genteel and handsome!'

"Can you beat it!? I ask you as an old friend! The bumptious swine didn't even have enough delicacy in what he probably thought of as love making to grant me the intimacy to call him Jack, or Harry, or Percival, or Happy Hooligan, or whatever else he's named. He's such an indescribable prig that he probably doesn't even allow *himself* to think of himself in terms of a first name.

"I just had time to get out the words, which must have come with something of a lilt: 'Yes, you just *wait* until I call you!'

"I'm ashamed to confess they were almost lost in a burst of laughter. It wasn't ladylike at all the way I laughed. It was belly-shaking laughter. Homeric laughter. Rabelaisian laughter, maybe. I couldn't stop.

"Lou, the cook, came back in and asked what was the matter. 'I can't explain,' I told her and went on laughing.

"What sort of people are you psychiatrists anyway?" she now asked her friend in her spirited, arch way, again enjoying her old friend's discomfiture, which was now almost lost in wonder and amusement. "I bet that bat-house troubadour went away thinking I had become hysterical with delight at the opportunity he offered."

"That might not be absurd after all," the friend murmured, remembering the self-possession and happy assurance with which Dr. ________ had emerged from the telephone booth that morning.

This case is offered for what it may be worth. No diagnosis of psychopathic personality has been made. Occasional news of him over the next few years indicated that he was still outwardly well adjusted. I believe it likely that he continues to prosper, and I have not the faintest notion that he will ever reach the wards of a psychiatric hospital except in the capacity of a physician and executive. He does not really succeed in impressing people of discernment, though he continues to think he succeeds in this. He impresses many people who are themselves essentially undiscriminating. He cannot tell these from others with sounder judgment and regards himself as a great success socially as well as financially.

Such a personality shows suggestions of an inner deviation qualitatively similar to what is found in the fully developed sociopath. The shrewdness is typical. Unlike others, such as Max, whose cleverness brings only momentary success in objective dealing with the world, this man's similar cleverness is applied with enough persistence for him to advance continuously. He advances financially and, within limits, even professionally. He is a smart fellow and, in a very superficial sense, has a glib facility in medical activities. In relations with the public he shows an excellent knack, an artful sense of showmanship.

For the more fundamental questions that immediately confront a person interested in psychiatry he apparently has no awareness, and therefore no concern. The problems of life that make up the chief and underlying interest for real psychiatrists do not exist for him. He is said to give many of his patients about what they feel they need. With relatively uncomplex and emotionally shallow persons his amazing self-confidence is perhaps more quickly effective than the deeper understanding, with its inevitable lack of certainties, that another sort of man would bring to his work.

His patients are reported to show improvement that compares favorably with that shown by most of the patients treated by physicians whose aims are more serious. We must not forget that pseudoscientific cultists frequently succeed in relieving psychoneurotic patients of their symptoms by absurd measures. These practitioners, if they work in accordance with the fundamental principles of their craft, have no awareness of the real problems underlying such symptoms and little or no ability to help patients understand and deal with these problems. Such a man as this appears to be similarly limited. If one imagines his attempting pertinent psychiatric study of a seriously motivated person, of a person whose world is quite foreign to him, the picture becomes farcical.

This man, then, the traits already mentioned notwithstanding, is one who, unlike the obvious psychopath, succeeds over many years in his outer adjustment. Granting that the behavior just described is fairly typical and is persisted in, the conclusion follows that inwardly he is very poorly adjusted indeed. The quality of happiness he knows and the degree of reality in which he experiences so much that is major in human relations are such that, despite his superficial success, he must fail to participate very richly in life itself.

Let it be pointed out that the drunkenness, immature sex attitudes, execrable taste, and deceit are not in themselves the basis for suspecting that this man is affected in some measure with the same disorder that affects the patients presented previously. Many readers would perhaps dismiss all this with the thought that our man might be more properly called a bad fellow and his status left at that. The significant points are these:

His impulse to drink does not seem to be motivated by the hope of shared gaiety. His attitude in sexual aims is so self-centered as to give the impression that even when carrying out intercourse with women he is essentially solitary, isolated in evaluations so immature that what satisfaction he achieves must lie in concepts of a phallic damaging and despoiling of the female with simultaneous reassurances to puerile concepts of his own virility. Such confusing and fragmentary achievement, common enough in a groping boy of 13, is a poor and pathologic substitute for fulfillment compatible with deep personality integration and is inadequate for one even remotely as near adult as what is implied by this man's outer surface.

His lack of taste and judgment in human relationships seems inconsistent with his opportunity to learn and with his ability to learn in other modes of knowing where such values and meanings do not enter. His apparent hypocrisy is probably not a conscious element of behavior. At least he is unaware of how it would seem to others, even if he assumed all the facts were known to them. It has, perhaps, never occurred to him that there might be people in the world who had other fundamental aims than his own dominant aim to drop the disguise in which he has acted his part perhaps not too comfortably during the week and plunge into what I would call activity more representative of perverse or disintegrative drives, of aims at sharp variance with everything his outer self seems to represent.

I am well aware that many basic impulses appear in forms not socially acceptable, that they might be called immoral, vulgar, or criminal or be described by other unpleasant words. The person here discussed, when seen without his mask, seems not to be directed in any consistent and purposive scheme by these socially unacceptable tendencies but largely to blunder about at their behest. In his outer front he functions in accordance with all the proprieties, large and small, but here the reality is thin and personal participation halfhearted. He is somewhat like a small boy who succeeds in maintaining decorum and even in getting a good mark for conduct while in the schoolroom under teacher's watchful eye. Though he looks attentive, he is only shrewdly compromising, biding his time to get at what is to him more important. When the bell rings and he escapes from what he finds to be an artificial situation, an area of formalities and polite pretenses, he becomes natural and plays in accordance with what he takes to be the actual rules and real aims of existence.

The small schoolboy learns eventually to reconcile what the classroom represented and what he sought in his hours of play. He finds in his work responsibilities and ways of celebrating much that is compatible, a core at least, that he can integrate into constructive, self-fulfilling, and, on the whole, harmonious expression of basic impulses.

In such a man as the one we are considering, little harmony of this sort appears. Unlike those presented as clinical psychopaths, he has learned to carry out the formalities rather consistently and appears as actually living in a constructive and socially adapted pattern. Actually this is a surface activity, a sort of ritual in which not much of himself enters. For his more natural and inwardly accepted impulses he has found little reconcilable with what he gives lip service to. So he must turn to patterns of behavior so immature and (subjectively) chaotic that they mock and deny all that his surface affirms.

The outer layers of socially acceptable functioning extend little deeper into affect than any other exercise empty of all but formality. He has apparently learned to carry out a lip service in matters that he finds unreal and tedious and to take pride in how well this is performed. As an alternative to the barren channels of formality, the inner man finds for the more valid fulfillment of real impulse only pathways or outlets that sharply deviate from the surface channels, that cannot in any way be integrated with them, and that in themselves remain relatively archaic, poorly organized, undirected toward any mature goal, and socially regressive or self-destructive.

It is confusing to interpret such a personality in terms of bad and good. From a psychiatric viewpoint, at least, such aspects of a maladjusted human being cannot be assessed authoritatively.

Years after the incidents recorded in this report, some news of the good doctor was received which I believe would stand as "Paradox in Paradise."

It was brought to the young psychiatrist who had accompanied Dr. __________ during the spree just cited by an earnest, middle-aged lady with a strong penchant for talking about psychology and psychiatry and psychoanalysis, about anything containing the prefix *psych* for that matter. Striking at once for her hearer's closest interests, she began to talk about a wonderful lecture she had recently heard in a distant town at some woman's club or literary society that was fostering the cause of mental hygiene.

The lecturer was marvelous, she insisted. He stirred up such enthusiasm that half the ladies present had begun to study psychology. And his subject! He talked about the queerest people! They were not exactly *insane,* but they really did the most fantastic things! They were even harder to understand than lunatics themselves! But the lecturer understood them, though he confessed in all modesty that some points about them were a puzzle even to one of his own experience. He was a most impressive person—so poised and authoritative, yet always quiet-spoken. He was such an *intellectual* person. A man of wide and profound culture. And such a gentleman!

"I declare, I believe half of the women in our club wished they could exchange roles with his wife! With all that grasp of psychology, just imagine what a husband he must be!"

She would like to learn more about these people . . . psychopathic personalities or psychopaths the doctor had called them.

And the doctor's name. . . . She uttered it in hushed tones of admiration.

section three · Cataloging the material

chapter 4 · Orientation

CONCEPTUAL CONFUSIONS WHICH CLOUD THE SUBJECT

While preparing the first edition of this volume, I was impressed and sometimes astonished by the dearth of pertinent material about the psychopath in most psychiatric textbooks. It seemed not only surprising but almost incredible to find how little space was devoted to this disorder. With psychopaths making up so large a proportion of the patients who must be dealt with, and their problems being so serious, it was indeed difficult to understand why they were almost ignored.

If the medical student, the resident physician, or the beginner in psychiatry could find little help from the textbooks, it would seem that he might obtain from monographs or special treatises the information he needed. Despite the existence of several large and scholarly volumes on the psychopathic personality, I was unable to discover anywhere a book that came to grips with the subject in such a way as to give real or practical assistance. There was, furthermore, relatively little published at the time in psychiatric journals that had much bearing on the urgent and major problems with which so many strove in helplessness and in confusion.

Through the literature of many decades pertinent articles were scattered. Some of these gave serious attention to the subject. Not always readily accessible to the average physician who dealt directly with these numerous patients, this largely buried but valuable material did not regularly influence methods or generally clarify the fundamental issues.

Surrounded by what seemed almost a conspiracy of silence, a desert of evasiveness or indifference, not only the relatives of the patients but also courts, physicians, and medical institutions had, it seemed, little to guide them in a task of the first order.

At present there are indications of more practical interest in the problem. Popular textbooks, it must be admitted, still have relatively little to say about this subject, but in their current treatment of the psychopath there is a happy departure from the once almost universal procedure of mixing the few pages or paragraphs on this subject with all manner of unrelated deficiencies as, for example, congenital organic brain diseases.

The confusion and equivocation in which our subject has been all but lost can be better understood from a historical survey. Since the first edition of this book was prepared, Maughs has published a thorough and valuable study of this sort. It is not practical here to do justice to the evolution of concepts that Maughs traces through more than a century and a half. A few points, however, have so much bearing on our central problem that they demand notice.

Early in the nineteenth century Pinel recorded his surprise in finding that many patients do not show the disordered reasoning assumed to be necessary for psychotic behavior. He is quoted by Maughs thus:

> I thought that madness was inseparable from delirium or delusion, and I was surprised to find many maniacs who at no period gave evidence of any lesion of the understanding.

Prichard's descriptions of a "moral insanity" and Benjamin Rush's beliefs about derangement of the "will" suggest that such patients as we now call psychopaths, or antisocial personalities, were observed and that the absence of delusion and irrationality of thought was noted. Maughs gives a most helpful account of the efforts to interpret such disorder in terms of disease that spares the intellect but attacks other "faculties" such as "moral affections," "will," "sense of Deity," and "emotions."

It is most interesting to note that these earliest observers* not only recorded that serious personality disorder occurred in the absence of "a lesion of the intellect" but also that they were strongly inclined to recognize it as illness, to distinguish it from ordinary crime or depravity.

Despite the fact that they dealt largely with philosophic abstractions and assumed various "faculties" which were treated as separate and established entities, their practical conclusions seem far more realistic than many subsequent concepts and sometimes perhaps more pertinent than those which now determine the medical and legal status of the psychopath.

Dr. Ordronaux, Professor of Medical Jurisprudence of Columbia University in 1873, expressed a contrary point of view that soon prevailed and, translated into other terms, represents rather accurately an attitude toward our problem that is still influential today. As quoted in part from Maughs, Ordronaux makes the following statement:

> Our moral nature is, like the mind, a special endowment. It feels, it is conscious. . . . Moral nature knows no alterations in rhythm, craves no rest, never sleeps voluntarily. The only disease to which moral nature is subject is sin.

Though still assuming that "intellect" and "moral nature" are in actuality "things" as separate and independent as the words used to designate them, Ordronaux is quite sure that one, unlike the other, is not subject to any sort of disease.

At this point it might be helpful to ask ourselves a few questions. In psychiatry as in most other fields of human endeavor the belief in faculty psychology has long been abandoned. Primarily through the persistent efforts of Adolf Meyer, nearly all medical workers agree today that we do not encounter a "mind" independent of a body, that we had best confine our attention to what we meet in experience, that is to say, a person who may show disorder in various aspects of his functioning. We reject the demand to deal separately with an "intellect," a "moral faculty," a "will," as if they were, apart from the words, things that can be isolated for study or for treatment.

In view of our generally avowed position in this matter, it is not a little surprising to find how concepts deeply rooted in the long-discarded faculty psychology enter, by the back door, and influence the attitudes and practices of today. A few of the many important points made by Korzybski are extremely pertinent here. Without attempting to go into the deep and general confusion and the ineffective procedures that can arise

*Pinel, Esquirol, Rush, Woodward, Conolly.

through the incompatibility of language and concept with fact, it is worth our while to consider for a moment what Korzybski and his co-workers refer to as consciousness of abstracting.

It is obvious to us today that what most psychiatrists and psychologists talked and wrote about some decades ago were verbal abstractions and that these were treated as if they referred to what can be met in experience. By juggling these verbal artifacts without realizing (and admitting) that they do not necessarily correspond to real and separate entities, logical and eloquent arguments can be made, but such philosophizing usually has little applicability to the world in which we live. In medical problems this method has been peculiarly unrewarding.

If we grant that *mind* and *body, thinking* and *feeling, moral faculty* and *intellect,* and *character* and *personality* cannot, except in language, be split apart and dealt with as clear-cut entities, let us keep this fact clearly in mind. This is not to say that such terms must not be used. It is neither practicable nor possible to avoid them. They convey something that is important. When the husband of a patient asks, "It's not her mind, is it Doc?" and gets the reassuring answer, "No, it's just her nerves," he may receive useful and valid information (that she is not psychotic). On the other hand, he may receive a good deal of information that is not only misleading but sometimes distinctly harmful. He may find himself automatically instructed to this effect:

1. His wife's trouble is confined to the peripheral nerves.
2. These nerves are weak (in the most literal sense) or perhaps frayed and a bit tangled.
3. The nerves have actually, as she has often told him, been jumping about in her body and knotting up in painful snarls.
4. She really has nothing wrong with her but is just putting on.
5. A little *active medicine* or a *nerve tonic* will cure the sickness, which is fortunately localized far from her "mind."
6. Since she got run down and developed nervous exhaustion, a lot of rest in bed is plainly the answer.

It is no doubt clear to us as psychiatrists that "nervous trouble" is a kind of "mental trouble," and we are not likely to be confused in such a way as the patient's husband. Nor are we likely, today, to believe that a neurosis is caused by toxins arising from sexual frustration or that it is something essentially different from a psychoneurosis. We are not likely to feel we are talking about a patient with ordinary psychosis ("mental illness") when we refer to a psychopath, despite the fact that our term unequivocally signifies illness of the "mind." To escape the unjustified implications of faculty psychology, we wisely avoid diagnosing "moral insanities," but we often turn to "neurotic character" as a term to indicate the same type of disorder. If we use the current nomenclature, we may classify those usually called psychopaths under the general term *personality disorder* and the subtype *antisocial personality.* Whatever terms are used, it is important for us to retain full realization that we abstract in a term or concept some aspect of what we meet only as an integrated entity.

The early material cited and discussed by Maughs makes clear the difficulties encountered approximately 100 or more years ago in trying to solve psychiatric problems on the assumptions of faculty psychology. Some believe that the chief medicolegal decisions today are determined almost entirely on the question of whether or not a "lesion of the intellect" can be demonstrated.

In more recent decades two tendencies particularly seem to have played a major and persistent role in isolating the psychopath from practical consideration and in concealing him in a strange and gratuitous confusion. One of these tendencies arose from efforts to group these patients with many other types by no means similar. The other seems to have proceeded from ambitious attempts to break down the psychopath's disorder by fine and largely imaginary distinctions, by all sorts of descriptive nuances and diagnostic deceit, into theoretical entities to be differentiated and classified under many subheadings.

These attempts at elaborate differentiation have been applied not to a distinguishable group having in common fundamental features that could be brought into conceptual focus but to an essentially heterogeneous referent. A good analogy would arise if someone set out to establish and list scores of inconsequential differences between Fords, Toyotas, Chevrolets, Cadillacs, and Lincolns by studying assiduously a general material in which automobiles, oxcarts, demolished freight cars, jet planes, rural woodsheds, and the village pump were undistinguished, embraced under a single term, and treated through such concepts as can be formed in such an approach. Would it not be wiser to put all our automobiles together in a field of reference before attempting to take further steps?

It is perhaps worthwhile to say here that the more types our writers enumerate and the more seriously they take these philosophic artifacts, the less likely is any relationship to be found between what is in the book and our direct experience with psychopaths. Before these fine distinctions can be made to any good purpose, there must first appear some recognition of the basic group that is to be further differentiated. This seems notably lacking where wordplay is most extensive and ambitious.

Either of the two practices just mentioned would in itself have introduced more than enough obscurity. Together they have worked to make a confusion unparalleled in the whole field of psychiatry.

As the psychoses were recognized and the psychoneuroses distinguished from them, it became increasingly popular to put virtually anything that failed to fit into these categories with the psychopath in a veritable diagnostic salad of incompatibles. The term *psychopathic personality,* of course, invites such practice with its literal applicability to all psychiatric disorders. The official term *personality disorder* does not totally avoid similar implications of a very broad application.

Early in the present century Meyer called attention to the importance of separating patients now generally called psychoneurotic from the heterogeneous conglomeration of types among which the psychopath was then, and is still to some degree, officially placed. Through persistent efforts the mental defective was also distinguished and today is considered apart.

When mentally defective patients, in all their degrees of disability, were not distinguished from the psychopath, while both were listed under the same official term, it is not surprising that many excellent observers found and reported physical abnormalities, stigmata of degeneration, and gross neural pathology in the general group. It is not remarkable to see that such findings became associated with (and regarded as characteristic of) not only the patients in whom they occurred but also with the psychopath and other unrelated patients, all of whom were considered together as closely related examples of a constitutional defect state. It is, however, truly remarkable that such errors persisted through the years and decades. A good example is afforded by material from Sadler's popular textbook published in 1936.

In this ponderous volume, totaling 1,231 pages of text, fewer than five pages were spared for our subject. After several descriptive statements that could apply accurately to the behavior of the real psychopath and that seem to indicate him as the subject under discussion, physical characteristics of "constitutional psychopathic inferiority" are given through an extensive quotation from another authority. Some of these physical characteristics, presumably of the psychopath, deserve a moment of consideration:

> The brain may be abnormally large or small or defective either in part or as a whole. The abnormalities may be due to defective development, injury, tumor, infection, or vascular accidents, such as cerebral hemorrhage, or to interference with the circulation of cerebrospinal fluid such as occurs in hydrocephalus. Associated with these abnormalities are weakness and paralyses of various parts of the body as well as varying degrees of intellectual defect. The spinal cord likewise may be affected with resulting weaknesses or paralyses. There may be gross physical defects in the development of the eyes, ears, nose, mouth, arms, hands, legs, feet, rectum, anus, and external urogenital organs. Minor physical defects sometimes referred to as stigmata of defective development include abnormalities of the cranium, malformations of the external ears, nose or mouth (abnormal spacing, position, or defective development of teeth; high-arched palate, harelip or cleft palate), webbing of fingers or toes, distorted or supernumerary digits, excessive amounts or absence of hair, undescended testicles and infantile uterus.

Just what bearing this curious compendium of deformities may have on the question of the psychopath I am scarcely prepared to say. A causal relation, to which Sadler does not openly commit himself but seems somewhat evasively to imply, is scarcely to be assumed, even if it is not to be dismissed at once as fantastic. None of the many hundreds of psychopaths whom I have observed showed any such pictures as one gets from reading this quotation in the context that is given. Although such stigmata and such gross brain changes are sometimes associated with mental deficiency, cerebral agenesis, and various organic diseases, they are certainly not regarded as characteristic of psychopathic personality. In fact, if such abnormalities as these were found in a patient, the diagnosis of organic brain disease, mental deficiency, or of some definite heredodegenerative condition would become inescapable and the diagnosis of *psychopathic personality* (or *personality disorder, antisocial type*) would become unlikely if not impossible.*

After other brief descriptions the author under discussion adds a statement that is all but incredible. Following the opinion that prognosis is hopeless for complete recovery, it is asserted that psychopaths are not likely to improve "unless a psychiatrist can take them in hand for six months to a year and teach them how to live." Under these conditions great improvement is considered probable. It is quite clear that more than a few different and extremely unlike things are being considered. Though all these are grouped under one name, they do not thereby gain homogeneity. Nor does it seem

---

*In Henry's original text, from which the quotation was taken by Sadler, this list of physical deformities and organic brain and spinal cord diseases and abnormalities precedes a description of mental deficiency, to which it has pertinent application.

helpful for purposes of description, study, or treatment to approach either the psychopath or patients of these other types in such a manner.

A few paragraphs beyond the account of physical defects and gross neurologic abnormalities just quoted we find the description of a subtype, "the feebly inhibited," which includes these interesting statements:

> On the functional side these individuals are notoriously subject to "general nervousness." "Specifically, we find tremors, facial or other tics (habit spasms), abnormal movements of the eyes, headaches, little attacks of dizziness, enuresis, prolonged throughout childhood, and so on." The organs of the special senses are particularly apt to show signs of inferiority; defective vision is very common.

Any person familiar with the psychopath as he is met in clinical experience will need no prompting to realize what confusion is likely to ensue if the medical student tries to reconcile books and facts at this point.

Let us give a little more attention to these statements. The book from which they are taken was published in 1936. The last quotation is to be found, repeated precisely to the last comma, in another volume by Sadler published in 1945. It is of interest to note that the entire passage also appears in *The Individual Delinquent* (William Healy, 1915), a work that expresses concepts widely accepted and congruent with the terminology at that time but at confusing variance with official standards in 1936* and long ago discarded by Healy. Though no longer representing the thoughts of the original author or the criteria of the American Psychiatric Association, this archaic concept is carried verbatim in a textbook published twenty-one years later and in another published thirty years later.

And with all this we find other statements, some applicable to the real psychopath and apparently so directed but plainly incongruous, if not indeed fantastic, if we attempt to correlate them with the material just quoted from the same volume. For instance, it is said of these people that "they suffer from no physical or mental disease that would account for their deficiency." (What about those brains abnormally large or small and defective in part or as a whole? What about tumor, infection, cerebral hemorrhage? What about paralyses and "gross physical defects of the . . . nose . . . legs . . . anus"?)

The confusion about our subject as it has been so often presented in psychiatric textbooks should not be peremptorily attributed to carelessness or ignorance on the part of the authors. It is worthwhile for us to remember that these authors are attempting to treat many disparate and not a few distinctly incongruous matters under a single heading. Even today our officially approved standards demand that a good many different disorders be so treated. Often we find much broader and more heterogeneous areas embraced, and such a motley conglomeration of diverse subjects appears under a single label that even the most sagacious author can say little without falling at once into paradox, error, and soon into absurdity. His statements may be sound, accurate, and entirely pertinent to the various subjects he, perchance, has in mind and at the same

---

*It is only proper to emphasize that Dr. Healy's subsequent writings do not suggest any identification of the type of patients we are discussing with other sorts of disorder related to organic brain disease. His work, on the contrary, stands out among the most valuable efforts of those who have helped clarify these matters.

time ring loud with nonsense as they strike willy-nilly upon other and alien subjects all forced under a single identifying term that applies to nothing except in language.

The second tendency, already mentioned, is illustrated in the brief space (five pages) of the textbook we have been discussing. Not only do we find many dissimilar subjects treated under one term, but also a record of ambitious attempts to devise subtypes on a superficially descriptive basis unrelated to the real and obvious differences (such as, for instance, between a patient with cerebral agenesis and a typical psychopath). We are given the various "types" as listed by Kraepelin, Schneider, and Partridge:

Kraeplin	*Schneider*	*Partridge*
1. The excitable	1. The hyperthymic	1. The delinquent
2. The unstable	2. The depressive	2. The inadequate
3. The impulsive	3. The insecure	3. Those with general incompatibility
4. The eccentric	4. The fanatic	
5. The liars and swindlers	5. The self-seeking	
6. The antisocial	6. The emotionally unstable	
7. The quarrelsome	7. The explosive	
	8. The affectless	
	9. The weak-willed	
	10. The asthenic	

To these Sadler adds his own list of types:

1. Kleptomania
2. Pathologic liars
3. Eccentrics
4. Sex abnormalities
5. The feebly inhibited

Is it an exaggeration if we say that the difficulties confronting the psychiatrist or layman who has had to approach the psychopath through such a tangle of concepts (and it has been the traditional method) are comparable with those which would be faced by a general practitioner discussing leukemia if this term meant also a broken leg, hemorrhoids, pregnancy, brain tumor, and the common cold? And if there were no other term available!

Throughout the second quarter of this century Kahn's treatise entitled *Psychopathic Personalities* was, judging by references in textbooks and in the psychiatric journals, generally regarded as the authoritative and the most useful source of information about our present subject. This I believe to be scarcely less unfortunate than paradoxical. Here we have a valuable and scholarly work by a distinguished psychiatrist, a large volume embodying the author's fundamental concepts of personality structure and psychopathology in general. But we find little or nothing in all this material that has any pertinent relation to our group of patients. We find, in fact, all the psychoneuroses treated under the heading *psychopathic personality* and a list of sixteen categories that seem occasionally to touch but never to clarify our subject. Kahn's use of the term *psychopathic personality* is, in my opinion, not only justifiable but more in accordance with its obvious literal meaning than our customary use. Such questions are, however, not particularly germane. The point that demands emphasis is that our chief scientific work generally regarded for a couple of decades as authoritative in the field turns out not to be a book about the psychopath but a careful and valuable study of other subjects. Among these subjects it is difficult to find material related to our problem.

In his work, which is primarily concerned with psychopathology in general, Kahn, in accordance with established practice, lists types that have been almost universally quoted as characteristic subdivisions into which the psychopath can be classified:

1. The nervous
2. The anxious
3. The sensitive
4. The compulsive
5. The excitable
6. The hyperthymic
7. The depressive
8. The moody
9. The affectively cold
10. The weak-willed
11. The impulsive
12. The sexually perverse
13. The hysterical
14. The fantastic
15. The cranks
16. The eccentric

The authors whom we have quoted and briefly discussed are not responsible for the confusion that surrounds the psychopath. Such an approach to the subject was the traditional approach that for decades prevailed in psychiatry. Even the most wise and painstaking efforts cannot clarify a subject unless the subject is available. Many of the works mentioned I hold in high respect. In them other subjects are handled in such a way that those who seek reliable information can find it without undue difficulty.

It is hoped that these points may help us keep in mind that in our attempts to understand the psychopath we must struggle not only with the intrinsic problem of trying to distinguish and evaluate a complex psychiatric disorder but also with an almost impregnable approach. To touch our subject itself we must somehow make our way through a surrounding zone dense with false or dubious assumptions, mined with terms that at the same time make sense and nonsense. The approach to our subject is, furthermore, still skillfully camouflaged by traditional influences that may, before we know it, have us talking about two or four or seven other things, no matter how earnestly we strive to speak of one at a time.

Since the last edition of this book was published, discussion of the psychopath has continued and further attempts have been made to evaluate his status. A remarkable, and curiously misleading, presentation of the subject was offered by a lay writer, Alan Harrington, first in the popular magazine *Playboy* and later in *Psychopaths,* a book amplifying his theme.

A serious and regrettable confusion, I believe, is likely to come from opinions quoted by this author that seem very plainly to advocate that the psychopath be admired, chosen as a leader, or at least as a model for others. Referring to one of these opinions, the author says, "The menacing psychopath is embraced. Incredibly . . . it seems at first shock . . . we are urged to turn into an 'antithetical' version of the outlaw and find our way to his radical vision of the universe."

Some of the people quoted or cited by the author of the *Playboy* article (and the subsequent book) seem to be spokesmen for, or prominent figures in, the recent movement of rebellion often referred to as the *counterculture.* In this movement we find zealots who embrace hallucinatory confusion under the influence of potentially brain-damaging psychedelic drugs and aggressively proclaim it as religious experience. Here, too, we find the antihero, often a figure flaunting treason and dishonor along with his unkept beard, barefootedness, and defiantly frayed blue jeans. In this so-called *counterculture* the *antihero* was not only welcomed but by some virtually enshrined. It has been fashionable also in this movement to degrade the high passion and glory of sexual love to a significance not far from that of a belch. Perhaps, in this general and heedless effort to reverse the basic values, almost anything traditionally regarded as undesirable, or despicable, might be automatically stamped with the sign of approval.

After many quotations from people who may be reflecting elements of this movement, the author himself encourages us to "ask . . . if the psychopath's time has come, [if] there may be a world-wide need for him." He goes on to say, "Could the coming of the psychopath be a natural and inevitable result of our drastically deteriorating environment (which helps fling him up) as well as one answer to it and, who knows, a potential remedy for such deterioration?"

Other opinions expressed by the author include these: "Although originally founded upon an anti-social condition, it [psychopathy] offers exciting new alternatives to the way we have lived until now. . . . the distinction blurs hopelessly between present day psychopathic patterns as observed in prisons, institutions and clinics, and equivalent behavior, which may often be put to use in good causes outside of these places. . . . would it be best," he asks, "to teach our children the psychopathic style in order that they may survive?" He speaks of "brilliant individuals among us that are basing their own lives on the psychopathic model" and, referring to them, he cites the opinion that "what was formerly diagnosed mental illness has turned into the new spirit of the age." He seems quite serious in repeatedly asking if we should imitate the psychopath, if we should "yield to insanity accepted as normal? Cultivate one's own latent psychopathy, perhaps trying to adapt it to good ends?" He also says, "Conceivably the times are calling for an idealized version of the psychopath as savior."

Other quotations are given from writers who claim that psychopaths should be considered as having found the great answers to life. In response to such opinions, the author asks, "Have we come to the hour of the psychopath, the advent of psychopathic man . . . [when] what was once presumed to be a state of illness is abruptly declared to be a state of health. . . . Can it be true that, with the dramatic appearance of the psychopathic ideal, a new man has come upon us, that in order to survive the turbulent years ahead, far from seeking to treat the psychopath in clinics, we should rather emulate him, learn how to become him?"

Such opinions as these, and many others quoted or expressed directly by the author, give rise to a number of thoughts. First, let me say that the question of whether or not it is desirable to be a psychopath seems not so much a real question as a pretext for sophistry, for a sophistry that is not only obvious but monumentally frivolous. It strongly suggests to me the sort of argument that might arise about whether or not a physician should use treatment in behalf of the patient or in behalf of the microorganisms that are in the process of killing him.

It is true that the psychopath is extremely difficult to understand or to explain. Confusion has often arisen about just what is indicated by the term. Any reasonable, sane person who feels or says that we should emulate the psychopath must, one might presume, have a poor understanding of what the term indicates and must, surely, be talking about something else. Textbooks over the years, as we know, have often listed widely differing disorders under this term. A sincere choice of the real psychopath as model or leader by anyone familiar with the subject would be beyond absurdity.

Even in these times of fiercely dictated permissiveness, this choice would have to be called by the currently censored but quite accurate terms *perverse* and *degenerate.* A true taste for the psychopath as leader or model, or as object of admiration, also suggests to me the peculiarly pathologic and unappealing aestheticism of Huysmans's fictional character, des Esseintes, who, after withdrawing from nearly all natural activities, takes another step:

> And a pale smile hovered over his lips when finally his servant brought him a nourishing enema compounded with peptone and informed his master that he was to repeat the little operation three times every twenty-four hours.
>
> The thing was successfully carried out and des Esseintes could not help secretly congratulating himself on the event which was a coping stone, the crowning triumph, in a sort, of the life he had contrived for himself. His predilection for the artificial had now, and that without any initiative on his part, attained its supreme fulfillment. A man could hardly go farther; nourishment thus absorbed was surely the last aberration from the natural that could be committed.
>
> What a delicious thing he said to himself it would be if one could, once restored to health, go on with the same simple regime. . . . Last but not least, what a direct insult cast in the face of old Mother Nature, whose never varying exigencies would be forever nullified.

The basic judgment and the moral orientation underlying a deliberate choice of the actual psychopath as model or leader could hardly deserve more consideration or respect than the judgment and orientation leading to a militant demand that Richard Speck be installed as National Supervisor of Nursing Education in the United States and that the Congressional Medal of Honor be awarded to the Boston Strangler.

CLARIFYING THE APPROACH

Despite the difficulties that have been discussed, efforts to study the psychopath have proceeded. No drastic change in the official psychiatric attitude has occurred, and no step has been taken to make it possible to deal satisfactorily with the disorder by medical methods. But information has been accumulating that may someday bring this about.

The studies of Partridge have been valuable in focusing attention on the type of patient who needs attention as a separate entity rather than in a confused group. In his writing can be found a discernible and well-presented clinical picture. Partridge's three general types include only psychopaths, and the relatively modest distinctions among them impress us as valid rather than imaginary. Here, too, we find a clear rejection of the time-honored assumption that psychopaths are marked by gross physical defects and "stigmata of degeneration" and that this disorder has been satisfactorily related to inborn defects. This valuable contribution, though largely ignored by many authorities, merits recognition.

Long ago, when the psychopath was, even more than at present, confusingly submerged in a nonspecific category (known only by terms applied also to a wide variety of gross physical defect states), Healy and those who worked with him began to emphasize the purposive or reactive nature of antisocial behavior. Careful attention was given to the emotional deprivations and distortions of aim that lay behind maladapted acts, and evidence of influences essentially psychogenic were noted and evaluated.

In work with juvenile delinquents, Healy pointed out that under similar conditions of insecurity or emotional deprivation one child might show anxiety and passive withdrawal and another, aggressive mischief, apparently in response to the personal stress. These observations have been helpful over the years in efforts to interpret and to deal with behavior disorder.

Although relatively neglected for a long period by those concerned with interpretive or causal as contrasted with simply descriptive formulations, the psychopath received attention from Alexander, who makes an interesting contrast between ordinary neurosis, in which repressed impulses find a symbolic or substitutive expression in subjectively unpleasant symptoms, and character neurosis, in which the unconscious drives are believed to appear in maladapted objective behavior. In both disorders unconscious conflict is postulated. In orthodox neurosis this conflict may give rise to conscious anxiety without visible source, or impulses (repressed and ungratified) may be manifested indirectly by displacement (as in obsessions and compulsions), or otherwise (as in conversion paralysis and anesthesia). In character neurosis, according to Alexander, unconscious impulses obtain a degree of fulfillment in another manner, by a pattern of pathologic behavior in which apparently purposeless and sometimes self-defeating antisocial acts are carried out persistently. This pattern is followed despite penalties and in the absence of adequate conscious incentive. This formulation has attracted much popular interest.

Alexander maintained, and many of his followers still maintain, that the antisocial conduct often represents an unconscious but purposive effort to obtain punishment in order to expiate and gain relief from (unconscious) feelings of guilt. As a hypothesis this is indeed ingenious and appealing. It has attracted many adherents. I have not been able, however, to discover such a sense of guilt or remorse (conscious or unconscious) in any of the psychopaths I have studied. Nor have I seen any convincing evidence of such unconscious guilt revealed in the work of Alexander or of other observers who accept his formulation. Such guilt is often assumed but, so far as I know, never demonstrated. I must therefore remain skeptical of this popular interpretation, however pleasant it might be to solve the problem of the psychopath by an interpretation so simple and so graceful.

The more experience I have had with psychopaths, the stranger it has seemed to me that a theory should insist that they have such deep and influential unconscious feelings of guilt when they are at the same time so plainly callous and free from remorse about grievous wrongs and crimes that they clearly recognize as their own. It strikes me as a quaint fantasy to assume without real evidence that they unconsciously go to such pains to obtain punishment and win redemption for unknown sins when they plainly and glibly ignore responsibility for every known misdemeanor and felony and pride themselves in evading penalties and in flouting the basic principles of justice.

The term *neurotic character* adopted by Alexander to designate the psychopath, although it may be of value in suggesting belief in a psychogenic etiology, is not conducive to progress in dealing with our problem. This point has been well emphasized by Karl Menninger in a discussion of the practical need of a new official name for the psychopath. As pointed out by Menninger, the word *character* in such a use offers possibilities of confusion. If one patient has a neurotic character and another a neurotic personality, then just what is a character? And just what is a personality? And just how do they differ? There is, we may emphasize again, a considerable possibility of arousing the ghosts of a faculty psychology in the use of these terms.

Menninger makes another point in speaking of neurotic character that I believe is of essential importance. "The condition" he writes, "is closer to a psychosis than to a neurosis and the term neurotic is, therefore, misleading."

A helpful study of the psychopath by Henderson presented in the Salmon Lectures (1938) and subsequently published called attention to the seriousness of the problem. From this presentation the reader is able to get clear ideas about actual patients as they appear clinically and the need for better methods of handling them.

Over a period of several decades Karpman also called attention to the psychopath, pointing out how little serious effort has been made by psychiatrists to understand or to deal with the essential problem. He maintained that psychogenic factors are responsible for the behavior disorder in many instances and believed that most patients classified as psychopathic personality should be called neurotic. A small residue of patients for whom he proposed the term *anethopath,* are, in Karpman's opinion, essentially unlike the others in that they are disabled by intrinsic defect rather than by dynamic psychopathologic reactions.

In these studies the very great egocentricity, the inability to form any important or binding attachment to another, the failure ever to realize and grasp the very meaning of responsibility, all features that I believe to be most essential, are emphasized by Karpman and made clear as seldom done in other literature on the psychopath. It is doubtful if anyone else has done more to elucidate this psychopathologic picture and similar antisocial behavior disorders.

In the system of classification that prevailed when the first two editions of this book were prepared, the diagnosis of psychopathic personality was listed among those conditions considered as being "without mental disorder." In the New York State Department of Mental Hygiene *Outlines for Psychiatric Care* the general term was subdivided as follows:

> *Psychopathic personality*
>
> With pathologic sexuality. Indicate symptomatic manifestations, e.g.: homosexuality, erotomania, sexual perversion, sexual immaturity.
>
> With pathologic emotionality. Indicate symptomatic manifestations, e.g.: schizoid personality, cyclothymic personality, paranoid personality, emotional instability.
>
> With asocial or amoral trends. Indicate symptomatic manifestations, e.g.: antisociality, pathologic mendacity, moral deficiency, vagabondage, misanthropy.
>
> Mixed types.

The first division, *pathologic sexuality,* will be discussed in Chapters 5 and 6. Suffice it to say here that only the last term, *sexual immaturity,* has been characteristic of our group.

In the second division, *pathologic emotionality,* the schizoid, cyclothymic, and paranoid personalities are regarded as relatively mild and relatively static deviations of the same types familiar in schizophrenia, manic-depressive psychosis, and paranoid psychosis. Their disorder or disability is very different clinically from that discussed in this volume. The typical psychopath shows little or no indication of suffering from a deviation in the direction of such a disorder as schizophrenia, manic-depressive psychosis, or paranoia but shows a disorder quite different. Characteristic schizoid or cyclothymic traits are not discernible features of the psychopath. Although psychopaths tend to blame their troubles on others, they do not, like patients with real paranoid deviation, organize and persistently follow out highly purposive plans or hold tenaciously to strong affective attitudes. Emotional instability is, in a shallow sense, applicable to the psychopath, but this quality scarcely seems an outstanding or fundamental deviation. Many, as a matter of fact, show less evidence of anxiety, uneasiness, and other reactions implied by emotional instability than the average person.

The descriptive terms included in the third category apply in varying degrees to many of the patients discussed here, but these scarcely seem either broad enough or deep enough to be of value as diagnostic formulations.

Under one term, *psychopathic personality,* we find grouped many types of disorder. These disorders have very little in common. One thing that has been presumed about some of them, that is, that they are relatively trivial as contrasted with extremely disabling conditions, we grant, so far as schizoid personality, cyclothymic personality, and paranoid personality are concerned. This characteristic of being an incomplete degree of various sorts of disorder we deny as applying to the subject of this volume. Only by a manipulation of verbal abstractions can such disorders be identified with the specific disorder shown by those regularly called psychopaths.

In the 1952 revision of the *Diagnostic and Statistical Manual* we find the general term *personality disorders* used to designate all the various items formerly listed under *psychopathic personality*—all these and several more.

Personality disorders

- Personality pattern disturbance
  - Inadequate personality
  - Schizoid personality
  - Cyclothymic personality
  - Paranoid personality
- Personality trait disturbance
  - Emotionally unstable personality
  - Passive-aggressive personality
  - Compulsive personality
  - Personality trait disturbance, other
- Sociopathic personality disturbance
  - Antisocial reaction
  - Dyssocial reaction
  - Sexual deviation; specify supplementary term
  - Addiction
    - Alcoholism
    - Drug addiction
- Special symptom reaction
  - Learning disturbance
  - Speech disturbance
  - Enuresis
  - Somnambulism
  - Other

Transient situational personality disturbance

- Gross stress reaction
- Adult situational reaction
- Adjustment reaction of infancy
- Adjustment reaction of childhood
  - Habit disturbance
  - Conduct disturbance
  - Neurotic traits
- Adjustment reaction of adolescence
- Adjustment reaction of late life

In this long list of items, *sociopathic personality disturbance, antisocial reaction,* is thus defined:

> This term refers to chronically antisocial individuals who are always in trouble, profiting neither from experience nor punishment, and maintaining no real loyalties to any person, group, or code. They are frequently callous and hedonistic, showing marked emotional immaturity, with lack of sense of responsibility, lack of judgment, and an ability to rationalize their behavior so that it appears warranted, reasonable, and justified.
>
> The term includes cases previously classified as "constitutional psychopathic state" and "psychopathic personality." As defined here the term is more limited, as well as more specific in its application.

Here the familiar psychopath could be accurately and officially classified. It seems to me regrettably confusing that under the same general heading of *personality disorders* there were still listed such astonishingly unallied minor difficulties as *learning disturbance, speech disturbance, enuresis,* and *somnambulism.*

Since the 1952 revision of the psychiatric nomenclature just mentioned, another revision of our official terminology was made. The following classification is given:

V. PERSONALITY DISORDERS AND CERTAIN OTHER NONPSYCHOTIC MENTAL DISORDERS (301-304)

301 Personality disorders
- .0 Paranoid personality
- .1 Cyclothymic personality ((Affective personality))
- .2 Schizoid personality
- .3 Explosive personality
- .4 Obsessive compulsive personality ((Anankastic personality))
- .5 Hysterical personality
- .6 Asthenic personality
- .7 Antisocial personality
- .81 Passive-aggressive personality
- .82 Inadequate personality
- .89 Other personality disorders of specified types
- [.9 Unspecified personality disorder]

In this classification we find a more distinct place for our subject than in the earlier schemes of classification. Here the psychopath is officially designated as personality disorder, antisocial type, a recognizable entity in a fairly large group of different and distinct disorders.

It is perhaps in silent recognition of the absurdities that prevailed for so long in our official categories that psychiatrists in practice still avail themselves of the more or less slang term which is a sort of nickname for our subject. When one psychiatrist on the staff of a state hospital, or at a meeting of the American Psychiatric Association, expresses to another some thought he has about the *psychopath,* it is immediately and plainly understood that he is not making reference to schizoid disorder or to sexual deviation *per se* but to a disorder nearly all psychiatrists recognize and recognize as distinct from the heterogeneous mess of unrelated disorders with which it was for so long officially listed. There is nothing vague about these patients clinically. Their course of conduct can be predicted with much greater accuracy than that of patients with defined psychoses.

Attempts to discuss this type of patient and to use the approved term *personality disorder* in its official meaning were until recently likely to be neither clear nor accurate. In fact, it was difficult not to talk nonsense if one bore in mind all the things that term was recognized as including.

The currently approved category *personality disorder, antisocial type* seems to offer an accurate term and to avoid the great confusion promoted by earlier schemes of classification. It is probable, however, that the older unofficial term *psychopath* will maintain its currency for a long time. All experienced psychiatrists are used to it, and few, if any, are likely to be misled by it.

chapter 5 · A comparison with other disorders

PURPOSE OF THIS STEP

Some material has been presented in which manifestations of the disorder occur. It is our task to arrange it in such a way that its features can be seen clearly and compared with the features of other disorders. Such a step should be helpful in our efforts to recognize what we are dealing with and to evaluate it. Let us compare these patients known as psychopaths with others showing clinical illness and deviated reactions or patterns of living. Significant details should emerge, differentiation should become clearer, and distinguishing features of our subject should become more apparent.

The contrast with some surrounding types is so obvious that only a few points need be made. In discussing other disorders not so clearly defined and those traditionally confused with the psychopath, more extensive consideration is demanded. When there are important common characteristics between the two groups compared, it may be worthwhile to go into even more detail and bring out all features that can be helpful in delineating our subject. Only a few paragraphs or pages will be given to the discussion of some items that follow. To others which deserve it, a great deal more space will be devoted.

In this chapter we shall consider the psychopath's relation to the following subjects:

1. The psychotic
2. Deviations recognized as similar to the psychoses but regarded as incomplete or less severe reactions
3. The psychoneurotic
4. The mental defective
5. The ordinary criminal
6. Other character and behavior disorders, including delinquency
7. A case showing circumscribed behavior disorder
8. Specific homosexuality and other consistent sexual deviations
9. The erratic man of genius
10. The injudicious hedonist and some other drinkers
11. The clinical alcoholic
12. Fictional characters of psychiatric interest
13. The psychopath in history

THE PSYCHOTIC

For the sake of emphasis let us first contrast very briefly the psychopath with the general group of psychotic patients to which he is considered not to belong. These, if their disorder is well advanced, are usually recognized by the law as "insane" and by the man on the street as irrational, irresponsible, plainly unable to accept the general facts accepted by humanity at large, and, furthermore, unable to provide for themselves or to remain safely or conveniently at liberty among their fellows. Such people frequently have beliefs that are not only false but bizarre, inconsistent, and nearly always impossible to remove even by convincing demonstrations of their impossibility. Ready examples are the belief of a soda jerk that he is an emperor dead a thousand years ago, a belief still maintained although the patient admits he is living in the twentieth century and realizes that he is in a psychiatric hospital and that he grew up in the local slums, and the belief of an inconspicuous clerk that a worldwide organization has been formed to persecute him because of jealousy aroused by the fact that his testicles are pure radium.

Many of these patients hear voices speaking to them and cannot be made to see that these are imaginary. To the layman they are plainly not people to reason with or to be relied on but are obviously "demented." It is apparent that they do and say foolish or fantastic things because their reasoning processes, not to speak of their perceptions, are gravely disordered or misdirected. Their general personality outlines are often distorted or sometimes even appear to be destroyed.

Patients in whom a milder psychosis exists usually show some of these specific peculiarities and always show general personality deviations which enable the psychiatrist eventually to place them in their proper classification. These patients with a milder disorder often are able to get along without serious difficulty in the community, just as a patient with mild influenza may not even go to bed whereas one with a severe attack may lie delirious, unable to sit up, and finally die. These milder degrees of psychosis, however, show the same type of disorder found in the more severe and obvious manifestations, just as the mild influenza attack is the same in type but not in degree as the serious one.

It is perhaps worthwhile to add here that not all those suffering from a typical psychosis, even when the disorder is serious in degree, give an obvious impression of derangement. Severe paranoid conditions, particularly those of the most malignant type, may exist for years in persons who lack all superficial signs that the layman often feels should be apparent to establish psychosis (insanity).

Sometimes such people appear not only normal but brilliant, and their powers of reasoning in all areas except those dominated by delusion are intact. The delusions themselves may even be withheld when the excellent judgment of the subject discerns that they will not be accepted by others or may interfere with psychotic plans toward which he is assiduously and ingeniously working. "Why, if I'd let the public in on these facts, a lot of fools might have thought I was insane," one such patient explained. Another patient, who had for years been hearing imaginary voices which he accepted as real, admitted that he denied this to the draft board because, "They might have thought something was wrong with my mind." He had been doing a satisfactory job and, on the surface, making a good social adjustment in his community. He was accepted for service in the army.

Another man with clear-cut paranoid delusions prospered for years by selling stocks and bonds to opulent widows and to others in whom his enthusiastic optimism and shrewd reasoning powers worked marvelous conviction. He was indeed persuasive. To my definite knowledge he induced a friend to believe that serious mental disorder threatened him, or was perhaps already present. Offering to help the friend, who naturally became alarmed, the paranoiac made arrangements for his hospitalization and, accompanying the other, had him voluntarily admitted to a psychiatric institution. After a period of observation the friend was found to be free of any such trouble. Months later the real patient's delusional system was elicited and his commitment deemed necessary.

Even today one often encounters popular misconceptions of what constitutes psychosis or seriously disabling "mental disorder" that seem to belong to earlier centuries. Even when a patient is speaking frankly and continually about hearing voices from the next county (or the next world), relatives occasionally express surprise at the opinion that anything could be wrong with his *mind,* insisting that he had been running the store as well as ever, adding up the accounts without error, and showing his usual common sense in daily affairs.

Fanatics and false prophets who show real but not so obvious signs of classic psychosis, as everyone must by now have learned, sometimes attract hundreds or thousands of followers who contribute large funds to projects founded on delusion. If news reports by many observers can be relied upon, even those showing plain evidence of very serious disorder, persons as fully psychotic as many on the wards of the state hospitals, also succeed in appearing to large groups not only as sage leaders or men with supernatural powers but also as God.

The psychopath, on the other hand, is free of all technical signs of this sort. There are no demonstrable defects in theoretical reasoning. At least he is free of them in the same sense that the general run of men and women are free. He carries out his activities in what is regarded as ordinary awareness of the consequences and without the distorting influences of any demonstrable system of delusions. His personality outline is apparently or superficially intact and not obviously distorted.

The diagnostic formulation *psychosis with psychopathic personality,* listed in the nomenclature that was official until 1952, deserves attention. Such a psychosis was thus defined by the *Outlines for Psychiatric Examinations* (1943):

> The abnormal reactions which bring psychopathic personalities into the group of psychoses are varied in form but usually of an episodic character. Most prominent are attacks of irritability, excitement, depression, paranoid episodes, transient confused states, etc. . . . True prison psychoses belong in this group.
>
> A psychopathic personality with a manic-depressive attack should be classed in the manic-depressive group and likewise a psychopathic personality with a schizophrenic psychosis should go in the dementia praecox group. Psychopathic personalities without episodic mental attack or psychotic symptoms should be placed in the group "without psychosis."

In agreement with Cruvant and Yochelson, I cannot see that anything was gained through such a classification. If a psychopath develops some other disorder such as schizophrenia or affective psychosis, the additional disorder can be listed properly without recourse to such an appellation as that just mentioned. So, too, if transient confusional states occur, they may be so classified in the psychopath as in others.

Such a category promoted confusion by implying the presence of a specific psychotic illness different from, and in addition to, the psychopath's essential disorder and that this, even if it is correctly listed as schizophrenia, or paranoid psychosis, needed the further qualification *with psychopathic personality.* The transient confusional states considered by some as a characteristic reaction of psychopaths to imprisonment are usually trivial (minor) additions to or complications of the very serious, incapacitating disorder that is fundamental. Such manifestations might be compared with those of a schizophrenic patient who by chance also develops temporary delirium.

If the psychopath develops a major or minor disorder of a type classed among "the psychoses," it can be signified by addition of the usual term, just as if he had developed brain tumor or peptic ulcer. There seems to be neither need of nor warrant for a hybridizing concept which does nothing to clarify but a good deal to cloud the issues. I am not sure there was ever much more need for "psychosis with psychopathic personality" than for "psychosis with red hair" or "neurosis with a Ph.D. degree." The current nomenclature appears better designed to avoid unnecessary confusions of this sort. Influences of the older terminologies, concepts, and classifications, however, probably still play a part in serious misunderstandings about the psychopath that have not yet been satisfactorily resolved.

DEVIATIONS RECOGNIZED AS SIMILAR TO THE PSYCHOSES BUT REGARDED AS INCOMPLETE OR LESS SEVERE REACTIONS

As noted earlier, conditions resembling psychoses but appearing incomplete or less severe are still classified officially under the same general diagnostic term as the disorder to which this book is devoted. Such an arrangement has been approved by some as a means of placing together groups assumed to be on the borderline of serious disorder with a genuine similarity in degree if not in type. There is another argument in favor of using one term to identify these diverse clinical realities. This arises from efforts to distinguish as active disease processes the psychoses and psychoneuroses from other conditions presumed to be circumscribed defect states or relatively static deviations. It is true that some genuine similarities can be discerned here among many of the diverse conditions listed under *personality disorders.* These similarities have, it seems to me, been given an undue importance.

It is far from proved that pathologic conditions that we call schizoid personality or paranoid personality begin at birth and remain unchanged throughout life. There is a vast range of difference in chronicity, reversibility, severity, and prognosis, throughout the schizoid disorders and, indeed, throughout the paranoid and affective disorders also. Much would be gained both logically and practically if in our official nomenclature we could place all essentially schizoid disorders in an appropriate category and then make what further distinctions are useful as to transiency, chronicity, and degree. Since schizoid manifestations vary from rapid processes to maladjustments apparently static, from relatively mild deviations and disabilities to total incapacity and maximum personality disintegration, let us then reflect these facts in our language. As a matter of fact, as every psychiatrist well knows, in many patients an initial disorder of slow or rapid progress (disease process) becomes static or relatively static at widely varying levels of deviation from the normal. So too, it seems, we should deal with affective and paranoid disorders. Without minimizing the fact that schizophrenia is an illness, it is perhaps more profitable to conceive of it as a complicated distortion of the life process (or, as has been said, *a way of life,* albeit an extremely pathologic way) than as a circumscribed external agency that selects and falls upon its victim. Active and progressive schizophrenic illness probably arises out of tendencies and influences not unlike those which underlie the milder and more static distortions we label as schizoid personality.

In many important respects it seems to me that the person who is called a psychopath or antisocial personality differs greatly from most people showing a schizoid, paranoid, or cyclothymic disorder or deviation in degree short of psychosis and in whatever state of chronicity. The psychopath varies not only in type but also in the severity of his specific disorder, which can range from a mild or borderline degree that allows him to conduct a relatively normal and acceptable life up through great degrees of disability. There are also behavior patterns of this sort which prove to be temporary.

It will perhaps be worthwhile to consider briefly an example from the secondary group distinguished under various subheadings (schizoid, cyclothymic, and others) and officially classed with the psychopath in a primary pigeon hole labeled *personality disorders.*

Well qualified for the diagnosis of schizoid personality is a 19-year-old whom I treated on several occasions. I would prefer to call his reaction one definitely schizoid in nature, very chronic and relatively static, and lacking most clinical features by which disorders otherwise similar are recognized as constituting "a psychosis." The first point that stands out in this patient is how obviously he differs from all psychopaths. On meeting him, it is immediately seen that he is a lonely person, one recognized as queer by all who encounter him. In discussing his recent attempt at suicide, he could give no good reason for his act. No evidence of depression was obtained. As if not knowing what else to say, he suggested he must have tried to kill himself "just out of curiosity." He had no positive convictions about a future life or interest in exploring such possibilities. He had been making good grades at college and he had no worries that he could express. His attempt at suicide had been authentic. Only by chance had he been discovered where he hung in a noose made by his belt. No evidence of delusions or hallucinations was ever elicited. A few excerpts from a report given by the college physician, who spent much time with him, are contributory:

> Oliver was recognized as a bit odd or eccentric since his coming here during the summer weeks of 19____. He worked quite willingly with sustained effort and application. Everyone liked him and although they protested his persistent pipe and untidy personal appearance (being unshaven, lax about clean garments and combed hair), they were amused and tolerant. He had the reputation of having superior intellectual capacity and that gave him the aura of a potential winner. The students included him in everything and he was a conflicting mixture of pathetic eagerness to be accepted as one of them and to be the lone wolf. He went through the motions of being one of the group but it all had to be within the boundaries of his own withdrawal pattern. Though unresponsive in regard to greetings and small talk, he would talk for hours about himself and his ideas and was eager for such expression.
>
> Girls interested him less. Actually, though he protested that he had an average interest in the other sex, he had very few dates with them. However, very recently he

groomed himself quite adequately and went to Foxbridge to visit a girl whom he used to date during his high school days and who is studying journalism there.

It was noted and accepted by everyone that Oliver would argue every point, in class and out, but much good-natured teasing caused him to restrain himself somewhat in this respect. However, I have noted in all my contacts with him a persistent negativistic attitude. He prided himself on always taking the opposite point of view and that his philosophy was quite peculiar to himself. He expressed a resentment of everything "expected" of him by way of the simplest courtesies and social amenities of any kind.

He is sure that there is nothing neurotic about himself and mentioned doctors and nurses other than yourself who have told him that they thought him to be all right. He exhibits an attitude toward his hospitalization quite similar to that toward his attempted suicide. His defense is thick and strong and he reacts with argument or denial to almost anything which is said which seems to imply that all is not quite as it should be with him. He said that you had told him that he would need some help and had better come to see me every few days. He thinks that is not necessary and I think he is right, for I can see no way to approach him even on the outskirts of his problem without stimulating a negative reaction on his part. I noted that same lack of insight as you, and it is so complete as to bar any psychotherapeutic relation. I left the way open for him to come at any time and I will indeed help if I can.

This fragment from Oliver's personal notes also brings out something about his state that is difficult to describe in any other way I know:

Loneliness
By
Oliver ________, Jr.

It is now long after the hour of midnight. I am alone, except for my pipe and my ever-active mind, in one of the front rooms.

God has created many horrible things, but the greatest of all those monsters is that intolerable loneliness that man calls Love, Sex, Self-Pity, Comradeship, *und so weiter.* I trust that you, as an individual, shall be able to grasp some vague notion of what I, as a purely abstract thinking-apparatus, am trying to convey to you.

Nothing in a State of Nothingness. Can you imagine a more comforting place? No emotions of fear, love, hate, anger, sympathy, pity. No materiality! No spirituality! No mentality! Nothing!!! The Hell of the Bible! The Heaven of the Bible! Paradise! Purgatory! and the Inferno!—all One!! All nothing!!!

Have you ever really delved deeply into why, for what purpose you were born or why anyone was born? To bear children? Yes, but dogs can do that gracefully. To build? To make money? You must leave all behind when you depart. You are unable to carry it with you.

The epicureans had a good idea when they said, "Eat, drink and be merry, for tomorrow we may die." But why eat, drink, and be merry? Why should one live, or the animals which are so very close below us? There is no God; there is no Heaven; there is no Hell; these are the dreams of baby minds. The Church, the Bible, Science, Spiritualism, and on and on and on can offer not a solitary shred of evidence that there is a God, Heaven, Hell, Devil, Angels. They are but wistful thinkers—the Church, the Bible, and Spiritualism. They are the idealists. Scientists are the realists, but they study nature. Why build machines? What can it matter to you personally one hundred years from now? You will be nothing. Nothing.

Am I insane? They say I am because I ask, "Why?" and there is no answer to that by anyone. "What?" can be answered. So can "When?" "Where?" "Who?" "How?" et cetera, but not "Why?" Healthy minds do not ask, "Why?" Normal people sleep and love, eat and drink, breathe and excrete, work and, perhaps, think—think, but only a little and only within the bounds of conventionality.

—*Oliver*

Oliver frequently writes letters to the newspapers commenting on such topics as politics, art, religion, and history. There is usually a bitterness in his comments and a kind of wit that seems to leaven his isolation. The brittle strangeness of manner, the inadequateness and inappropriateness of his affective reactions can only be appreciated in direct contact. An excerpt from one of his letters to the newspaper follows:

It was just a fairly good "B" picture. There was nothing in it that I had not seen numbers of times before at the movies. I did not think it dirty. I thought it to be just what it was—a literally cheap film. Artists only would have banned it. On the other hand, I found the decidedly wicked picture ________ to be the funniest screened attraction I'd ever seen (I saw it on my return trip in Atlanta). . . .

Miss Smith, please find your glasses! My morals are evaporating!

Oliver ________, Jr.

At the end of a letter to his father he signs himself:

With a heart of gold (hard and yellow), I close,

Your oldest son,
Oliver ________, Jr.

This is a person who, despite his superior intelligence and his awkward gestures at being sociable, is recognized at once as extremely eccentric, if not indeed bizarre, by his classmates as well as by the expert. Evidence of his psychiatric trouble is apparent, and no trained observer would confuse him with the psychopath. A history is not necessary to surmise that he has had difficulties and that further difficulties lie ahead. Although his personality is not outwardly fragmented, it immediately gives clues to the fact that here experience is not what others find it. Such a patient sometimes gives the impression that through him one comes in closer touch with what is most specific and inexplicable in schizophrenia, what is usually blurred or hidden in the chaos of the overt psychosis. Superficially nothing could be more different from what he presents than the socially smooth psychopath who has an explanation for everything, an easy cordiality for everyone. His bitterly authentic seriousness and his capacity for hurt and suffering also contrast with the psychopath.

In many patients the disturbance classed as schizoid personality might be more accurately regarded as masked schizophrenia or, as has been sometimes said, "ambulatory" schizophrenia. Although the more gross technical signs of psychosis are not evident on the surface, many of these patients have a very serious disorder within. The tendency to call their condition schizoid personality (and therefore label them as definitely "sane") sometimes results in their being incorrectly treated. Very dangerous tendencies, well concealed, may emerge into tragic acts.

Some years ago a young woman regarded as seclusive, a bit peculiar, and withdrawn by her acquaintances called a major-league baseball player to her hotel room on the pretext of grave and urgent business. The business was not what might be expected from such a call by a young woman to a man whom she had never met personally but had seemed to admire, hero-worship, and brood over for a long time in yearning fantasies. According to newspaper accounts, the woman, with no explanation or reason she could explain afterward, shot the ballplayer in a genuine attempt to kill him and one that barely failed to do so.

I cannot offer a diagnosis on this patient whom I have never seen. Her behavior and her personal characteristics as disclosed in the press are, however, entirely typical of patients with masked but real and serious schizoid disorder. Such patients are perhaps more accurately indicated by the term *masked schizophrenia* than by *schizoid personality,* which may, artificially and unrealistically, ignore the true state of very ill and dangerous persons and classify them with those presumably deviated in mild degree.

Some patients of this sort eventually show themselves to be psychotic, and it then becomes apparent that a serious inner disorder has, perhaps for many years, been masked by the minor overt peculiarities that constitute what is generally regarded as schizoid personality. Sometimes in patients with masked schizophrenia the serious inner pathology is so well concealed that the patient may be almost indistinguishable from the typical psychopath. It is important to keep in mind that the excellence of the superficial aspect of the patient (whether he be called a masked schizophrenic or a psychopath) gives no reliable indication of how serious the inner, concealed, and at the time undemonstrable pathology may prove to be or how disastrously and unpredictably it may be expressed when it erupts into disastrous antisocial behavior. Like the very dangerous and profoundly ill ambulatory schizophrenic patient whose central disorder is well masked and not yet demonstrable, the psychopath has a concealed but very real and grave pathology. Unlike other types of masked psychosis, the central personality "lesions" of the psychopath are not covered over by peripheral or surface functioning suggestive of some eccentricity or peculiarity of personality but by a perfect mask of genuine sanity, a flawless surface indicative in every respect of robust mental health.

The example of schizoid personality or masked schizophrenia just presented under the pseudonym *Oliver* is obviously distinguishable from the psychopath. His outer aspect contrasts vividly with the smooth and deceptive disguise of the typical psychopath. There are, however, other masked schizophrenics who resemble the typical psychopath much more closely. I have seen a number of patients who were classified by able and experienced psychiatrists as typical psychopaths (antisocial personalities) and by others, equally able, as very well masked schizophrenics. About these patients the difference of judgment lay in estimates of how effectively the surface function masked the inner disorder and gave an appearance of full health. There was usually no disagreement in the conclusion by all the psychiatrists that an underlying disorder was severe and maximally disabling. The deceptive qualities of the excellent disguise, the perfection of the mask, afford no reliable indication that the true condition is mild or moderate and no assurance that it may not be far more serious than the disability of some patients in whom auditory hallucinations and bizarre delusions can be readily demonstrated.

It is perhaps pertinent to mention here that there are other disguises behind which other serious personality disorders mislead us. Chamberlain was among the first who ably emphasized what he refers to as cryptic depression. Patients so affected may complain only of headache, nausea, a pain in the back, or weakness. On repeated questioning, some will admit depression as a minor element in the situation. Others will deny it convincingly and show no evidence of it. I have seen many such patients in whom the history of previous depressive psychosis, many details of the patient's personality, and the prompt response to electric shock therapy give indirect but convincing evidence of the invisible illness. Here it might be said that the potentially more serious condition appears only in a substituted reaction that seems to constitute a compromise or a disguise.

Under the term *pseudoneurotic schizophrenia,* Hoch and Polatin discuss what every psychiatrist has often encountered—the patient who gives one the feeling that he must be a schizophrenic but in whom none of the specifically characteristic features of psychosis can be demonstrated. Often the only complaints are of vague or minor physical discomforts. Sometimes other features that literally indicate a psychoneurosis, and this only, constitute all that can be brought out. Such patients do not express delusions. They deny hallucinations and show no disorder of thinking as this is ordinarily described and no mannerisms or bizarre overt attitudes. They are never grossly irrational in what they express. The history does not show them psychotically deviated in their general behavior until, perhaps, some irreparable psychotic act occurs. Their lack of insight (broader and more profound than in the psychoneurotic patient) and a peculiar emotional deficit and distortion make the examiner realize, without being able to prove it, that he is dealing with schizophrenia. At length the examiner becomes convinced that these patients do not normally experience and evaluate the basic issues of life and that this difference is of the sort and degree not found except in schizophrenia. Some of these people eventually develop delusions and hallucinations, but many go on year after year fully masked by the psychoneurotic facade.

The patient who is seriously schizophrenic but whose basic disorder is masked by the outer appearance of neurosis or by what seems to be only minor eccentricities or schizoid traits can nearly always be readily distinguished from the true psychopath. As mentioned previously, however, there are sometimes masked schizophrenics whose outer appearance is more like that of the true psychopath.

Guttmacher discusses these patients in a very interesting paper and designates them by the term *pseudopsychopathic schizophrenia.* The type of patient discussed by Guttmacher may appear for many years to be a typical psychopath and show all the features in his behavior that are characteristic. Some of these patients do not show the outer eccentricities and oddnesses that usually distinguish the masked schizophrenic. Occasionally they may be almost as outgoing, charming in manner, and almost as free from apparent abnormality as the classic psychopath. As pointed out by Guttmacher, sometimes such a patient will eventually develop a full-blown and obvious schizophrenic psychosis.

It might be argued that the psychosis has developed independently of the psychopathic defect, but I think it much more likely that a serious central disorder was present all the time and that eventually it has become manifest through the disruption of the formerly perfect superficial function and outer appearance. Such developments as these lead me to believe not only that the central disorder in the psychopath may perhaps be similar in degree to that in schizophrenia but also that there may be more similarity in quality than is generally recognized.

An interesting comparison between thoroughly masked schizophrenia and the disorder of the psychopath can be found in the fictional characters Judd Steiner and Artie Straus as they are presented by Meyer Levin in his novel *Compulsion.* Judd Steiner, the fictional representative of Nathan Leopold, gives a strong impression of a deep schizoid disorder masked by generally sane behavior and great intellectual brilliance. Artie

Straus, who is modelled on the novelist's conception of Loeb, emerges in the book as a remarkably well-drawn figure of the classic psychopath. The author admits that his fictional characters are not necessarily true interpretations of the actual characters whose utterly unprovoked sensational murder of a teenaged boy startled and horrified the world in 1924. This long-deliberated and ingeniously planned murder for a thrill suggests a callousness and cynicism that are difficult to describe and still astonishing to contemplate. Both the similarities and the differences between Judd and Artie are wonderfully and convincingly conveyed by Levin in his book and should stimulate interest in everyone concerned with the basic problems of psychiatry.

There is little point in devoting space to detailed accounts of paranoid or cyclothymic personalities. In some degree such characteristics can be seen among anyone's acquaintances, and to name a quantitative point at which they warrant a diagnosis is not easy. Nor is it possible to lay down specifications that will enable one to delineate confidently where paranoid personality ceases and paranoid state or paranoid psychosis begins. So it is with depressions. Where the depth of negative affect permissible to a cyclothymic personality ceases and that of "neurotic depression" begins is perhaps even more difficult to define than where, at greater depths, the disorder should properly be pronounced depressive psychosis. There is about all this much to suggest that traditional concepts have attributed to our terms a good deal more authority than clinical facts uphold.

I find it helpful to consider all schizoid reactions, of whatever degree or course of development, as qualitatively similar, whether or not they are sufficiently disabling to merit such a term as psychosis. So, too, the affective and paranoid reactions seem to fall naturally each into its primary group rather than into other pigeonholes (on the basis of degree) which may give rise to confusion.

The characteristic disorder of the psychopath is usually not difficult to distinguish from these other disorders, but like all of them, it, too, is seen in the widest variations of degree, in manifestations ranging from isolated character traits in a successful person, or brief episodes of delinquency in adolescence, to disability far greater than that shown by many of the psychotic patients committed to institutions.

THE PSYCHONEUROTIC

People who suffer from personality disorders that cause them to be anxious, restless, unhappy, and obsessed with thoughts they themselves recognize as absurd but who are, in the lay sense, altogether sane have for years been classed as psychoneurotic. They recognize reason in general, often admit that their symptoms arise from emotional conflicts, and are free from delusions and hallucinations.

Sometimes their complaints are chiefly physical, of fatigue, of numbness, of indigestion, even of paralysis. Often they will not admit that this numbness or indigestion or paralysis could possibly be related to emotional difficulty, and indeed they themselves may be unaware of conflict. They are often resistant to reasoning but more in the sense of a person with strong prejudices than of one with delusions or with intellectual dilapidation. Sometimes they feel strong fears that they may carry out acts which they dread and which would indeed be tragic or criminal, but they recognize the nature of these acts and do not carry them out. Other acts, apparently senseless but relatively harmless, they do carry out, recognizing the absurdity of feeling that they must do so but becoming anxious if they resist the impulse.

In general, psychoneurotic people recognize objective reality and try to adapt themselves like most others to the ways of society. Patients with traditional psychoneurosis are not characterized by antisocial activity or by striking inability to pursue ordinary goals. Their symptoms handicap them often, but in a way we readily understand. Anxiety, for instance, can make special difficulties for a salesman or obsessive manifestations can handicap a banker, a scholar, or a housewife. These patients as a group are sharply characterized by anxiety and by the various symptomatic schemes that apparently arise from the anxiety and that look as if they were measures employed in reaction to the anxiety and in efforts to relieve it.

It is true that many patients with conversion symptoms do not show what is ordinarily conveyed by the word *anxiety* or by *tension, fear, distress,* and similar terms. Many psychiatrists believe that in such instances the paralysis (or the blindness) may be a substitute for conscious anxiety and probably a defense against it, a means of preventing it or controlling it. The rather remarkable calmness shown by such patients has often been pointed out. Not a few psychopathologists maintain that there is an "unconscious anxiety" or what might be thought of as something embryonic, underlying, or incipient that would be anxiety if not converted into the physical manifestation.

Certainly it may be said about psychoneurosis, as the term is officially used and most widely accepted, that patients with this kind of disorder usually find their symptoms unpleasant, consciously suffer from them, and complain.

On the contrary, those called psychopaths are very sharply characterized by the lack of anxiety (remorse, uneasy anticipation, apprehensive scrupulousness, the sense of being under stress or strain) and, less than the average person, show what is widely regarded as basic in the neurotic. It is very true that Alexander and others who use his terminology and accept his interpretations refer to behavior disorders as character neuroses. Karpman feels that most (but not all) patients who are classed as psychopaths should be grouped with the neurotic or the psychotic group. So far as its implication of causal factors is concerned, the term *neurotic* has undeniably valuable applications for those who feel that they have discovered such causes; but its tendency otherwise to identify the psychopath with hysteria, anxiety reactions, or ordinary obsessive-compulsive disorders is likely to cause confusion and make for practical difficulties.

If the psychopath really has a neurosis, it is a neurosis that is manifested in a fundamentally different life-pattern from classic neurosis, manifested, one might say, in a pattern that is not only different but opposite. Alexander and others have made this quite clear, and the interpretation of the psychopath's behavior as symptomatic "acting out" against his surroundings, in contrast with the development of anxiety or headache or obsession is, it seems to me, an interesting formulation. It is of obvious importance to respect this polar difference between how the psychopath is going to behave socially and what can be expected of patients with somatization or conversion. I do not believe that psychopaths should be identified with the psychoneurotic group, for this would imply that they possess full social and legal competency, that they are capable of handling adequately their own affairs, and that they are earnestly seeking relief from unpleasant symptoms.

There are disorders in which the two diverse types of reaction (developing subjectively unpleasant symptoms versus callously carrying out socially destructive acts) seem to exist in the same symptom. The so-called pyromaniac (and kleptomaniac) often seems motivated by forces similar to the classic obsessive-compulsive patient who corrects the alignment of objects on the bureau forty times a day and who is painfully and over-scrupulously preoccupied with fears that he may harm his child. Such a patient detests the acts he carries out as a sort of ritual to mitigate his subjective distress and is by no means likely to harm the child. He is, in fact, horrified by these thoughts (fears) and is nearly always conscientious to an excessive degree.

On the other hand, as Fenichel has pointed out, the patient abnormally impelled to commit arson or theft (or sex murder) is not committing an act in which scrupulous feelings play a direct or major role and (despite possible ambivalence) gains excitement and consciously satisfies strong drives. The distinction emphasized by Fenichel between ego-syntonic and ego-alien motivations (compulsive acts of caution versus so-called compulsive antisocial acts) is a fundamental point and brings out a distinction not merely of degree but of quality. Behavior that Fenichel classifies as impulse neurosis seems to lie in an area where the unlike (and, as a rule, mutually exclusive) manifestations of the psychopath and the classic obsessive-compulsive patient both play a part together, the two customary opposites approaching and perhaps merging, paradoxically, in the antisocial act.

This particular mingling of influences (or merging of pictures) ordinarily quite different (and mutually exclusive) is not unique in psychiatry. Is there anyone who has not seen patients manifesting genuine manic and genuine catatonic features? Has any psychiatrist failed to note obsessive reactions that are colored with genuine delusion?

Despite any confusions that arise in arguments about psychopathology (dynamic or descriptive) in regard to the psychopath, all, I believe, will agree that his clinical manifestations are easily distinguished from the syndromes now classified as psychoneurosis. It is doubtful if in the whole of medicine any other two reactions stand out in clearer contrast.

The true psychopaths personally observed have usually been free, or as free as the general run of humanity, from real symptoms of psychoneurosis. The psychoneurotic patient, furthermore, is usually anxious to get over his symptoms, while the psychopath does not show sincere evidence of regretting his conduct or of intending to change it.

Caldwell has effectively set down outstanding differences between these two clinical pictures. Our point can be clarified by quoting him:

	Feeling	*Thinking*	*Acting*
1. Ego-enhancement (psychopathic)	Hedonistic Callous Emotionally immature	Irresponsible Rationalistic	Antisocial Impulsive Defiant Explosive
2. Ego-depreciation (neurotic)	Apprehensive Anxious Fearful Depressed Helpless Inferior Jealous	Stereotyped in fantasies Preoccupied with moral and religious ideas Obsessive	Antisocial Asocial Shy, sensitive Hesitant Indecisive Suggestible Overly protective Sexually conditioned Timorous Passive

Some observers believe that the presence of what has long been known as psychoneurosis is sufficient reason for questioning the diagnosis of psychopathic personality. In the study just referred to, Caldwell reports neurotic manifestations in patients whose chief features were plainly those of the psychopath. I believe that the two types of reaction are not characteristically seen together, but perhaps there are no two pathologic syndromes in psychiatry, however distinct, that may not sometimes overlap.

THE MENTAL DEFECTIVE

The mental defective often behaves foolishly or ineffectively and, if the defectiveness is great, may show prolonged and serious maladjustment in ordinary surroundings. In contrast with the psychopath, however, the mental defective is obviously stupid, and his follies may be understood readily as depending on his lack of intelligence, a handicap that is easily demonstrated. This can be measured with some accuracy in psychometric examinations. Many low-grade defectives show developmental deficiencies or other organic changes in their actual brain structure. The psychopath, on the other hand, is often, if not usually, of superior intelligence when measured scientifically. Some of his accomplishments also indicate he has ability that is average or better when he is using it. He often gives the impression in conversation of excellent intellect and is plainly a very different person from the mental defective. Though in England the psychopathic personality was still until fairly recently sometimes referred to by the expressive term, *moral imbecile,* the distinction from intellectual imbecility has always been clearly recognized.

Serious defects in ordinary intelligence naturally handicap a subject, naturally make it difficult for him to learn complicated relationships between cause and effect, and limit his critical ability in choosing wisely among the many courses of conduct offered every day. The defective is likely to be susceptible to false counsel and prone to overlook the more remote and subtle consequences that may follow the gratification of a petty impulse. Unlike the psychopath, mental defectives show limitations of judgment in theoretical situations. They are often unable to express adequate comprehension of mistakes they have made or wrongs they have done. They do not outline, even verbally, ingenious plans for the future or discuss their total situation in such a way as to give a convincing impression of wisdom and reliability. They cannot simulate successfully deep contrition, purpose, and understanding. The badly handicapped mental defective may repeat time after time acts that result in loss or harm to others and to himself. His limitation in reasoning about facts that play a part in such consequences usually offers a satisfactory explanation of his disability.

This disability is considered by courts before which the defective may be tried for misdemeanors or felonies and which may be called upon in efforts to hospitalize him or in other ways to safeguard and help him. It is not only admitted that intellectual defect diminishes judgment and legal responsibility, but varying degrees of defect are recognized and, for practical purposes, accepted as implying degrees of competency.

If a high-grade moron commits murder, his relatively slight defect will be regarded as slight by the jury. The idiot or the imbecile will, however, be properly considered as one with a disability that may have played a major part in such an act. So, too, there has usually not been much difficulty in having the idiot committed (if necessary, against his own will and judgment) to a medical institution where he can be protected and cared for. No jury, however, not even a jury of morons, would deprive of his legal freedom a man showing no more defect than what is customary with an I.Q. of 70.

It is important for us to note that particularly in the question of commitment for a mental defective, varying degrees of disability are recognized and are regarded as affecting competency in varying degrees. In determining the presence of disability and its degree, the record of the defective's actual behavior is not ignored. Psychometric tests furnish evidence that helps the psychiatrist to classify patients properly as idiots, imbeciles, or morons, and this evidence contributes to medicolegal decisions concerning competency. The need for institutionalization in a defective is, however, demonstrated more effectively by his acts than by his I.Q. In contrast, we find that no matter how much evidence of incompetency emerges in the psychopath's record, this classification alone is (officially) regarded as establishing complete sanity, absolute competency.

THE ORDINARY CRIMINAL

Although efforts have been made to interpret criminalism as a form of mental disorder and many criminal careers have been expounded as reactions to emotional conflict, the sort of person described here shows the following important points of distinction from the typical criminal:

1. The criminal usually works consistently and with what abilities are at his command toward obtaining his own ends. He sometimes succeeds in amassing a large fortune and may manage successfully and to his own profit a racket as complicated as a big business. The psychopath very seldom takes much advantage of what he gains and almost never works consistently in crime or in anything else to achieve a permanent position of power or wealth or security. Mercier long ago made the following statement quoted by Henderson:

> There are persons who indulge in vice with such persistence, at a cost of punishment so heavy, so certain, and so prompt, who incur their punishment for the sake of pleasure so trifling and so transient, that they are by common consent considered insane although they exhibit no other indication of insanity.

The man who is essentially criminal may then be regarded as consistently purposive, whereas the psychopath seems hardly purposive at all in comparison. To say the least, the pattern of his actions over any fairly long range of time indicates little that the observer can understand as what a human being would consciously choose. The patient himself sometimes convincingly denies any particular temptation driving him toward the situations to which his behavior repeatedly leads.

2. The criminal ends, though condemned, can usually be understood by the average man. The impulse to take money, even unlawfully, in order to have luxuries or power otherwise unobtainable, is not hard to grasp. The criminal, in short, is usually trying to get something we all want, although he uses methods we shun. On the other hand, the psychopath, if he steals or defrauds, seems to do so for a much more obscure purpose. He will repeatedly jeopardize and sometimes even deliberately throw away so much in order

to seek what is very trivial (by his own evaluation as well as by ours) and very ephemeral. He does not utilize his gains as the criminal does. Sometimes his antisocial acts are quite incomprehensible and are not done for any material gain at all.

3. The criminal usually spares himself as much as possible and harms others. The psychopath, though he heedlessly causes sorrow and trouble for others, usually puts himself also in a position that would be shameful and most uncomfortable for the ordinary man or for the typical criminal. In fact, his most serious damage to others is often largely through their concern for him and their efforts to help him.

4. The typical psychopath, as I have seen him, usually does not commit murder or other offenses that promptly lead to major prison sentences. This is true of the disorder as I present it in what I consider a pure culture. A large part of his antisocial activity might be interpreted as purposively designed to harm himself if one notices the painful results that so quickly overtake him. Of course I am aware of the fact that many persons showing the characteristics of those here described do commit major crimes and sometimes crimes of maximal violence. There are so many, however, who do not, that such tendencies should be regarded as the exception rather than as the rule, perhaps, as a pathologic trait independent, to a considerable degree, of the other manifestations which we regard as fundamental. It is, of course, granted that when serious criminal tendencies do emerge in the psychopath, they gain ready expression, and that no punishment can discourage them. Psychopaths who commit physically brutal acts upon others often seem to ignore the consequences. Unlike the ordinary shrewd criminal, they carry out an antisocial act and even repeat it many times, although it may be plainly apparent that they will be discovered and that they must suffer the consequences.

Many people, perhaps most, who commit violent and serious crimes fail to show the chief characteristics that so consistently appear in the cases we have considered. Many, in fact, show features that make it very difficult to identify them with this group. The term *psychopath* (or *antisocial personality*) as it is applied by various psychiatrists and hospital staffs sometimes becomes so broad that it might be applied to almost any criminal. Granting the essential vagueness of the term, and disputing no one's right to it, I (who am using it only for convenience) maintain that the large group of maladjusted personalities whom I have personally studied and to whom this diagnosis has been consistently applied differs distinctly from a group of ordinary criminals. The essential reactive pattern appears to be in many important respects unlike the ordinary criminal's simpler and better organized revolt against society and to be something far more subtly pathologic. It is my opinion that when the typical psychopath, in the sense with which this term is here used, occasionally commits a major deed of violence, it is usually a casual act done not from tremendous passion or as a result of plans persistently followed with earnest compelling fervor. There is less to indicate excessively violent rage than a relatively weak emotion breaking through even weaker restraints. The psychopath is not volcanically explosive, at the mercy of irresistible drives and overwhelming rages of temper. Often he seems scarcely wholehearted, even in wrath or wickedness. Jenkins, in making distinctions between the dyssocial type of sociopathic personality and the antisocial type, brings out important points. Criminals, despite the fact that they break the laws of society, are often loyal to each other and can sometimes pursue a common cause consistently. Jenkins distinguishes these as dyssocial personalities from the truly antisocial personalities who cannot maintain loyalty even to each other in a common defiance of society or in any consistent revolt.

Most typical psychopaths, despite their continually repeated transgressions against the law and the rights of others and their apparent lack of moral compunction, seem to avoid murder and other grave felonies that remove them indefinitely from free activity in the social group. Most of these people carry out antisocial acts that would seem to make it likely for them to be confined most of their lives in penal institutions but often succeed, through the efforts of their families or through their equivocal medicolegal status, in escaping punishment altogether or in being released long before the expiration of ordinary terms of confinement. It should be emphasized, nevertheless, that there are other typical psychopaths (antisocial personalities) who, in addition to the usual and familiar pattern of incompetent maladjustment and deliberate folly, proceed to carry out crimes of the greatest magnitude, including premeditated, unprovoked, and trivially motivated murder.

When such crimes are committed and he is convicted of them, the real psychopath usually seems as free of remorse, as unperturbed, and as secure in a callous equanimity as when he has been detected in forgery, theft, adultery, or perjury—or after he has squandered in some idle and transient whim all the funds upon which his wife and children are depending to keep them from hardship and bitter poverty over the next few years.

The reactions of a young man convicted of murder some years ago are illustrative. The reports indicate that he had enjoyed the advantages of wealth and a highly respectable family background but suggest that he had shown capricious irresponsibility and repetitious, unprovoked, antisocial activities over a long period.

After learning that his mother was going to take a trip by airplane, he made some careful and rather elaborate plans. These included taking out flight insurance on her life for a considerable sum of money and payable to himself. He also succeeded in placing a time bomb in his mother's luggage and set it to explode during the flight. His efforts were successful. The plane was demolished and all persons aboard, including his mother, were killed. Some of this young man's reactions, as reported by the press, suggest that the chance of obtaining the insurance money was perhaps less stimulating to him that what he took to be the sporting qualities and challenges of the exploit. He apparently had no grudge against his mother or other reason to wish her ill.

Accounts in newspapers and magazines of this young man's trial suggest an insouciance and easy equanimity under circumstances that would naturally evoke extreme remorse, dread, and other desperately serious emotions. He often seemed to be enjoying his role and to delight in having the opportunity to be at the focal point of so much attention and publicity. He appeared to be entirely free of sorrow over the death of his mother and also free of shame at being proved guilty of such a horrible and unprovoked mass murder.

In *Newsweek* magazine the following items were reported:

> At times, he watched the proceedings with wide, staring eyes that showed no emotion; at other times he read a book, *The Mask of Sanity,* by Dr. Hervey Cleckley.
>
> When the verdict was announced he bit his lower lip, but otherwise remained impassive. His wife, Gloria, 22, the mother of his two small children, broke down and sobbed hysterically.

Some accounts of this trial lead one to feel that the murderer might have found amusement, or some other sort of satisfaction, in what he regarded as an important and dramatic role and one in which he could display himself to advantage.

Some psychiatrists might say that this young man's apparent nonchalance under these circumstances should be taken as indicating that he was motivated by an unconscious sense of guilt which he now found satisfaction in expiating. Perhaps so. But I remain skeptical of this hypothesis until I see some concrete evidence of its validity. Evidence, let us remember, cannot be obtained by free surmises and interpretations based on the projection of mere assumptions into a theoretically constructed but still invisible unconscious. The attitude of this young man toward his brutal and senseless crime and toward the death of his mother, it seems to me, is consistent with the amazing lack of capacity for love and normal human feelings that is typical of the psychopath. His amusement and apparent satisfaction in his prominent role in court also impress me as typical of the psychopath's egocentricity, his relish for many of his uninviting and antisocial deeds, and his feeling of petty satisfaction in cleverly carrying out acts that would overwhelm others with tragic sorrow and humiliation.

If there is no positive motivation toward major goals, no adequate inhibition by revulsion from what is horrible or sordid, it is perhaps more understandable that the rudderless and chartless facsimile of a full human being may flounder about in trivialities or in tragic blunders and see little distinction between them.

OTHER CHARACTER AND BEHAVIOR DISORDERS, INCLUDING DELINQUENCY

Those who repeatedly commit antisocial acts or continue to carry out behavior in other ways unacceptable to the group and incompatible with good standing among one's fellows are often referred to as delinquents. Truly felonious deeds are not regarded as characteristic of delinquency so much as repetitiveness in misdemeanor or impropriety. In contrast with the orthodox criminal and to some degree like the psychopath, the delinquent often shows lack of sufficient conscious motivation to account for his conduct. Though delinquency is not a diagnostic term, it has value in that it indicates character and behavior disorders lying between the criminal and psychopathic extremes. Transient episodes of poorly adapted behavior, particularly in the juvenile, are included. Many of the things which the psychopath does are typical of the delinquent but seem to constitute only a part of his life expression, perhaps a relatively small part. Motivation also can often be discovered in the delinquent. Such motivation may be imperfectly understood by the patient and may arise indirectly from circumstances, within and without, which he fails to recognize or to evaluate properly.

Ordinary delinquency might be thought of as a relatively mild disorder with fair prognosis similar in its outer clinical manifestations to the malignant and sweeping disorder found in the full-blown psychopath. As a pathologic reaction, as a kind of maladaptation, there are important resemblances and correlations. Hysterical dissociation and the sort of personality dissociation or disintegration found in schizophrenia also have something in common as well as important differences.

In one the disintegrative process is more superficial and self-limited, often of brief duration; in the other this process may continue until the entire personality is fragmented and no longer recognizable and the organism is incapable of functioning even at the lower levels accepted as characteristic of a human being. In repetitive delinquent behavior the subject often seems to be going a certain distance along the course that a full psychopath follows to the end. In the less severe disorder antisocial or self-defeating activities are frequently more circumscribed and may stand out against a larger background of successful adaptation. The borderlines between chronic delinquency and what we have called the psychopath merge in this area. Although anxiety, remorse, shame, and other consciously painful subjective responses to undesirable consequences are deficient in both as compared with the normal, this callousness or apathy is far deeper in the psychopath. The deficiency is also far more successfully masked.

It is worthwhile to emphasize that many who, as they mature, become well-adjusted people and happy and distinguished citizens can look back to incidents of unprovoked misconduct which, if habitual, might constitute delinquency. If such isolated fragments not only persisted but took precedence in the entire life scheme and became in fact the major expression of the personality, behavior would emerge having much in common with the case histories given in this book.

Many stable and productive adults are known by me (and others, no doubt, by the reader) who can be clearly identified earlier in life as members of destructive gangs which, on Halloween or on other special occasions, carried out raids in the residential section, hurling brickbats about, smashing windows, removing wrought-iron gates, puncturing automobile tires, and shooting about rather wildly with air guns or small-caliber rifles. Some remembered as special leaders in these activities became properly respected bankers, Rotarians, physicians, deacons, professors, attorneys, and scoutmasters.

A happy husband and father who is also an outstanding civic leader recalls with some retroactive bewilderment his membership in a select club at college in which the chief topic at meetings consisted of obscenely boastful accounts of recent enterprises in miscegenation. In this particular setting, that of an isolated rural community in the South, such relations in themselves implied a maximum of scatalogic contempt for the partner, a peculiarly derogatory aim in the act, that even the language customarily used in such reminiscences could not adequately convey.

Another conventional and well-adjusted adult recalls an incident after a beer party following the last football game of the season when a fair proportion of the celebrants went out together to a pasture and there pursued and constrained a number of cows in efforts to achieve sexual relations with the fairly patient but reluctant animals.

A kindly and eminently responsible medical colleague reports numerous episodes from his adolescent days in a farming community. Among many other fumbling and confused ventures in the masculine approach, he remembers finding amusement and delight in joining with other boys to make the rounds of rural outhouses where young ladies, like all other local people, in response to natural demands, exposed to those strategically placed the most secret regions of the body through familiar apertures. Those who lay in wait now made stealthy use of bamboo switches or small branches to titillate the relatively immobilized and vulnerable ladies at this vividly inopportune moment. Strange girls visiting in the community gave special impetus to these gross but hilarious improprieties.

Numerous instances come to mind of young women, who, after episodes of damaging promiscuity not accounted for by erotic passion, achieve a better evaluation of such acts and, as they mature, integrate their impulses in such a way as to find security, personal fulfillment, and adequate sexual response in stable and faithful marriages. A transient episode in a woman about 30 years of age is also pertinent to the discussion.

Despite very unhappy marital relations, she had scrupulously refrained from indulging in any sexual activity except with her husband until shortly after their divorce. Then, for reasons she could not explain, she found herself susceptible to almost any overture, and, in fact, made it all too plain that she was available. There occurred a series of unrewarding sexual relations with strangers who casually picked her up, with some salesmen who happened to appear at the door, and with acquaintances of long standing (some of whom she considered distinctly unattractive). After some months of this behavior she reoriented herself and has since then been leading her customary conventional life.

Temporary periods of distinctly delinquent behavior are apparently not uncommon even in careers on the whole successful and constructive. More protracted or habitual reactions of this sort result in disordered patterns that approach in varying degrees the pattern of the psychopath.

Confused manifestations of revolt or self-expression are, as everyone knows, more likely to produce unacceptable behavior during childhood and adolescence than in adult life. Sometimes persistent traits and tendencies of this sort and inadequate emotional responses indicate the picture of the psychopath early in his career. Sometimes, however, the child or the adolescent will for a while behave in a way that would seem scarcely possible to anyone but the true psychopath and later change, becoming a normal and useful member of society. Such cases put a serious responsibility on the psychiatrist.

A patient I once saw affords an excellent example. A 15-year-old high school boy, the son of respectable and God-fearing parents, attacked with considerable violence and apparently tried to rape a 9-year-old girl. When interviewed, he showed indifference, despite the fact that the girl's father had threatened him with death and tried to seize him. He denied actual rape and spoke calmly of the whole affair as if it were a minor matter, such as, for instance, breaking a neighbor's window. He later tried to excuse himself by inventing a palpably absurd story about being drugged with marijuana given him in the form of cigarettes by a Mephistophelian stranger. This boy's parents were severely pious and straitlaced. Much of his teaching had apparently implied that a minor oath or any preoccupation with thoughts of sex should be regarded as soul-devouring. He seemed indeed much like a psychopath, but might his conduct not have been the result of an ordinary adolescent drive emerging in a mind relatively without restraining principles partly because of the very fact that absurd trifles had been so magnified by his teaching that he saw all prohibited things at a level of importance and had dismissed all as absurd because so many indeed were? In such a case I feel that the child should be given benefit of the doubt until evidence of a persistent pattern is thoroughly established.

A 16-year-old boy was sent to jail for stealing a valuable watch. Though apparently content and untouched by his situation, after a few questions were asked he began to seem more like a child who feels the unpleasantness of his position. He confessed that he had worried much about masturbation, saying he had been threatened and punished severely for it and told that it would cause him to become insane.

He also said no one liked him, that he talked and yelled too much, and that no one would play with him. While speaking of this he seemed to echo a real worry, to reenact a former attitude to a perplexity and trouble that he once felt. At the moment this boy seemed accessible, and it was felt his problem might be understood, as many of the behavior problems of children and adolescents can be understood. In the next moment, however, hope faded, and it became apparent that the boy was not now taking seriously what he might once have taken seriously. I could not reach a level of any inward reality. There remained only the mimicry of feeling that, if it ever existed, had now vanished. Of course, it cannot be stated positively that there was no genuine feeling. It cannot be known that a schizophrenic who fails to turn his head when told of a tragedy fails to suffer. We often feel with strong conviction, however, that the schizophrenic does not appreciate such events in the ordinary sense and as people who are not schizophrenic appreciate them. With similar conviction I believe that this boy was no longer aware of serious conflict or suffering or humiliation either about masturbation, about his present status in jail, or about the almost unbelievable series of absurd, shameful, and fruitless acts that had occupied him for years. He was entirely rational in the ordinary sense and of average intellectual capacity.

He admitted having broken into his mother's jewelry box and stolen a watch valued at $150.00. He calmly related that he exchanged the watch for 35 cents' worth of ice cream and seemed entirely satisfied with what he had done. He readily admitted that his act was wrong, used the proper words to express his intention to cause no further trouble, and, when asked, said that he would like very much to get out of jail.

He stated that he loved his mother devotedly. "I just kiss her and kiss her ten or twelve times when she comes to see me!" he exclaimed with shallow zeal. These manifestations of affection were so artificial, and, one might even say, unconsciously artificial, that few laymen would be convinced that any significant feeling, in the ordinary sense, lay in them. Nor was his mother convinced.

A few weeks before this boy was sent to jail, he displayed to his mother some rifle cartridges. When asked what he wanted with them, he explained that they would fit the rifle in a nearby closet. "I've tried them," he announced. And in a lively tone added, "Why, I could put them in the gun and shoot you. You would fall right over!" He laughed and his eyes shone with what seemed a small but real impulse.

This might be considered merely childish jest. A normal child might, of course, say such a thing, and in a normal child it would be merely a jest. I believe that this boy also spoke in jest, but I fear that he might carry out the jest, not with bitterness or hate in the ordinary sense but merely because the fancy struck him and because the death of his mother would mean so little to him that it cannot be counted in the ordinary terms of human emotion.

This boy's history showed, over a period of several years, dozens of episodes similar to the present. His misdeeds were apparently without purpose. He gained nothing, took little or no precaution against detection, and seemed to be unmoved by punishment. He is mentioned here because I could not help but wonder if a few years earlier he perhaps did feel shame and insecurity and might have been amenable to teaching. It was difficult to say whether his behavior disorder would tend to improve or be substantially modified by ordinary treatment or whether this was an early stage of the psychopath's career.

A CASE SHOWING CIRCUMSCRIBED BEHAVIOR DISORDER

When behavior disorder is circumscribed, in a child or in an adult, one may sometimes feel that symptomatically the patient resembles a psychopath but that a different sort of personality lies behind the manifestation. Instead of essential indifference to the pathologic situation, we sometimes see genuine zeal to avoid the faulty and self-damaging acts. It is not rare to find relatively normal attitudes to most aspects of life and sometimes healthy and admirable personality features.

In such patients, unlike psychopaths, it is more often possible to bring out valid responses and to learn about experiences and relations that have been influential over years and that may have played an important part in causing the poorly adapted behavior. Strong indications can sometimes be found that inner and poorly understood emotional confusions and conflicts are provoking repetitive rebellious and ineffective antisocial conduct. A brief discussion of one such patient may be germane.

This young woman in her middle twenties voluntarily sought help from an internist widely known for his interest in personality problems; he referred her for psychiatric treatment. Her spontaneous complaint was of sexual promiscuity which she feared would damage her socially. She expressed the opinion that, aside from what these doings might cause others to think of her, she herself deemed them wrong and highly undesirable.

A virgin until approximately two years earlier, she had since that time had full sexual relations with over twenty different men. She denied any personal attachment or romantic attitudes toward these partners, to whom she had yielded casually, promptly, and apparently without conflict or indecision. She had obtained pleasant reactions from the physical contact and after the first few ventures began to respond regularly with genital orgasm. She had never entertained illusions to the effect that any of this considerable group of men were enamored of her and said she had no desire to bring out such feelings in them. Her appearance was distinctly attractive and her figure particularly well endowed with anatomic features likely to arouse and enhance erotic interest.

An articulate and apparently a candid woman, she showed little reluctance to discuss either her sexual adventures or any other material. In most respects she showed evidence of better than ordinary maturity and a considerable sophistication without affectedness. Her general intelligence was even better than might have been expected from her good record at college and subsequent success in her work.

In journalism she had made rapid progress as a writer of advertisements and of feature articles on the daily paper in one of the largest cities in her state. She did not write the society news or obituaries or deal chiefly with material usually reserved for the novice reporter, but often discussed politics, scientific developments, and economic problems. Nothing in her appearance or manner suggested masculine characteristics, tastes, or attitudes. She dressed in such a way as to make the most of her looks and had interests and hobbies predominately feminine.

Although the excitement of physical relations seemed to have been genuine and full orgasm occurred and left her without the feeling that anything might be lacking, the experiences reported impressed the examiner, in some important respects, as relatively shallow. She gave as her reason or motive for doing what she regarded as wrong (and as unwise) a mounting sense of tension and a specific desire that she found too strong to resist. It seemed likely that she was really influenced by natural feelings of this sort but not to any unusual degree.

In fact, it was chiefly the matter of relieving a trivial or, at most, a rather moderate need than of being driven by intense passions or allured by breathtaking or exquisite possibilities of fulfillment.

Although she had made her charms fully available to so many men, she usually permitted only a single encounter of this sort. Shortly after the beginning of her promiscuity she had continued with one partner through three dates at intervals of several days, and a few months later she equaled this record with another man. Several other times she had repeated her adventure with the same partner through two sessions.

The rule for many months had, however, been one night with almost anybody but two with none. Considering her physical attributes and personal attractiveness, it is not surprising that those who had been so generously treated, often on the first date, wished to continue. She felt not only an aversion for this but also for seeing or having anything further to do with the partner. She realized that after such full and prompt compliance or cooperation at the beginning it would be difficult indeed to keep matters more or less platonic thereafter.

She was cognizant of the old analogy between getting the first olive out of a bottle and getting the first kiss and of its even greater applicability to what she had offered without even initial delay or any impediment whatsoever.

This did not, however, appear to be the chief factor in her breaking off relations. There was a primary loss of interest in the partner. No evidence emerged of an appreciable sense of shame on her part or of uneasiness about meeting unflattering attitudes and appraisals that might develop toward a woman who lets herself be taken so readily.

Nor did she worry about perhaps drawing out strong feelings in the partner, about his developing a binding attachment that might cause him distress. She was not, so far as she was aware, designing her conduct so as to enjoy the frustration or disappointment of all these men by cutting them off so abruptly from a quite lively pleasure they had reason to hope would remain available.

Completion of the sexual act was not followed by remorse or self-recrimination. Relieved and pleased, she had no wish for any sort of personal closeness or intimacy with her companion but, on the other hand, she did not feel strong revulsion. She had not sought personal intimacy in the beginning, and nothing happened, despite rather delightful somatic sensations, that gave incentives in this direction. After satisfaction occurred, she did not react with negative feelings toward sexuality or promiscuity as she might had there been strong conscious conflict between an intensely passionate yearning and the ordinary resistances to such conduct under such conditions. She evaluated her behavior as wrong, dangerous, and puzzling, but this evaluation was steady. Her attitude did not lead to a fierce struggle against the impulses toward such behavior, succumb temporarily to overpowering passions, and then arise to invoke shame and bitter regret.

She did not feel impelled by any special need for variety in changing her partners so promptly and in embracing so many, nor did she have the mistaken idea, so commonly encountered in problems of female promiscuity, that she was proving her charms and sex appeal by the fact that so many men had relations with her. She had been popular with men for a long time before her present habits began, and she realized better than most women that almost any female, even one of distinctly mediocre attractions, would not have trouble in getting seduced by practically any number of males alert for opportunities of free entertainment of this sort.

Though sometimes succumbing with almost unparalleled rapidity as soon as her date began his advances, she often pretended to be reluctant and made him go through a good many overtures, both verbally and with caresses, before cooperating.

She could not, however, recall having even once, since over a year previously, failed in full cooperation on the man's initial attempt. Although not unresponsive sensually to kisses and caresses, it was not the heightening or prolongation of ecstatic pleasure that prompted her to hold out for a while and allow these preliminaries to run their course.

She expressed, in fact, a preference for "going on, getting to it, and getting it over with." She distinctly enjoyed observing with skepticism a man's efforts to pretend he might be taking her seriously, his tactics in going through rituals of deception so common and sometimes rather elaborate, which the predatory male uses to get his way with the ladies. She was not conscious, during early discussion of these matters, of any real hate or contempt but admitted it made her feel that by seeing through these hypocritical ruses and pseudoemotional maneuvers she was getting the better of the man in their encounter.

It had not occurred to her that this would be regarded by most as an almost fantastically inaccurate way of scoring in such a contest, since the adversary never failed to gain all his ends. She admitted awareness that men would be inclined to take her lightly, to say the least, on finding that she could be so casually induced to have intercourse, and by so many. She seemed to regret this and to show some concern about it, but hardly to do so in ordinary or adequate degree.

She admitted that the feeling of satisfaction and superiority she attained through her prompt recognition of the date's concealed intentions and through inwardly mocking him in the steps he took to work the situation toward seduction while pretending other attitudes was distinctly pleasant to her and that she valued it highly.

The more this was discussed, the larger part she estimated it to have played in her motivations. She did not recognize any deeply derogatory attitude in this but found in it something more like the thrill of a game in which one enjoys outwitting and defeating, according to fair rules of the contest, an opponent who is not disliked or despised because of this. She did not feel tempted to show that she saw through the date's pretenses by her manner and attitude, by so telling him, or by making him fail to achieve his obvious aims with her.

As about other matters, she entered frankly into the discussion of relations she had previously maintained with an older woman. The patient voluntarily brought up this subject and did not seem to have had any intention to evade it.

Shortly after moving to the city where she now worked, she had met this woman, who immediately showed warm cordiality and treated her with attention that suggested both affection and admiration. This new friend, although almost fifteen years older than the patient, was youthful in appearance and in spirit, attractive to men, and extremely intelligent. She and her husband also were on the faculty of a local college. This woman, whose knowledge of literature, music, and of many other matters was considerable, seemed to the patient distinctly the most delightful and understanding person encountered in all her life.

A tremendous new interest was aroused in my patient, who found in fiction, poetry, psychological books, and in almost all the activities of life, meaning and delight she had never before discovered or deemed possible.

She felt uniquely understood and really cared for in a way that made everything she had regarded in the past as understanding and love seem perfunctory and trivial. For the first time she felt very close to someone and was thus able, for the first time, to realize that this had heretofore been missing.

The patient had been popular with both girls and boys and had never considered herself as lonely or isolated. Her friendship with other girls had, she now discovered, been relatively superficial. She realized more clearly also how little her popularity with boys had led to any personal intimacy or valuable shared understanding. She learned far more in a short time from this new friend than she had during all the years at college, and what she learned filled life with interest, humor, and all sorts of marvelous pleasures and goals.

She found confirmation of attitudes she had developed toward many of the conventional and uninspiring ideas, demands, limitations, and expectations she had encountered in her family. Achieving what she felt was new and real understanding which she could apply to conflicts and uncertainties that had troubled her as long as she could remember, she now felt secure, independent, and almost triumphantly eager for the future and its opportunities.

Soon her friend's husband had to go elsewhere for several months of work on a research project. She welcomed the opportunity to give up her own quarters and stay in the house of this wonderful and inspiring guide and benefactress. Despite the complications and interruptions of her hostess's two small children (whom the patient seemed to enjoy playing with and to love), there were greater opportunities for listening together to symphonies, for reading aloud Shakespearean plays, and for discussion over a few drinks until long past midnight.

She shared her friend's room and soon was sleeping in the same twin bed with her, both finding the nearness and the contact delightful. Lying together in the dark, thrilled with evidences of being understood and loved, she liked to talk and to listen and to have close physical contact with her idol. Both women, made lively and articulate by cocktails and by delight, found it easy to murmur to each other all sorts of things concerning admiration and love and what each meant to the other.

From close embraces, to kisses, to mutual masturbation, things proceeded without our patient's giving very distinct thought to whether or not there was anything homosexual, anything perverse or queer about such practices. The older and more sophisticated of the two was the other's symbol of the ideal. What she approved and considered natural and delightful was almost automatically accepted by the other.

Furthermore, she got the strangest new delights from what happened while they were in bed together. She had, as a matter of fact, not only erotically exciting sensations but distinct orgasms from the digital caresses and stimulations of the other. She did not think of herself and the other woman as something equivalent to husband and wife or as one pretending to be a man and the other acting the part of a woman under such circumstances. Both were women, in the patient's feelings, but there were wonderful and unforeseen revelations, sensual as well as intellectual and otherwise, in all this prized experience.

She was not preoccupied with resentment toward the absent husband. Without quite knowing why, she would not have wanted him to know every detail about what she and his wife did. But he did not loom in her concepts as a distinct rival, nor did their mutual masturbation seem to intrude distinctly into the areas supposedly reserved for husbands and wives. She was more concerned about the fact that her main source of happiness would be curtailed, that she could not be so often with this wonderful person after the husband returned and she went back to her regular quarters.

The sensuous feelings and the startlingly delightful and new experience of orgasm were all tied in with her affection and love and unstinted admiration for the wonderful person who had brought so much to her. She had learned something about homosexuality not only from books but from her efforts several years earlier as president of a students' honorary society at college to help a freshman who had shown what seemed to her serious and regrettable tendencies of this sort. It sometimes occurred to her that what she and the totally wise friend did might be regarded as perverse or like the misdeeds of that girl at college, but such thoughts had little more force in her evaluation of the acts than some farfetched philosophic abstraction which might be literally true in syllogisms but without relation to actualities of experience. These sexual activities were a private and secret delight, one part of the many things they shared and into which no one else entered.

As she discussed this matter, freely and without hedging or apparent shame, she seemed to have little or no fear that she might be homosexual. I also felt that she was probably not what this term indicates in its reference to full and fixed lesbian women. Her physically erotic relations with the other woman had been in some respects a substitutive practice, though what it might stand for was not well formulated among her goals. Her reaction, in certain aspects, seemed akin to what a normal, adolescent boy might experience in masturbating while immersed in vivid fantasies of intercourse with the image of the girl he has chosen as a sweetheart and wants someday to marry.

There was, however, an important difference. She had no definite referential imagery in which a male figure could be located as the personally and fully embraced partner in the world of delightful feelings that were evoked. There was no channellized structure, as in the example of the romantically masturbating boy, to conduct her aspirations toward a real and well-defined goal. Although there were resemblances, her experience apparently lacked features essential to the persistent pattern of true homosexuality. In the first rewarding intimacy she had experienced with another human being, this delightful and exciting physical contact seemed wonderful, and she found it in no way disturbing or objectionable.

Such a situation could scarcely have arisen for a man under similar circumstances without vastly more pathologic actualities and consequences, for in the virgin male genital aims are nearly always clearer and less ambiguously merged in general and nonsexual personal relations.

After some months of what had been the most delightful time in this patient's life, her beloved friend and idol announced that their relations must be terminated. The young girl could not conceive of any valid reason for such a decision. The articulateness of her preceptor failed at the task of making clear or acceptable what was, nevertheless, made final. Soon afterward this indescribably wise and wonderful being moved away, her husband having been given a position much to his advantage at a university in another section of the country.

The young lady we are concerned with was puzzled, sad, and hurt beyond anything that she could express or explain. After having for the first time in her life exposed and offered her intimacy, love, adoration, longings, and everything else that she had always automatically and fearfully guarded, she found herself rejected. Her emotional commitment had led to loneliness and frustration and to the shame and hurt of being discarded.

It was not difficult for this intelligent girl to begin discovering that without knowing it she had for some time been deliberately and actively engaged in the process of throwing herself away. She had been thrown away by the only person to whom she had offered and fully given herself. Unable to make verbal comment on her hurt and betrayal, she formulated and, in another way, expressed comment in behavior that spoke with more authority than any language. She began to understand that by so damaging herself she was, not in the mere light symbols of language but in terms more concrete, trying to explain to the one who had rejected her how much this rejection hurt. This could not be adequately conveyed without pain also to the one her desperate message must reach. The banishment inflicted by this other, she had already found, constituted a wall that could be penetrated, if at all, only by an emotional projectile of great traumatic force.

Going back a little farther, let us consider the situation of this girl prior to her meeting with the older woman. Since she could first remember, it had seemed obvious to her that civilization was devised in such a way as to give the human male many undeserved advantages over the human female. Little boys could wander off on tree-climbing, hiking, or other adventures, but little girls were more restricted. Men became airplane pilots, surgeons, generals, whereas nearly all women, as she saw it, became wives who day after day performed routine household tasks, washed dishes, nursed babies, and seldom got out to have any fun, even at night.

Furthermore, husbands did not seem to find wives attractive. Even the funny papers joked about how dull a wife was as compared with the stenographer and showed husbands on every possible occasion gleefully slipping away from prosaic and dowdy figures at home to get "a night out with the boys." As her life progressed, she had steadily encountered facts to corroborate the implications of an old saying fairly common in her childhood, "Why you can't get any more lift out of that than out of kissing your own wife."

When she had wanted to be a general or a cowboy leader in those early games in the park, the others laughed at her and said she was only a girl. Facts such as her being able to run faster and climb better than some of the boys did not matter. No, the decisions were all determined by the irrelevant point about her being a girl.

She had to stay at home sometimes and help her mother with the dishes or other tasks. Daddy, after reading the morning paper, went off and stayed the whole day among all the excitements of town. There is no need to give much from the thousands of incidents, real and familiar to anyone, which she encountered and from which she logically derived her distorted convictions that active and exciting lives are open to men whereas women are expected to live in the circumscribed orbit of a house, carrying out repetitious tasks and dull, petty, routines and often becoming creatures of convention, careless of their looks, shapeless, and uninspiring.

In her reactions to these formulations she did not derive envy and admiration for man as compared with woman. It was not through any real virtue or superiority that males had all the interesting work and freedom and fun. It was because of conventions and rules, based not on facts but on tradition, that men had this advantage.

They were often smug enough and biased enough to think they deserved such a break. Women, not taking the trouble to think things through, placidly accepted such an arrangement. She did not want to be a man or more like a man, but she was determined to evade as much as possible these artificial impediments. Instead of throwing her life away in a meek gesture to empty conventions, she would go after the interesting things. The success and independence she might achieve, the fun she might have, would, aside from their intrinsic value, be a comment on the fallacies she had detected and would oppose.

Under hypnosis and narcosis as well as in unaltered awareness, she gave much detail that filled in a convincing picture of her childhood environment. Hundreds of memory items emerged to disclose her father not as cruel but as an arbitrary and moody disciplinarian in small matters. Her parents did not (to her) seem to find intimacy, fulfillment, or very much real fun together in their marriage.

The mother (in her eyes) lived in trivial activities and was bored, boring, and fretful but unaware of the reasons. The patient's outlook and aims had slowly taken form in reaction to the model of marriage she found, or thought she found, in her home. As she grew, she discovered in her general surroundings thousands of items that seemed to support and that further shaped opinion and inclination.

It should not be assumed that the marriage of these parents was all that it appeared to the little girl. Details of it which she encountered at susceptible moments might be accurate without being representative of the whole. So, too, as she grew and observed the world about her, she found facts that continued to confirm her early evaluations.

Anyone can find dull housewives and distant, bored husbands. Everyone knows that the immature male may take advantage of the "double standard" and try to see how far he can get with women under the pretense of love, only to react with the precise and unflattering opposite of love in degree proportionate to their acquiescence. During an early discussion of the disadvantages of marriage for women, the patient cited as evidence two young couples who often went together on car trips, the two husbands sitting together in front, the wives ignored on the rear seat. All the observations given as evidence by the patient seemed to be true and accurate. Her interpretations also seemed, for the specific instances she cited, correct.

If a man and a woman value so much the opportunity to be together on dates, why should they almost immediately after marriage so change as to choose even a person of the same sex to sit by in preference to the mate? Custom or courtesy might suggest that, as in seating arrangements at dinner parties, husbands and wives, in this limited sense, be swapped about. But can anything except the absence of basic sexual and personal interest make men turn regularly to men and women to women on occasions when married couples gather? The patient found in scores of incidents she had observed indications that these couples were not particularly close to each other or having much fun together.

Among other examples she pointed out how often at parties the husbands drifted or sometimes almost raced for the kitchen, where, in purely male company, they spent much of the evening, frankly oblivious of the wives stranded together in the living room.

I could not but agree with her that such behavior was consistent with and might indicate serious attrition, if not indeed the unhappy and untimely death, of what it is natural to seek in heterosexual love relations. Her basic concept can, perhaps, be conveyed by a joke she told. It is an old joke, but expressive:

A husband who habitually paid little attention to his wife did not even look up from his paper when she came down one day in a new and breathtaking dress. She tried in vain to make him notice and admire it. She was a good-looking and voluptuous woman and resented being ignored. Not succeeding in getting the husband to raise his eyes even momentarily to regard her, she ran back upstairs. Resolved to shake him from his lethargy, she stripped and came down again, completely naked. Announcing she was on her way downtown to shop, she paused for his appraisal. Finally she succeeded in getting him to glance up from the paper. Before returning to peruse it, he indifferently remarked, "Umph! Need a shave, don't you."

Among her married friends she had observed many wives who received strict allowances dealt out to them as if they were children or servants by husbands who would not even divulge to their mates and reputed equals any fundamental information about the family's finances. Everything concerning their business affairs, to which these husbands seemed to devote most of their lives and interest, was withheld from wives who were, the patient felt, appraised as too inconsequential or undeserving to share in these matters sacred to the male world.

Many of her conclusions might apply correctly to the specific cases from which she drew them. She had, apparently, with precocious accuracy, sensed and ferreted out negative points in specific husbands and specific wives that others, accepting more optimistic generalizations, would have overlooked. Her ideologies and the general shaping of her aims and actions had been strongly conditioned by the implicit assumption that all marriage was necessarily what she had seen it to be in many instances. Argument with her about this overgeneralization would scarcely have altered her fundamental outlook.

In the course of time, however, as she brought up the concrete details of experience with increasing amounts of affect, she became aware of distortions and evasions formerly screened by her dogmatic ideologies. Eventually she could see (and feel) that it was her mother (or the image she had made of her mother as a child) which she had rejected and that this did not demand rejection of the feminine role itself. She could see also that while she had determined not to accept all the limitations she believed inherent in woman's status sociologically, this distortion had not extended into deeper biologic levels. She had not, in turning from the mother, identified herself with her father and determined to *be* a man. Had this occurred, far more serious problems might have arisen.

Marriage was very strongly rejected as an ambition. Reactions to her mother and to her father apparently combined in this negative force and contributed to a distorted response to this major feminine role. She examined again and felt again the effects upon her of her older brother. It was he for whom money had to be saved so that he could go to medical school. She recalled that at first she had been very fond of him and proud of him. As she continued to reorient herself to what had appeared to be preference on the parents' part for his ambitions, while deprivations were demanded of her so that he could attain the independence of being a physician, she became better able to see these things in the general context of her life.

Incidents scorned at the time and since then neglected, when now recalled and reappraised, indicated parental pride in her also. It became possible for her to see that this had not been sufficiently valued by her because it was pride in her as a girl and for qualities unlike those she specifically needed for competition with her brother.

It is impossible to set down here all the myriad events that came up for this girl's reappraisal or the affective reactions and shaping of attitudes that, seen as a whole, seemed to account for her rejection of marriage and fear to give herself in any deep, personal intimacy with men. Nothing that is said as a generalization about her life pattern can convey what emerged as she reproduced it in the concrete form of innumerable incidents. Nor would any explanation in general terms have been useful in her efforts to reorient herself as were the explanations she herself gradually arrived at.

The sexual relations with men, begun several months after the break with her lesbian partner, soon convinced her of something she had not wanted to admit at the time—that the sexual organs of man and woman are appropriately designed for contact and work together in such a way as to get better sensual results than anything possible with two female bodies, which are not anatomically equipped for such a feat. She was forced to admit this although she continued to deny all possibility of other genuine and happy relations between man and woman.

This at first was a blow to her, for she sought to preserve in idealized perfection her concept of the relation with the other woman as being in every respect superior to anything possible between woman and man. She had jealously guarded those feelings and impulses which, in being bestowed, constitute falling in love. In her sexual activities with the series of men she went to unusual lengths in trying to keep her sensations and all relations and contacts of any importance to herself confined, localized, and impersonal. Capacities to love another, to give genuine intimacy (herself) to another, drawn out initially by the homosexual partner, were less deeply buried than before and therefore demanded more vigilant protection from arousal by man.

In having intercourse with men she continued also her old competition with the other sex, rejecting them as lovers or needed complements to herself in personal matters, but seeking to outwit them or to find some basis, however farfetched and flimsy, on which she could mock them in their sexual tactics.

Her promiscuous relations appeared eventually to the patient as having been used to carry out several purposes simultaneously:

1. They satisfied a need for sensual pleasure and orgasm that had, since her experiences with the woman, become clearer and more urgent.
2. By cheapening herself as a sexual object, she expressed reproach and criticism of one who had discarded her and made a protest against being so treated.
3. She reaffirmed her rejection of woman's role in marriage by caricaturing in her own attitude the personal relations of the heterosexual act.
4. She found an aspect of the situation, however farcical and insubstantial, by which she could think of herself as mocking the man (his not realizing she knew what he was after).
5. She tried to ensure her freedom from any need of marrying by getting localized genital pleasures and relief while keeping distinctly withdrawn from truly personal relations.
6. By changing partners on each occasion, she expressed her freedom from attachment and her disdain for any important relationship in connection with the act.

This practice also made it impossible for an attachment to develop and threaten the sort of lonely security she had built up over so many years.

It took her much less time and effort to reach the foregoing conclusions than to realize emotionally that she had, without suspecting it, been very much influenced by a need (not admitted) to find something she had never realized was desirable and necessary until she had sensed a misleading clue to it in her close personal relations with the older woman.

It was more difficult still for her to accept the possibility that anything of this nature might be worth seeking in a man. This possibility did not become acceptable to her so much through its direct examination or continuing reappraisal of what she had experienced with the woman, but chiefly, it seemed, through the relation of present and recent matters, to aims, attitudes, and reactions recognizable in her childhood and, under varying aspects, in the year-by-year pattern of her life. She at first brought out material with little affective reaction to it. Later her feelings about incidents already mentioned were allowed expression.

It was less difficult for her to give up her sexual promiscuity than to alter her attitude toward marriage. Even the possibility that male and female have personality features and resources for erotic relations with each other comparable to the situation anatomically (which she had found so superior to the deviated homosexual experience) was something it took her much time to accept.

The fear, born in her childhood, of losing that freedom which would enable her to escape the fate she saw as inevitable for every housewife, strove long and stubbornly against the recognition of anything that might modify her concepts and her affective reactions to them. These concepts, warning her perpetually from within, had, it seems, blocked many nascent impulses that might have led her years ago into experiences that could not but modify her basic fear. Not by reasoning alone but only by experiencing something directly, something directly between herself and man, was it likely that sufficient modification could occur for her to continue improvement.

From a small and very reluctant beginning, such experiences developed, and with them came changes of attitude extending much deeper than the presence or absence of the symptoms she had once expressed in her behavior.

No attempt has been made to bring out anything very deep or remarkable about this patient. She illustrates, however, several points useful for our purpose. The outlandishly promiscuous and poorly motivated sexual activity that constituted the objective clinical manifestation of her trouble was entirely typical of what we find in the real psychopath. Her conduct in this respect would seem to argue well for that diagnosis. The lack of adequate conscious purpose, of anything resembling irresistible passion or even strong ordinary temptation, to account for such inappropriate and unrewarding behavior seems even more characteristic than the bare deeds.

Important distinctions can be made, however, between this localized expression and the similar but generalized malfunctioning that distorts the psychopath in all his serious performances. Not only was this young lady consistently successful and purposive in her work and in all other social relations, but her emotional attitudes and responses in almost every situation except those centering about sexual aims were normal and adequate. In the erotic situation she not only behaved unwisely and unsuccessfully but also showed evidence of distorted evaluations, of affective confusion, and of serious deficit. In a crude analogy it might be said that her pathology compared with the widespread pathology of the psychopath somewhat as a carbuncle caused by a staphylococcic infection compares to staphylococcic septicemia.

Despite many superficial resemblances to serious and predominant homosexual reactivity and life patterning, she had retained, beneath the surface, biologic and fundamental heterosexual potentiality. Her experiences with the seriously deviated woman awakened or liberated needs and capacities for close, devoted, and understanding human relations. In the framework of this broad awakening, genital impulses were also stimulated, though misdirected. For the patient, it appears that she found in the experience with the older woman expression for much that she had missed long ago in parental relations as well as in friendships and the usual heterosexual gropings of adolescence.

The somewhat clarified and freed genital impulses did not seem to be integrated into the broader pattern of personal arousal in such a way as to constitute real and firmly fixed homosexuality, but rather, they appeared to accompany, in a confusing but addictive sense, the other and surrounding affective capacities and urges as all emerged. In a confusion which she could not evaluate, reacting to several important needs or urges, she hit upon the maladapted behavior pattern in which she presented herself.

Her personality as a whole remained sufficiently intact or normally functional for her to give to the physician and to herself an account of earlier experiences and her reactions to them sufficiently valid for plausible explanation of the disordered behavior to emerge. The awareness of important influences shaping the pattern of behavior made available to the patient (as well as to the observer) some understanding of this pattern. On the basis of this, slowly but progressively, helpful modifications were made by the patient in her evaluations and in her adaptation.

It is quite possible that in the fully disordered psychopath similar but far more complicated causative influences exist behind the clinical manifestations. In the real psychopath a gross lack of sincerity and insight seriously impedes all efforts to obtain information essential to interpretation. We must also consider the possibility that the psychopath may be born with a biologic defect that leaves him without the capacity to feel and appreciate the major issues of life or to react to them in a normal and adequate manner.

SPECIFIC HOMOSEXUALITY AND OTHER CONSISTENT SEXUAL DEVIATIONS

When the first edition of this book was written, it had for many years been customary to use the term *sexual psychopath* to designate homosexuals, sadists, masochists, and also people specifically inclined toward exhibitionism, voyeurism, fetishism, cross-dressing, and pedophilia. Included at times with these deviations under the concept of *sexual psychopathy* were also types of abnormal behavior designated as erotomania and sexual immaturity. For many years before and after the initial publication of *The Mask of Sanity* this custom had authoritative sanction in our nomenclature.

This I believe tended to promote confusion and foster the belief that these, or most of these, sexual disorders, deviations, or anomalies, along with the disorder of the psychopath or antisocial personality, were all types or variations of a unitary basic abnormality. Even now in our latest official nomenclature we find what I, and I believe most other psychiatrists, regard as the real psychopath included with all the recognized sexual deviations under the general heading *personality disorders.*

It is true that some sexually aberrant patients show additional pathologic features. Sometimes, but by no means regularly or even frequently, these features include those typical of the psychopath (true antisocial personality). This relatively rare mixing of features, however, has never seemed to me an adequate reason for identifying the two groups, or even for assuming that they are in fundamental respects closely related.

No one is more ready than I to agree that the real psychopath's sexuality is abnormal. The schizophrenic, the patient with organic brain disease, the paranoid, and many other types of psychiatric patients also carry out deviated sexual activity, and in those who do not one often finds indications of extremely deviated attitudes about the basic erotic orientations. Yet we would not find it profitable to give up our distinguishing terms for these disorders and merge them as types under a general term that also embraces the sexual disorders. Such a scheme would, no doubt, tend in time to blur our concepts about what we are dealing with.

It impresses me as inaccurate to assume that homosexuals as a class show the general life pattern of gratuitous folly and purposelessness so typical of the psychopath. It seems unlikely that more than a small percentage of homosexuals ever come to the attention of psychiatrists at all. Fewer by far are admitted to psychiatric hospitals. Whether or not the Kinsey Report correctly estimates the proportion of male homosexuals in the nation, it seems obvious that they are far from rare in almost any community. As noted previously, some deviates of this sort also show the more generalized and even the typical maladjustment seen in the psychopath, but the two groups, neither in medical practice nor in a survey of the community, seem to coincide. There is, indeed, some overlapping, but this is true of most psychiatric conditions.

It would seem remarkable if any physician of experience could not call to mind a great many distinct and overt homosexuals who continue to lead peaceful, productive, and socially useful lives and who cannot, even by the most violent imaginative tour de force, be identified with the psychopath as he is here presented. It could hardly be said that characteristically these deviated people fail to show kindness and consideration for the rights of others, that they are incapable of gratitude, affection, or compassion. Only confusion is promoted by efforts to identify them as a group with the gross pattern of failure and the profound, generalized incompetency of the other life pattern.

In the homosexual group are found people active and persistent in the promotion of painting, music, literature, and other expressions of art or learning, and reliable leaders in civic enterprises. In these endeavors they do not, usually, give evidence of such inconsistency and shallowness as we see in the other disorder.

Among these better adjusted homosexuals are seen successful lawyers, artists, bankers, and scholars, who appear in their nonsexual activities to show persistent purpose and evidence of responsibility. There are also less successful but industrious and peaceful citizens who year after year carry out their duties in humbler occupations and regularly fulfill obligations to dependents.

When we consider people of this sort, and it is not unlikely that they constitute a majority of homosexuals, it is not surprising to see that Greenspan and Campbell long ago made this statement:

> The homosexual is so unlike the psychopath that it is hardly conceivable that the most popular classification places him as a subgroup of the psychopathic personality. [They add] However, there are possible two reasons for this error. One, any sexual anomaly, even in the minds of physicians, is unequivocally associated with antisocial behavior and therefore akin to psychopathic personality. Two, an occasional psychopath will admit to homosexual activities, thereby substantiating this impression.

That some homosexuals show persistent and gross maladaptation all through their pattern of living seems less remarkable than that so many avoid what is typical of the psychopath or of the schizophrenic. It seems to me unlikely that the typical homosexual can escape deep frustration in what is perhaps the most fundamental aspect of living. The mockery and scorn that deviation of this sort often evokes from society and the almost inevitable efforts at secrecy and pretense to which its victims are usually driven are likely to act as significant distorting forces on the whole personality. Because they have to suppress, evade, and implicitly deceive so much about something so vital every day of their lives, it is perhaps remarkable that homosexuals can adjust successfully or with dignity in any phase of living.

Another much more complicated factor has also impressed me as contributing to the difficulties of the homosexual's life. Many of those who discussed their problems with me fully have left me with the conviction that the ideal mate they seek is not another homosexual but a normally oriented person of their own sex. This need would lead to a futile quest for the impossible and bring not only inevitable frustration and repeated disillusionment but also, as can easily be seen, would make for pessimistic and cynical attitudes about love.

In the early years of my psychiatric practice this frequently recurring feature of the homosexual's need and quest was vividly illustrated for me by an athletic and successful young man. With frankness and dignity he discussed numerous and diverse erotic experiences, all with other men. The more he conveyed to me about his reactions, the more it seemed clear that he felt a paradoxical distaste for the available homosexual partners with whom he sought physical satisfaction or relief from tension. It seemed also that he could not, despite his freely admitted homosexuality, wholeheartedly identify himself with the group. In his complexly mixed feelings there seemed to be negative elements not unlike those so often found in the ordinary man's reactions to those he thinks of as "gay." At his deeper levels of feeling he seemed to reject other homosexuals from full acceptance, either in the role of erotic partners or as objects of fraternal fellowship.

In sharp contrast to these negative reactions, and ambivalent reactions, toward his fellows, this man expressed pure adoration and unqualified admiration for a young heterosexual male whom he seemed to regard as the ideal, the ultimate, erotic choice. His longing for this unattainable figure seemed completely free from the negative qualities that marred his pleasure with available homosexual partners. In referring to the normally oriented young man who had so powerfully, but unwittingly attracted him, the patient exclaimed, "He was just a typical, clean-cut American boy." His yearning and his almost ecstatic admiration seemed not only genuine but touched with grief and reverence that brought a lyric note to the ordinarily banal words he seized upon as if in desperate need to convey something complex and specific. With emphasis this man repeated, "He was a perfectly typical young American boy! A clean-cut American boy!"

Indications of a similar choice for the normally oriented and unavailable person of the same sex have often been evident in homosexuals I have since encountered. I have wondered if this specific emotional demand is not far more common among homosexuals than is generally recognized. I have indeed wondered if it might, in some degree, be universal. If so it could account for tragic difficulties in mating.* It is well, however, to avoid sweeping generalizations on the basis of one's necessarily limited experience.

Some other types of sexual behavior regarded as abnormal have in the past been classified under such terms as *erotomania* and *sexual immaturity.* So far as erotomania is concerned, the following points may be made: Most psychopaths known to me have shown little compunction about seeking sexual gratification. They are so frequently found in brothels and with other professional vendors of erotic wares that one might at first glance conclude that they indeed suffer from erotomania.† A closer consideration of the circumstances, however, reveals that the psychopath is not pushed into these situations by an excessivley vigorous eroticism but that even the feeblest and most transient impulse will cause him to seek gratification with partners and in environments shunned by a person with ordinary judgment and discretion and taste. It is indeed open to question whether the impulse is more than feeble in the sense of genitalized sexuality, to say nothing of mature sexuality. Sometimes the male psychopath, after carefully setting the stage for seduction, will instead of achieving intercourse, straightway drink himself into the purgatorial nirvana of maudlin semiconsciousness, leaving his partner to nurse and pamper him. In my experience the typical psychopath of either sex does not appear to have a sexual drive, normal or perverse, of sufficient vigor to account for the poor judgment shown in what seems rather to be a vague blundering along the roads of folly and frustration toward what is essentially life rejection. There are, of course, persons activated by strong libidinous drive who often commit extremely indiscreet deeds and who sometimes even bring disaster on themselves. These, however, do not impress me as fundamentally similar to the psychopath.

Sexual immaturity can be more aptly used, in my opinion, as a term to describe all psychopaths than to segregate any particular group of them.

Masochism, sadism, bestiality, fetishism, necrophilia, voyeurism, and the terms for various other perversions would seem to imply people who consistently sought definite erotic satisfaction in one or more of these ways and in whom this quest was a major and persistent life aim. Taken in this sense, such characteristics are not particularly common in the psychopaths whom I have studied. Psychopaths, of course, show a carelessness about drifting with virtually any impulse. But they do not regularly give the impression that efforts to attain specific gratification of this sort play an important role in their conduct or could account for their generalized patterns of failure.

In a broader sense it might be said that the apparently willful persistence with which they bring humiliation and emotional suffering upon those who love them, as well as

---

*I have discussed these questions at length in another work, *The Caricature of Love*.

†Such a conclusion would, however, be as seriously wrong as to assume that the inveterate reader of sentimental rhymes gave evidence of a strong inclination for poetry or that the empty and aggressive braggart were really of stoic fiber.

failure and unpleasant circumstances upon themselves, marks all psychopaths as both sadists and masochists. Only in this sense, however, are these impulses common or consistent, and the gratification is probably not the directly erotic sensation enjoyed by perverts who literally whip others or have themselves whipped. I get the impression that a great many of the people who have attracted attention primarily as sadists have many characteristics of the classic psychopath. Certainly they seem to show extreme callousness to the suffering of others. The lives of other famous sadists strongly suggest the influence of deep schizoid disorder. It has been already stated that true psychopaths with serious tendencies to perpetrate violent crimes do exist. The real psychopath who is a real (persistently organized) sadist, of course, ranks as an extremely dangerous person. Like all psychopaths, he is unlikely to be greatly altered by punishment or training or treatment, and he constitutes a grave problem. People of this type are often responsible for perverse and murderous attacks on children frequently noticed in the newspapers.

If true and full sadistic tendencies are combined with the psychopath's lack of compunction, a formidable menace to others is likely to emerge. Let us consider Neville G. C. Heath, who within a period of three weeks committed two of the most gruesome sexual murders and mutilations ever to be reported.

According to reliable evidence, some of which was brought out at his trial, this man followed an extremely irresponsible career for many years. On several occasions he was court-martialed and discharged from the military service. Forgeries, thefts, housebreaking, impersonation of an officer, fraud, and many elaborate episodes of swindling brought him repeatedly to the attention of the police. The history available about this handsome, intelligent, attractive and carefree antisocial figure prior to his two sadistic murders strongly indicates the typical psychopath.

His record as a charmer among the ladies is difficult to match. Many intelligent, lovely, and wealthy young women apparently succumbed to his quickly irresistible wooing and, with rapture and pride, considered themselves engaged to him until he disappeared after ingeniously borrowing or otherwise obtaining large sums of money from their families. He was regularly able to convince not only the women but also their families that he was a man of great distinction and tremendous financial resources. One report indicates that while on a sea voyage he seduced a young Hungarian beauty and also her similarly enticing and voluptuous mother. After the mother and daughter discovered that he had been alternating his sexual attentions between them, with convincing vows of eternal fidelity to both, they maintained a fierce and idealistic loyalty to Heath and each sought diligently to obtain financial advantages for him through intercession with the husband (of the older) and father (of the younger), who had not, because of urgent and important business responsibilities, been able to accompany them on the voyage. This is apparently a typical example of Heath's ability to impress others, including very learned and intelligent people, with his appearance of profound sincerity and of innumerable other virtues and remarkable abilities and achievements.

The sexually perverse murders carried out by this handsome, athletic young man of idealistic and intensely virile appearance were acts of memorable brutality and horror. Each of the two young women tortured and killed by Heath within a period of three weeks was cruelly butchered. The sexually sadistic quality of Heath's behavior on these two occasions is made plain by the nature of the mutilations. A nipple was bitten entirely from one girl's breast. Much of the breast itself had been chewed and mangled to bloody pulp. With the other girl this had almost been accomplished. At the autopsy both showed that some instrument, perhaps a poker, had been thrust with violence into the vagina, rupturing it and damaging the abdominal viscera. In one of the victims the poker had apparently been driven far up into the abdominal cavity and twisted about with great violence. One body had been lashed severely by a heavy, metal-tipped whip. The nude bodies were found covered with clotted blood. The abdomen of one woman had been ripped open so extensively that the intestines emerged and spread sickeningly over the area about her body. One deep gash started below the genital organs and extended up into the breast. Heath is described as being extremely calm and poised and entirely free of remorse after these deeds. After the first murder he spoke with great interest about accounts of it in the newspapers, expressed opinions about how the gruesome wounds might have been inflicted, and even communicated with the police, offering to help them discover the murderer.

The victims were tightly bound and gagged. Points brought out at the autopsies indicate that Heath wanted the women to remain alive as long as possible to experience the agony resulting from his vicious torture and that he seemed to relish the butchery particularly while the victims still remained conscious and capable of feeling it. Apparently he also found perverse sexual satisfaction in continuing after death the gruesome and protracted mutilation of the bodies.

Those who devoutly believe that the psychopath carries out crimes because of an inner, unconscious sense of guilt and a need (also unconscious) to seek punishment in persistent efforts to gain expiation might say that Heath's getting in touch with the police and offering them advice after the first butchery and murder, and his making himself conspicuous at the scene of the first crime, afford proof of their assumptions. It appears to me, however, that such an argument ignores the peculiar and astonishing callousness of psychopaths and also ignores the fact that they appear to take a positive and boastful delight in showing off in the midst of their uninviting, destructive, and antisocial achievements. They often seem to relish this as an exhibition of their prowess. I think it much more likely that such a man as Heath would want to savor the afterglow of his perverse and sadistic crime, to exult in his success, and to flaunt his ability to hoodwink the police than that he would be unconsciously seeking punishment in order to ease a conscience which was causing him great remorse of which he remained unaware.

THE ERRATIC MAN OF GENIUS

Rather curiously, one might at first think, many persons widely recognized as geniuses have been placed by various writers in the classification of psychopathic personality. The vagueness and plasticity of the term as it was for so long officially used seems still to promote it's being stretched in practice to cover nearly any type of abnormal behavior imaginable, and the literal or etymologic connotation is, of course, no less all-embracing.

It is true that a number of celebrities presented in school books as ornaments of our civilization are credited with isolated acts that would do justice to the cases discussed in this book. Some of the great figures in history, literature, philosophy, and art are said even to have behaved continually in abnormal patterns.

The concept of genius as a type of madness is particularly associated with Lombroso, who, in 1888, with *The Man of Genius,* advanced his familiar hypothesis that genius is a degenerative psychosis, a sort of "moral insanity" which may at times take the form of other mental disorders but which preserves certain distinguishing characteristics.

Grasset, following a similar line of thought, gives some striking examples. Tolstoi is said to have lashed himself with ropes and to have fallen a considerable distance while attempting to fly before he became preoccupied with wondering seriously whether to abandon civilization for a primitive life in the desert. Jean Jacques Rousseau's many false starts as medical student, clockmaker, theologian, painter, servant, musician, and botanist are noted, as well as his curious letter addressed to God Almighty which he placed under the altar of Notre Dame. Rousseau's expressed repugnance toward the normal sex act is also noted. Schopenhauer's peculiarities, long famous, are reviewed by Grasset. His abnormal attitude of esthetic distaste toward woman, his morbid suspiciousness which led him to write even trivial notes in dead languages, and his occasional assaults on unsuspecting bystanders who he fancied were talking about him all suggest a deep-seated maladjustment.

Unusual and apparently irrational behavior has indeed been so commonly reported in the lives of those acclaimed as great artists and thinkers that there is a popular tendency to regard it as the rule rather than the exception. Vincent Van Gogh's career is a familiar example. His justly celebrated exploit in cutting off his own ear and sending it to a prostitute of Arles is one of many.

Richard Wagner, according to some of his biographers, manifested an utter disregard for the feelings and the rights of others, a petty vanity, and sometimes a callousness almost worthy of the psychopath. Nordau has indeed said that Wagner is accused of having "a greater degree of degeneracy than all the other degenerates heretofore seen put together!"

Jonathan Swift, in his poem *The Lady's Dressing Room* and in other writings, manifests an attitude so basically distorted that it is difficult not to believe he was a very ill man psychiatrically. In an interesting discussion of life-rejecting attitudes and their relation to obsessive disorder, Straus makes clear something that is probably not only pertinent to that syndrome but also to other psychiatric conditions. The basic emotional judgment expressed by Swift might, if it were an unconscious stratum in the psychopath, play an important part in his clinical manifestations. The life of this learned, conscientious and brilliant man does not, however, show behavioral features that would in any way suggest his being classed in our group, nor do the other celebrated figures mentioned above, despite these reports of eccentricity and of various psychiatric manifestations.

Is it not pertinent here to ask ourselves again, What is a genius? In the dictionary, among other definitions, we find, "a man endowed with transcendant ability." Shall we conclude that the authentic genius will demonstrate more than ordinary wisdom in the conduct of his life? Or should we consider his books or his music or his statuary apart from his personal acts? Shall we say that his creative productions furnish the evidence of superior wisdom or of essential greatness that he may have failed to display in his role as a husband, father, friend, or citizen?

It seems reasonable to argue that we should gratefully accept the work of the poet and artist for what positive qualities we find in the work, itself, and that we can ignore altogether, if we choose, the life of the man who produced it. May there not be truth and beauty quite genuine in the creative artist's experience but which he cannot apply consistently in the conduct of his own life? It seems reasonable to believe that this is likely.

On the other hand, if the productions of the artist, the poems, novels, or paintings themselves, reflect gruesomely distorted or perverse appraisals of life, is it not natural for us, when we recognize this, to feel distaste? If malignantly perverse attitudes are presented, disguised, or partly disguised, as verities enshrined by art, it seems reasonable to believe that the unwary may be seriously confused or misled. Such qualities in art might justifiably be recognized and proclaimed as pathologic.

Throughout Europe and America, Paul Verlaine is acclaimed as an important figure in world literature. In our colleges and universities young people are encouraged to admire his works and to recognize him as a rare and wonderful spirit, towering above the level of common humanity. The sordid folly, the senseless and distasteful misconduct, parasitism, indolence, depravity, and irresponsible squandering reported as habitual of Verlaine might make it difficult for some, despite his established reputation as a poet, to believe he was a man of superior qualities and sensibilities. Others may assume that this man's unprovoked and truly murderous assaults on a close friend and also on Arthur Rimbaud, his favorite homosexual intimate, and on his mother arose from the turbulent passions of a great creative artist. Could such acts and the general conduct of his life be related to callousness, perversity, and a deficiency of basic human reactions? It has been said that "probably the greatest misfortune ever to befall Paul Verlaine in his tragedy-riddled career was the fact that he was sentenced to only two years in jail—instead of life imprisonment—for the attempted murder of Arthur Rimbaud." These two years have been judged by some as the least miserable and humiliating, the most nearly normal years of his adult life.

For centuries moralists have sometimes condemned the artist's life as licentious, as given over to sensual delights, to violent and exquisite but unconventional erotic pursuits and consummations. Others have argued, often indignantly, that the creative genius is exempt from our ordinary standards of behavior, that his mighty passions justly sweep aside ethical barriers suitable for lesser men, and that his vast spiritual fulfillments and accomplishments not only excuse but even sanctify conduct that in others might be classed as irresponsible or even criminal. The immature and the naive often picture those who choose the bohemian life as virile standard-bearers of youth, gallant rebels against puritanical restrictions, strong men who claim a rich and lusty fulfillment of what Eros demands.

It is popularly believed also that the genius is neglected or, through outrageous injustice, even condemned by his contemporaries because they are too stupid to understand him and to recognize his superior wisdom and spiritual values. According to legend, subsequent generations at last catch on or wake up and come to see that the creative artist was right and the surrounding social group stupidly wrong. Those who do not in retrospect justify and romantically glorify the poet's or musician's actual conduct often conclude that his productions show that he understood or felt more profoundly than ordinary men the issues of human life and that his lofty and magnificent being reveals itself to us through his cantos, his odes, or his symphonies.

We find in Thomas Mann's appraisal of Dostoevski viewpoints not entirely the same as those just mentioned. It is plain that he regards the venerated Russian novelist as profoundly disordered, as perhaps chief among "the great sinners and the damned, the sufferers of holy disease. . . . I am," Mann says, "filled with awe, with a profound, mystic, silence-enjoining awe, in the presence of the religious greatness of the damned, in the presence of genius of disease and the disease of genius, of the type of the afflicted and the possessed, in whom saint and criminal are one." Mann feels that Dostoevski was personally preoccupied with fantasies of bestial brutality such as the rape of a girl child he described in Stavrogin's confession. "Apparently this infamous crime constantly occupied the author's moral imagination."

Mann apparently does not regard Dostoevski as great despite his disease or as redeemed by art from what he finds in "the criminal depths of the author's own conscience." To the contrary, he identifies disease and genius:

> The disease bears fruits that are more important and more beneficial to life and its development than any medically approved normality. The truth is that life has never been able to do without the morbid, and probably no adage is more inane than the one which says that "only disease can come from the diseased." Life is not prudish and it is probably safe to say that life prefers creative, genius-bestowing disease a thousand times over to prosaic health; prefers disease, surmounting obstacles proudly on horseback, boldly leaping from peak to peak, to lounging, pedestrian healthfulness. Life is not finical and never thinks of making a moral distinction between health and infirmity. It seizes the bold product of disease, consumes and digests it, and as soon as it is assimilated, it is health. An entire horde, a generation of open-minded, healthy lads pounces upon the work of diseased genius, genialized by disease, admires and praises it, raises it to the skies, perpetuates it, transmutes it, and bequeathes it to civilization, which does not live on the home-baked bread of health alone. They all swear by the name of the great invalid, thanks to whose madness they no longer need to be mad. Their healthfulness feeds upon his madness and in them he will become healthy.
>
> In other words, certain attainments of the soul and the intellect are impossible without disease, without insanity, without spiritual crime, and the great invalids are crucified victims, sacrificed to humanity and its advancement, to the broadening of its feeling and knowledge—in short, to its more sublime health. . . . They force us to re-evaluate the concepts of "disease" and "health," the relation of sickness and life; they teach us to be cautious in our approach to the idea of "disease," for we are too prone always to give it a biological minus sign.

Mario Praz, in his well-known work *The Romantic Agony,* makes this comment about the French decadents:

> [They] found or thought they found in the novels of Dostoevski a sadism which had become more mystical and more subtle, no longer limited to the grossness of physical torture but penetrating like a worm-hole into all moral phenomena. . . . they found also a thirst for the impossible, and impotence elevated to the height of a mystical ecstasy. . . . In Sade and in the sadists of the "frenetique" type of Romanticism it is the integrity of the body which is assaulted and destroyed, whereas in Dostoevski one has the feeling . . . of the "intimacy of the soul brutally and insolently violated."

Unlike Thomas Mann, Praz does not express a belief in any mystical value superior to that of health in such reactions or claim that they save subsequent generations from madness. He does, however, present much evidence to support his argument that in the work of many important literary figures generally regarded as geniuses it is the pathology itself that has won admiration and been acclaimed as beauty or wisdom. He offers many examples of the influence of the Marquis de Sade, and of his tastes, in the writings of Baudelaire, Verlaine, Swinburne, Flaubert, Gautier, Huysmans, and others too numerous to mention here.

The rapt attention that Praz demonstrates in the literary productions of this large group for literal algolagnia is complicated by many nuances of perversion. Truly corrupt and appalling depravities of taste and impulse are expressed, some passing beyond the antisocial or the unnatural and well deserving to be called antibiologic. Sexual inversion sometimes overreaches itself into rapturous praise and lustful yearning for such tragic monstrosities as those exemplified by the literal hermaphrodite. Pain, disfigurement, torture, putrefaction, disgrace, ennui, death, profanation, and nearly all things detestable to sane men are, according to the argument by Mario Praz, esthetically invoked, equivocally identified as love or glory, and treated with perverse veneration. Through the sensibilities of these famous decadents, woman is enthusiastically perceived as an overpowering, murderous vampire, man as a furtive and gelded weakling. Necrophilia and coprophilia apparently have attractions for at least a few of the group presented by Praz. In some of their writings delight is expressed not merely in things naturally disgusting, but in disgust itself.

The pathology and perversion of axiomatic human values demonstrated by Praz in the literary productions he discusses are indeed profound. If these productions represent the life experience of the authors, accurately reflect their taste and judgment, it is difficult to refrain from asking why they should be accepted as intellectual or spiritual superiors qualified to enlighten or inspire ordinary men and women.

If Baudelair or Swinburne achieves a genuine excellence of art in poetry, need we concern ourselves with its substance, with what human values it proclaims or implies, or with what kind of personal experience it embodies or reflects? Can we appraise the worth of this poetry as art entirely apart from its content? If the viewpoints and emotional reactions that produced it are psychotic or obviously perverse, must we say that this is irrelevant, that it has nothing to do with the greatness of the poet? Or of the poetry?

Perhaps this can be done by the critic of art who in his role ceases to react as a human being. To the ordinary man, and probably to the physician, esoteric attempts to isolate art from biologic experience, to consider it without reference to the personal emotion it reflects or evokes, are likely to appear speciously mystical and unenticing.

Baudelaire's actual life is reported as that of a feeble and affected eccentric, a wastrel apparently without normal passions or friendships. Dyeing his hair green and sometimes leading a live lobster through the streets on a pale blue ribbon, he lived, at times, in an atmosphere chiefly of vexation and disgust, with an ignorant mulatto girl for whom his attachment is said to have been "cerebral rather than sensuous." Some of his biographers concluded that he may have been sexually impotent. His reported disdain for ordinary morality was apparently surpassed by his repulsion at prospects of physical relations with beautiful and intelligent women.

Can it be said, despite his unenviable personal career, that Baudelaire's art establishes him as a very great man, a lofty spirit resplendent above the ordinary and deserving our reverent admiration? Before trying to answer such a question is it not reasonable to inquire into what sorts of judgment and feeling, what evaluations of experience—ethical, esthetic, or otherwise—are reflected in this work? If we find in it wisdom and beauty, something to sustain or enrich lesser men, it might be argued that we should ignore the conduct of his life and bow our heads in acknowledgment of his message.

Praz credits Baudelaire's poetry with having given "a psychological turn to the refinements of perversity" and in it finds a vividly persistent taste for joy in damnation, an insistence on achieving religious beliefs in order to enhance the shame and horror of desecrating them. Here the sexual mate emerges scarcely at all except in terms of derisive obscenity or hideous monstrosity. Not occasionally but pervasively we see that "inversion of values which is the basis of sadism, vice [representing] the positive active elements, virtue the negative and passive. Virtue exists only as a restraint to be broken." Actual voluptuousness is travestied, achieving little or no recognition except in perverted forms of physical brutality or moral abuse. Praz not only speaks of but amply illustrates Baudelaire's "inexhaustible need to be occupied with macabre and obscene subjects." His works are shown to abound in enthusiastic references to nearly all those defilements, reversals, butcheries, and abortions of basic human feeling embodied in the Black Mass and apparently relished there so avidly by J. K. Huysmans. The fraudulent or counterfeit is regularly accorded superiority over the actual. Baudelaire states that it is his purpose to "extract beauty out of evil." It is doubtful if such an extract can be made beautiful or valuable through being renamed, however melodiously, or through being welcomed, however lyrically. Ignominy is rapturously embraced and pronounced sublime. Ennui is accepted as an esthetic triumph. Perhaps nothing is more typical of how this genius reacted to life than his famous statement: "Woman is natural, that is to say abominable."

A recent biographer speaks of Baudelaire as "a soul of such profound spirituality and a mind of such heightened sensibility." We are also told that, "through his own sufferings he came to understand the sufferings of mankind." Do his works really reveal this spirituality and understanding? Have the courts who during his life condemned *Les Fleurs du Mal* as "an outrage upon morals and decency" been proved stupidly wrong?

"I have loved overmuch," Swinburne says. The youthful and the naive often believe him. The surging rhythms of his verse, the sumptuous imagery, the cumulative efflorescence of his alliteration readily stir the uninitiated. Many who encounter Swinburne during high school or college assume he speaks for the hot desire of youth, that the fervor of his poetry is a quintessential fervor of Eros. He is often pictured by the unsophisticated as a gallant, vital figure, the sensuous and virile bard of passionate love and physical ardors. Even those who ordinarily reject poetry, having vaguely relegated it to the province of bookish pedants or to the effeminate, sometimes respond to lines from "Dolores" or "The Garden of Proserpine." During the imperious urges, the inarticulateness, and the confusion of a first love, they may find in Swinburne an intensity that seems to match their wildest aspirations. His brilliantly ringing lines must, they believe, represent a noble pagan vigor, a spirit so strong and vital that it sweeps through ordinary restraints and conventional artificialities. His voice is often taken to be the mighty voice of a lover calling on life to flood and fecundate parched deserts of asceticism and negation, on nature to flower in ultimate fulfillment.

In the vivid urgency to consummate amorous desires which society insists they defer and only dream about for so long, the normal boy and girl may read from the following lines in "Dolores":

By the ravenous teeth that have smitten
Through the kisses that blossom and bud,
By the lips intertwisted and bitten
Till the foam has a savour of blood.
By the pulse as it rises and falters,
By the hands as they slacken and strain,
I adjure thee respond from thine altars,
Our Lady of Pain.

They often find reflected in this something of the vigor of their natural impulses. Anticipating sexual fulfillments that must be delayed, they normally picture these fulfillments as hot-blooded, wholehearted, and breathtaking. Perhaps such a term as "Our Lady of Pain" is surprising, but, after all, sorrow is often mentioned in connection with love. The heart aches, and in separation there is suffering.

Continuing, they find Swinburne thus speaking of a female figure:

As of old when the world's heart was lighter,
Through thy garments the grace of thee glows,
The white wealth of thy body made whiter
By the blushes of amorous blows,
And seamed with sharp lips and fierce fingers,
And branded by kisses that bruise;
When all shall be gone that now lingers,
Oh, what shall we lose?

Normally oriented young people will probably assume that the poet is referring to sexual ardor. What matters an accidental bruise or abrasion from embraces and caresses exchanged in the joy and vigor of amorous consummation? Ordinary readers may be puzzled when the female is referred to thus:

Fruits fail and love dies and time ranges;
Thou art fed with perpetual breath,
And alive after infinite changes,
And fresh from the kisses of death;
Of languors rekindled and rallied,
Of barren delights and unclean,
Things monstrous and fruitless, a pallid
And poisonous queen.

Perhaps they are puzzled. But after all, poetry, they remember, is not necessarily literal like a blueprint or like a pamphlet giving instructions about how to repair radios. Their uncertainties are dissolved in the stimulation of:

Thou wert fair in the fearless old fashion,
And thy limbs are as melodies yet,
And move to the music of passion
With lithe and lascivious regret.

They will probably continue to feel that Swinburne is dealing with the passions they feel even after he says:

> I could hurt thee—but pain would delight thee;
> Or caress thee—but love would repel;
> And the lovers whose lips would excite thee
> Are serpents in hell.

After all, the real speech between lovers is seldom exact. Literally inappropriate words are often risked to convey opposite meanings, perhaps through efforts to register intensity about what cannot be adequately defined or soberly conveyed as a matter of fact.

From what is known of Swinburne's life, it seems unlikely that he could have "loved overmuch." He apparently had little or no interest in normal relations with women. This was so conspicuous that his close friend Rossetti is said to have bribed a particularly enterprising and alluring lady with ten pounds to evoke in him some amorous response. After her best efforts she confessed her failure and returned the money. After repeatedly showing himself unable to avoid disastrous drinking or to handle his ordinary affairs with minimum competency, the poet spent nearly all his adult life living with his bachelor friend and protector Watts-Dunton, who apparently acted as an informal guardian or voluntary lay attendant.

The evidence according to Praz strongly indicates that Swinburne habitually sought bizarre satisfactions and shames in "queer houses" where flagellation was practiced as a substitute for, or a mockery of, biologically oriented sexual relations. Since early in life he pored over the writings of the Marquis de Sade, for whom he is said to have maintained not only a strong affinity but, indeed, hero worship. The poet's writings copiously illustrate his concept of sensual pleasure and of "love" as painful brutality and foul humiliation. It is difficult to find in them, or from what is reported of his life, anything to indicate that he enjoyed an appreciable awareness of what women mean to ordinary men, or of human love.

Praz presents strong evidence that in Swinburne's poetry recurrent reflection of a most malignant sadism become at times frankly cannibalistic and that he projects perversion and morbid derogation into the surrounding universe. When Swinburne writes of "the mute melancholy lust of heaven," according to Praz, "heaven merely reflects the mute melancholy lust of the poet himself."

Depicting in "Anactoria" what he apparently means to be taken for sexual love, Swinburne is sometimes explicit:

> I would my love could kill thee; I am satiated
> With seeing thee live, and fain would have thee dead.
> I would earth had thy body as fruit to eat,
> And no mouth but some serpent's found thee sweet.
> I would find grievous ways to have thee slain,
> Intense device, and superflux of pain;
> Vex thee with amorous agonies, and shake
> Life at thy lips, and leave it there to ache;
> Strain out thy soul with pangs too soft to kill,
> Intolerable interludes, and infinite ill;
> Relapse and reluctation of the breath,
> Dumb tones and shuddering semitones of death.

• • •

Ah that my lips were tuneless lips, but pressed
To the bruised blossom of thy scourged white breast!
Ah that my mouth for Muses' milk were fed
On the sweet blood thy sweet small wounds had bled!
That with my tongue I felt them, and could taste
The faint flakes from thy bosom to the waist!
That I could drink thy veins as wine, and eat
Thy breast like honey! that from face to feet
Thy body were abolished and consumed,
And in my flesh thy very flesh entombed!

• • •

. . . Oh that I
Durst crush thee out of life with love, and die,
Die of thy pain and my delight, and be
Mixed with thy blood and motion into thee!
Would I not plague thee dying overmuch?
Would I not hurt thee perfectly? not touch
Thy pores of sense with torture, and make bright
Thine eyes with bloodlike tears and grevious light?
Strike pang from pang as note is struck from note,
Catch the sob's middle music in thy throat,
Take thy limbs living, and new-mould with these
A lyre of many faultless agonies?

It may be that Baudelaire, or that Swinburne, shows sufficient mastery over the rhythms and the other technicalities of poetry to be correctly classified as a genius. Is it, however, even sane to argue that the basic tastes and judgments expressed or implied on human life in the lines just quoted should be accepted as superior to those of the ordinary man? Regularly reversing the most axiomatic human orientations, do these not stand as expressions in art of what has been unforgettably illustrated in conduct by such figures as Jack the Ripper, Gilles de Rais, and Neville George Clevely Heath? Can these tastes and judgments be regarded as anything but obvious manifestations of disease, of disease that is uninviting and malignant?

Praz, in his detailed and serious study, offers impressive evidence of the influence exerted by earlier exponents of the pathologic and perverse on subsequent artists and literary figures of similar inclination. The Marquis de Sade apparently is accepted as a true prophet or seer by Baudelaire and Gautier; these in turn profoundly influence Swinburne, Oscar Wilde, d'Annunzio, Octave Mirbeau, J. K. Huysmans, Barbey d'Aurevilly, and scores of others.

If we conclude that some men accepted as superior to the common stature of humanity prove, on closer acquaintance with their artistic works, no less than with their lives, to be not great and admirable figures in the ordinary meaning of such terms, how shall we try to explain their continuing recognition as remarkably inspired or enlightened personages? An attempt to answer this question adequately would lead us far afield. One point, however, may be briefly noted.

If there are among those commonly accepted as geniuses some who could be better classified as apostles of disease and negation, it is scarcely surprising that they continue to gain disciples. The malignant perversions of the Marquis de Sade are accepted by Baudelaire and Swinburne as a rich gospel of estheticism. The schizoid misogyny of August Strindberg, listed in encyclopedias as Sweden's foremost literary figure, prompts him to hail publicly and reverently as a genius the pathetic Viennese youth, Otto Weininger, who expressed a similar schizoid misgoyny in fantastic terms shortly before taking his own life. Pathologic reactions expressed in art apparently appeal to persons similarly disordered. Finding the normal premises of human life unacceptable, the ordinary biologic goals invisible or illusory, they seem to welcome the viewpoint of those who in poetry or philosophy reflect a life rejection they share. It is not difficult to see how such viewpoints may appear as manifestations of superior esthetic sensibility, as a special wisdom, to new cults of intellectual defeatists and deviates who gather in succeeding generations.

If it is true that some creative artists of great renown show both in their conduct and their work indications of serious personality disorder, how shall we class them? Are some of those established by tradition as high priests of truth, beauty, and inspiration really members of the clinical group we call psychopaths? Although some of their works convey reactions and evaluations as inadequate as those of the typical psychopath and as incompatible with even minimum standards of human feeling and behavior, we should not necessarily identify their disorder with that of the patients presented in this book. Sexual deviation with its inevitable frustrations and reversals of response and masked but profound schizoid disorder formulated in disdainful misanthropy and life perversion seem more likely to account for the tastes and viewpoints revealed by these talented people. None of the creative artists thought by Mario Praz to be dominated by sadistic influences, and none of the others mentioned in this chapter, impress me as people who should be classified primarily with the true psychopath.

In contrast with them, the typical psychopath does not labor consistently to express in art pathologic reactions or distorted appraisals of life. In words the typical psychopath characteristically gives normal evaluations, defines excellent moral standards, and enthusiastically claims the accepted goals and aims of civilized man as his own. He is often an articulate spokesman for the good life. If the sort of patient described here should have sufficient talent and industry to produce works accepted as valuable literature or art, I do not think it likely he would in them try to express nihilistic or perverse attitudes. Whatever he might express would probably be as spurious, as little representative of authentic human experience, as his convincing but empty promises, his eloquent protestations of a love he does not feel. His production, however brilliant technically, would be a valid rendering of neither health nor disease but a counterfeit.

Is it possible that behind the psychopath's disorder there once lay extraordinary potentialities? I have seen other types of people who in critical periods of development seemed to face problems that arose largely from their own precocity, their own distinctly superior qualities. Such patients sometimes seem, it might be said, to have advanced intellectually and in some respects emotionally so far ahead of what is average that they encounter problems and pressures which demand greater general maturity than it has been possible for them to acquire, although their general maturity may well excel the average. Patients in such situations have been observed who, it seemed, were being pushed into various patterns of psychiatric illness, pushed toward clinical psychoneurosis or possibly even toward schizophrenia, by factors brought into play more through the indirect effects of their superiority than by any specific personality deficits.

Although excellent capacity is of value in efforts to work through problems, to avoid dangerous pathologic reactive patterns, it is also, I believe, possible that high magnitudes of emotional and other functional potentiality may have something to do with the degree of destructiveness when regressive withdrawals and disintegrative forces set the course. A man of unusual integrity and loyalty is likely to be more severely damaged than a man mediocre in these respects if complicated and confusing situations cause him to make grave errors in his business (or in his decision as an officer during combat) that result in disaster for which he holds himself responsible. Abandonment or betrayal by a fiancé or mate is likely to put stress upon persons in direct proportion to the depth of genuineness with which the other is loved. Persons of great dignity and pride may find it necessary to destroy their own life under circumstances in which those with a shallower scope of feeling can adjust with only moderate emotional damage.

The possibility that a once great capacity for positive living may have played some part in the development of the psychopath's negative (destructive) patterns is, I believe, worthy of careful consideration. Certainly these patterns are thorough and uncompromising (no halfway measure), and if they do represent something purposive, though consciously involuntary, their effectiveness suggests an invisible purpose of uncommon force. If the psychopath's disorder could be shown to arise in some such fashion, it is so subtle and so monumentally effective a job that it is easy to imagine that the potentialities represented here in reverse might deserve the estimate of genius. No real evidence, however, has been presented to support this purely speculative hypothesis.

THE INJUDICIOUS HEDONIST AND SOME OTHER DRINKERS

Those who devote their lives unduly to sensual pleasure are popularly regarded by more sober and restrained members of society as wicked or depraved. By his fellows who are especially austere the ways of the careless bon vivant are often attacked with thunderous vigor and even, by certain extremists, held as largely responsible for the ills of mankind.

It is well known, of course, that a large number of human beings, during their development, pass through a stage of recklessness in which strong drink and casual lovemaking are snatched at injudiciously. These jejune efforts to drink life to the lees sometimes bring embarrassment or misfortune to young people. Having tried out his wings of independence or of revolt and usually having received a fair number of bumps, jolts, or bruises, the average fledgling learns his way about and ceases to lay aside altogether his judgment and common sense when in pursuit of pleasure.

Ordinary people, young or old, if they contract a venereal disease, become illegitimately pregnant, lose their jobs because of excessive drinking, or suffer some other sharp reverse, observe the sequence of cause and effect and try to adapt themselves so as not to suffer in the same way again. Indeed, even a severe headache or other unpleasant features prominent in the aftermath of late hours and excessive drinking will cause the normal person to avoid waking in the same condition the next day. Sometimes, of course, indiscretion is piled on indiscretion and the bout of dissipation causes prolonged discomfort. The general rule, however, is to learn, even if slowly, by experience.

A significant difference then between the man popularly regarded as a dissipated person and the psychopath is that the former, even though he breaks over into indiscretion from time to time on occasions of excitement, tends to be guided by painful consequences. More important still, the ordinary hard drinker or high liver appears plainly to be motivated by pleasure principles which we can all understand.

What difference will one more drink make? What spoilsport insists on leaving? Words and ideas come to him. The occasion grows more festive and he more sparkling. Perhaps he is putting his best foot forward before some attainable or unattainable lady or merely embracing in good fellowship and understanding some group which he finds, in the general merriment, better able to know and value him. Someone breaks into song, snatches of poetry are quoted, each man gives tongue to his special enthusiasm or his special dislike. There is laughter, merriment, play, the dance. The general effort is toward life, toward a more full and active living.

Sometimes these activities in the relatively make-believe world of synthetic freedom, these pursuits of joy that are often not quite joy itself, make real living, or one's ordinary capacity to live, seem drab or feeble by comparison. Sometimes it seems desirable to shirk the harder, soberer transactions of the day and exist chiefly for the escape into another world which is not quite one's own. In varying degree, depending on how sound is one's integration and how obdurate one's insight, persons profit by experience and limit these indulgences in accordance with the hard and inescapable facts of self and of the objective world.

In the wide range of the accepted normal, various degrees of responsibility, various ethical and esthetic standards, various demands of ambition, and various exigencies of the next day or of the next decade must be reckoned with before one even comes to the question of whether drinking and conduct under the influence of alcoholic drink constitute a psychiatric illness. Even when a person arrives at the point where a definite illness or maladjustment unquestionably exists, many psychopathologic pictures must be considered and discarded before segregating the particular picture that we will, lacking a better name, call the psychopath.

For the Methodist pastor in Paris, Alabama, to drink at all would indicate some maladaptation of the man to his way of life. Yet the Anglican vicar in Stoke Poges or the priest in Amalfi may take his port or his Vino Orvieto Bianco Secco without arousing our suspicion. The middle-aged bachelor whose only tasks are to clip coupons and squire admiring dowagers about his gardens may regularly sip whiskey and soda for hours past midnight without invoking the significant consequences that such doings would bring to a surgeon called on for major emergencies several nights a week or to a young and ambitious businessman who must face a hard day's work each morning at 8 o'clock.

Several young doctors of philosophy might gather on Saturday night and hurl loud argumentative words about until dawn, consuming no mean quantities of whiskey while the structure of the hypothalamus, the prose of James Joyce, the sexuality of Sappho, and the ideas of Norbert Wiener or of Arnold Toynbee are discussed, challenged, and defended. A couple of friendly mill workers whose wives are out of town might settle down some evening before a holiday in a barroom and drink through stages of shouting conviviality, loud song, blustering amorousness with prostitutes, to snoring stupefaction. Such activities might be defended as human by some critics, assailed as wicked by others, and interpreted, perhaps, as efforts to escape the routine of the classroom or of home and factory by still others.

Two lovers who cannot for economic or legal reasons have each other freely under the same roof may on every available occasion lie in each other's arms until 3 A.M. in a parked automobile, having sexual intercourse as frequently as their abilities will permit. They may drink enough whiskey to blur recognition of the inevitable morrow, pouring out their feeling and fantasy to each other in a transient delirium of bliss. Each may suffer definite impairment of effectiveness at work, fatigue, headache, nausea, and many other discomforts day after day from deficient sleep and superfluous alcohol. They may be condemned as unconventional, sinful, or foolish by other people of various viewpoints. But their conduct has little in common with that of the psychopath. They feel that the game is worth the candle and they mean to play it.

A man whose desire for his wife has palled may at every party he attends drink too much, sway a little as he goes from group to group, try to make minor overtures to nearly every woman he encounters, and, with the slightest encouragement, attempt seduction. Such a man, most people would perhaps agree, is maladjusted in the sense that he is far from happy in his life situation. His efforts to gain happiness may incur social disapproval of varying degree, be they adroit or ludicrous. Whatever of his other life plans or his ideologies he is ignoring, he is still moved by a fundamentally normal drive, that is, to accomplish sexual relations with a woman who appeals to him.

Another man may successfully avoid drinking to excess but also seek every opportunity to seduce female acquaintances, whether or not they are wives or sisters or sweethearts or daughters of his friends. He may try to induce the woman he seeks to drink to excess and so facilitate his purpose. This man might be called a sorry fellow by some, a fiend by others, or a latent homosexual by still others. Again he might be explained as one whose unconscious sense of inferiority or whose unrecognized sexual immaturity demands compensation for his inadequacy, or his regular failure to achieve mature fulfillment with each love object. Still another observer might regard him as a shrewd, cynical person who merely knows how to get what he wants and is above ordinary compunction. In some patients represented by the last example I have observed attitudes, personality mechanisms, and efforts at adjustment that have considerable resemblance to those of the psychopath. In the psychopath, however, is found a far greater regression, a failure to follow out consistently any aim that could be understood by the normal man, and a general disorganization of the whole life plan. The spite reaction may be fundamental in the complete psychopath, but it is directed less consistently toward bringing about an actual sexual union than in untranslatable activities. It is also less obvious and more deeply concealed, not only from the patient but also from the observer. He may start on his spree with such an objective consciously before him, but he will occasionally pour into himself not stimulating but emetic or soporific doses of alcohol and end by vomiting in the bed or falling limp on the floor long before any other aim is achieved.

There are scores of patterns in which superficially hedonistic behavior can be seen to represent an escape from or a compensatory reaction to some emotional problem that the person has not solved. The man so attached to his mother that his mature sex aims are distorted may over years maintain a reputation for heavy and boisterous drinking, for being a great man about town with the women.

Deep marital unhappiness may lead one or both partners of a married couple to dull the edges of frustration by drinking regularly to excess or by whooping it up at parties in a relatively vain pursuit of excitement and fulfillment. I have known successful businessmen and professional men who, over the years, have each day consumed astonishing amounts of alcohol. Among these are persons who, sober or under considerable influence, remain reliable, pleasantly sociable, and quite themselves. In such cases it must be granted that the excessive drinking, whatever its value as an anodyne, usually constitutes a problem in itself. It is not uncommon to find persons who continue to make a successful adjustment in general, despite the fact that they drink considerably more than many psychopaths. The distinguishing point is that gross changes from a normal attitude and from normal behavior do not occur and a whole life plan is not demolished.

There are people who may drink regularly to excess to enliven a career that has fallen into boredom or relative idleness but who find a level of intake at which they make an adjustment. Here the drinking is perhaps hit upon to kill time or as a substitute for the diversity and activity lacking in their daily routine. Although persons of this sort may lose control of the situation and become alcoholics in the clinical sense, many continue to maintain themselves without help. Drinking in such cases may be thought of as a handicapping factor, but, since there are few responsibilities or vivid interests to demand full activity, the subject remains able to carry on his attenuated career.

Specifically disturbed emotional and social relations may result not only in alcoholism as a distinct illness but also in excessive indulgence over years or decades without progressive loss of control. Persons with varying components of latent homosexuality often find a partial and disguised outlet for their impulses in frequent and injudicious alcoholic sessions with stag groups. Mildly schizoid personalities shut off from close personal contacts and lacking in occupations or preoccupations may solitarily consume alcohol in excess but avoid any spectacular behavior attributable to drink.

Other types who use alcohol as a partial anesthetic include such figures as O'Malley in Donn Byrne's story, who closes his career as a broken man, wandering from tavern to tavern drinking steadily to excess. A brilliant, able, and charming person in his ordinary life, he submits to this transformation when life holds nothing more for him. His love object, whom he lost because of her being driven to an Anglican nunnery by religious or pseudoreligious manifestations, had come to play so important a part in his life that she could not be replaced. Without her it was a relief for him to avoid full awareness, which he did by drink. He is pictured as a man old before his time, shabby, aimless, slightly intoxicated nearly always, and looking forward to nothing particular except perhaps death. This, too, is drinking unlike drinking to be happy. It is, however, far from the bellowing, vociferous episodes and the lyings-out of the psychopath. In O'Malley's case the cause of his drinking is readily visible, and his choice of a means to an end is not without logic and purpose. There is no effort on O'Malley's part to make himself objectionable to others or to create shocking and fantastic situations. He quietly becomes a drunkard to dull his sorrow and seeks only to be let alone.

The psychopath, then, in my opinion, is something very much more than the ordinarily dissipated or profligate person, even though the latter happens to be extremely injudicious. An important mark of distinction is that the profligate is usually after what everyone can see is a kind of pleasure or is seeking simple relief from pain we can conceive, whereas the psychopath seldom drives at anything that looks very much like pleasure or necessary analgesia.

Another type of behavior sometimes confused with the psychopath's life pattern might be represented by the fairly common case of the married man, well established in business and fond of his children, who throws away his security and his respectable position to seek love with some woman who cares nothing for him and on whom he soon throws away what he has. It might be said that such a man is rash or even foolish and some may call him depraved. But the appeal that drives him to his folly is one that most normal people have no difficulty in understanding. Love is well known for its power to make even sages give all, and some commitments between man and woman are all but impossible to explain. A man may give up all the fruits of his life to fulfill a definite erotic impulse. But the psychopath's impulse is not the result of fatal infatuation, nor is it so well formulated and comprehensible as the desire of a man for a woman's body.

The wrecked career of the psychopath is sometimes used by reformers and prohibitionists who crusade against alcohol and vice in general as an example of what dissipation will do to those who essay the primrose path. Well meant though such warnings may be, they are based on a premise of doubful validity. What drives the psychopath on in his career is not in any ordinary sense the love of wine or song or women. Whiskey is sometimes one of his means to an end, and certainly it aids him in his spectacular exploits, but it is not a primary cause in his life scheme. Though many may come to grief in such pursuit, they are scarcely more likely to become psychopaths than they are to become schizophrenics.

> To drift with every passion till my soul
> Is a stringed lute on which all winds can play,
> Is it for this that I have given away
> Mine ancient wisdom and austere control?
>
> • • •
>
> Surely there was a time I might have trod
> The sunlit heights, and from life's dissonance
> Struck one clear chord to reach the ear of God:
> Is that time dead?
>
> *Oscar Wilde*
> "Helas"

Such drifting with passions may indeed prevent the development of greatness and cheat the drifter of achievement and of deep happiness. There are many ways in which a man can waste his energy, cheapen his emotional powers, and bring about his maladjustment. There are many ways, perhaps, by which a man can fall into mental disorders and many types of disorder into which he can fall. Flowers of evil, whether splendid, redolent and darkly glittering, or mediocre, may choke out the blossoms ordinarily considered desirable. But the psychopaths whose stories are offered here do not seem driven wildly and at random by such winds of passion as those referred to in Oscar Wilde's familiar verse, nor is it likely that their souls are played upon like stringed lutes. One may listen indefinitely for the tragico-romantical notes of such a vibration, but he will listen in vain. The winds of passion are blowing almost imperceptibly, if at all, and no strings are in the lute. No vivid *fleurs du mal* will be culled from this garden, for the garden is barren.

THE CLINICAL ALCOHOLIC

The term *clinical alcoholic* is chosen for convenience to signify the large group of pathologic drinkers who are still making some genuine effort to adjust in normal life but are using drink to escape reality, which they cannot quite face, and, by a vicious cycle, are making themselves steadily more inadequate to face this reality. Such drinkers may, in several respects, be contrasted with the psychopath (antisocial personality) just as the nonalcoholic neurotic contrasts with the psychotic patient.

Like that of the psychopath, their drinking is not primarily for pleasure or has at least ceased to afford much pleasure. They often give a strong impression of drinking to avoid sober self-appraisal or some other aspect of reality. With alcohol they can remain a little more comfortably and longer in the false world of fantasy or in analgesia. They are often introverted people, often tender-minded and shy. Alcohol enables them to be less self-conscious and to make their way with greater ease into the social group. They become more and more disabled for real life, and reverses owing directly or indirectly to their alcoholism accumulate, making it ever more urgent for them to escape into the numbness of drink.

To a certain point this picture is not unlike that of the psychopath. Perhaps the psychopath sometimes arrives at his life scheme by way of phases almost identical with those of some neurotic drinkers, and perhaps the neurotic drinker may regress to levels at which he can be plainly recognized as a psychopath. Some of the patients described here as partial psychopaths might be placed by some observers in the class of neurotic drinkers.

For the purpose of drawing a useful distinction, however, the following points are offered:

Often the neurotic drinker wants to get well. This may not be obvious, but with proper psychiatric treatment it may be possible to obtain sincere cooperation. Although the neurotic drinker lacks insight and often cannot get well by his unaided efforts, he retains a capability of gaining insight, and good improvement is often possible under treatment. The psychopath's actual conduct when drinking, and sometimes when sober, is bizarre, often shameful and shocking, and actively damaging to himself. In the neurotic drinker such tendencies, if present, are much less pronounced.

The neurotic drinker on his spree is unintentionally destroying his chances for success and happiness, but this does not appear to be his fundamental aim; his fundamental aim apparently is to avoid facing his failures. Although this aim may be present in the established psychopath, it is not easily or regularly discernible. The latter appears to be driving primarily at evading, or ignoring, or destroying life itself, that is to say, life in the sense of social attainments and subjective integration.

Drinkers who can be classed as neurotic show better capacity for insight and may come voluntarily to seek treatment or may be persuaded by relatives to do so. The psychopath will not come voluntarily, except when he seeks hospitalization to avoid legal action, and he cannot be persuaded to carry out sincerely any therapeutic program.

To summarize, then, it may be said that the neurotic drinker is capable of insight and wants to get well. The psychopathologic picture is more readily comprehensible in terms of cause and effect and, under favorable conditions, is perhaps reversible. The psychopath, on the other hand, despite his superficial appearance of being a normal man, shows in his whole behavior pattern deviation and disorder that seem fundamental. His real drives, when one tries to surmise them from his reactions, strike the observer as foreign to ordinary human impulse. The process, if reversible at all, is not ordinarily found to be so. Apparently there is no latent insight that can be aroused or sincere desire to become well or, rather, to become like other men. I do not mean to state dogmatically that the psychopath's illness is irreversible but merely that in my own experience it has, in typical cases, proved to be so. It may be said that the process of schizophrenia as compared with hysteria is relatively less reversible, that it ordinarily brings about a greater and deeper disintegration of the personality. Despite this fact, schizophrenics often recover. Perhaps the psychopath, too, can recover. Perhaps some generally satisfactory means of treating him can eventually be devised.

Taking the group of chronic alcoholics as a whole, we are likely to find here people in whom the excessive drinking is a common symptom of underlying disorders that vary widely in type and in degree somewhat as we might say that fever may arise from a bad cold, measles, pneumonia, tuberculosis, meningitis, and other differing illnesses too numerous to list.

Alcoholics Anonymous, whose excellent work it is appropriate to mention here, has, in my experience with this group as a whole, appeared to be one of the most valuable therapeutic agencies available. Many gravely maladjusted patients in whom alcoholism was at the same time a disabling symptom and a secondary but major causal agent in disastrous life patterns have, through this agency and its program, made changes and progress that with no exaggeration can be called remarkable. Some patients whose behavior and emotional attitudes definitely suggested the psychopath's disorder have to my knowledge not only avoided for years the disabling effects of their former drunkenness but also other unrewarding and antisocial activities. Whether or not these were psychopaths in the full and deepest sense is not a question that can be answered confidently.

It is my belief that this type of disorder, like all other psychiatric disorders, may be seen in almost limitless variations of degree and severity. We see the utterly disorganized schizophrenic who has for twenty years been on the worst ward of a state hospital, and we also see schizoid reactions and limitations that persist for decades in people who continue to be self-supporting and to a considerable degree socially competent. I recall one patient who has expressed to me delusions typical of full-blown schizophrenia over some years and who is still an able worker with many pleasant social relations and recreational activities. Many more come to mind whose delusions are less extreme but who for decades have manifested autistic withdrawal, oddities, emotional distortions, and impairments consistent only with a schizoid reaction.

We also see manifestations identical with those of full-blown schizophrenia in every respect except their transiency. A 30-year-old man who, after taking a small dose of testosterone, experienced not only hallucinatory sexual and spiritual sensations within himself but also in others will serve as an excellent example. Vivid delusions were very prominent for approximately a week. These included an absolute conviction that all virtuous women at the mere sight of him caught the impact of magic, glowed with a fire both erotic and holy, and were visibly transformed. It was also his belief that this caused harlots who might sense his powers a block off to run up alleyways in shame. For several days, through false perceptions, he specifically "felt" men and women some miles away responding viscerally, intellectually, and spiritually, and in diverse ways, to what had miraculously become incarnate in his person. After being psychotic for a week and without specific treatment, he regained insight, lost his schizophrenic symptoms, and has for a number of years remained entirely free of them.

In the other disorder, that of the psychopath, I believe there also occur similar variations in chronicity, in severity, in completeness, in depth, and in every other respect. Although malignancy and irreversibility seem typical of the psychopathology as we meet it clinically in its advanced or long-fixed forms, outwardly similar behavioral and character patterns sometimes prove reversible. Few, if any, features of the full psychopath are more impressive than his inability to respond with consistent acts or in other ways that would indicate deep or genuine desire to change his situation. In therapeutic programs it is characteristic of him not to make valid or persistent efforts to cooperate. In their relations with Alcoholics Anonymous, psychopaths sometimes show at first what seems extraordinary zeal, sincerity, and promise, only to reveal after varying intervals that the whole matter was only a sort of prank or lightly taken adventure in versatile careers of self-ruin.

Fundamental points in the Alcoholics Anonymous system of group therapy and self-reorganization are the following:

1. The need for a most profound intention (an authentic and major desire) to overcome one's disability.
2. The necessity for extensive and basic changes in attitude and orientation at the core of the personality

At both of these points we find in the full psychopath an almost uniquely unfavorable situation. Although I know of nothing available today that can be counted on to succeed regularly, the evidence has suggested that Alcoholics Anonymous may in some cases affect favorably latent resources very difficult to reach by most methods in patients showing reactions that may have something in common with those of the typical psychopath.

FICTIONAL CHARACTERS OF PSYCHIATRIC INTEREST

Characters from literature, it may be argued, not being real people, are therefore of no value in the discussion of a medical problem. It can scarcely be doubted, however, that genuinely creative writers have often presented personalities more fully and more truly than we can readily get to know them in life. And sometimes minor writers succeed in portraying personalities that seem to be reliably true. The characters of the novelist and the dramatist are, furthermore, accessible to all who care to read about them, unlike the patient who has been seen and studied but cannot be presented personally to the reader. For the purpose of this discussion I feel that several points can be made by citing fictional characters, some of whom I believe have been no less faithfully drawn than patients reported in psychiatric examinations. Whether real people exist like them or not is beside the point, since I do not mean to use them as evidence to establish any conceptions of psychopathology but to illustrate personality reactions, whether real or imaginary, that I shall attempt to relate to the reactions considered in this volume.

Those who spend their lives in serious effort to put down in various forms a reflection of their human experience must sometimes encounter psychopathy or at least fragments of such behavior, hints of such an attitude. Abstruse and complex psychopathologic features of many types have for centuries emerged in literary creations and seem to emerge sometimes through an inexplicable insight of the poet, novelist, or dramatist, who, by his special talent, may successfully convey what he has accurately sensed in the life about him. What he senses may not be discernible to many, and it may be most difficult to convey by the direct textbook methods. The possibility of help from this source in efforts to gain understanding of the by no means simple riddle of the psychopath is a possibility that should not be rejected.

Certain personalities have been described and perhaps exist in actual life, who, unlike the ordinary criminal, seem to live by hate and cherish destructiveness not so much to gain power or material benefits but because they grow to love hate and destructiveness. The character Heathcliffe as presented in *Wuthering Heights* by Emily Brontë might be chosen as a puzzling example of misanthropy, ruthlessness, and maladjustment that has little in common with ordinary viciousness. Heathcliffe works to destroy others and to destroy what is generally regarded as happiness for himself as well. He unquestionably falls within the scope of psychopathology, a strange, terrible, and compelling figure. But he has little specific kinship with the personalities discussed here. He is strong, he is persistent, and his emotion, however distorted, appears greater by far than that of the average man. He never loses his imposing dignity, even though this dignity might be regarded as a dignity of evil. He remains integrated, not only superficially but profoundly. The personalities described in this book, in contrast, show no consistent pursuit of what might be called evil; their exploits are fitful, buffoonish, and unsustained by any obvious purpose. Consistent hatred of others is not a guiding line in their life scheme. And in Heathcliffe we find evidence of more than ordinary love for Kathy, of love that appears to be genuine and changeless despite the fact that it is a major factor behind his destructiveness.

It is not common to find in literature characters that could be grouped with the patients studied here. Creative artists have often presented the villain, the psychotic, the psychoneurotic, the erratic genius, the weak, the strong, the wise, and the stupid; but we seldom find in imaginative writing anyone who could fit the picture that emerges as we consider the histories in this book. Often, however, we find characters who in some aspect or in some phase of their activities suggest what we have seen in the psychopath, and we find others no less abnormal whose qualities may be used in contrast.

Iago in *Othello,* perhaps the most interesting and ingenious creation of vindictiveness known to man, carries out his schemes of hate and treachery without adequate motivation in the ordinary sense. In *King Lear* the cruelty of Edmund, bastard son of Gloucester, is plainly pathologic. Herr Naphta in Thomas Mann's *The Magic Mountain* although a professional Christian in holy orders, is addicted to destructiveness despite his great intellectual powers. All these characters are consistent, effective, and, despite their interesting psychiatric aspects, remote from the psychopath.

Mr. Micawber in *David Copperfield* and Tolstoi's Stepan Arkadyevitch Oblonsky in *Anna Karenina* are convincing examples of people who do not seem to learn by experience and who cannot, in important matters, be relied on by others. But neither shows the active pattern of self-defeat with which we are familiar. Both seem to represent ordinary human frailties that are much exaggerated. Falstaff *(Henry II)* indulges in outlandish excesses with sack, falls into humiliating situations repeatedly without evincing ordinary shame, and shows himself callous to the appeal of dignity and honor. Yet we sense in him a strong tide of normal, even if superficial, life, some Rabelaisian gusto, which makes his follies stand out in sharp contrast to the activities of the psychopath. He is bent on animal pleasure and coarse merriment whatever they may cost. We can understand him whether we should like to emulate him or not.

Mr. Burlap in Aldous Huxley's *Point Counter Point* is presented as a pious lecher, a literary windbag, and a hypocritical opportunist. He impresses the average reader as a most unpleasant personality, and he is portrayed as lacking many of the emotional capacities that the psychopath also lacks. His opportunism works to his material advantage, and he is steady in his aims and in his progress. However inconsistent or hypocritical his affect, it seems more real than what we see in the psychopath. In the same novel we find in Maurice Spandrell a man who seems to love cruelty and to love it best in its most unpleasant forms. Despite his inexcusable practices, we feel in him extraordinary emotional richness and a peculiar but impressive latent integrity which are in contrast to the cold-bloodedness and viciousness appearing in his outer life. It is plain that a personality disorder exists, but it is not the type of disorder with which we are here concerned.

Dostoevski's Prince Myshkin in *The Idiot,* a person of great wisdom and spiritual insight, yet eccentric and in some ways inadequate, might be called a psychopath by writers who use this term loosely for maladjusted or uneven geniuses. He is, however, a person who feels more profoundly than the ordinary man the very aspects of life to which our patients are numb.

In the figure of Zuleika Dobson, Max Beerbohm gives an impression not so much of indicating a personality, even in caricature, as of lightly embodying his fantasy. This wraithlike figment is used to suggest a carelessness about the fate of others, a preoccupation with trivialties, an absolute and mysterious incapacity for serious emotion that, in a way both outlandish and whimsical, echoes something of the psychopath. She nevertheless succeeds consistently in her aims.

Ibsen's Peer Gynt, although he, too, belongs perhaps in Elfland and very little in the ordinary world, shows a capacity for spiritual failure, an almost perverse unreliability, and an insousciance in self-frustration that suggests a translation of our problem, or some aspect of it, into poetry.

The children presented by Richard Hughes in *A High Wind in Jamaica* and those very different children Henry James gives us in *The Turn of the Screw* suggest an incapacity for normal feeling, an unalterable, subtle, and sinister resistance to human approach that might be compared to the callousness of the psychopath. Both authors seem to be more concerned with general aspects of life or of evil, however, than with a personality disorder.

Ferenc Molnar's Liliom, an altogether astonishing character to the average reader or theater-goer, fails all who trust him and fails himself with the prodigious consistency of a real psychopath. His final manifestation of the old inadequacy, even after being brought back from the dead to earth, really suggests that the dramatist may have had in mind something like the psychopath as we know him. His power to arouse inalienable devotion in women is also as impressive as what we see in real patients. Liliom's suicide, his capacity to admit his misdeeds with what impresses one as a measure of sincerity, his warmth, and his depicted strength and fearlessness all stand out in contrast, however, to the personality patterns discussed in this book.

In Proust's *Remembrance of Things Past* the Baron de Charlus, a masterpiece of psychopathology no less than of literary creation, would of course be classed as a psychopath in the broad and once orthodox meaning of the term. This most imposing and vivid character shows not only homosexuality but a taste for flagellation and other deviations of the sexual impulse, and he shows them as they can seldom be appreciated from the reading of textbooks. There is much about Charlus to suggest that he also shares in some measure the special disorder that we treat here. He seems to care little for the rights of others or for their suffering. He is found repeatedly in fantastic and shameful situations. Much of his abnormal behavior becomes more comprehensible, however, once we grant the authenticity of his abnormal sexual cravings. There are indications of a real learning and a more nearly sincere culture than in the personalities we describe here. A paradoxical and fragmentary but not totally false dignity in his living contrasts with the psychopath's great lack in this respect.

Charlus might justifiably be classed as a partial psychopath, at least. As in some psychopaths seen clinically, he has specific sex deviations which are basic (as contrasted with incidental careless acts of perversion) and which readily account for much of his folly. This figure is depicted as surpassingly haughty in cultural and social aloofness, as a superesthete who aggressively represents almost an apotheosis of the secondary defensive reactions pointed out as typical of the real homosexual by Greenspan and Campbell.

Such a figure as Jondrette (or Thénardier) of *Les Miserables* shows petty opportunism, little ability to profit by mistakes, an extreme degree of selfishness, and a talent for failure. Although these are superficially suggestive of the psychopath, I believe that Jondrette and others like him are conceived as rascals with a better organized antisocial revolt than what is seen in the psychopath. Svidrigailov in *Crime and Punishment* is more strange than Jondrette and appears for a time entirely callous to such feelings as pity or pride. He finally shows a magnanimity that distinguishes him from our subject.

Many female characters have been presented by novelists and dramatists as astonishingly faithless and astonishingly deficient in the stronger, richer emotions. In some of these the spiritual limitation appears to be absolute and unchangeable. Nina Leeds of Eugene O'Neill's *Strange Interlude* was regarded by some critics as shameless, immoral, and self-seeking to an extreme degree. The still celebrated Scarlett O'Hara in *Gone With the Wind,* in some contrast to Nina, fails regularly to respond to sincere emotion in her lovers and pursues above all else aims that are fundamentally egocentric and trivial. Nina Leeds, however, seems capable of real feeling toward her first lover, and her reactions after his death, all of which are based on strong emotional drives, can be understood without assuming the same type of disorder postulated in the psychopath. In fact, she shows very little in common with such a disorder.

Scarlett O'Hara, in my opinion, is a very convincing figure and really shows some of the emotional impoverishment described here in the patients presented as partial psychopaths. Her incapacity for a true commitment in love is apparently unmodifiable; her egocentricity is basic. She seems to be without means of understanding the strong emotions in those about her or of having adequate awareness of what makes them act when they act in accordance with principles they value. Unlike the complete psychopath, she successfully pursues ends that lead to her material well-being and she avoids putting herself in positions of obvious folly and shame. In her, however, we sense an inward hollowness and a serious lack of insight.

An interesting feature of *Gone With the Wind* and one that illuminates an important distinguishing characteristic of the psychopath can be found in a comparison between Scarlett O'Hara and Captain Rhett Butler. Although the captain's conduct is often at variance with most ethical standards, although he evades joining wholeheartedly in the war effort and even seeks to gain personal profit through complications of the war, he can hardly fail to give readers the impression of a man warmly and deeply human. If his objective misdemeanors and other bits of wrongdoing are added up and balanced against Scarlett's actions in the book, it is possible that his score would be technically worse and that he would be more liable to legal action and social censure.

Scarlett, as a matter of fact, is kind in the shallower ranges of feeling, rather consistently considerate about all matters except the most vital. The real contrast becomes clear when fundamental personal issues are at stake. Here Captain Butler's nuclear integrity and his valid reactions of love and compassion are communicated not so much by narration and exposition or by what he directly says as in small reflections of his essential personality that cumulatively reveal him.

It might be argued that of the two, Scarlett, as depicted in the novel, is on the whole a more conforming person, one who can better avoid conduct that will bring about social retaliation. Without attempting a judgment based on ethical absolutes, which is not the province of this book, one can show a significant contrast between what appears to be the inmost core of each. As indicated already, the fictional Scarlett O'Hara would be a poor representative of the clinical psychopath, but limitations in her personality so effectively brought out in the novel seem closely related in quality to the more disabling deficit that I believe is fundamental in the enigmatic disorder.

Anyone concerned at all with psychiatry is likely to find in Jenny Hagar Poster Evered of *The Strange Woman* (Ben Ames Williams) detail and concreteness familiar in the direct study of patients but hard to put into medical histories. In that she does not respect the rights of others and particularly in that she reacts in anything but a normal way in the deepest personal relations, Jenny might be proclaimed a psychopath whose deviation is extraordinarily complete. Sharply distinguishing points emerge when we consider the persistent purposiveness, the strong and sustained malice with which this woman works to destroy all happiness for children, husbands, and paramours. A conscious brutality prevails. Destructive impulses are directed consistently by open hate.

In contrast with this picture of a well-organized paranoid life scheme, we find the typical psychopath not consistently seeking to inflict major disaster on anyone. More characteristic is the psychopath's pettiness and transiency of affect (both positive and negative) and his failure to follow a long-range plan, either for good or for evil. The emotional damage he may (and often does) inflict on others, including mate, parents, and children, is not, it seems, inflicted for any major voluntary purpose or from a well-focused motive but from what weighs in at little more than whim or caprice. He does not seem to intend much harm. In the disaster he brings about he cannot estimate the affective reactions of others which are the substance of the disaster. A race of men congenitally without pain sense would not find it easy to estimate the effects of physical torture on others. A man who had never understood visual experience would lack appreciation of what is sustained when the sighted person loses his eyes. So, too, the real psychopath seems to lack understanding of the nature and quality of the hurt and sorrow he brings to others.

In contrast to anything of this sort, Jenny shows a rather accurate awareness of how it is going to hurt as she skillfully, and in response to consistent impulse, pursues her plans. All this is very typical of severe paranoid reactions seen clinically. Jenny is also depicted as having components of overt sadomasochistic deviation. Elements of callousness (from incomplete comprehension) are probably necessary for such reactions. Followed far enough inside the surface of action and consciousness, such callousness might be found based on similar pathology to that which constitutes the psychopath's basic incompleteness. As clinical pictures, nevertheless, there is more to contrast than to identify the two life schemes.

To illustrate a feature of what I shall subsequently try to formulate as the psychopath's real underlying condition, the remarkable character of Adrian Harley in George Meredith's *The Ordeal of Richard Feveral* offers an excellent example. This "wise young man" makes a very successful and comfortable adjustment to life in its exterior aspect. He is, of course, no psychopath in the full sense as this disorder as described here. He is a most shrewd, urbane, and learned person. His learning is, furthermore, in the humanities. Yet his incapacity to feel the actual living, the tragedy and joy that are so real to Richard and to Lucy Desborough, is absolute. He does not apparently intend to be cruel, but, perhaps chiefly because of a particular blindness, his shrewdness is used consistently to bring about disaster. He is entirely without insight and remains unable to see that he has seriously damaged others. No schizophrenic could be less cognizant of what existence means to Richard and Lucy than Adrian Harley as he stands with them on a terrace in the Isle of Wight chanting Greek hexameters into the sunset. If we consider such an emotional limitation as that seen in Scarlett O'Hara or in Adrian Harley as similar to what is seen in the psychopath, we must admit that many persons regarded as normal show less marked limitations of the same sort. This, I believe, is entirely true, just as many ordinary persons are slightly schizoid or slightly cyclothymic.

In the literature of this century such characters as Jeeter Lester of *Tobacco Road* (Erskine Caldwell) and Pop-Eye of *Sanctuary* (William Faulkner) deserve brief consideration. The first of these seems to learn little indeed by experience. He is callous to many situations involving himself and others that the ordinary man could scarcely bear. Jeeter Lester impresses me, however, as very little akin to the psychopath. His shiftlessness and resignation are entirely passive. He is to some extent a natural victim of his surroundings. He shows no active drive toward such folly and failure as lure the psychopath, but merely an aimless drifting. He is, despite all his frailities and follies, somehow warm with humanity.

The other figure, Pop-Eye, is depicted as a malign and vindictive man who pursues criminal aims successfully though somewhat peculiarly. His delight in watching the girl he has chosen for himself ravished by another man is extraordinary in the annals of orthodox criminal taste but is comprehensible in terms of voyeurism and masochism and especially in view of his own sexual impotence. An incompletely overt homosexuality is perhaps even more strongly contributory to this choice of role. Although there are features in common, he does not belong among the personalities discussed here.

In Don Birnam, hero of *The Lost Week-End* (Charles Jackson), we find a psychiatric presentation of remarkable force. Beneath the surface of alcoholic addiction very complicated and subtly distorted causal factors reveal themselves. Eventually a picture emerges in which important features of the psychopath are discernible. There are also contrasts. In Birnam awareness of major frustration is more clear, and anxiety and despair are not successfully avoided. What has happened and is still happening is bizarre and terrifying to the subject, since he retains some important degree of insight. When measured against the typical psychopath, this rather remarkable fictional creation suggests another comparison.

Several times patients in early, incomplete schizophrenic reactions have impressed me with varying degrees of ability to see or sense the strangeness and gravity of the processes operant within themselves. In sharp contrast to the ordinary patient with schizophrenia, in whom unawareness and indifference characterize the subject's attitude to all that is so obviously grotesque or tragic to the observer, these patients reacted to some degree as if with the fear, bewilderment, and horror that might be expected in one who recognizes such changes as occurring within himself. Many schizophrenics may show anxiety, alarm, and other strong affective reactions toward other matters, particularly toward delusional projection. This very different atypical residue of insight struck me not only as a remarkable feature but as one affording the observer an unusual viewpoint—the viewpoint of seeing, to some degree, this indescribable process through the eyes of the subject. Ordinarily the disintegration in schizophrenia is such, in specific quality whatever the degree, that the patient does not see the changes in himself with sufficient accuracy to react to them vividly or with anything like the emotional responses of an ordinary person.

In Don Birnam a good many things are revealed as within or near his own comprehension which suggest what may lie beneath the reactive patterns of the psychopath but, if there, are so far beneath that the typical psychopath is unaware of them and indifferent. The observer also has peculiar difficulty in gaining direct access to what may be beneath the surface. Although it may not be accurate to give the unqualified diagnosis to this marvelously interesting fictional patient, it is undeniable that he shows, very convincingly, important features of the psychopath.

A literary creation who impresses me as remarkably like a psychopath in the full sense is Dostoevski's senior Karamazov, father of the wonderful and puzzling brothers who themselves offer so much of interest to the psychiatrist. The elder Karamazov is not only free from major human feelings, but he also drives actively at folly. He shows a greedy relish for the very sort of buffoonery and high jinks that the psychopath seeks. He has no regard apparently for consequences and cannot be persuaded by reason or appealed to by sentiment. He appears superficially to be a man of strong passions, but in my opinion this is only an appearance. He does not pursue selfish or vicious ways consistently in the aim of self-interest. He immerses himself in indignity for its own sake. He does outrageous things, especially to his son Dimitri, yet he is not adequately motivated by consistently vindictive or cruel impulses.

The personality and behavior of Mildred as she appears in *Of Human Bondage* (Somerset Maugham) also have features that are difficult to reconcile with anything except this disorder, and this disorder in a serious degree. To petty, affective promptings this girl responds appropriately as a rule. All the stimuli that in the normal person evoke serious and lasting responses she perceives little more than a blind man perceives the sunset. Her positive responses to the trivial, the cheap, and the vulgar are understandable in view of the affective limitations so memorably revealed. It is not through savage and violent impuses that she mangles or destroys, but because only mild affect is necessary for action when the larger emotional consequences are invisible. They are invisible not through lack of rational foresight but through specific and more profound defects of evaluation. It is not at all necessary to assume genuine cruelty of any magnitude in Mildred as she reviles the man who has so convincingly demonstrated love for her and whom she wounds as only he could be wounded by the final epithet—*cripple.* So far as she can tell, she is doing little more than what anybody might do if moderately irked.

Like the full psychopath, Mildred cannot continue to provide successfully for her material needs. Unlike what is typical, she does not appear to be especially clever or to have great superficial charm and promise. Nevertheless, she illustrates, perhaps even more accurately than Karamazov the father, some of the features that seem to be fundamental in our subject.

I have seldom seen in fiction so complete and so faithful a portrayal of the psychopath as in the character Rags in *The Story of Mrs. Murphy* (Natalie Anderson Scott). No attempt is made to explain why this man behaves as he does. He is revealed, not by efforts at description and exposition, but with rare fidelity in the concrete rendering of his behavior. The author of this book understands something fundamental about the true psychopath that often is notably lacking in textbook accounts. This is communicated in a form singularly impressive and worthy of careful study.

One would not ordinarily expect to find among the comic cartoon strips of the daily newspapers enlightening information about psychiatric disorder. Nevertheless, in the strip "Judge Parker" an excellent presentation of the psychopath has been made to the public in the unforgettable character Sandra Deare. It is remarkable that so accurate and informative a treatment of such a problem could be given in this medium. This can be better understood when it is known that the creator of "Judge Parker" is a psychiatrist, Dr. Nicolas Dallis, who uses a pseudonym to indicate his authorship. I believe that this serious and wonderfully effective portrayal of the psychopath has served an important purpose in conveying to the public valuable knowledge about the psychopath's peculiar status and perplexing problems.

In many respects the most realistic and successful of all portrayals of the psychopath is that presented by Mary Astor in *The Incredible Charlie Carewe.* The rendition is so effective that even those unfamiliar with the psychopath in actual experience are likely to sense the reality of what is disclosed. The subject is superbly dealt with, and the book constitutes a faithful and arresting study of a puzzling and infinitely complex subject. Charlie Carewe emerges as an exquisite example of the psychopath—the best, I believe, to be found in any work of fiction.

The Incredible Charlie Carewe should be read not only by every psychiatrist but also by every physician. It will hold the attention of all intelligent readers, and I believe it will be of great value in helping the families of psychopaths to gain insight into the nature of the tragic problem with which they are dealing, usually in blindness and confusion.

THE PSYCHOPATH IN HISTORY

Over a period of many decades psychiatrists and sometimes other writers have made attempts to classify prominent historical figures—rulers, military leaders, famous artists and writers—as cases of psychiatric disorder or as people showing some of the manifestations associated with various psychiatric disorders. Many professional and lay observers in recent years have commented on the sadistic and paranoid conduct and attitudes reported in Adolf Hitler and in some of the other wartime leaders in Nazi Germany. Walter Langer, the author of a fairly recent psychiatric study, arrives at the conclusion that Hitler was "probably a neurotic psychopath bordering on schizophrenia," that "he was not insane but was emotionally sick and lacked normal inhibitions against antisocial behavior." A reviewer of this study in *Time* feels that Hitler is presented as "a desperately unhappy man . . . beset by fears, doubts, loneliness and guilt [who] spent his whole life in an unsuccessful attempt to compensate for feelings of helplessness and inferiority."

Though the term *psychopath* is used for Hitler in this quotation, it seems to be used in a broader sense than in this volume. Hitler, despite all the unusual, unpleasant, and abnormal features reported to be characteristic of him, could not, in my opinion, be identified with the picture I am trying to present. Many people whose conduct has been permanently recorded in history are described as extremely abnormal in various ways. Good examples familiar to all include Nero and Heliogabalus, Gilles de Rais, the Countess Elizabeth Báthory and, of course, the Marquis de Sade. I cannot find in these characters a truly convincing resemblance that identifies them with the picture that emerges from the actual patients I have studied and regarded as true psychopaths.

In the lives of many painters, sculptors, poets, and other writers who have gained a place in history we find reports of inconsistency and irresponsibility that sometimes do suggest the typical psychopath. Benvenuto Cellini, whose story has been recorded in such detail by his own hand, seems in more respects, perhaps, than any other creative artist who gained lasting renown to have followed a pattern similar to that of my patients. Nevertheless, he worked consistently enough to produce masterpieces that centuries later are still cherished.

During recent years several figures have become prominent in the daily news whose reported behavior is spectacular and difficult to explain in terms of normal human emotions. One of these, who referred to himself as Son of Sam, apparently devoted his efforts to finding heretofore unknown to him amorous couples secluded in cars and blowing out their brains. In seeking to account for such behavior, most psychiatrists would probably think of severe schizophrenic psychosis rather than of the reactions of the typical psychopath. Charles Manson, who remains prominent in the history of crime, was apparently able to lead a group of people who devoutly believed in him and followed his instructions to the point of committing multiple murders without understandable motivation. This strange leader, it seems to me, can be more plausibly explained as probably influenced by paranoid psychosis or paranoid schizophrenia than as a psychopathic personality.

Let us turn now to a much earlier historical figure, a military leader and statesman who is not likely to be forgotten while civilization as we know it remains on earth. I first encountered him during a course in ancient history when I was in high school. I had not at that time heard of a psychopath. The teacher did not try to classify him medically or explain his paradoxical career in psychologic terms. I felt, however, that this gifted teacher shared my interest and some of my bewilderment as the brilliant, charming, capricious, and irresponsible figure of Alcibiades unfolded in the classroom against the background of Periclean Athens. None of my immature concepts of classification (good man, bad man, wise man, foolish man) seemed to define Alcibiades adequately, or even to afford a reliable clue to his enigmatic image.

The more I read about him and wondered about him, the more he arrested my attention and challenged my imagination. All reports agreed that he was one of the chief military and political leaders of Athens in her period of supreme greatness and classic splendor during the fifth century B.C. This man led me to ponder at a very early age on many questions for which I have not yet found satisfactory answers. According to my high school history book,

> He belonged to one of the noblest families of Athens, and was a near kinsman of Pericles. Though still young, he was influential because of his high birth and his fascinating personality. His talents were brilliant in all directions; but he was lawless and violent, and followed no motive but self-interest and self-indulgence. Through his influence Athens allied herself with Argos, Elis, and Mantinea against the Lacedaemonians and their allies.

The result of this alliance led Athens into defeat and disaster, but Alcibiades on many occasions showed outstanding talent and succeeded brilliantly in many important affairs. Apparently he had great personal charm and easily aroused strong feelings of admiration and affection in others. Though usually able to accomplish with ease any aim he might choose, he seemed capriciously to court disaster and, perhaps at the behest of some trivial impulse, to go out of his way to bring down defeat upon his own projects. Plutarch refers to him thus:

> It has been said not untruly that the friendship which Socrates felt for him has much contributed to his fame; and certain it is, that, though we have no account from any writer concerning the mother of Nicias or Demosthenes, of Lamachus or Phormion, of Thrasybulus or Theramenes, notwithstanding these were all illustrious men of the same period, yet we know even the nurse of Alcibiades, that her country was Lacedaemon, and her name Amycla; and that Zopyrus was his teacher and attendant; the one being recorded by Antisthenes, and the other by Plato.

In the *Symposium,* one of his most celebrated dialogues, Plato introduces Alcibiades by having him appear with a group of intoxicated revelers and burst in upon those at the banquet who are engaged in philosophical discussion. Alcibiades, as presented here by Plato, appears at times to advocate as well as symbolize external beauty and ephemeral satisfactions as opposed to the eternal verities. Nevertheless, Plato gives Alcibiades the role of recognizing and expounding upon the inner virtue and spiritual worth of Socrates and of acclaiming this as far surpassing the readily discerned attainments of more obviously attractive and superficially impressive men. Plato devotes almost all of the last quarter of the *Symposium* to Alcibiades and his conversation with

Socrates. His great charm and physical beauty are emphasized repeatedly here.

Early in his career Alcibiades played a crucial role in gaining important victories for Athens. Later, after fighting against his native city and contributing substantially to her final disaster, he returned to favor, won important victories again for her, and was honored with her highest offices. In the Encyclopaedia Brittanica I read:

> Alcibiades possessed great charm and brilliant abilities but was absolutely unprincipled. His advice whether to Athens or to Sparta, oligarchs or democrats, was dictated by selfish motives, and the Athenians could never trust him sufficiently to take advantage of his talents.

And Thucydides says:

> They feared the extremes to which he carried his lawless self-indulgence, and . . . though his talents as a military commander were unrivalled, they entrusted the administration of the war to others; and so they speedily shipwrecked the state.

Plutarch repeatedly emphasizes the positive and impressive qualities of Alcibiades:

> It was manifest that the many wellborn persons who were continually seeking his company, and making their court to him, were attracted and captivated by his brilliant and extraordinary beauty only. But the affection which Socrates entertained for him is a great evidence of the natural noble qualities and good disposition of the boy, which Socrates, indeed, detected both in and under his personal beauty; and, fearing that his wealth and station, and the great number both of strangers and Athenians who flattered and caressed him, might at last corrupt him, resolved, if possible, to interpose, and preserve so hopeful a plant from perishing in the flower, before its fruit came to perfection.

Despite the talents and many attractive features of Alcibiades, some incidents appear even in his very early life that suggest instability, a disregard for accepted rules or commitments, and a reckless tendency to seize arbitrarily what may appeal to him at the moment. Plutarch tells us:

> Once being hard pressed in wrestling, and fearing to be thrown, he got the hand of his antagonist to his mouth, and bit it with all his force; when the other loosed his hold presently, and said, "You bite, Alcibiades, like a woman." "No," replied he, "like a lion."

On another occasion it is reported that Alcibiades with other boys was playing with dice in the street. A loaded cart which had been approaching drew near just as it was his turn to throw. To quote again from Plutarch:

> At first he called to the driver to stop, because he was to throw in the way over which the cart was to pass; but the man giving him no attention and driving on, when the rest of the boys divided and gave way, Alcibiades threw himself on his face before the cart and, stretching himself out, bade the carter pass on now if he would; which so startled the man, that he put back his horses, while all that saw it were terrified, and, crying out, ran to assist Alcibiades.

Alcibiades, one of the most prominent figures in Athens, an extremely influential leader with important successes to his credit, became the chief advocate for the memorable expedition against Sicily. He entered enthusiastically into this venture, urging it upon the Athenians partly from policy, it seems, and partly from his private ambition. Though this expedition resulted in catastrophe and played a major role in the end of Athenian power and glory, many have felt that if Alcibiades had been left in Sicily in his position of command he might have led the great armada to victory. If so, this might well have insured for Athens indefinitely the supreme power of the ancient world. The brilliant ability often demonstrated by Alcibiades lends credence to such an opinion. On the other hand, his inconsistency and capriciousness make it difficult, indeed, to feel confident that his presence would necessarily have brought success to the Athenian cause. If Athens had succeeded in the expedition against Syracuse the history of Greece and perhaps even the history of all Europe might have been substantially different.

Shortly before the great Athenian fleet and army sailed on the Sicilian expedition, an incident occurred that has never been satisfactorily explained. Now when Athens was staking her future on a monumental and dangerous venture, there was imperative need for solidarity of opinion and for confidence in the three leaders to whom so much had been entrusted. At this tense and exquisitely inopportune time the sacred statues of Hermes throughout the city were mutilated in a wholesale desecration.

This unprovoked act of folly and outrage disturbed the entire populace and aroused superstitious qualms and fears that support of the gods would be withdrawn at a time of crucial need. Alcibiades was strongly suspected of the senseless sacrilege. Though proof was not established that he had committed this deed which demoralized the Athenians, the possibility that Alcibiades, their brilliant leader, might be guilty of such an idle and irresponsible outrage shook profoundly the confidence of the expeditionary force and of the government. Many who knew him apparently felt that such an act might have been carried out by Alcibiades impulsively and without any adequate reason but merely as an idle gesture of bravado, a prank that might demonstrate what he could get away with if it should suit his fancy. Definite evidence emerged at this time to show that he had been profaning the Eleusinian mysteries by imitating them or caricaturing them for the amusement of his friends. This no doubt strengthened suspicion against him as having played a part in mutilating the sacred statues.

On a number of other occasions his bad judgment and his self-centered whims played a major role in bringing disasters upon Athens and upon himself. Though this brilliant leader often appeared as a zealous and incorruptible patriot, numerous incidents strongly indicate that at other times he put self-interest first and that sometimes even the feeble lure of some minor objective or the mere prompting of caprice caused him to ignore the welfare and safety of his native land and to abandon lightly all standards of loyalty and honor.

No substantial evidence has ever emerged to indicate that Alcibiades was guilty of the sacrilegious mutilation of the statues. He asked for an immediate trial, but it was decided not to delay the sailing of the fleet for this. After he reached Syracuse, Alcibiades was summoned to return to Athens to face these charges. On the way back he deserted the Athenian cause, escaped to Sparta, and joined the enemy to fight against his native city.

It has been argued that Alcibiades could not have been guilty of the mutilation since, as a leader of the expedition and its chief advocate, he would have so much to lose by a senseless and impious act that might jeopardize its success. On the other hand, his career shows many incidents of unprovoked and potentially self-damaging folly carried out more or less as a whim, perhaps in defiance of authority or as an arrogant gesture to show his immunity to ordinary rules or restrictions. It sometimes looked as though the very danger of a useless and uninviting deed might, in itself, tempt him to flaunt a cavalier defiance of rules that bind other men. If Alcibiades did play a part in this piece of egregious folly, it greatly augments his resemblance to the patients described in this book. Indeed it is difficult to see how anyone but a psychopath might, in his position, participate in such an act.

In Sparta Alcibiades made many changes to identify himself with the ways and styles of the enemy. In Athens he had been notable for his fine raiment and for worldly splendor and extravagance. On these characteristics Plutarch comments thus:

> But with all these words and deeds and with all this sagacity and eloquence, he mingled the exorbitant luxury and wantonness in his eating and drinking and dissolute living; wore long, purple robes like a woman, which dragged after him as he went through the marketplace, caused the planks of his galley to be cut away, that he might lie the softer, his bed not being placed on the boards but hanging upon girths. His shield, again, which was richly gilded had not the usual ensigns of the Athenians, but a Cupid holding a thunderbolt in his hand, was painted upon it. The sight of all this made the people of good repute in the city feel disgust and abhorrence and apprehension also, at his free living and his contempt of law as things monstrous in themselves and indicating designs of usurpation.

In contrast to his appearance and his habits in the old environment, we find this comment by Plutarch on Alcibiades after he had deserted the Athenian cause and come to live in Sparta and throw all his brilliant talents into the war against his native land:

> The renown which he earned by these public services, not to Athens, but to Sparta, was equalled by the admiration he attracted to his private life. He captivated and won over everybody by his conformity to Spartan habits. People who saw him wearing his hair cut close and bathing in cold water, eating coarse meal and dining on black broth, doubted, or rather, could not believe that he had ever had a cook in his house or had ever seen a perfumer or had ever worn a mantle of Milesian purple. For he had, as it was observed, this peculiar talent and artifice of gaining men's affection, that he could at once comply with and really embrace and enter into the habits and ways of life, and change faster than the chameleon; one color, indeed, they say, the chameleon cannot assume; he cannot himself appear white. But, Alcibiades, whether with good men or with bad, could adapt himself to his company and equally wear the appearances of virtue or vice. At Sparta, he was devoted to athletic exercises, was frugal and reserved; in Ionia, luxurious, gay and indolent; in Thrace, always drinking; in Thessaly, ever on horseback; and when he lived with Tisaphernes, the king of Persia's satrap he exceeded the Persians themselves in magnificence and pomp. Not that his natural disposition changed so easily, nor that his real character was so variable, but whether he was sensible that by pursuing his own inclinations he might give offense to those with whom he had occasion to converse, he transformed himself into any shape and adopted any fashion that he observed to be agreeable to them.

At Sparta Alcibiades seemed to strive in every way to help the enemy defeat and destroy Athens. He induced them to send military aid promptly to the Syracusans and also aroused them to renew the war directly against Athens. He made them aware of the great importance of fortifying Decelea, a place very near Athens, from which she was extremely vulnerable to attack. The Spartans followed his counsel in these matters and, by taking the steps he advised, wrought serious damage to the Athenian cause. The vindictive and persistent efforts of this brilliant traitor may have played a substantial part in the eventual downfall of Athens. Even before he left Sicily for Sparta Alcibiades had begun to work against his native land in taking steps to prevent Messina from falling into the hands of the Athenians.

Eventually a good many of the Spartans began to distrust Alcibiades. Among this group was the king, Agis. According to Plutarch:

> While Agis was absent and abroad with the army, [Alcibiades] corrupted his wife, Timea, and had a child born by her. Nor did she even deny it, but when she was brought to bed of a son, called him in public, Leotychides, but amongst her confidants and attendants, would whisper that his name was Alcibiades, to such a degree was she transported by her passion for him. He, on the other side, would say in his vain way, he had not done this thing out of mere wantonness of insult, nor to gratify a passion, but that his race might one day be kings over the Lacedaemonians.

It became increasingly unpleasant for Alcibiades in Sparta despite his great successes and the admiration he still evoked in many. Plutarch says:

> But Agis was his enemy, hating him for having dishonoured his wife, but also impatient of his glory, as almost every success was ascribed to Alcibiades. Others, also, of the more powerful and ambitious among the Spartans were possessed with jealousy of him and prevailed with the magistrates in the city to send orders . . . that he should be killed.

Alcibiades, however, learned of this, and fled to Asia Minor for security with the satrap of the king of Persia, Tisaphernes. Here he found security and again displayed his great abilities and his extraordinary charm. According to Plutarch:

> [He] immediately became the most influential person about him; for this barbarian [Tisaphernes] , not being himself sincere, but a lover of guile and wickedness, admired his address and wonderful subtlety. And, indeed, the charm of daily intercourse with him was more than any character could resist or any disposition escape. Even those who feared and envied him, could not but take delight and have a sort of kindness for him when they saw him and were in his company, so that Tisaphernes, otherwise a cruel character, and above all other Persians, a hater of the Greeks, was yet so won by the flatteries of Alcibiades that he set himself even to exceed him in responding to them. The most beautiful of his parks containing salubrious streams and meadows where he had built pavilions and places of retirement, royally and exquisitely adorned, received by his direction the name of Alcibiades and was always so called and so spoken of.
>
> Thus, Alcibiades, quitting the interest of the Spartans, whom he could no longer trust because he stood in fear of Agis, the king, endeavored to do them ill offices and render them odious to Tisaphernes, who, by his means, was hindered from assisting them vigorously and from finally ruining the Athenians. For his advice was to furnish them but sparingly with money and so wear them out, and consume them insensibly; when they had wasted their strength upon one another, they would both become ready to submit to the king.

It is not remarkable to learn that Alcibiades left the service of the Persians. It does seem to me remarkable, however, after his long exile from Athens, his allegiance to her enemies and the grevious damage he had done her, that he was enthusiastically welcomed back to Athens, that he again led Athenian forces to brilliant victories, and that he was, indeed, given supreme command of the Athenian military and naval forces. His welcome back to Athens was enthusiastic. According to Plutarch, "The people crowned him with crowns of gold, and created him general, both by land and by sea." He is described as "coming home from so long an exile, and such variety of misfortune, in the style of revellers breaking up from a drinking party." Despite this, many of the Athenians did not fully trust him, and apparently without due cause, this time, he was dismissed from his high position of command. He later retired to Asia Minor where he was murdered at 46 years of age, according to some reports for "having debauched a young lady of a noble house."

Despite the widespread admiration that Alcibiades could so easily arouse, skeptical comments were made about him even before his chief failures occurred. According to Plutarch, "It was not said amiss by Archestratus, that Greece could not support a second Alcibiades." Plutarch also quotes Timon as saying, "Go on boldly, my son, and increase in credit with the people, for thou wilt one day bring them calamities enough." Of the Athenians' attitude toward Alcibiades, Aristophanes wrote: "They love and hate and cannot do without him."

The character of Alcibiades looms in the early dawn of history as an enigmatic paradox. He undoubtedly disconcerted and puzzled his contemporaries, and his conduct seems to have brought upon him widely differing judgments. During the many centuries since his death historians have seemed fascinated by his career but never quite able to interpret his personality. Brilliant and persuasive, he was able to succeed in anything he wished to accomplish. After spectacular achievement he often seemed, carelessly or almost deliberately, to throw away all that he had gained, through foolish decisions or unworthy conduct for which adequate motivation cannot be demonstrated and, indeed, can scarcely be imagined. Senseless pranks or mere nose-thumbing gestures of derision seemed at times to draw him from serious responsibilities and cause him to abandon major goals as well as the commitments of loyalty and honor. Apparently his brilliance, charm, and promise captivated Socrates, generally held to be the greatest teacher and the wisest man of antiquity. Though Alcibiades is reported to have been the favorite disciple and most cherished friend of the master, it can hardly be said that Socrates succeeded in teaching him to apply even ordinary wisdom consistently in the conduct of his life or to avoid follies that would have been shunned even by the stupid.

According to the Encyclopaedia Brittanica; "He was an admirer of Socrates, who saved his life at Potidaea (432), a service which Alcibiades repaid at Delium; but he could not practice his master's virtues, and there is no doubt that the example of Alcibiades strengthened the charges brought against Socrates of corrupting the youth."

When we look back upon what has been recorded of Alcibiades, we are led to suspect that he had the gift of every talent except that of using them consistently to achieve any sensible aim or in behalf of any discernible cause. Though it would hardly be convincing to claim that we can establish a medical diagnosis, or a full psychiatric explanation, of this public figure who lived almost two and a half thousand years ago, there are many points in the incomplete records of his life available to us that strongly suggest Alcibiades may have been a spectacular example of what during recent decades we have, in bewilderment and amazement, come to designate as the psychopath.

During this brief period Greece, and Athens especially, produced architecture, sculpture, drama, and poetry that have seldom if ever been surpassed. Perhaps Greece also produced in Alcibiades the most impressive and brilliant, the most truly classic, example of this still inexplicable pattern of human life.

chapter 6 · A clinical profile

SYNOPSIS AND ORIENTATION

In an earlier chapter it was noted that an attempt would be made to follow the general methods of science. Let us stop for a moment to orient ourselves. In Section Two some examples of the material were offered and certain observations recorded. In Chapters 4 and 5 an effort was made to consider traditional concepts of the problem and to differentiate broadly the subject of this study from certain other personality reactions. These may be regarded as preliminary steps in the process of sifting and arranging our observations into some sort of order for the purpose of giving them, as much as possible, distinct and comprehensible form. To take another step in this process, let us now attempt to put down in more concise statement the general facts of behavior and appearances of emotion and purpose that emerge from our recorded observations and that appear to be common qualities of the group in question.

Before going on to the perhaps still unanswerable questions of why the psychopath behaves as he does or of how he comes to follow such a life scheme, let us, as was just suggested, attempt to say what the psychopath is in terms of his actions and his apparent intentions, so that we may recognize him readily and distinguish him from others.

We shall list the characteristic points that have emerged and then discuss them in order:

1. Superficial charm and good "intelligence"
2. Absence of delusions and other signs of irrational thinking
3. Absence of "nervousness" or psychoneurotic manifestations
4. Unreliability
5. Untruthfulness and insincerity
6. Lack of remorse and shame
7. Inadequately motivated antisocial behavior
8. Poor judgment and failure to learn by experience
9. Pathologic egocentricity and incapacity for love
10. General poverty in major affective reactions
11. Specific loss of insight
12. Unresponsiveness in general interpersonal relations
13. Fantastic and uninviting behavior with drink and sometimes without
14. Suicide rarely carried out
15. Sex life impersonal, trivial, and poorly integrated
16. Failure to follow any life plan

SUPERFICIAL CHARM AND GOOD "INTELLIGENCE"

More often than not, the typical psychopath will seem particularly agreeable and make a distinctly positive impression when he is first encountered. Alert and friendly in his attitude, he is easy to talk with and seems to have a good many genuine interests. There is nothing at all odd or queer about him, and in every respect he tends to embody the concept of a well-adjusted, happy person. Nor does he, on the other hand, seem to be artificially exerting himself like one who is covering up or who wants to sell you a bill of goods. He would seldom be confused with the professional backslapper or someone who is trying to ingratiate himself for a concealed purpose. Signs of affectation or excessive affability are not characteristic. He looks like the real thing.

Very often indications of good sense and sound reasoning will emerge, and one is likely to feel soon after meeting him that this normal and pleasant person is also one with high abilities. Psychometric tests also very frequently show him of superior intelligence. More than the average person, he is likely to seem free from social or emotional impediments, from the minor distortions, peculiarities, and awkwardnesses so common even among the successful. Such superficial characteristics are not universal in this group but they are very common.

Here the typical psychopath contrasts sharply with the schizoid personality or the patient with masked or latent schizophrenia. No matter how free from delusions and other overt signs of psychosis the schizoid person may be, he is likely to show specific peculiarities in his outer aspect. Usually there are signs of tension, withdrawal, and subtle oddities of manner and reaction. These may appear to be indications of unrevealed brilliance, perhaps even eccentricities of genius, but they are likely to complicate and cool easy social relations and to promote restraint. Although the psychopath's inner emotional deviations and deficiencies may be comparable with the inner status of the masked schizophrenic, he outwardly shows nothing brittle or strange. Everything about him is likely to suggest desirable and superior human qualities, a robust mental health.

ABSENCE OF DELUSIONS AND OTHER SIGNS OF IRRATIONAL THINKING

The so-called psychopath is ordinarily free from signs and symptoms traditionally regarded as evidence of a psychosis. He does not hear voices. Genuine delusions cannot be demonstrated. There is no valid depression, consistent pathologic elevation of mood, or irresistible pressure of activity. Outer perceptual reality is accurately recognized; social values and generally accredited personal standards are accepted verbally. Excellent logical reasoning is maintained, and, in theory, the patient can foresee the consequences of injudicious or antisocial acts, outline acceptable or admirable plans of life, and ably criticize in words his former mistakes. The results of direct psychiatric examination disclose nothing pathologic—nothing that would indicate incompetency or that would arouse suspicion that such a man could not lead a successful and happy life.

Not only is the psychopath rational and his thinking free of delusions, but he also appears to react with normal emotions. His ambitions are discussed with what appears to be healthy enthusiasm. His convictions impress even the skeptical observer as firm and binding. He seems to respond with adequate feelings to another's interest in him, and, as he discusses his wife, his children, or his parents, he is likely to be judged a man of warm human responses, capable of full devotion and loyalty.

ABSENCE OF "NERVOUSNESS" OR PSYCHONEUROTIC MANIFESTATIONS

There are usually no symptoms to suggest a psychoneurosis in the clinical sense. In fact, the psychopath is nearly always free from minor reactions popularly regarded as "neurotic" or as constituting "nervousness." The chief criteria whereby such diagnoses as hysteria, obsessive-compulsive disorder, anxiety state, or "neurasthenia" might be made do not apply to him. It is highly typical for him not only to escape the abnormal anxiety and tension fundamentally characteristic of this whole diagnostic group but also to show a relative immunity from such anxiety and worry as might be judged normal or appropriate in disturbing situations. Regularly we find in him extraordinary poise rather than jitteriness or worry, a smooth sense of physical well-being instead of uneasy preoccupation with bodily functions. Even under concrete circumstances that would for the ordinary person cause embarrassment, confusion, acute insecurity, or visible agitation, his relative serenity is likely to be noteworthy.

It is true he may become vexed and restless when held in jails or psychiatric hospitals. This impatience seems related to his inability to realize the need or justification for his being restrained. What tension or uneasiness of this sort he may show seems provoked entirely by external circumstances, never by feelings of guilt, remorse, or intrapersonal insecurity. Within himself he appears almost as incapable of anxiety as of profound remorse.

UNRELIABILITY

Although the psychopath is likely to give an early impression of being a thoroughly reliable person, it will soon be found that on many occasions he shows no sense of responsibility whatsoever. No matter how binding the obligation, how urgent the circumstances, or how important the matter, this holds true. Furthermore, the question of whether or not he is to be confronted with his failure or his disloyalty and called to account for it appears to have little effect on his attitude.

If such failures occurred uniformly and immediately, others would soon learn not to rely upon psychopaths or to be surprised at their conduct. It is, however, characteristic for them during some periods to show up regularly at work, to meet their financial obligations, to ignore an opportunity to steal. They may apply their excellent abilities in business or in study for a week, for months, or even for a year or more and thereby gain potential security, win a scholarship, be acclaimed top salesman; or be elected president of a social club or perhaps of a school honor society. Not all checks given by psychopaths bounce; not all promises are uniformly ignored. They do not necessarily land in jail every day (or every month) or seek to cheat someone else during every transaction. If so, it would be much simpler to deal with them. This transiently (but often convincingly) demonstrated ability to succeed in business and in all objective affairs makes failures more disturbing to those about them.

Furthermore, it cannot be predicted how long effective and socially acceptable conduct will prevail or precisely when (or in what manner) dishonest, outlandish, or disastrously irresponsible acts or failures to act will occur. These seem to have little or no relation to objective stress, to cyclic periods, or to major alterations of mood or outlook. What is at stake for the patient, for his family, or for anybody else is not a regularly determining factor. At the crest of success in his work he may forge a small check, indulge in petty thievery, or simply not come to the office. After a period of gracious and apparently happy relations with his family he may pick a quarrel with his wife, strike her, drive her from the house, and then throw a glass of iced tea in the face of his 3-year-old son. For the initiation of such outbursts he does not, it seems, need any great anger. Moderate vexation usually suffices.

The psychopath's unreliability and his disregard for obligations and for consequences are manifested in both trivial and serious matters, are masked by demonstrations of conforming behavior, and cannot be accounted for by ordinary motives or incentives. Although it can be confidently predicted that his failures and disloyalties will continue, it is impossible to time them and to take satisfactory precautions against their effect. Here, it might be said, is not even a consistency in inconsistency but an inconsistency in inconsistency.

UNTRUTHFULNESS AND INSINCERITY

The psychopath shows a remarkable disregard for truth and is to be trusted no more in his accounts of the past than in his promises for the future or his statement of present intentions. He gives the impression that he is incapable of ever attaining realistic comprehension of an attitude in other people that causes them to value truth and cherish truthfulness in themselves.

Typically he is at ease and unpretentious in making a serious promise or in (falsely) exculpating himself from accusations, whether grave or trivial. His simplest statement in such matters carries special powers of conviction. Overemphasis, obvious glibness, and other traditional signs of the clever liar do not usually show in his words or in his manner. Whether there is reasonable chance for him to get away with the fraud or whether certain and easily foreseen detection is at hand, he is apparently unperturbed and does the same impressive job. Candor and trustworthiness seem implicit in him at such times. During the most solemn perjuries he has no difficulty at all in looking anyone tranquilly in the eyes. Although he will lie about any matter, under any circumstances, and often for no good reason, he may, on the contrary, sometimes own up to his errors (usually when detection is certain) and appear to be facing the consequences with singular honesty, fortitude, and manliness.

It is indeed difficult to express how thoroughly straightforward some typical psychopaths can appear. They are disarming not only to those unfamiliar with such patients but often to people who know well from experience their convincing outer aspect of honesty. A saying current among psychiatric residents, secretaries, medical associates, and others familiar with what goes on in my office may illustrate this point. The saying is in substance that excellent evidence for the diagnosis of psychopathic personality can be found in my own response to newcomers who seek to borrow money or cash checks. It is rather generally believed that only psychopaths are successful and that in typical cases success is inevitable. Although I argue that some exaggeration has perhaps colored this story and overemphasized the infallibility of my reaction as a test, I must admit there is much truth in the matter. Even after so many years of special interest in the subject, I am forced to confess that fairly often observers have had the opportunity to make a snap diagnosis from my response to this sort of appeal and see it gain full confirmation in subsequent events. I might add that no such loan has ever been repaid and that all such checks have bounced.

After being caught in shameful and gross falsehoods, after repeatedly violating his most earnest pledges, he finds it easy, when another occasion arises, to speak of his *word of honor,* his *honor as a gentleman,* and he shows surprise and vexation when commitments on such a basis do not immediately settle the issue.

The conception of living up to his word seems, in fact, to be regarded as little more than a phrase sometimes useful to avoid unpleasantness or to gain other ends. How inadequate such ends may be to account for the psychopath's neglect of truth can be shown in a brief example:

In a letter to his wife, at last seeking divorce and in another city, one patient set down dignified, fair appraisals of the situation and referred to sensible plans he had outlined for her security. He then added that specified insurance policies and annuities providing for the three children (including their tuition at college) had been mailed under separate cover and would, if she had not already received them, soon be in her hands. He had not taken even the first step to obtain insurance or to make any other provision, and, once he had made these statements in his letter, he apparently gave the matter no further thought.

LACK OF REMORSE AND SHAME

The psychopath apparently cannot accept substantial blame for the various misfortunes that befall him and that he brings down upon others. Usually he denies emphatically all responsibility and directly accuses others as responsible, but often he will go through an idle ritual of saying that much of his trouble is his own fault. When the latter course is adopted, subsequent events indicate that it is empty of sincerity—a hollow and casual form as little felt as the literal implications of "your humble and obedient servant" are actually felt by a person who closes a letter with such a phrase. Although his behavior shows reactions of this sort to be perfunctory, this is seldom apparent in his manner. This is exceedingly deceptive and is very likely to promote confidence and deep trust. More detailed questioning about just what he blames himself for and why may show that a serious attitude is not only absent but altogether inconceivable to him. If this fails, his own actions will soon clarify the issue.

Whether judged in the light of his conduct, of his attitude, or of material elicited in psychiatric examination, he shows almost no sense of shame. His career is always full of exploits, any one of which would wither even the more callous representatives of the ordinary man. Yet he does not, despite his able protestations, show the slightest evidence of major humiliation or regret. This is true of matters pertaining to his personal and selfish pride and to esthetic standards that he avows as well as to moral or humanitarian matters. If Santayana is correct in saying that "perhaps the true dignity of man is his ability to despise himself," the psychopath is without a means to acquire true dignity.

INADEQUATELY MOTIVATED ANTISOCIAL BEHAVIOR

Not only is the psychopath undependable, but also in more active ways he cheats, deserts, annoys, brawls, fails, and lies without any apparent compunction. He will commit theft, forgery, adultery, fraud, and other deeds for astonishingly small stakes and under much greater risks of being discovered than will the ordinary scoundrel. He will, in fact, commit such deeds in the absence of any apparent goal at all.

Yet we do not find the regularity and specificity in his behavior that is apparent in what is often called compulsive stealing or other socially destructive actions carried out under extraordinary pressures that the subject, in varying degrees, struggles against. Such activities, and all disorder distinguished by some as impulse neurosis, as we have mentioned, probably have important features in common with the psychopath's disorder. In contrast, his antisocial and self-defeating deeds are not circumscribed (as, for example, in pyromania and kleptomania), and he shows little or no evidence of the conscious conflict or the subsequent regret that are not regularly absent in these other manifestations. Again the comparison of a circumscribed dissociation typical of hysteria with the general ego disintegration of schizophrenia may be usefully cited.

Objective stimuli (value of the object, specific conscious need) are, as in compulsive (or impulsive) stealing, inadequate to account for the psychopath's acts. Evidence of any vividly felt urge symbolizing a disguised but specifically channelized, instinctive drive is not readily available in the psychopath's wide range of inappropriate and self-defeating behavior. Two incidents in typical cases are offered.

1. An 18-year-old boy often stole objects for which he had some use, but stealing was not a dominant feature in his almost universally manifested maladjustment. Drifting one day into church, he chose to remain after services and speak personally with the clergyman. As might be expected, he made a profound impression and, spontaneously professing conversion, brought justifiable pride to his counselor. Although disappointed because this new religious attitude did not curtail the boy in his flagrant truancy, his desultory cheating in examinations, and his lying, the clergyman worked hopefully and assiduously with him. On one occasion, after hanging around game rooms and street corners until 3 A.M., the youth explained his tardiness to his parents in a vivid account of having been injured while wrestling at the school gymnasium. He had, he explained to them, spit up blood and so was taken in an ambulance to the hospital emergency room, where he was treated by the family physician. He gave realistic detail about difficulties in locating the physician, the spirit of emergency prevailing, and techniques of treatment. This story was elaborated despite his knowledge that the next day he was, in the company of his father, going to visit this very physician (for a previously made appointment) and that all he said would be proved untrue.

Despite repeated and versatile acts inconsistent with the boy's profession of religion, the patient clergyman, naturally impressed with one who seemed so sincere and whose stated attitudes were so admirable, did not lose hope and at times even became quite optimistic. This optimism was particularly shaken after the discovery that his convert had, during communion, succeeded in stealing one of the small glass goblets used in the ceremony.

2. Stealing was a very minor feature of Anna's career, a few details of which were cited in Chapter 2. While on parole for the afternoon from a private psychiatric institution, she accepted the hospitality of an old friend who had planned tea and sandwiches for several rather demure women whose common interest centered on church activities. While accompanying her hostess on a preparatory visit to a large grocery store, the patient, as if by whim, slipped into her ample handbag a bottle of vitamin tablets, a package of cream cheese, and a tin of anchovy paste. On arriving at the house (prior to the gathering), she presented all but the vitamin tablets to her hostess as a contribution to the party. She was a woman of considerable wealth and had funds with her. She apparently realized that her theft might be detected and would almost surely be suspected. In carrying out the act she behaved with what can perhaps best be called moderate caution. Apparently she was not strongly influenced by fears of being caught. Nor, on the other hand, did she seem to be seeking purposively but unconsciously any specific thrill, masochistic or otherwise, that might arise in this event. Nothing about her reactions to this and scores of similar acts ever suggested an irresistible force compelling her on against her judgment and will.

POOR JUDGMENT AND FAILURE TO LEARN BY EXPERIENCE

Despite his excellent rational powers, the psychopath continues to show the most execrable judgment about attaining what one might presume to be his ends. He throws away excellent opportunities to make money, to achieve a rapprochement with his wife, to be dismissed from the hospital, or to gain other ends that he has sometimes spent considerable effort toward gaining. It might be said that he cares little about financial success and little about regaining his wife, but it is difficult indeed to say that he is not extremely eager to get out of the psychiatric hospital where he has been locked up for months with other patients whom he regards as "lunatics" and who are, indeed, not desirable associates for the average man or for him. Be it noted again that the psychopath appears as unwilling to remain in a psychiatric hospital and as impatient to regain his freedom as would be the normal man. I have not in these patients ever found reliable evidence that unconsciously they seek and enjoy as punishment such confinement.

This exercise of execrable judgment is not particularly modified by experience, however chastening the experiences may be. Few more impressive examples of this could be offered from the records of humanity than the familiar one of the psychopath who, in full possession of his rational faculties, has gone through the almost indescribably distasteful confinement of many months with delusional and disturbed psychotic patients and, after fretting and counting the days until the time of his release, proceeds at once to get drunk and create disorder which he thoroughly understands will cause him to be returned without delay to the detested wards. It is my opinion that no punishment is likely to make the psychopath change his ways. Punishment is not, of course, regarded as an appropriate measure in medical treatment. It is, however, often considered and administered by legal authorities. And it must be remembered that at present the law deals with these patients more frequently than physicians deal with them.

Despite the extraordinarily poor judgment demonstrated in behavior, in the actual living of his life, the psychopath characteristically demonstrates unimpaired (sometimes excellent) judgment in appraising theoretical situations. In complex matters of judgment involving ethical, emotional, and other evaluational factors, in contrast with matters requiring only (or chiefly) intellectual reasoning ability, he also shows no evidence of a defect. So long as the test is verbal or otherwise abstract, so long as he is not a direct participant, he shows that he knows his way about. He can offer wise decisions not only for others in life situations but also for himself so long as he is asked what he would do (or should do, or is going to do). When the test of action comes to him, we soon find ample evidence of his deficiency.

PATHOLOGIC EGOCENTRICITY AND INCAPACITY FOR LOVE

The psychopath is always distinguished by egocentricity. This is usually of a degree not seen in ordinary people and often is little short of astonishing. How obviously this quality will be expressed in vanity or self-esteem will vary with the shrewdness of the subject and with his other complexities. Deeper probing will always reveal a self-centeredness that is apparently unmodifiable and all but complete. This can perhaps be best expressed by stating that it is an incapacity for object love and that this incapacity (in my experience with well-marked psychopaths) appears to be absolute.

Terms in use for what we experience as emotion contain much ambiguity, and their referential accuracy is limited. This contributes to confusion and paradox, which are difficult to avoid in attempts to convey concepts about such a matter.

In a sense it is absurd to maintain that the psychopath's incapacity for object love is absolute, that is, to say he is capable of affection for another in literally no degree. He is plainly capable of casual fondness, of likes and dislikes, and of reactions that, one might say, cause others to matter to him. These affective reactions are, however, always strictly limited in degree. In durability they also vary greatly from what is normal in mankind. The term *absolute* is, I believe, appropriate if we apply it to any affective attitude strong and meaningful enough to be called love, that is, anything that prevails in sufficient degree and over sufficient periods to exert a major influence on behavior.

True enough, psychopaths are sometimes skillful in pretending a love for women or simulating parental devotion to their children. What part of this is not pure (and perhaps in an important sense unconscious) simulation has always impressed this observer as that other type of pseudolove sometimes seen in very self-centered people who are not psychopaths, which consists in concern for the other person only (or primarily) insofar as he enhances or seems to enhance the self. Even this latter imitation of adult affectivity has been seldom seen in the full-blown psychopath, although it is seen frequently in those called here partial psychopaths. In nonpsychopaths a familiar example is that of the parent who lavishes money and attention on a child chiefly to bask in the child's success and consciously or unconsciously to feel what an important person he is because of the child's triumphs. Although it is true that with ordinary people such motives are seldom, if ever, unmixed, and usually some object love and some self-love are integrated into such attitudes, in even the partial psychopath anything that could honestly be called object love approaches the imperceptible.

What positive feelings appear during the psychopath's interpersonal relations give a strong impression of being self-love. Some cynical psychologists and philosophers have, of course, challenged the existence of any love that is not on final analysis selfish, saying that the mother who gives up her own life for her child really does so because it would be more painful to her to see the child perish. Without attempting to take up the cudgels in this interesting dispute, it will suffice to say that whatever normal and highly developed and sincere object love may actually be, it is, whether judged behaviorally or intuitively, something that impresses the ordinary observer as definitely unlike anything found in the psychopath.

The psychopath seldom shows anything that, if the chief facts were known, would pass even in the eyes of lay observers as object love. His absolute indifference to the financial, social, emotional, physical, and other hardships that he brings upon those for whom he professes love confirms the appraisal during psychiatric studies of his true attitude. We must, let it never be forgotten, judge a man by his actions rather than by his words. This old saying is especially significant when it is the man's motivations and real feelings that we are to judge. This lack in the psychopath makes it all but impossible for an adequate emotional rapport to arise in his treatment and may be an important factor in the therapeutic failure that, in my experience, has been universal.

GENERAL POVERTY IN MAJOR AFFECTIVE REACTIONS

In addition to his incapacity for object love, the psychopath always shows general poverty of affect. Although it is true that he sometimes becomes excited and shouts as if in rage or seems to exult in enthusiasm and again weeps in what appear to be bitter tears or speaks eloquent and mournful words about his misfortunes or his follies, the conviction dawns on those who observe him carefully that here we deal with a readiness of expression rather than a strength of feeling.

Vexation, spite, quick and labile flashes of quasi affection, peevish resentment, shallow moods of self-pity, puerile attitudes of vanity, and absurd and showy poses of indignation are all within his emotional scale and are freely sounded as the circumstances of life play upon him. But mature, wholehearted anger, true or consistent indignation, honest, solid grief, sustaining pride, deep joy, and genuine despair are reactions not likely to be found within this scale.

Craig said long ago that patients who suffer from hysteria do not react with awe, reverence, wonder, or pity. Often they do not, it might be said, appear capable of achieving in sincerity the major emotions, although their protestations of such emotions are prominent and their show of feeling is sometimes so vigorous that the observer is often misled to believe that they are in tragic grief or remorse. Although such a diminution of emotional range, especially along the deeper notes, may be seen in the patient with hysteria, in the psychopath it is very much more far-reaching, profound, and final. Even in the situations of squalor and misery into which he repeatedly works himself, when confined in jails and what he regards as lunatic asylums, after throwing away fortunes or catching and transferring gonorrhea to his bride—even under these circumstances he does not show anything that could be called woe or despair or serious sorrow. He becomes vexed and rebellious and frets in lively and constant impatience when confined, but he does not grieve as others grieve.

Psychopaths are often witty and sometimes give a superficial impression of that far different and very serious thing, humor. Humor, however, in what may be its full, true sense,* they never have. I have thought that I caught glimpses of it in psychopaths and, despite a typical history, was inclined to question the diagnosis. Further observation of these patients gave convincing evidence that the apparent humor, like the apparent insight, was really an artifact.

One might feel a superficial inclination to credit with humor the patient described under "The Psychopath as Scientist" who, after his lamentable marriage to the very unprepossessing streetwalker, laughed and admitted that the joke was on himself. At first glance such a reply might appear to be the valiant humor of a man who can smile in any adversity. And, indeed, it might be correctly judged as this if the speaker showed any evidence of feeling his adversity or accepting his responsibility. But in this instance the only convincing appraisal is that "he jests at scars who never felt a wound." When the normal man makes a gay or ironic quip on the subject of his own adversity, we may justifiably applaud it as humor. If the quip concerns an adversity that scarcely touches the maker, it is as empty of humor as the empty boldness of a daredevil who wagers his fortune in a dice game where no one is playing for keeps.

In such a discussion only personal opinions of what is real humor and what is not real humor can be expressed. Everyone's capacity to appreciate or appraise such a quality varies, no doubt, as widely as one's sense of what is beautiful.

The emotional poverty, the complete lack of strong or tragic feeling universally found in all the psychopaths personally observed, has caused me considerable bewilderment in connection with frequent references in the literature to the powerful instinctual drives and passions said to be manifested in such people. Although weak and even infantile drives displaying themselves theatrically in the absence of ordinary inhibitions may impress the layman as mighty forces, it is hardly to be concluded that wise and deeply experienced psychiatrists would be similarly deceived. Perhaps such descriptions apply to other types of personality than that discussed here. And since, as I have already stressed, our aim is to present a type of personality disorder well known and believed to be a clinical entity rather than to argue about names, efforts will be limited to describing and trying to interpret the material at hand.

In considering the general shallowness of affect common to all members of this series in connection with their incapacity for object love, there is temptation to wonder about the possible interdependence of these faculties. Is it possible for tragic or transforming emotion to arise in any person without that peculiar and indescribable personal com-

*Carlyle said, "True humour springs not more from the head than from the heart; it is not contempt, its essence is love; it issues not in laughter, but in still smiles which lie far deeper. It is a sort of inverse sublimity, exalting, as it were, into our affections what is below us."

mitment to another? Or, if not to another human being, at least to some abstraction well outside the self?

SPECIFIC LOSS OF INSIGHT

In a special sense the psychopath lacks insight to a degree seldom, if ever, found in any but the most seriously disturbed psychotic patients. In a superficial sense, in that he can say he is in a psychiatric hospital because of his unacceptable and strange conduct, and by all other such criteria, his insight is intact. His insight is of course not affected at all with the type of impairment seen in the schizophrenic patient, who may not recognize the fact that others regard him as mentally ill but may insist that he is the Grand Lama and now in Tibet. Yet in a very important sense, in the sense of realistic evaluation, the psychopath lacks insight more consistently than some schizophrenic patients. He has absolutely no capacity to see himself as others see him. It is perhaps more accurate to say that he has no ability to know how others feel when they see him or to experience subjectively anything comparable about the situation. All of the values, all of the major affect concerning his status, are unappreciated by him.

This is almost astonishing in view of the psychopath's perfect orientation, his ability and willingness to reason or to go through the forms of reasoning, and his perfect freedom from delusions and other signs of an ordinary psychosis.

Usually, instead of facing facts that would ordinarily lead to insight, he projects, blaming his troubles on others with the flimsiest of pretext but with elaborate and subtle rationalization. Occasionally, however, he will perfunctorily admit himself to blame for everything and analyze his case from what seems to be almost a psychiatric viewpoint, but we can see that his conclusions have little actual significance for him. Some of these patients mentioned spoke fluently of the psychopathic personality, quoted the literature, and suggested this diagnosis for themselves. Soon this apparent insight was seen to be not merely imperfect but a consistent and thorough artifact. Perhaps it was less a voluntary deception than a simulation in which the simulator himself fails to realize his lack of emotional grasp or that he is simulating or *what* he is simulating. The patient seems to have little or no ability to feel the significance of his situation, to experience the real emotions of regret or shame or determination to improve, or to realize that this is lacking. His clever statements have been hardly more than verbal reflexes; even his facial expressions are without the underlying content they imply. This is not insight but an excellent mimicry of insight. No sincere intention can spring from his conclusions because no affective conviction is there to move him.

Such a deficiency of insight is harder to comprehend than the schizophrenic's deficiency, for it exists in the full presence of what are often assumed to be the qualities by which insight is gained. Yet the psychopath shows not only a deficiency but apparently a total absence of self-appraisal as a real and moving experience. Here is the spectacle of a person who uses all the words that would be used by someone who understands, and who could define all the words but who still is blind to the meaning. Such a clinical picture is more baffling to me than any of the symptoms of schizophrenia, on which attempts have been made to throw some light by psychopathologic theories. Here we have a patient who fulfills all the ordinary theoretical criteria of a "sound mind," and yet with this apparently sound mind is more incomprehensible than the psychotic patient.

What I regard as the psychopath's lack of insight shows up frequently and very impressively in his apparent assumption that the legal penalties for a crime he has committed do not, or should not, apply to him. This astonishing defect in realization often seems genuine, as the patient protests in surprise against the idea that prison might be anticipated for him, as for others under similar circumstances. He frequently reacts to such an idea as if to something unexpected and totally inappropriate. This characteristic has already been mentioned in the discussion of Gregory in Chapter 2.

Some observers believe that what the psychopath expresses about himself and his situation constitutes insight and merits such a term. I cannot agree with this opinion. The chief and most valid connotations of the word disappear in such an application. Profoundly psychotic patients whose gross lack of insight would be admitted by all sometimes express opinions that, if fully meant and appreciated, would indicate an insight that is plainly not there. A few brief examples may help:

A young man with a very active manic psychosis was interviewed some years ago. He whistled, shouted, winked, expressed the belief that he controlled the movements of the sun by his glance, sang snatches of bawdy songs, announced himself as a "sort of Messiah," and laid claim to the sexual vigor of seven bulls. Leaping about in a hospital shirt he had torn almost to shreds, he found exposed wires at a place on the wall from which he had torn the electric fixtures.

Seizing and releasing them and seizing them again, he got good jolts of the city current, which he relished, apparently interpreting the sensation as a manifestation of his own vitality. When asked if he felt anything was wrong with him mentally, he shouted in glee, "Sure, Doc, I'm crazy as a coot! I'm nuts I tell you. Crazier than anybody you ever saw!"

Another patient on a closed ward, a man badly disabled for years by obvious schizophrenia, often shouted out to the passerby, "Simple case of dementia praecox, Doc, simple case of dementia praecox," pointing to himself several times. Despite the chance diagnostic accuracy of what he said, this patient, like the one just mentioned, had little grasp of his situation and almost no real appreciation of his disorder and its meaning. Another manic patient not only spoke words that correctly indicated a good deal about his situation but even hammered out with a metal object he had obtained these letters in deep gashes in the wood door: "Bug house nutty."

Indications of serious impairment of insight abound in the psychopath's reactions after his failures have been undeniably demonstrated or his antisocial acts detected. The persistent tendency to ask for recommendations from those they have every reason to know cannot furnish anything but a negative report fatal to their plans has been illustrated. Such decisions in highly intelligent people can hardly mean less than that something crucial is absent from the realization of their status.

The calm assurance with which they report a successful rehabilitation in the midst of flagrant and immediate maladjustment often does not seem so much a real effort to deceive as an indication that the patient himself is greatly deceived. Despite his awareness of major facts, the pivotal significance of these facts seems not to be in his evaluations.

After a peculiarly overt and spectacular succession of failures, thefts, truancies, falsehoods, and expulsion from school, a young man had to be sent home to a distant state by his aunt and uncle with whom he had been staying. They had taken him in the hope that he might do better in another environment. His parents, after years of struggle, had found no solution.

All the details of his recent failure and disaster were factually known to him and had been discussed with his aunt and uncle. They made no effort to deceive him about why he had to be sent home. The physician to whom he wrote the letter which follows had also been frank with him. The letter was mailed a couple of days after he returned in what to another person could not have seemed less than total failure and disgrace.

> Dear Doctor:
>
> Arrived home safe and sound. I really was astonished at the great change in this small, typical, mid-western town when I pulled into it on Sunday. . . . I'm getting on fine here with Mother and Father. I feel like a different fellow. Dr. _______ I don't know how I'll ever thank you for what you did for me down there. It was my chance to straighten out and I took it. I believe I can say I did a good job of it. I don't know whether I could have done it alone. But the main thing is it's done and I want you to know I appreciate your help.
>
> Well, I have to go now. . . .

He also mentioned in other correspondence that he was helping his brother, who had shown some delinquency, to see the light, explaining that if he himself had been able to do such a thorough job the brother might profit and direct himself by the example, might, indeed, pull himself together, and "be a real man too." While writing to this effect, he continued the typical behavior without modification.

Let us consider a man whose wife, after many years of struggle equal to that of others discussed in some detail here, had left him and was seriously considering divorce. It is difficult to imagine a situation in which the necessity of permanent separation could be more clear or imperative. Nor is it likely that any patient described here has given a marital partner more reason to feel this need or has more fully demonstrated that, no matter what he said, he would continue to behave, toward her and in general, just as he had since their marriage. A few excerpts from his letters to the wife are illuminating:

> You will never be happy either by yourself or with some other man . . . we have too much in common. . . . I have no reason to lie or to misrepresent things to you now, even though I did try to explain it to you before. . . . There'll be another day, so I'm told and believe, and even though I don't expect to get proper judgment here on earth from you and yours I will up there and if I'm wrong I'm willing to suffer for eternity. . . .
>
> I do love you. I've never loved anyone else since childhood. . . . If I kill myself my blood will be on your hands . . . it will be heavy on your heart and soul. . . . All wrongs will be righted on Judgment Day. . . . You should have stuck by me—should never have left me. . . . I've suffered now really more than I can stand. . . . You think it will bring you happiness to be rid of me. . . . I sincerely hope and pray that it does if you do such a thing. I wish I could feel likewise . . . and believe everyone is at fault but me.

There is more in all this than simply false promises and fraudulent efforts to persuade the wife not to get a divorce. There is also indication of inability in his fundamental reactions to size up normally what he has done, what he is, and what he has been.

UNRESPONSIVENESS IN GENERAL INTERPERSONAL RELATIONS

The psychopath cannot be depended upon to show the ordinary responsiveness to special consideration or kindness or trust. No matter how well he is treated, no matter how long-suffering his family, his friends, the police, hospital attendants, and others may be, he shows no consistent reaction of appreciation except superficial and transparent protestations. Such gestures are exhibited most frequently when he feels they will facilitate some personal aim. The ordinary axiom of human existence that one good turn deserves another, a principle sometimes honored by cannibals and uncommonly callous assassins, has only superficial validity for him although he can cite it with eloquent casuistry when trying to obtain parole, discharge from the hospital, or some other end.

As in attempting to delineate other aspects of the psychopath, we find ourselves again confronting paradox. Although he can be counted on not to be appreciably swayed in major issues by these basic rules, we often find him attentive in small courtesies and favors, perhaps even habitually generous or quasi-generous when the cost is not decisive. Occasionally his actions may suggest profound generosity in that large sums are involved or something presumably of real value is sacrificed. Usually, however, these appearances are deceiving.

The psychopath who squanders $1,000 on a prostitute usually seems not to share very actively in the distressing worry and deprivation that his wife and children (or his parents) may experience quite substantially. The motives of a boy at boarding school who casually sells his new clothes to buy candy bars and soft drinks (for the whole dormitory) seem to lack an important dimension of magnanimity. This dimension could be presumed if after his extravagance the boy set to work assiduously in efforts to carry the burden he had created.

In relatively small matters psychopaths sometimes behave so as to appear very considerate, responsive, and obliging. Acquaintances who meet them on grounds where minor issues prevail may find it difficult to believe that they are not highly endowed with gratitude and eager to serve others. Such reactions and intentions, although sometimes ready or even spectacularly facile, do not ever accumulate sufficient force to play a determining part in really important issues. The psychopath who causes his parents hardship and humiliation by repeatedly forging checks and causes his wife anguish by sordid (and perhaps halfhearted) relations with another woman may gain a considerable reputation in the community by occasionally volunteering to cut the grass for the frail old lady across the street, by bringing a bottle of sherry over now and then to bedridden Mr. Blank, or by leaving his work to take a neighbor's injured cat to the veterinarian.

Outward social graces come easily to most psychopaths, and many continue, throughout careers disastrous to themselves and for others, to conduct themselves in superficial relations, in handling the trivia of existence, so as to gain admiration and gratitude. In these surface aspects of functioning, the typical psychopath (unlike the classic hypocrite) often seems to act with undesigning spontaneity and to be prompted by motives of excellent quality though of marvelously attenuated substance.

FANTASTIC AND UNINVITING BEHAVIOR WITH DRINK AND SOMETIMES WITHOUT

Although some psychopaths do not drink at all and others drink rarely, considerable overindulgence in alcohol is very often prominent in the life story. Delirium tremens and other temporary psychoses owing directly to alcohol were not commonly found in the hundreds of patients observed by me. The view of some professional moralists to the effect that demon rum is the fundamental cause of disaster such as that of the psychopath appears to have little claim to validity. It has been pointed out already that an irreconcilable difference in primary aim appears to exist between the ordinary person who drinks too much and the psychopath. This may be restated briefly as follows: The ordinary drinker gets into trouble by drifting with enthusiasm into the opinion that if two or six or eight drinks have made him feel so good, another (or two more or perhaps five more) will make him feel just so much better. Such rationalizations may assist the normal drinker, especially if he has serious fundamental conflicts, in a progress toward becoming a neurotic drinker or toward an alcoholic breakdown.

I cannot say that it is impossible in certain persons for a state of mental disorder identical with that described here as psychopathic personality to be reached eventually in this way. Often, however, these neurotic drinkers, in sharp contrast with the psychopath, worry about their state when sober, are capable of making an earnest effort to get well under psychiatric treatment, and lack most of the deeper personality features of the psychopath. Even in the neurotic drinker it is more often an independent and preexisting personality maladjustment rather than the alcohol which is primarily causal. Many psychiatric observers make this vividly clear and no less convincing. An interesting interpretation of alcoholism from a psychoanalytic viewpoint has been offered by Knight.

A major point about the psychopath and his relation to alcohol can be found in the shocking, fantastic, uninviting, or relatively inexplicable behavior that emerges when he drinks—sometimes when he drinks only a little. It is very likely that the effects of alcohol facilitate such acts and other manifestations of the disorder. This does not mean, however, that alcohol is fundamentally causal. Good criteria for differentiation between psychopaths and others who drink, moderately or excessively, can be found in what tendencies emerge after similar amounts have been consumed.

A peculiar sort of vulgarity, domineering rudeness, petty bickering or buffoonish quasi maulings of wife, mistress, or children, and quick shifts between maudlin and vainglorious moods, although sometimes found in ordinary alcoholics with other serious patterns of disorder, are particularly typical of the psychopath and in him alone reach full and precocious flower. Even in the first stages of a spree, perhaps after taking only two or three highballs, he may show signs of petty truculence or sullenness but seldom of real gaiety or conviviality. Evidence of any pleasurable reaction is characteristically minimal, as are indications that he is seeking relief from anxiety, despair, worry, responsibility, or tension.

Alcohol, as a sort of catalyst, sometimes contributes a good deal to the long and varied series of outlandish pranks and inanely coarse scenes with which nearly every drinking psychopath's story is starred. Free from alcohol, such a patient would scarcely sit under a house all night idly striking matches, or, concealing himself behind book stacks, urinate from the window of a public library on passersby in the street below. Nor would he, like the psychopathic son of a prominent family, suddenly, as a prank, decide to climb into a tree at a busy street corner, where he deliberately undressed, shouting wildly and puerilely to draw public attention. This man could not be persuaded to withdraw until the local fire department was called to remove him. The alcohol probably does not of itself create such behavior. Alcohol is not likely to bring out any impulse that is not already potential in a personality, nor is it likely to cast behavior into patterns for which there is not already significant subsurface predilection. The alcohol merely facilitates expression by narcotizing inhibitory processes. In cases of this sort very little narcotizing may be needed. The oil that lubricates the engine of an automobile neither furnishes the energy for its progress nor directs it.

Psychopaths often indulge in these strange performances after drinking relatively little. They know perfectly well what they have done before when drinking and, with these facts squarely before their altogether clear and rational awareness, decide to drink again. It is difficult indeed for me to see any substantial grounds for placing the responsibility for the drinking psychopath's deeds primarily on alcohol instead of on the disorder which, in ways no less serious even if less spectacular, he shows also when entirely sober.

Although his most theatrical exploits in public are usually carried on when drinking, the psychopath, even after he has been free from all alcohol for months, as for instance, when he is in a psychiatric hospital, retains all the essential personality features that have been mentioned. These show little or no tendency to diminish when he cannot drink. These words translated from Aeschylus, "Bronze is the mirror of the form; wine of the heart," express something pertinent about alcohol and man, whether the man be ill or well.

All the curious conduct reported in patients who drank and who were presented here occurred in the absence of delirium tremens, alcoholic hallucinosis, or any other of the well-known psychoses owing directly to intoxication. Of course, such psychotic conditions may occur in psychopaths and in neurotic drinkers. It is important to keep such symptoms separate, since they are clearly due to another type of mental disorder.

Most of this asocial, unacceptable, and self-defeating behavior associated with the psychopath's drinking seems to occur without the benefit of extreme inebriation. If actual confusion from alcohol prevailed or states of genuine amnesia were induced before the grotesque shenanigans began, intoxication could more plausibly be suspected of playing a larger causal role. The psychopath often reacts in this typical way while in perfect orientation, with unclouded awareness and in anything but the deeply drugged state thought by some to be a prerequisite.

For whatever reason the psychopath may drink, it is true that, in contrast with others who use alcohol to excess, he hits upon conduct and creates situations so bizarre, so untimely, and so preposterous that their motivation appears inscrutable. Many of his exploits seem directly calculated to place him in a disgraceful or ignominious position. He often chooses pranks and seeks out situations that would have no appeal for the ordinary person, whether the ordinary person be drunk or sober. The observer sometimes wonders if a truly astonishing ingenuity or an actively perverse inventiveness is directing the psychopath, so consistently does he bring off scenes not only uncongenial but even unimaginable to the average man.

Furthermore, these exploits seem to such little purpose, almost as hard to understand on the assumption that they are for amusement or play as on the grounds of utility. One patient with numerous other outstanding incidents in his career, while sitting at a formal dinner party given by friends in honor of his birthday, turned cooly and spat with deliberation on the cake as it was brought to his side for him to cut.

One patient who developed typical symptoms early in life showed, long before he had ever touched anything alcoholic, prankish tendencies worth noting here. When taken into a store by his parents to be fitted with new clothes, he often allowed intestinal gas to pass quietly but with vivid olfactory manifestations. Considerable embarrassment and vexation were experienced by the clerks and by his parents, but he was never ruffled and apparently took mild or moderate pleasure in the situation. He occasionally resorted to these tactics while riding with his parents and dignified company in a car when the windows were tightly closed because of cold weather. A few times he discomfited his family considerably by the same means in church. At first the parents accepted his apologies after reprimands and they were inclined to believe his innocent-faced explanation that an involuntary lapse of control had occurred. The timing of events and the predilection for close places and special surroundings, as well as the emergence of other behavior, convinced them in time that these acts were deliberate.

Another young psychopath who had never encountered liquor of any sort did many things that would not attract the ordinary mischievous teenager. Finding time a little heavy on his hands (and his parents out of the house for a few hours), he took tools from the cellar and, working with no little skill and dispatch, got the connections of the bathroom toilet apart, put into the outlet pipe a small electric motor, and then carefully reconnected the fixture. The subsequent flooding, mess, trouble, and expense did not seem to give him hilarious mirth or vindictive satisfaction. Certainly he showed no evidence of such feeling in a degree to warrant his risking the punishment he received.

The pranks or buffoonery of the sober adult psychopath naturally differ somewhat from those typical of adolescence or earlier. With a few drinks the similarity of the adult's behavior often increases.

SUICIDE RARELY CARRIED OUT

Despite the deep behavioral pattern of throwing away or destroying the opportunities of life that underlies the psychopath's superficial self-content, ease, charm, and often brilliance, we do not find him prone to take a final determining step of this sort in literal suicide. Suicidal tendencies have been stressed by some observers as prevalent. This opinion, in all likelihood, must have come from the observation of patients fundamentally different from our group, but who, as we have mentioned, were traditionally classified under the same term. It was only after a good many years of experience with actual psychopaths that I encountered my first authentic instance of suicide in a patient who could be called typical.

Instead of a predilection for ending their own lives, psychopaths, on the contrary, show much more evidence of a specific and characteristic immunity from such an act. This immunity, it must be granted, is, like most other immunities, relative.

Although suicide, then, cannot be named an impossibility among this group, its unlikelihood still merits strong emphasis. Since most psychopaths do not remain hospitalized or under other protective supervision, the rarity of this act becomes more significant. Also worth nothing is the fact that most real psychopaths, not once or a few times but habitually, work themselves into situations that might strongly prompt the normal man to end his own life. Since suicidal threats, like promises and well-formulated plans to adopt a new course, are so frequently offered by these patients, there is good reason to keep in mind the fact that they are nearly always empty. Many bogus attempts are made, sometimes with remarkable cleverness, premeditation, and histrionics.

SEX LIFE IMPERSONAL, TRIVIAL, AND POORLY INTEGRATED

The psychopath's sex life invariably shows peculiarities. The opinion has already been expressed that homosexuality and the other specific deviations, though of course occurring in psychopaths, are not sufficiently common to be regarded as characteristic. Evidence of consistent, well-formulated deviation was extremely rare in a large group of male psychopaths personally observed in a closed psychiatric institution. Among male and female subjects seen as outpatients and in general hospitals, such complications, though more frequent, do not seem to be a distinguishing feature. If we take another viewpoint and consider the group who come or are sent to the physician primarily for sexual deviation, we find again some patients with behavior patterns resembling in various degrees that of the real psychopath. These patients are probably not typical of the deviate group as a whole, whose members much more frequently show different fundamental patterns of adjustment and maladjustment.

Unmistakable psychopaths who do not show evidence of strong or consistent deviated impulses but who nevertheless occasionally carry out abnormal sexual acts have been seen much more often than those in whom the two fundamental patterns seem to overlap. This is not surprising in view of the psychopath's notable tendencies to hit upon unsatisfactory conduct in all fields and his apparent inability to take seriously what would to others be repugnant and regrettable. The real homosexual seeking an outlet for his own impulses often finds it possible to engage the psychopath in deviated activities, sometimes for petty rewards, sometimes for what might best be called just the hell of it.

It has been said that some people whose sexual activities are normal under ordinary circumstances may, in the absence of normal opportunities, resort to immature or abnormal practices as a substitutive measure. It is not hard to believe that a man of orthodox sexuality, if stranded and alone for years on an uninhabited island, might develop impulses toward masturbation. Some studies of prisoners give the impression that mutual masturbation and far more abnormal relations occur in persons who, when not confined, sought only heterosexual intercourse. Surely every psychiatrist has seen people whose sexual aims are usually directed toward the other sex but whose orientation is so confused, and whose evaluation of sexual experience is so trivial, that they sometimes also engage in homosexual and abnormal relations.

In psychopaths and in many other people who cannot be correctly placed with the well-defined homosexual group, there are varying degrees of susceptibility or inclination to immature or deviated sex practices. In contrast with others, the psychopath requires impulses of scarcely more than whimlike intensity to bring about unacceptable behavior in the sexual field or in any other. Even the faintest or most fleeting notion or inclination to forge a check, to steal his uncle's watch, to see if he can seduce his best friend's wife, or to have a little fling at fellatio is by no means unlikely to emerge as the deed. The sort of repugnance or other inhibiting force that would prevent any or all such impulses from being followed (or perhaps from even becoming conscious impulses) in another person is not a factor that can be counted on to play much part in the psychopath's decisions.

The activities of a typical patient of this sort whom I once studied are highly illustrative. This 27-year-old man, honor graduate of a college despite great irregularity in his studies, had for a number of years followed a career so similar to those of the other patients cited that there is no point in going into detail. He showed no indications of ordinary homosexuality in manner, dress, physique, or in personality features. He had been rather active in heterosexual relations since about 15, his partners being professionals, girls of respectable family, and married women.

All of these relations had apparently been to him more or less equivalent and entirely without personal significance. He admitted having once or twice, and more or less experimentally, submitted to the wishes of a homosexual and also to a couple of blundering ventures into deviated activity while drinking with others apparently more like himself. These did not seem to give him any particular satisfaction, and there is reason to believe that he distinctly preferred what he did with women. To the patient, any idea that he might be a homosexual seemed absurd.

In the absence of any persistent or powerful urge in this specific direction, the patient, apparently without much previous thought, hit upon the notion of picking up four black men who worked in the fields not far from his residence. In a locality where the Ku Klux Klan (and its well-known attitudes) at the time enjoyed a good deal of popularity, this intelligent and in some respects distinguished young man showed no compunction about taking from the field these unwashed laborers, whom he concealed in the back of a pickup truck, with him into a well-known place of amorous rendezvous. At the place he chose, a motel was discreetly set up in such a way that women brought by men to them for familiar purposes could enter without the possible embarrassment of being identified by the management. Despite these facilities, suspicion arose, and the patient was surprised by the man in charge of the resort while in the process of carrying out fellatio on his four companions. He had chosen to take the oral role.

When seen not long after this event, the young man was courteous but a trifle impatient about how long he might have to be hospitalized. He showed some concern with what use psychiatric examination might be in helping him avoid the term of imprisonment that would, according to the law, befall him if he should be convicted of the charges made by the proprietor and which he did not deny. This possibility did not, however, greatly alarm him.

He had often evaded penalties for antisocial acts in the past, and he had a good deal of easy confidence. Although he expressed regret and said his prank was quite a mistake, he seemed totally devoid of deep embarrassment. On the whole, his attitude might be suggested by such phrases as "Well, boys will be boys," or "Now wasn't that a foolish damn thing for me to do." These were not his literal words, but they are congruent with his behavior. By some legal step, his family, whose members were wealthy and influential, succeeded in having him avoid trial. Finding himself free, he left against medical advice within a few days.

As might be expected in view of their incapacity for object love, the sexual aims of psychopaths do not seem to include any important personality relations or any recognizable desire or ability to explore or possess or significantly ravish the partner in a shared experience. Their positive activities are consistently and parsimoniously limited to literal physical contact and relatively free of the enormous emotional concomitants and the complex potentialities that make adult love relations an experience so thrilling and indescribable. Consequently they seem to regard sexual activity very casually, sometimes apparently finding it less shocking and enthralling than a sensitive normal man would find even the glance of his beloved.

None of the psychopaths personally observed have impressed me as having particularly strong sex cravings even in this uncomplicated and poverty-stricken sense. Indeed, they have nearly all seemed definitely less moved to obtain genital pleasure than the ordinary run of people. The impression one gets is that their amativeness is little more than a simple itch and that even the itch is seldom, if ever, particularly intense.

The male psychopath, despite his usual ability to complete the physical act successfully with a woman, never seems to find anything meaningful or personal in his relations or to enjoy significant pleasure beyond the localized and temporary sensations. The female, whether or not she has physiologic orgasm, behaves in such a way as to indicate similar evaluations of the experience. Even these sensations seem to wither precociously and leave the subject a somewhat desiccated response to local stimuli. Sensations so isolated are, no doubt, peculiarly vulnerable to routine and to its justly celebrated antidotes for excitement.

What is felt for prostitute, sweetheart, casual pickup, mistress, or wife is not anything that can bring out loyalty or influence activities into a remedial or constructive plan. Nor do sexual desires always seem to compete successfully against such trivial impulses as wanting to hang about street corners or idle in juke joints where the psychopath may, by tampering with slot machines or cheating at dice or cards, pick up a little change and demonstrate his cleverness to the other fellows. So little is apparently found in heterosexual experience that deviate impulses (even when weak) are sometimes accepted and acted upon largely because of reasons like the reason why all cats look gray at night.

For the person who has ever known even one mature and normal erotic fulfillment, it is impossible to imagine turning by choice to a biologically inappropriate partner or placing partial or deviated aims above what has been so obviously well designed for the purpose. What the human organism shows anatomically is scarcely more clear than the emotional evidence, at physiologic as well as at broader interpersonal levels of reactivity. Even from more remote and less tangible sociologic aspects, nature has left no room here for doubt. It is difficult, without postulating an extremely dulled or otherwise inhibited sensual response in heterosexual experience, to account for the psychopath who can drift into deviate pranks as approximations or acceptable novelties in the same field. It has been said that "the thalamus outdid itself in devising pleasures to go with the conjugating act itself." Without great support from ethics or convention, it seems these would suffice for normal choice in the intact personality.

The familiar record of sexual promiscuity found in both male and female psychopaths seems much more closely related to their almost total lack of self-imposed restraint than to any particularly strong passions or drives. Psychopaths sometimes seem by preference to seek sexual relations in sordid surroundings with persons of low intellectual or social status. Often, however, the convenience by which what is little more than a whim can be gratified may play a greater part in this than specific preference. Another and more serious kind of sordidness also seems to constitute real inducement.

Entanglements that go out of their way to mock ordinary human sensibility or what might be called basic decency are prevalent in their sexual careers. To casually "make" or "lay" the best friend's wife and to involve a husband's uncle or one of his business associates in a particularly messy triangular or quadrilateral situation are typical acts. Such opportunities, when available, seem not to repel but specifically to attract the psychopath. Neither distinct appeal of the sex object nor any formulated serious malignity toward those cuckolded or otherwise outraged seems to be a major factor in such choices. There is more to suggest a mildly prankish impulse such as might lead the ordinary man to violate small pedantic technicalities or dead and preposterous bits of formality as a demonstration of their triviality.

Sexual exploits often seem chosen almost purposively to put the subject himself, as well as others, in positions of sharp indignity and distastefullness. The male psychopath who goes through legal matrimony with the whore he has picked up for the evening furnishes a clear example. And so does the well-born woman who submits to several men in rapid succession, none of whom takes the least trouble to conceal his contempt for her. I have seen psychopaths who seriously attempted to seduce sisters, mothers-in-law, and even their actual mothers. One boasted to his wife in glowing details of his erotic feats with her mother and with his own. His excellent talents at lying lead me to doubt the truth of his claims. I have little doubt, however, that he would not have hesitated to carry out all that he boasted of if the women had allowed him to proceed.

Beneath his outwardly gracious manner toward women and his general suavity and social charms, the male psychopath (or part psychopath) nearly always shows an underlying predilection for obscenity, an astonishingly ambivalent attitude in which the amorous and excretory functions seem to be confused. He sometimes gives the impression that an impulse to smear his partner symbolically, and even to wallow in sordidness himself, is more fundamental than a directly erotic aim, itself hardly more to him than a sort of concomitant and slightly glorified back scratching.

FAILURE TO FOLLOW ANY LIFE PLAN

The psychopath shows a striking inability to follow any sort of life plan consistently, whether it be one regarded as good or evil. He does not maintain an effort toward any far goal at all. This is entirely applicable to the full psychopath. On the contrary, he seems to go out of his way to make a failure of life. By some incomprehensible and untempting piece of folly or buffoonery, he eventually cuts short any activity in which he is succeeding, no matter whether it is crime or honest endeavor. At the behest of trivial impulses he repeatedly addresses himself directly to folly. In the more seriously affected examples, it is impossible for wealthy, influential, and devoted relatives to place the psychopath in any position, however ingeniously it may be chosen, where he will not succeed eventually in failing with spectacular and bizarre splendor. Considering a longitudinal section of his life, his behavior gives such an impression of gratuitous folly and nonsensical activity in such massive accumulation that it is hard to avoid the conclusion that here is the product of true madness—of madness in a sense quite as real as that conveyed to the imaginative layman by the terrible word *lunatic.* With the further consideration that all this skein of apparent madness has been woven by a person of (technically) unimpaired and superior intellectual powers and universally regarded as sane, the surmise intrudes that we are confronted by a serious and unusual type of genuine abnormality. Not merely a surmise but a strong conviction may arise that this apparent sanity is, in some important respects, a sanity in name only. When we consider his actual performance, evidence of mental competency is sorely lacking. We find instead a spectacle that suggests madness in excelsis, despite the absence of all those symptoms which enable us, in some degree, to account for irrational conduct in the psychotic.

section four · Some questions still without adequate answers

chapter 7 · What is wrong with these patients?

A BASIC HYPOTHESIS

Now that we have proceeded with our task through the stages of (1) presenting observations of the gross material and (2) sifting and tabulating as conveniently and intelligibly as we were able the pertinent residue of our data, let us attempt the next step. This will consist in searching for some concept or formulating some theory that might satisfactorily account for the facts observed. Much of the material appears contradictory, not only in the ordinary world of average or normal living but even in the world of mental disorder commonly granted to be less readily comprehensible in terms of ordinary reason. Even the accepted postulates that help us come to some understanding of the patient with hysteria or the delusional schizophrenic seem at first to fail when applied to the psychopathic, or antisocial, personality.

A patient whose fragmented personality prevents him from becoming aware of significant facts and puts him at the mercy of phantasies indistinguishable from what is real may conduct himself in a fashion that strikes us as altogether absurd and irrational if we fail to take into consideration this fragmentation. A man who is sane by the standards of psychiatry, aware of all the facts which we ourselves recognize, and free from delusions but who conducts himself in a way quite as absurd as many of the psychotic becomes another problem altogether. The observer is confronted with a paradox within the already baffling domain of mental disorder.

In the attempt to arrive at an applicable conception, one consistent with the facts of our observation, I find it necessary first of all to postulate that the psychopath has a genuine and very serious disability, disorder, defect, or deviation. To say that he is merely queer or perverse or in some borderline state between health and illness does little or nothing to account for the sort of behavior he demonstrates objectively and obviously. The practice, quite popular until recent years, of classifying the disorder of these patients, no matter how plain their incapacity to lead normal lives, as (1) no nervous or mental disease and (2) psychopathic personalities, whatever the sanctions afforded by tradition, emerges not only as a misleading practice but also as sometimes promoting absurdity when we honestly examine the material to which such terms are applied.

Let us for a moment consider the essential evidence brought out in staff meetings on which experienced psychiatrists establish in an obvious case the diagnosis of schizophrenia and on which legal action is taken to declare the patient psychotic and incompetent (insane) and commit him for treatment. In the brief summarizing statement to support such opinions we often find such words as these:

> The history shows that he has failed repeatedly to make a satisfactory adjustment in the social group. His actions indicate serious impairment of judgment and show that he cannot be relied upon to conduct himself with ordinary regard for the safety of himself or of others. His irrational and unacceptable behavior has, furthermore, occurred without normal or adequate motivation. He shows no real insight into his condition and tends often to project the sources of his troubles to the environment. His emotional reactions are grossly impaired and he has repeatedly shown inappropriate or inadequate affect. We may say, then, that he is psychotic, incompetent, incapable of carrying on the usual activities of life, and in need of close supervision.

Such facts have often over many decades constituted more convincing evidence for the diagnosis of schizophrenia than the delusions and hallucinations also frequently present but sometimes not demonstrable in that psychosis. All of the statements just recorded (excepting only the one word *psychotic*) may be applied with full validity to the psychopath. This, of course, does not make him a patient with schizophrenia, but it does, I maintain, afford grounds, that cannot be dismissed lightly, for saying he has a grave psychiatric deficit. Although I insist on the gravity of his abnormality, I frankly admit that it is a different kind of abnormality from all those now recognized as seriously impairing competency. It is an abnormality that differs more widely in its general features from any of those than they differ from one another.

The first and most striking difference is this: In all the orthodox psychoses, in addition to the criteria just mentioned, or to some of these criteria, there is a more or less obvious alteration of reasoning processes or of some other demonstrable personality feature. In the psychopath this is not seen. The observer is confronted with a convincing mask of sanity. All the outward features of this mask are intact; it cannot be displaced or penetrated by questions directed toward deeper personality levels. The examiner never hits upon the chaos sometimes found on searching beneath the outer surface of a paranoid schizophrenic. The thought processes retain their normal aspect under psychiatric investigations and in technical tests designed to bring out obscure evidence of derangement. Examination reveals not merely an ordinary two-dimensional mask but what seems to be a solid and substantial structural image of the sane and rational personality. The psychopath, might, then, be thought of, in the full literal sense, as an example of what Trélat meant to designate by his expressive term *la folie lucide.* Furthermore, this personality structure in all theoretical situations functions in a manner apparently identical with that of normal, sane functioning. Logical thought processes may be seen in perfect operation no matter how they are stimulated or treated under experimental conditions. Furthermore, the observer finds verbal and facial expressions, tones of voice, and all the other signs we have come to regard as implying conviction and emotion and the normal experiencing of life as we know it ourselves and as we assume it to be in others. All judgments of value and emotional appraisals are sane and appropriate when the psychopath is tested in verbal examinations.

Only very slowly and by a complex estimation or judgment based on multitudinous small impressions does the conviction come upon us that, despite these intact rational processes, these normal emotional affirmations, and their consistent application in all directions, we are dealing here not with a complete man at all but with something that suggests a subtly constructed reflex machine that can mimic the human personality perfectly. This smoothly operating psychic apparatus reproduces consistently not only specimens of good human reasoning but also appropriate simulations of normal human emotion in response to nearly all the varied stimuli of life. So perfect is this reproduction of a whole and normal man that no one who examines the psychopath in a clinical setting can point out in scientific or objective terms why, or how, he is not real. And yet we eventually come to know or feel we know that reality, in the sense of full, healthy experiencing of life, is not here.

Fortunately for the purpose of this discussion, but unfortunately indeed in any other light, an objective demonstration is available that coincides perfectly with our slowly emerging impression. The psychopath, however perfectly he mimics man theoretically, that is to say, when he speaks for himself in words, fails altogether when he is put into the practice of actual living. His failure is so complete and so dramatic that it is difficult to see how such a failure could be achieved by anyone less defective than a downright *madman** or by a person totally or almost totally unable to grasp emotionally the major components of meaning or feeling implicit in the thoughts that he expresses or the experiences he appears to go through. In the actions of his living, then, he confirms our subjective impression, or it might be said that our surmise coincides with the objective and demonstrable facts.

During my early observation of psychopaths that preceded publication of the first edition of this book I was so much impressed with the degree of maladjustment in these patients that I felt at the time, and said, they should be called psychotic. Subsequent consideration led me long ago to change this opinion and to find myself in complete accord with Richard L. Jenkins, who wrote:

> Hervey Cleckley, in *The Mask of Sanity,* expresses the belief that the psychopathic personality is a psychosis not technically demonstrable, maximally concealed by an outer surface of intact function and manifested only in behavior. The disagreement I would express with this intriguing definition is that, to me, it strains the concept of psychosis past the breaking point. A psychosis is a major mental disorder. A psychopathic personality shows not a disorder of personality but rather a defect of personality, together with a set of defenses evolved around that defect. The defect relates to the most central element of the human personality: its social nature. The psychopath is simply a basically asocial or antisocial individual who has never achieved the developed nature of *homo domesticus.*

There is another important point against classifying the psychopath's grave defect with the psychoses. Though I believe he is in degree as maladjusted for leading an acceptable life as the psychotic patient, I do not believe there are similar reasons to consider him legally irresponsible or morally blameless for the frauds he perpetrates and the crimes he may commit.

---

*This violent and unfortunate term I use with apology but cannot spare here because of its clear-cut emphasis.

Let us, then, assume, as a hypothesis, that the psychopath's disorder, or defect, or his difference from the whole or normal or integrated personality consists of an unawareness and a persistent lack of ability to become aware of what the most important experiences of life mean to others. By this is not meant an acceptance of the arbitrarily postulated values of any particular theology, ethics, esthetics, or philosophic system, or any special set of mores or ideologies, but rather the common substance of emotion or purpose, or whatever else one chooses to call it, from which the various loyalties, goals, fidelities, commitments, and concepts of honor and responsibility of various groups and various people are formed. Let us assume that this dimension of experience which gives to all experience its substance or reality is one into which the psychopath does not enter. Or, to be more accurate, let us say that he enters, but only so superficially that his reality is thin or unsubstantial to the point of being insignificant. Let us say that, despite his otherwise perfect functioning, the major emotional accompaniments are absent or so attenuated as to count for little. Of course he is unaware of this, just as everyone is bound, except theoretically, to be unaware of that which is out of his scale or order or mode of experience. If we grant the existence of a far-reaching and persistent blocking, absence, deficit, or dissociation of this sort, we have all that is needed, at the present level of our inquiry, to account for the psychopath.

The effort to express what is meant by experiencing life in a full sense, or by awareness of a solid emotional contact, runs through the psychoanalytic literature, which so often stresses the difference between an actual, or emotionally participating, understanding of some important situation and a mere verbal or academic understanding, however complete in that dimension. This point is also implicit in the concepts of Adolf Meyer's psychobiology, which, by its very definition of terms, shows that it is striving to emphasize the wholeness of experience or the full meaning of reactions. Among lay observers of human problems and human values is sometimes found a sharp awareness of the very point I mean to stress in trying to describe the so-called psychopath.

A poet of our century, Donald Parson, chilled by the dead perfection of the celebrated glass flowers at Harvard, seems to see and translate into metaphor and allegory something closely related to the problem of the personalities discussed here and whose outer state I am trying to describe as a mask of sanity:

> I stand in wonder. What amazing art!
> No counterfeit is this, but counterpart
> Itself, carved with the infinite detail
> That makes the plodding step of patience fail.
> From life's authentic prompt-book is this leaf,
>
> • • •
>
> Farewell, stark forms. No more can you beguile,
> You wear the sleety artificial smile
> That freezes as it falls. My earthly flowers
> Can hear the wing-beat of the flying hours
> And, blushing for your deep immortal lie,
> Are unafraid—nay, eager—proud—to die.
> So shall they burgeon with a sweeter breath
> Because, like us, they wait the frost of death.
>
> "Glass Flowers"

Although to the casual reader these words may suggest more readily the obvious artificiality familiar in the schizophrenic and the schizophrenic's withdrawal from the pain and pleasure of objective life, a point may be made that the full implication of the poem more properly bears on the state of these personalities we now discuss.

Such outward perfection as that seen in the glass flowers at Harvard and such complete lack of participation in the essence of life and mortality suggest wonderfully the situation that we mean to portray in the personalities described in this volume. The schizophrenic does not preserve the intact outer form and function of a complete personality, but the psychopath does.

Without suffering or enjoying in significant degree the integrated emotional consequences of experience, the psychopath will not learn from it to modify and direct his activities as other men whom we call sane modify and direct theirs. He will lack the real driving impulses that sustain and impel others toward their various widely differing but at least subjectively important goals. He will naturally lack insight into how he differs from other men, for of course he does not differ from other men as he sees them. It is entirely impossible for him to see another person from the aspect of major affective experience, since he is blind to this order of things or blind in this mode of awareness.

It must be granted of course that the psychopath has some affect. Affect is, perhaps, a component in the sum of life reactions even in the unicellular protoplasmic entity. Certainly in all mammals it is obvious. The relatively petty states of pleasure, vexation, and animosity experienced by the psychopath have been mentioned. The opinion here maintained is that he fails to know all those more serious and deeply moving affective states which make up the tragedy and triumph of ordinary life, of life at the level of important human experience. Such capacities vary widely, of course, among normal people and are perhaps proportionate to the general personality development, or, in a far-reaching sense, to true cultural level. The scope or the substantiality of such reactions, if they could be accurately and objectively estimated, would, perhaps more than any other criteria, make it possible to judge how successful and how complete an experiment in nature a particular person has proved to be. A Beethoven, a Dante, or an Aeschylus, if his real inner life is faithfully represented in his works, would probably present no less a contrast in this aspect with the illiterate and unimaginative peasant or the successful pickpocket than in objective accomplishments. Nevertheless, no normal person is so unevolved and no ordinary criminal so generally unresponsive and distorted that he does not seem to experience satisfaction, love, hate, grief, and a general participation in life at human personality levels much more intense and more substantial than the affective reactions of the psychopath. My concept of the psychopath's functioning postulates a selective defect or elimination that prevents important components of normal experience from being integrated into the whole human reaction, particularly an elimination or attenuation of those strong affective components which ordinarily arise in major personal and social issues.

However intelligent, he apparently assumes that other persons are moved by and experience only the ghostly facsimiles of emotion or pseudoemotion known to him. However quick and rational a person may be and however subtle and articulate his teacher, he cannot be taught awareness of significance which he fails to feel.* He can learn to use

*"Intellect is invisible to the man who has none." (From Schopenhauer's *Essays,* "Our Relation to Others.")

the ordinary words and, if he is very clever, even extraordinarily vivid and eloquent words that signify these matters to other people. He will also learn to reproduce appropriately all the pantomime of feeling; but, as Sherrington said of the decerebrated animal, the feeling itself does not come to pass.

Even his splendid logical faculties will, in real life situations, produce not actual reasoning but that imitation of reasoning known as rationalization, for in the synthesis by which reasoning contributes to sound judgment, the sense of value, that is, the value of truth and feeling, cannot be missing. When this is missing, the process is only rationalization, something which, however technically brilliant, does not satisfactorily guide and shape action. And no difference between the two is more fundamental.

When we conceive of the thought, the emotional responses, the general psychic processes, and the behavior of a person in whom is postulated a defect of this sort, we have arrived at something identical or all but identical with the psychopath as he appears in actual life.

When we say that a disorder at deep levels of personality integration prevents experience from becoming adequately meaningful to the subject, we become vulnerable to the accusation of talking nonsense. It is easy indeed to become unclear, if not to appear actually ridiculous, in attempting to express a point, however tentatively, on these fundamental matters. A reviewer in the *New England Journal of Medicine* says of the concept here advanced:

> If that [understanding of the meaning of life] is the disease from which the psychopathic inferior suffers, this term can be applied to most of us and certainly to the reviewer, since, so far as he knows, no one has yet given us an insight into the meaning of life.

Such a comment is appealing and not without humor, but it scarcely meets the issue in a responsible manner. We need not assume that a normal man understands the ultimate purpose of life or even that he is remotely near final accuracy in his evaluations of his own bits of experience in order to believe that the psychopath is, in comparison, seriously disabled by the specific deficiency we are attempting to formulate.

Although "meaning" or "the meaning of life" can be applied to a philosophic or religious system that attempts to explain man and the universe, it must be obvious that such an application is not intended here. By saying that a good deal of the affective substance that people find in life experiences is lacking in the psychopath's responses, we seek only to point out that he is not adequately moved and that he does not find subjective stimuli to make the major issues of life matter sufficiently to promote consistent striving. Furthermore, he cannot achieve true and abiding loyalty to any principle or any person. It is difficult, perhaps, to express anything about such a matter without inviting misunderstanding. Such an affective alteration of fundamental experience is generally granted in the schizophrenic, who shows superficial indications of it. In the psychopath, although it is so strongly indicated by his conduct, this alteration is well masked by his misleading surface. It should not be said that such an estimate can be scientifically proved in either case, or that any subjective state in another can be so established.

In Brenden Maher's important work devoted to current problems of psychiatry and psychology published in 1973, I find support and encouragement in this comment on subsequent studies of the psychopath:

Dr. Cleckley's book, *The Mask of Sanity,* has been the stimulus for most of the experimental research that has been conducted into the problem of psychopathy. It is one of the best examples available of careful clinical observation leading to hypotheses (not conclusions) which can then be put to controlled test. The wealth of clinical anecdote with which each point is illustrated renders it difficult to find any one sequential extract from the book that might serve to present his hypotheses in a systematic fashion. The extract in this volume consists of several portions of the text selected and assembled to be maximally coherent, while letting Cleckley's own views be presented in his own words.

From Cleckley's hypothesis there has developed naturally a major interest in the psychobiology of the psychopath's emotional experience—or lack of it. A *prima facie* credence must be given to the possibility that the psychopath is deficient in those bodily responses that give rise to the emotional experiences of anxiety, pity and the like. Hare, one of the major investigators of the present time, examines this explanation and presents the pertinent data in his paper here. The paper is not previously published elsehwere and it provides a new synthesis of findings from several related lines of research on the topic.

THE CONCEPT OF MASKED PERSONALITY DISORDER OR DEFECT

Let us consider further the concept of disorders or defects that are deeply or centrally located. The contrast between such a pathology and one that is peripheral and visible can be demonstrated readily in speech disorders.

The man whose tongue has been severely mutilated is not able to pronounce his words clearly. Perhaps he can only mutter unintelligibly. Even a child or a savage can see where the trouble is and understand why function is disrupted. If the hypoglossal nerves are cut, the tongue, although itself unmarred, will not move and words cannot be uttered. An observer may detect the paralysis and in time note that the tongue has shrunk in size. There are, to be sure, some changes discernible at the outer aspect of the organism, but these are less obvious and less gross than the visible swelling, the bruises, and the lacerations that are present when the tongue itself has been directly injured.

Should localized damage occur much farther away in the motor cortex of the brain or in the pyramidal tract, the tongue itself will maintain its normal size and appearance. Although it cannot be voluntarily used to produce speech, or for other purposes, considerable reflex movement may occur. With none of these three lesions have we encroached upon the understanding of language or upon its use except through one of its peripheral instruments, the tongue. All three of these patients can read and think verbally without impairment. All can write as articulately as before.

If localized destruction is visited upon neurons in another part of the brain (let us refer to this area roughly and inexactly as the quadrilateral space of Marie), the tongue remains anatomically sound and able to perform all ordinary movements. The entire physiologic apparatus whereby words are sounded remains intact—intact and controlled by conscious volition. The patient can protrude his tongue and move it from side to side as directed. He can speak also, in contrast to our last two examples, and, unlike the one whose tongue was directly injured, his words may be clearly and accurately pronounced.

Often, however, the phrase or sentence he utters will not be what he means to say. Perhaps it will carry little or no suggestion of what he wishes to tell us. Perhaps it will amount to a rough approximation or an awkward circumlocution that indirectly gives us a clue. Perhaps some word irrelevant to his actual thought will be repeated over and over.

Attempting to ask for his pen, he may say, "Ben—Ben—then—then" and, perhaps gesturing with his hand in sign language, at length indicate more to us by the words, "what you write with." Perhaps in attempting to tell us good morning or to inquire about the health of our aunt, he may, to his embarrassment, shout, "Doggone, doggone, son of a bitch, you bastard." This is indeed clear, but it has nothing to do with what he has tried to express.

Various degrees of impairment may be found in those aphasias classified by Henry Head as verbal, nominal, or syntactic. Some aphasic patients may utter clear sounds but fail to put syllables together into words. Others may hit upon words but not succeed in making comprehensible sentences or even phrases. Many of those seriously affected by such a disorder understand simple statements made by others. Some can communicate with us far better in writing than by the spoken word. In most, however, along with a serious defect in their own meaningful use of speech, we find some impairment in the understanding of spoken or written language. Even those considerably handicapped in reading, speaking, writing, or grasping the significance of what they are told may retain a relatively good use of "inner speech" and may be able still to make silent use of words for thinking or reasoning. Such people are aware of their difficulty and realize in exasperation that they cannot say what they intend and that language once quite familiar has, for them, somehow lost much of what it formerly conveyed.

In discussing these three types of dysarthria we proceeded from the periphery of the functional unit (the injured tongue) inward (the severed hypoglossal nerves) to the relatively central point of the cerebral motor cortex. When we then consider in comparison to dysarthria the aphasias, we find that this entire motor apparatus that produces words is unimpaired, and also unimpaired is the sensory system by which language, written or spoken, is accurately perceived. We confront now a deeper disorder. In a sense we may say, roughly and imperfectly, that the instrument itself is unimpaired but the player has lost some of his ability to use it accurately for his purposes. Let us modify this and say that the player (if he is to represent something very inexactly suggested by "mind" or "personality") is not in immediate contact with the instrument and does not directly use it as, for instance, a pianist who strikes the keys or man at the telephone who puts the receiver to his ear. In our far from adequate analogy let us assume a complicated system of processes between the hand and the keys, between the ear and the receiver.

To produce speech there must be between the operator and his mechanism for uttering words other instrumentalities of evaluation whereby the words are chosen and used to express his purpose. So, too, between the correctly received perception (auditory or visual) and its understanding must come processes of recognition and association and integration, the complex shaping of significance that is grasped as a whole, before a real message can be completed. As Suter suggested, speech may be thought of as coming about "as a result of the functioning of a very elaborate kind of reflex arc made up of (1) an afferent, sensory, or receptive part; (2) a central, associative or elaboration part; and (3) an efferent, motor or expressive part."

Speech disorder resulting from damage to the neural mechanisms of (2), on which depend the elaboration of concepts and the association of words with referents in the person's life experience and designated by Suter as anomia, may be thought of as more central than those chiefly limited to (1) or (3), where the defect is, in a sense, more external.

Henry Head described under the term *semantic aphasia* a disorder of language still more central, more (functionally) proximal in the dimension, or area, or direction that (2) serves to indicate. This disorder he believed is related to pathology at, or near, the supramarginal gyrus. Semantic aphasia, according to Head, is "characterized by want of recognition of the ultimate significance and intention of words and phrases . . . loss of power to appreciate or formulate the general conclusion of a connected train of thought." The person with semantic aphasia "may understand a word or short phrase and can appreciate the various details of a picture but the significance of the whole escapes him."

In semantic aphasia, in which, so to speak, the lesion is more central than in other aphasias, the language function can usually produce more words and better phrases than in verbal or syntactic aphasias, but these have far less meaning or use to the patient. The vehicles or vessels of speech are readily made but emerge empty, devoid of the content they ordinarily define. The patient may enunciate clear, grammatical sentences, but they are irrelevant to any intention of his and do not convey even the distorted hints of valid statement often successfully transmitted by the jargon or the circumlocutions of a patient whose aphasia is more peripheral. In the latter, intentions can be realized inwardly and communicated to some degree by gestures or pantomime, or verbal fragments and approximations. In semantic aphasia, as described by Head, inner speech or verbal thought is seriously crippled, and the patient usually cannot formulate anything very pertinent or meaningful within his own awareness. He cannot by gestures or verbal approximations hint at his message because he lacks the inner experience on which a message might be formulated. If he could do this, the more peripheral difficulties that mar the speech in verbal aphasia would not lie in his way and his thought would proceed to articulate expression. But he has no inner production of thought and feeling to transmit. The instrumentalities for language are apparently adequate. They do in fact still perform smoothly but more or less reflexly and apart from inner purpose, manufacturing phrases and sentences but doing so automatically. But the language does not represent or express anything meaningful.

It might be said that the very severe inner disorder of language in semantic aphasia is to a considerable degree masked by the mechanical production of a well-constructed but counterfeit speech carried on in some degree of independence by an undirected outer apparatus that has become virtually disconnected from inner purpose. Like real speech, it appears to represent the inner human intention, thought, or feeling, but actually it is an artifact. Behind the superficially good (clear, grammatical) speech there is little or nothing to be symbolized and conveyed. This stands in contrast to the gross superficial disorder of communication in verbal aphasia, in which inner purposes can still be intelligently formulated and, however awkwardly and indirectly, are often communicated with some degree of success to another.

We need not assume Head's interpretation of the aphasias to be entirely and finally correct if it will by analogy help us formulate and clarify a concept of personality disorder, a concept in which the deeper and less obvious levels of function can be compared and contrasted with more superficial aspects of behavior. Let us use the analogy not as evidence for the concept but only as a means of stating it.

Let us consider several familiar types of psychiatric illness with this aim in mind. The patient with a toxic-delirious psychosis (for example, delirium tremens) shows a maximum of disorder in his superficial aspect. He may not recognize his whereabouts and may scream at nonexistent monsters or belabor the empty air with a broomstick to fight off poison-spitting bugs a yard long which he sees pursuing him. As he leaps over the bed or brandishes a chair, wild-eyed, disheveled, and half-clad, any layman can recognize him as ill and no doubt admit his disorder is mental (that he is "crazy"). Nothing conceals his psychosis. Delusions, hallucinations, confusion, loss of basic orientations, and irrational conduct are obvious everywhere in his immediate area of contact with the surroundings. Despite the spectacular impressiveness of his manifestations, he is very likely to recover, perhaps in a few days. Although intense, his pathology is in some respects relatively superficial.

On the other hand, the hebephrenic patient sometimes maintains excellent orientation and calmness. Despite hallucinations and delusions, which he often keeps largely to himself, he may carry on clerical work without supervision and do so logically and effectively. It is not difficult for the physician to demonstrate convincing evidence of the patient's grave disorder, but this is usually less obvious, less vivid peripherally, let us say, than in the first example. As a matter of fact, the uninformed layman (especially if a close relative) will sometimes insist for a while that "it can't be his mind, Doc, it must just be his nerves." Members of the family may argue that because he has kept his accounts straight at the store where he worked and showed intelligence about other matters, he must have a relatively minor psychiatric disorder. The outer form of normal behavior may be much better preserved in such a patient than in one with delirium tremens despite the fact that beyond this relatively thin functional shell the basic foundations of his personality are in chaotic devastation, and despite the fact that his disorder is maximally malignant, extending deeply into the core of his being.

A patient with early paranoid schizophrenia is likely to be free of those outer manifestations of mental illness which distinguish the hebephrenic. His reasoning powers may be truly excellent, his emotional reactions appropriate, and his general behavior effective. It might be difficult indeed to find any point at which we can truthfully say his abilities, in the ordinary sense, are impaired by disease. He may be a brilliant and delightful companion at a dinner party and may discuss politics, business, or philosophy with high intelligence and learning. Well concealed beneath all this exterior functional perfection is a serious disorder which may influence him to direct his unblemished talents toward useless or highly undesirable goals or perhaps to carry out, conscientiously and effectively, disastrous antisocial aims. If we consider personality function somewhat as we did the more circumscribed function of speech, we might say that what is pathologic or defective in the paranoid patient must be more centrally situated, more difficult to discern or to demonstrate from the outside. Yet such a disability is not mild. It is as real and often as serious as hebephrenia. Some paranoid patients, particularly those with paranoia vera, show no signs at all of psychiatric impairment that can be demonstrated regularly. If brought to the courts, they may successfully establish their sanity before judge and jury, sometimes excelling their medical and legal examiners in the exercise of reason. Not rarely they attract supporters or disciples in the community who enthusiastically follow their advice. In such patients, despite the impressive outer layers of unimpaired function, psychosis is genuine and severe.

The delusions of some paranoiacs are circumscribed—confined to conviction about what is indisputably possible or even plausible. A man may, for instance, believe his wife is unfaithful. Sometimes it is difficult to prove objectively that this belief is a delusion rather than a sane mistake, or, indeed, a fact. The pathologic substructure or inner lesion, so to speak, that gives rise to his delusion is not directly accessible to our scrutiny. From that point out, we might say, he behaves rationally. His functions peripheral to this disturbed level may proceed sanely and effectively.

The delusional belief in paranoia, although often not intrinsically absurd or irrational, allows the trained observer to realize eventually that such a patient is psychotic despite the unimpaired operation of his exterior functions. This psychosis is extremely well disguised by the covering layers of sanity. The delusion, once it is recognized, gives us a reliable clue to the extremely serious disorder beneath, somewhat as specific notes in the percussion of a chest reveal indirectly to an internist the presence of a lung cavity despite the unmarred exterior of the body.

In some cases of schizophrenia no delusion or other manifestation technically indicative of psychosis can be elicited. In contrast with paranoia, not even one circumscribed but distinct clue can be offered by the examiner as evidence of a true mental disorder. Under such terms as simple, masked, or ambulatory schizophrenia many of these cases have been described. The psychiatrist who recognizes the psychosis in such a patient is often at a loss to explain his conclusion. He senses a peculiar emotional deficit and distortion and is able to realize that the person does not normally experience and evaluate the basic data of life and that this deviation is of the quality and the degree characteristic of schizophrenia. Let us not deny that the psychiatrist may sometimes erroneously come to such a conclusion. He must rely on a clinical judgment, not on objective scientific evidence. The experienced wine taster may, it is said, detect that his beverage comes from grapes grown on the east rather than the west side of some hill in Touraine. Experts may reliably distinguish in an obscure painting the hand of Benozzo Gozzoli from that of a talented imitator. Perhaps few psychiatrists develop so sure and fine a knack of diagnosing schizophrenia in these cryptic cases. It is true, nevertheless, that experience sometimes enables them to apprehend correctly such a disorder in those who show no objectively demonstrable sign of psychosis. Some of these patients are more dangerous than many who hallucinate, express delusions, and show gross irration ality.

Most of these masked schizophrenics do not present an outer aspect that appears entirely normal. A brittleness, an indefinable peculiarity of manner, fine details of posture or gesture, and nuances of expression and attitude may cumulatively contribute to the psychiatrist's impression. Many subliminal or almost subliminal items of perception may be sensed in such a person and correctly identified with similar real but not quite expressible qualities familiar to the observer because he has previously sensed them in hundreds of closely studied schizophrenic patients who also showed gross and indisputable manifestations of psychosis. What is thus sensed may reveal to the psychiatrist that such a patient is emotionally far out of contact in basic human relations and inadequately influenced by sane motives.

Such patients with schizophrenia suggest in some respects the psychopath in that their major abnormality, their real pathology, is chiefly within and largely concealed by good reasoning and by ability, at least for intervals, to go through the motions of what looks like a sane pattern of life. Occasionally such a patient will address an insulting letter to the President, attempt to hang himself, announce the discovery of perpetual motion, or wander off from home and let no one know whether he is dead or alive for a couple of months, without being able to give any good reason for such acts and apparently without feeling that an explanation is in order. After following for years obviously queer, distorted, and socially restricted, but apparently not psychotic, careers, a few commit without provocation murder or some other tragic misdeed, for which they show little evidence of remorse or other adequate and understandable reactions.

Such patients in some respects, particularly in their central emotional deficit, may seem closer to the psychopath than to the ordinary state hospital schizophrenic. There are, however, important differences. The psychopath's outer mask of mechanically correct peripheral functioning is immeasurably more deceptive. The masked schizophrenic outwardly shows no obvious or expected signs of traditional psychosis, but he does not achieve the socially appealing presence, the warm, easy manners, or the false promise of strong and superior character and human qualities that are so bewildering in the psychopath. Real peculiarities, cool and strange alterations of emotion, social isolation, and a profound and indefinable queerness emerge in outer aspects of the cryptic schizophrenic. Such signs, except to the expert, do not suggest psychosis or adequately warn us that gross and malignant alterations exist beneath such a surface. But the evidence of something schizoid, or something queer and not precisely normal, is usually apparent.

The surface of the psychopath, however, that is, all of him that can be reached by verbal exploration and direct examination, shows up as equal to or better than normal and gives no hint at all of a disorder within. Nothing about him suggests oddness, inadequacy, or moral frailty. His mask is that of robust mental health. Yet he has a disorder that often manifests itself in conduct far more seriously abnormal than that of the schizophrenic. Inwardly, too, there appears to be a significant difference. Deep in the masked schizophrenic we often sense a cold, weird indifference to many of life's most urgent issues and sometimes also bizarre, inexplicable, and unpredictable but intense emotional reactions to what seems almost irrelevant. Behind the exquisitely deceptive mask of the psychopath the emotional alteration we feel appears to be primarily one of degree, a consistent leveling of response to petty ranges and an incapacity to react with sufficient seriousness to achieve much more than pseudoexperience or quasi experience. Nowhere within do we find a real cause or a sincere commitment, reasonable or unreasonable. There is nowhere the loyalty to produce real and lasting allegiance even to a negative or fanatic cause.

Just as meaning and the adequate sense of things as a whole are lost with semantic aphasia in the circumscribed field of speech although the technical mimicry of language remains intact, so in most psychopaths the purposiveness and the significance of all life-striving and of all subjective experience are affected without obvious damage to the outer appearance or superficial reactions of the personality. Nor is there any loss of technical or measurable intelligence.

With such a biologic change the human being becomes more reflex, more machinelike. It has been said that a monkey endowed with sufficient longevity would, if he continuously pounded the keys of a typewriter, finally strike by pure chance the very succession of keys to reproduce all the plays of Shakespeare. These papers so composed in the complete absence of purpose and human awareness would look just as good to any scholar as the actual works of the Bard. Yet we cannot deny that there is a difference. Meaning and life at a prodigiously high level of human values went into one and merely the rule of permutations and combinations would go into the other. The patient semantically defective by lack of meaningful purpose and realization at deep levels does not, of course, strike sane and normal attitudes merely by chance. His rational power enables him to mimic directly the complex play of human living. Yet what looks like sane realization and normal experience remains, in a sense and to some degree, like the plays of our simian typist.

The various differences between central and peripheral speech disorders cannot of course be pronounced identical with similar differences between masked and obvious psychiatric disorders. In Henry Head's interpretation of semantic aphasia we find, however, concepts of neural function and of its integration and impairment that help to convey a hypothesis of grave personality disorder thoroughly screened by the intact peripheral operation of all ordinary abilities. In relatively abstract or circumscribed situations, such as the psychiatric examination or the trial in court, these abilities do not show impairment but more or less automatically demonstrate an outer sanity unquestionable in all its aspects and at all levels accessible to the observer. That this technical sanity is little more than a mimicry of true sanity cannot be proved at such levels. Only when the subject sets out to conduct his life can we get evidence of how little his good theoretical understanding means to him, of how inadequate and insubstantial are the apparently normal basic emotional reactions and motivations convincingly portrayed and enunciated but existing in little more than two dimensions.

What we take as evidence of his sanity will not significantly or consistently influence his behavior. Nor does it represent real intention within, the degree of his emotional response, or the quality of his personal experience much more reliably than some grammatically well-formed, clear, and perhaps verbally sensible statement produced vocally by the autonomous neural apparatus of a patient with semantic aphasia can be said to represent such a patient's thought or carry a meaningful communication of it.

Let us assume tentatively that the psychopath is, in this sense, semantically disordered. We have said that his outer functional aspect masks or disguises something quite different within, concealing behind a perfect mimicry of normal emotion, fine intelligence, and social responsibility a grossly disabled and irresponsible personality. Must we conclude that this disguise is a mere pretence voluntarily assumed and that the psychopath's essential dysfunction should be classed as mere hypocrisy instead of psychiatric defect or deformity?

Let us remember that his typical behavior defeats what appear to be his own aims. Is it not he himself who is most deeply deceived by his apparent normality? Although he deliberately cheats others and is quite conscious of his lies, he appears unable to distinguish adequately between his own pseudointentions, pseudoremorse, pseudolove, and the genuine responses of a normal person. His monumental lack of insight indicates how little he appreciates the nature of his disorder. When others fail to accept immediately his "word of honor as a gentleman," his amazement, I believe, is often genuine. The term *genuine* is used here not to qualify the psychopath's intentions but to qualify his amazement. His subjective experience is so bleached of deep emotion that he is invincibly ignorant of what life means to others.

His awareness of hypocrisy's opposite is so insubstantially theoretical that it becomes questionable if what we chiefly mean by hypocrisy should be attributed to him. Having no major values himself, can he be said to realize adequately the nature and quality of the outrages his conduct inflicts upon others? A young child who has no impressive memory of severe pain may have been told by his mother it is wrong to cut off the dog's tail. Knowing it is wrong, he may proceed with the operation. We need not totally absolve him of responsibility if we say he realized less what he did than an adult who, in full appreciation of physical agony, so uses a knife. Can a person experience the deeper levels of sorrow without considerable knowledge of happiness? Can he achieve evil intention in the full sense without real awareness of evil's opposite? I have no final answer to these questions.

Attempts to interpret the psychopath's disorder do not, of course, furnish evidence that he has a disorder or that it is serious. For reliable evidence of this we must examine his behavior. Only here, not in psychopathologic formulations, can we apply our judgment to what is objective and demonstrable. Functionally and structurally all is intact on the outside. Good function (healthy reactivity) will be demonstrated in all theoretical trials. Sound judgment as well as good reasoning are likely to appear at verbal levels. Ethical as well as practical considerations will be recognized in the abstract. A brilliant mimicry of sound, social reactions will occur in every test except the test of life itself. In the psychopath we confront a personality neither broken nor outwardly distorted but of a substance that lacks ingredients without which normal function in major life issues is impossible.

Any method that offers the possibility of adding objectivity to our appraisals is indeed stimulating and welcome anywhere in psychiatry but particularly so in this more than ordinarily confusing problem.

Simon, Holzberg, and Unger, impressed by the paradox of the psychopath's poor performance despite intact reasoning, devised an objective test specifically to appraise judgment as it would function in real situations, as contrasted with theoretical judgment in abstract situations.

These workers are aware that the more complex synthesis of influences constituting what is often called judgment or understanding (as compared to a more theoretical "reasoning") may be simulated in test situations in which emotional participation is minimal, that rational factors alone by an accurate aping or stereotype can produce in vitro, so to speak, what they cannot produce in vivo. Items for a multiple choice test were selected with an aim of providing maximal possibilities for emotional factors to influence decision and particularly for relatively trivial immediate gratification impulses to clash with major, long-range objectives. The same items were also utilized in the form of a completion test. The results of this test on a group of psychopaths tend to support the hypothetical interpretation attempted in this book.

If such a disorder does indeed exist in the so-called psychopath, it is not remarkable that its recognition as a major and disabling impairment has been long delayed. Pathologic changes visible on the surface of the body (laceration, compound fractures) were already being handled regularly by medical men when the exorcism of indwelling demons retained popular favor in many illnesses now treated by the internist. So, too, it has been with personality disorders. Those characterized by gross outward manifestations have been accepted as psychiatric problems long before others in which a superficial appearance of sanity is preserved.

Despite the lack of academic symptoms characteristic of those disorders traditionally classed as psychosis, the psychopath often seems, in some important respects, but not in all, to belong more with that group than with any other. Certainly his problems cannot be dealt with, medically or by any other means, unless similar legal instrumentalities for controlling his situation are set up and regularly applied.

I believe that if such a patient shows himself grossly incompetent in his behavior, he should be so appraised. If it is necessary to change some of our legal criteria to make attempts at treatment or urgently needed supervision possible for him, the most serious objections are primarily theoretical. Perhaps our traditional definitions of psychiatric disability can stand alteration better than these grossly defective patients and those about them can stand the present farcical and sometimes tragic methods of handling their problems.

This is not to say that all people showing features of this type should be regarded as totally disabled. It is here maintained that this defect, like other psychiatric disorders, appears in every degree of severity and may constitute anything from a personality trait through handicaps of varying magnitude, including maximal disability and maximal threat to the peace and safety of the community.

FURTHER CONSIDERATION OF THE HYPOTHESIS

In attempting to account for the abnormal behavior observed in the psychopath, we have found useful the hypothesis that he has a serious and subtle abnormality or defect at deep levels disturbing the integration and normal appreciation of experience and resulting in a pathology that might, in analogy with Henry Head's classifications of the aphasias, be described as semantic. Presuming that such a patient does fail to experience life adequately in its major issues, can we then better account for his clinical manifestations? The difficulties of proving, or even of demonstrating direct objective evidence for, hypotheses about psychopathology (or about ordinary subjective functioning) are too obvious to need elaborate discussion here.

If the psychopath's life is devoid of higher order stimuli, of primary or serious goals and values, and of intense and meaningful satisfactions, it may be possible for the observer to better understand the patient who, for the trivial excitement of stealing a dollar (or a candy bar), the small gain of forging a $20.00 check, or halfhearted intercourse with an unappealing partner, sacrifices his job, the respect of his friends, or perhaps his marriage. Behind much of the psychopath's behavior we see evidence of relatively mild stimuli common to all mankind. In his panhandling, his pranks, his truancy, his idle boasts, his begging, and his taking another drink, he is acting on motives in themselves not unnatural. In their massive accumulation during his career, these acts are impressive chiefly because of what he sacrifices to carry them out. If, for him, the things sacrificed are also of petty value, his conduct becomes more comprehensible.

Woolley, in an interesting interpretation of these patients, compared them with an otherwise intact automobile having very defective brakes. Such an analogy suggests accurately an important pathologic defect which seems to exist. In contrast with an automobile, however, the braking functions of the human organism are built into the personality by reaction to life experience, to reward and punishment, praise and blame, shame, loss, honor, love, and so on. True as Woolley's hypothesis may be, it seems likely that more fundamental than inadequate powers to refrain is the inadequate emotional reactivity upon which the learning to refrain must be based. Even with good brakes on his car, the driver must have not only knowledge of but also feeling for what will happen otherwise if he is to use them correctly and adequately.

Some of the psychopath's behavior may be fairly well accounted for if we grant a limitation of emotional capacity. Additional factors merit consideration. The psychopath seems to go out of his way to make trouble for himself and for others. In carelessly marrying a whore, in more or less inviting detection of a theft (or at least in ignoring the probability of detection), in attempting gross intimacies with a debutante in the poorly sheltered alcove just off a crowded dance floor, in losing his hospital parole or failing to be with his wife in labor just because he did not want to leave the crap game at midnight (or at 3 A.M.)—in such actions there seems to be not only a disregard for consequences but an active impulse to show off, to be not discreet but conspicuous in making mischief. Apparently he likes to flaunt his outlandish or antisocial acts with bravado.

When negative consequences are negligible or slight (both materially and emotionally), who does not like to cut up a little, to make a bit of inconsequential fun, or perhaps playfully take off on the more sober aspects of living? Dignity might otherwise become pompousness; learning, pedantry; goodness, self-righteousness. The essential difference seems to lie in how much the consequences matter. It is also important to remember that inclination and taste are profoundly shaped by capacity to feel the situation adequately. A normal man's potential inclination to give the pretty waitress $100.00 would probably not reach awareness in view of his knowledge that this would result in his three children's not having shoes or in his having to humiliate himself by wheedling from a friend a loan he will never repay.

If, as we maintain, the big rewards of love, of the hard job well done, of faith kept despite sacrifices, do not enter significantly in the equation, it is not difficult to see that the psychopath is likely to be bored. Being bored, he will seek to cut up more than the ordinary person to relieve the tedium of his unrewarding existence. If we think of a theater half-filled with ordinary pubertal boys who must sit through a performance of *King Lear* or of Beethoven's *Ninth Symphony,* we need ask little of either imagination or memory to bring to mind the restless fidgeting, the noisy intercommunication of trivialities, the inappropriate guffaws or catcalls, and perhaps the spitballs or the mischievous application of a pin to the fellow in the next seat.

Apparently blocked from fulfillment at deep levels, the psychopath is not unnaturally pushed toward some sort of divertissement. Even weak impulses, petty and fleeting gratifications, are sufficient to produce in him injudicious, distasteful, and even outlandish misbehavior. Major positive attractions are not present to compete successfully with whims, and the major negative deterrents (hot, persistent shame, profound regret) do not loom ahead to influence him. If the 12-year-old boys could enjoy *King Lear* or the *Ninth Symphony* as much as some people do, they would not be so restless or unruly. If the son of a family long honored in the community (and husband of a wife at her wits' end) felt about going to jail and about being widely known as a jailbird, as most people do, he could not, after dozens of brief incarcerations, drop in on somewhat similar acquaintances (just back at work after their own periods of detention) and gaily twit them with such greetings as, "What kind of a bird can't fly?"

In a world where tedium demands that the situation be enlivened by pranks that bring censure, nagging, nights in the local jail, and irritating duns about unpaid bills, it can well be imagined that the psychopath finds cause for vexation and impulses toward reprisal. Few, if any, of the scruples that in the ordinary man might oppose and control such impulses seem to influence him. Unable to realize what it meant to his wife when he was discovered in the cellar flagrante delicto with the cook, he is likely to be put out considerably by her reactions to this. His having used the rent money for a midnight long-distance call to an old acquaintance in California (with whom he bantered for an hour) also brings upon him censure or tearful expostulation. Considering himself harrassed beyond measure, he may rise from the dining room table in a petty tantrum, curse his wife violently, slap her, even spit on her, and, further annoyed by the sudden weeping of their 6-year-old daughter, throw his salad in the little girl's face before he strides indignantly from the room.

His father, from the patient's point of view, lacks humor and does not understand things. The old man could easily take a different attitude about having had to make good those last three little old checks written by the son. Nor was there any sense in raising so much hell because he took that dilapidated old Chevrolet for his trip to Memphis. What if he did forget to tell the old man he was going to take it? It wouldn't hurt him to go to the office on the bus for a few days. How was he (the patient) to know the fellows were going to clean him out at stud or that the little bitch of a waitress at the Frolic Spot would get so nasty about money? What else could he do except sell the antiquated wreck? If the old man weren't so parsimonious, he'd want to get a new car anyway!

And why did he (the father) have to act so magnanimous and hurt about settling things last Saturday night down at the station? You'd think from his attitude that it was the old man himself who'd had to put up with being cooped in there all those hours with louse-infested riffraff! Well, he'd thanked his father and told him how sorry he was. What else could a fellow do? As for that damned old car, he was sick of hearing about it. His grudge passing with a turn of thought, he smiles with half-affectionate, playfully cordial feelings toward the old man as he concludes, "I ought to tell him to take his precious old car and stick it up his ________ !"

Lacking vital elements in the appreciation of what the family and various bystanders are experiencing, the psychopath finds it hard to understand why they continually criticize, reproach, quarrel with, and interfere with him. His employer, whom he has praised a few hours before, becomes a pettifogging tyrant who needs some telling off. The policeman to whom he gave tickets for the barbecue last week (because he is such a swell guy) turns out to be a stupid oaf and a ________ meddler who can't mind his own business but has to go and arrest somebody just because of a little argument with Casey in the Midnight Grill about what happened to a few stinking dollar bills that were lying on the bar.

Adolescents who feel a need to kick over the traces often seek to do so in unconventional, spectacular, daring, and sometimes shocking acts that often are motivated primarily by impulses of defiance. Similar impulses of defiance no doubt contribute to the psychopath's behavior. Figures representing authority or respectability naturally irk him. They are smug and meddlesome in his eyes and tempt him to show them what he really can do. If he cannot actually remember his parents, on the eve of a whipping, telling him "this is going to hurt me more than it does you," he, like all people, gets the idea. Through the damage he does to himself he has a way of getting back at or disciplining them, along with his wife, his friends, and all sorts of self-righteous people who volunteer to "do him good" and to meddle.

It is not necessary to assume great cruelty or conscious hatred in him commensurate with the degree of suffering he deals out to others. Not knowing how it hurts or even where it hurts, he often seems to believe that he has made a relatively mild but appropriate reprimand and that he has done it wth humor. What he believes he needs to protest against turns out to be no small group, no particular institution or set of ideologies, but human life itself. In it he seems to find nothing deeply meaningful or persistently stimulating, but only some transient and relatively petty pleasant caprices, a terribly repetitious series of minor frustrations, and ennui.

Like many teenagers, saints, history-making statesmen, and other notable leaders or geniuses, he shows unrest; he wants to do something about the situation. Unlike these others, as Lindner has so well and convincingly stressed, he is a "rebel without a cause." Reacting with something that seems not too much like divine discontent or noble indignation, he finds no cause in the ordinary sense to which he can devote himself with wholeheartedness or with persistent interest. In certain aspects his essential life seems to be a peevish bickering with the inconsequential. In other aspects he suggests a man hanging from a ledge who knows if he lets go he will fall, is likely to break a leg, may lose his job and his savings (through the disability and hospital expenses), and perhaps may injure his baby in the carriage just below. He suggests a man in this position who, furthermore, is not very tired and who knows help will arrive in a few minutes, but who, nevertheless, with a charming smile and a wisecrack, releases his hold to light a cigarette, to snatch at a butterfly, or just to thumb his nose at a fellow passing in the street below.

In his work on obsessive disorder, Straus brings out and develops a concept very germane to the present discussion. Beneath severe obsessive disorder he often finds indications of a distaste for life as it is ordinarily lived, a nauseous rejection of what is normally most appealing, and an attitude toward the world that finds in our chief sources of joy the equivalent of decay and filth. These observations are interesting and extraordinarily articulate. They seem to elucidate from an independent viewpoint other and important aspects of what has elsewhere been presented as confusion of love and hate.

It is impossible to give briefly an adequate account of what Straus brings out. Its relation to our subject is of interest. The psychopath does not seem to share the obsessive patient's specific pathologic evaluations, but he also reacts to the milieu of human life as if it had been altered in its essential qualities. The alteration in the psychopath is by no means similar to what Straus depicts. The obsessive patient, according to Straus, spends his life desperately trying to avoid what he finds so disgusting and horrible. The psychopath looks as if he were reacting to what is trivial by showing that he just doesn't give a damn. Having no major goals or incentives, he may be prompted by simple tedium to acts of folly or crime. Such prompting is not opposed by ordinary compunction or concern for consequences.

The psychopath certainly does not seem to be warding off anything similar to what the obsessive patient solemnly seeks to ward off with disgust. He may, however, be flouting something very different in an unrecognized or pooly recognized mockery or travesty whereby he demonstrates that he is not emotionally involved.

The lack of aversion to conduct and situations which to the normal man are repulsive is striking and paradoxical in the psychopath. This is no less impressive than the disgust Straus finds in obsessive patients. It might in fact be regarded as an equally basic alteration of the normal reaction but an alteration toward the other extreme. The opposite reactions of depression and manic euphoria have been interpreted as diverse responses to an identical inner pathologic situation. The prude and the pathologically wanton often seem to be influenced chiefly by the same misconception of sexuality as being intrinsically ignoble and, to the female, degrading. So, too, the active life rejection believed by Straus to underlie obsession and the indifference to major human values underlying the psychopath's life scheme may themselves be thought of as profoundly pathologic reactions in opposite directions.

A world not by any means identical but with some vivid features of both these underlying situations can be found in Huysmans' *Against the Grain* and in Jean-Paul Sartre's *Nausea.* In the satirical novels of Evelyn Waugh, also, an atmosphere difficult to describe sometimes develops—an atmosphere that may give the reader awareness of attitudes and evaluations genuinely illustrative of deeply distorted or inadequate reactions to life.

In none of this fiction does one find evidence of the obsessive patient's reaction to what he scrupulously rejects as if it were filth. The leading characters depicted therein show a peculiar cynicism which is more conscious and directed and purposive than the behavior of the psychopath. But none of the characters presented show even an approximate awareness of what is most valid and meaningful and natural in human beings. A negative response to life itself, an aversion at levels more basic than ordinary morals or the infraconscious foundations of taste and incentive, is conveyed subtly and impressively.

It is difficult to illustrate by incident, by the expressed attitude of the characters depicted, or by any clearly implied evaluation of the authors the specific quality of what is evoked in these novels as the essence of an unhappy, mutilated, and trivial universe in which all the characters exist. The sense of pathology pervades to levels so deep that rational scrutiny cannot reach and meet the fundamental implications; nor can inquiry satisfactorily demonstrate its precise source. If the actual world and man's biologic scope were only that conveyed in these interesting works, it would perhaps be less difficult to account for obsessive illness and for the psychopath's career as reasonable reactions to a situation where no course is possible except one profoundly pathologic in one way or another.

Thoughtful contemplation of what is depicted in these works of fiction suggests a world as fundamentally altered as what Straus presents as the world of the obsessive patient. In the effective and terse implication of general emotional incapacity in these characters, the authors succeed in evoking awareness of a sort of quasi life restricted within a range of staggering superficiality. This, rather than those aspects of the works which apparently brought them popularity, may deserve high literary appraisal as concise and valuable communications of something that is by no means easy to convey in direct language. Such a superficiality and lack of major incentive or feeling strongly suggest the apparent emotional limitations of the psychopath.

In his discussion of what arouses disgust in his obsessive patients, Straus brings out memorable points. Not by literal falsification of objective facts but by seeing and feeling these facts in a pathologic mode is the world altered. He says:

> Curls on a head look lovely and attractive, but the same hair found in the soup is disgusting; perhaps we should like to cut one of these curls as a souvenir, but we should be disgusted to collect the hair left in a comb. Saliva spit out is disgusting, an expression of our contempt, but on fresh lips and tongue the saliva is not disgusting. Separation from the integrity of the living organism turns the physiognomy from delight to disgust. This transition indicates a transition from life to death; it signifies decay. Disgust is directed more against decay, the process of decomposition, than against the dead. A skeleton, a mummy, may be frightening, even horrible, but not as disgusting as a cadaver which has just been brought from a river to the morgue.

Through the writings of Jonathan Swift excellent illustration is given of a peculiar distortion of those sympathetic relations which constitute the very essence of biology. It is not the charm of a lovely woman that attracts Swift's attention but the fact that she has sweat pores, excretions. Similar pathologic preoccupations with decay have also been noted by Havelock Ellis and cogently discussed. To the psychopath the basic axioms of life must seem different from what they seem to normal people and also very different from what they seem to people with severe obsessive disorders. Obsessive patients, according to the concept of Straus, are unable to appreciate what is normally obvious about many positive aspects of experience. This underlying and often unrecognized attitude can be better illustrated than described. Let us consider briefly an item that is vividly pertinent:

A young man who apparently was not quite happy in his marriage had been seen occasionally with other women. According to rumor, he had been or was about to be unfaithful to his wife. A cousin, also married and a few years older, was, in my presence, attempting to bring the other fellow to his senses. The counselor was a man of remarkable learning and intellect. He did not approach the problem by harping on conventional morality or the personal injustice that the other's wife might be done. Maintaining a light touch, half-teasing in his remarks but also seriously trying to be helpful, he spoke of how often young married men drift astray. He made, in a playful, unmoralizing style, some good arguments for avoiding adultery. Then, as if to diminish the temptations that he felt might be troubling the young man, he said: "Remember that when you kiss a girl you are sucking on the end of a tube twenty-five feet long and that the other end is filled with ----."*

Exposition or further discussion can contribute little or nothing to the remark as it stands. Whether the estimated length of the gastrointestinal tract is accurate or not has little pertinence. No one can argue with the literal truth of the counselor's statement. But who can avoid wondering about what might have led to the arrival at such a conception of a woman's kiss? And to such a response to such a stimulus?

What Straus and Havelock Ellis have brought out is not discernible in the reactions of the psychopath. It is, as a matter of fact, somewhat veiled in the reactions of most

*The speaker did not have symptoms of obsessive-compulsive neurosis or any features of the psychopath.

obsessive patients. Observation of the psychopath makes it increasingly plain, however, that he is not reacting normally to the surroundings that are ordinarily assumed to exist. I cannot clearly define the specific milieu that such a patient encounters and to which his reactions are related. There is much to suggest that it is a less distinctly or consistently apprehended world than what Straus describes as the inner world of the obsessive patient. It is my belief that it may be a world not less abnormal and perhaps more complexly confusing. We should remember, however, that we have no direct evidence to prove that a deficiency or distortion of this sort exists in the unconscious core of the psychopath. We can only say that his behavior strongly and consistently suggests it. This discussion has been based, of course, on a hypothesis that the psychopath has a basic inadequacy of feeling and realization that prevents him from normally experiencing the major emotions and from reacting adequately to the chief goals of human life.

There are other theories that attempt to explain the disorder without taking into consideration the question of such a defect. Alexander has assumed that the psychopath's behavior arises from forces similar to those which in the psychoneurotic are by many believed to be the fundamental cause of his distressing symptoms. Postulating unconscious conflict and repressed impulses also in the psychopath, he was led to believe that the antisocial, unprofitable, and self-damaging acts of the psychopath are purposive and unconsciously motivated expressions of the conflict. In the classic neurosis, subjective symptoms develop and the patient complains of weakness, headache, or obsessions or develops compulsive rituals, conversion paralysis, blindness, and so on. As these manifestations are thought by some to be reactions of the organism to inner stress, reactions that serve the purpose of protection, relief of anxiety, and gratification (by substitution or displacement) of rejected or frustrated impulses, so, too, according to Alexander, the pathologic behavior of the other type of patient is an acting out of impulses similarly neurotic. Thus interpreted, the psychopath has, in a sense, genuine and adequate reasons (like the neurotic for his symptoms) for the apparently foolish and uncalled-for things he does that damage himself and others. He himself does not know the reasons or clearly recognize his aims or the real nature of the impulses, and his acts do not constitute a wise solution for his problem; but the acts, according to Alexander, are purposive. This concept of the psychopath as acting out the neurotic problem (in contrast with the more passive development of ordinary symptoms) has been accepted by many psychoanalysts. It is an interesting concept, but it rests chiefly on psychoanalytic theories and assumptions about the unconscious and not upon regularly demonstrable evidence.

Some interpretations of schizophrenia assume that it is largely through the relatively undamaged remnants of the personality that the positive features of the psychosis emerge. If the process is complete, if the personality has, so to speak, entirely dissolved in the underlying id, the machinery to express most of the usual symptoms will be lacking. In response to stress and conflict, what remains of the personality produces, by familiar mechanisms, most of what is generally regarded as characteristic of the disorder. The more fundamental feature, and the one that particularly distinguishes schizophrenia from the psychoneuroses, is the disintegration of the personality. In the psychopath we maintain there is also a generalized abnormality or defect of the personality that can be compared with schizophrenia and contrasted with ordinary psychoneurosis (in which the personality is "intact" and the organism maintains "sane" social relations). It cannot be said that the disorder is that of schizophrenia, but in the whole of the patient's life we find such inadequacy of response, such failure of adaptation, that it seems plausible to postulate alterations more fundamental and more extensive than in classic psychoneurosis.

Beyond the symptomatic acts of the psychopath, we must bear in mind his reaction to his situation, his general experiencing of life. Typical of psychoneurosis are anxiety, recognition that one is in trouble, and efforts to alter the bad situation. These are natural ("normal") whole personality reactions to localized symptoms. In contrast, the severe psychopath, like those so long called psychotic, does not show normal responses to the situation. It is offered as an opinion that a less obvious but nonetheless real pathology is general, and that in this respect he is more closely allied with the psychotic than with the psychoneurotic patient. The pathology might be regarded not as gross fragmentation of the personality but as a more subtle alteration. Let us say that instead of macroscopic disintegration our (hypothetical) change might be conceived of as one that seriously curtails function without obliterating form.

In addition to outwardly visible demolition or shattering in material structures, other changes may occur. These may be intracellular and leave the appearance unchanged but greatly alter the substance. Colloidal variations in concrete may rob it of its essential properties although the appearance of the material remains unaltered. Steel under certain conditions is said to crystallize and lose much of its strength. The steel so affected looks the same as any other, and no outer evidence of the molecular rearrangement which has so greatly altered the substance can be detected. For the purpose of analogy, one can consider not only intracellular or molecular but also intramolecular changes. Let us think of the personality in the psychopath as differing from the normal in some such way. The form is perfect and the outlines are undistorted. But being subtly and profoundly altered, it can successfully perform only superficial activities or pseudofunctions. It cannot maintain important or meaningful interpersonal relations. It cannot fulfill its purpose of adjusting adequately to social reality. Its performance can only mimic these genuine functions.

Karl Menninger in *Man Against Himself* picturesquely developed the argument that antisocial behavior sometimes represents an indirect search for punishment, a veiled but essentially self-destructive activity. The hypothesis of an active "death instinct" advanced by Freud is, in this dramatic study, applied to many types of disorder. In localized symptoms, as well as in broad maladjustments, self-damaging impulses are interpreted as fulfilling their negative purpose.

In the patients presented here the general pattern of life seems to be more complex. Although thefts are sometimes committed, checks forged, and frauds perpetrated under circumstances that invite or even assure detection, similar deeds are also frequently carried out with shrewdness and foresight that are difficult to account for by such an interpretation. It is also characteristic for the real psychopath to resent punishment and protest indignantly against all efforts to curtail his activities by jail sentences or hospitalization. He is much less willing than the ordinary person to accept such penalties. In the more circumscribed symptoms of acting out, in many of the disorders referred to by Fenichel as impulse neuroses, the unconscious but purposive quest for punishment might more plausibly be conceived of as a major or regular influence. The validity of such an assumption, however, whether or not it is plausible, must be determined by what actual evidence can be produced to establish it, and not by mere surmises and inferences about what may or may not be in the unconscious.

ASPECTS OF REGRESSION

The persistent pattern of maladaptation at personality levels and the ostensible purposelessness of many self-damaging acts definitely suggest not only a lack of strong purpose but also a negative purpose or at least a negative drift. This sort of patient, despite all his opportunities, his intelligence, and his plain lessons of experience, seems to go out of his way to woo misfortune. The suggestion has already been made that his typical activities seem less comprehensible in terms of life-striving or of a pursuit of joy than as an unrecognized blundering toward the negations of nonexistence.

Some of this, it has been suggested, may be interpreted as the tantrumlike reactions of an inadequate personality balked, as behavior similar to that of the spoiled child who bumps his own head against the wall or holds his breath when he is crossed. It might be thought of as not unlike a man's cutting off his nose to spite not only his face, but also the scheme of life in general, which has turned out to be a game that he cannot play. Such reactions are, of course, found in nearly all types of personality disorder or inadequacy. It will perhaps be readily granted that they are all regressive. Behavior against the constructive patterns through which the personality finds expression and seeks fulfillment of its destiny is regressive activity although it may not consist in a return, step by step, or in a partial return to the status of childhood and eventually of infancy. Such reactions appear to be, in a sense, against the grain of life or against the general biologic purpose.

Regressive reactions or processes may all be regarded as disintegrative, as reverse steps in the general process of biologic growth through which a living entity becomes more complex, more highly adapted and specialized, better coordinated, and more capable of dealing successfully or happily with objective or subjective experience. This scale of increasing complexity exists at points even below the level of living matter. A group of electrons functioning together makes up the atom, which can indeed be split down again to its components. The atoms joining form molecules, which, in turn, coming together in definite orderly arrangement, may become structurally coordinating parts of elaborate crystalline materials; or, in even more specialized and complex fashion, they may form a cell of organic matter. Cells of organic matter may unite and integrate to form the living organism we know as a jellyfish. Always the process is reversible; the organic matter can decompose back into inorganic matter.

Without laboriously following out all the steps of this scale, we might mention the increasing scope of activity, the increasing specialization, and the increasing precariousness of existence at various levels up through vertebrates and mammals to man. All along this scale it is evident that failure to function successfully at a certain level necessitates regression or decomposition to a lower or less complicated one. If the cell membrane of one epithelial unit in a mammalian body becomes imporous and fails to obtain nutriment brought by blood and lymph, it loses its existence as an epithelial cell. If the unwary rabbit fails to perceive the danger of the snare, he soon becomes in rapid succession a dead rabbit, merely a collection of dead organs and supportive structures, protein, fat, and finally, inorganic matter. The fundamental quest for life has been interrupted, and, having been interrupted, the process goes into reverse.

So, too, the criminal discovered and imprisoned ceases to be a free man who comes and goes as he pleases. A curtailment in the scope of his functioning is suffered—a regression in one sense to simpler, more routine, and less varied and vivid activities. The man who fails in another and more complex way to go on with life, to fulfill his personality growth and function, becomes what we call a schizophrenic. The objective curtailment of his activities by the rules of the psychiatric hospital are almost negligible in comparison with the vast simplification, the loss of self-expression, and the personal disintegration that characterize his regression from the subjective point of view. The old practice of referring to the extremely regressed schizophrenic as leading a vegetative existence implies the significance that is being stressed.

Regression, then, in a broad sense may be taken to mean movement from richer and more full life to levels of scantier or less highly developed life. In other words, it is relative death. It is the cessation of existence or maintenance of function at a given level.

The concept of an active death instinct postulated by Freud has been utilized by some to account for socially self-destructive reactions. I have never been able to discover in the writings of Freud or any of his followers real evidence to confirm this assumption. In contrast, the familiar tendency to disintegrate, against which life evolves, may be regarded as fundamental and comparable to gravity. The climbing man or animal must use force and purpose to ascend or to maintain himself at a given height. To fall or slide downhill he need only cease his efforts and let go. Without assuming an intrinsic death instinct, it is possible to account for active withdrawal from positions at which adaptation is unsuccessful and stress too extreme. Whether regression occurs primarily through something like gravity or through impulses more self-contained, the backward movement (or ebbing) is likely to prompt many sorts of secondary reactions, including behavior not adapted for ordinary human purposes but, instead, for functioning in the other direction. The modes of such reactivity may vary, may fall into complex patterns, and may seek elaborate expression.

In a movement (or gravitational drift) from levels where life is vigorous and full to those where it is less so, the tactics of withdrawal predominate. People with all the outer mechanisms of adaptation intact might, one would think, regress more complexly than can those who react more simply. The simplest reaction in reverse might be found in a person who straightway blows out his brains. As a skillful general who has realized that the objective is unobtainable withdraws by feints and utilizes all sorts of delaying actions, so a patient who has much of the outer mechanisms for living may retire, not in obvious rout but skillfully and elaborately, preserving his lines. The psychopath as we conceive of him in such an interpretation seems to justify the high estimate of his technical abilities as we see them expressed in reverse movement.

Unlike the general with the retreating army in our analogy, he seems not still devoted to the original contest but to other issues and aims that arise in withdrawal. To force the analogy further, we might say that the retiring army is now concerning itself with looting the countryside, seeking mischief and light entertainment. The troops have cast off their original loyalties and given up their former aims but have found no other serious ones to replace them. But the effective organization and all of the technical skills are retained.

F. L. Wells has expressed things very pertinent to the present discussion. A brief quotation will bring out useful points:

> The principle of substitutive reactions, sublimative or regressive in character, has long been known, but Kurt Lewin's . . . experimental construction of the latter is

> especially apt, if not unquestionable mental hygiene. A child, for example, continually impelled to open a gate it is impossible for him to open, may blow up in a tantrum, grovel on the ground, till the emotion subsides sufficiently for him to become substitutively occupied, as with fragments of gravel and other detritus he finds there, by which he forgets his distress about the gate. Lewin, perhaps unaware of the status of this and allied observations (and their symbols) in psychiatric history, gives it the name "going out of the field": the background is that enunciated by Woodworth and by James before him, not to say Adolf Meyer, Janet, Jung, and the psychoanalytic group generally. The human personality has the adaptive property of finding satisfactions at simpler levels when higher ones are taken away, fortunately so if this keeps him out of a psychosis, otherwise if it stabilizes him in contentment at this lower level ("going native") or if the satisfactions cannot be found short of a psychosis (MacCurdy, . . .). All such cases have the common regressive factor of giving up the higher-level adjustment (opening the gate) with regressive relief at a lower level (playing with the gravel).

Another illustration given by Wells emphasizes features of the concept that are valuable to us:

> Consider, for example, the group of drives that center about the concept of self-maintenance, the "living standards" of civilization. This means the pursuit of the divers means to surround oneself with the maximum of material comfort in terms of residence, food, playthings, etc., for the purchase of which one can capitalize his abilities. That the normal individual will do this to a liberal limit is taken in the local culture as a matter of course, probably more liberally than the facts justify. For this pursuit involves a competitive struggle beset also with inner conflicts (e.g., ethical), which by no means everyone is able to set aside. Among regressions specific to this category are those undertakings of poverty common to religious orders, but this regression is quite specific, since these orders often involve their members in other "disciplines" from which the normal individual would flee as far (Parkman, . . . Chap. 16). It is quite certain, though hard to demonstrate objectively, that many an individual in normal life regresses from these economic conflicts only in less degree. He does not take the vow of poverty like the monastic, nor does he dedicate himself to the simplified life of the "South Sea Island" stereotype, but he prefers salary to commission, city apartment to suburban "bungalow," clerical work to (outside) sales.

A thought expressed by William James and quoted by Wells deserves renewed attention:

> Yonder puny fellow however, whom everyone can beat suffers no chagrin about it, for he has long ago abandoned the attempt to "carry that line," as the merchants say, of Self at all. With no attempt there can be no failure; with no failure no humiliation. So our self-feeling in this world depends entirely on what we back *ourselves* to be and do. It is determined by the ratio of our actualities to our supposed potentialities; a fraction of which our pretentions are the denominator and the numerator our success: thus, Self-esteem 3 Success/Pretensions. Such a fraction may be increased as well by diminishing the denominator as by increasing the numerator. To give up pretensions is as blessed a relief as to get them gratified; and where disappointment is incessant and the struggle unending, this is what men will always do. The history of evangelical theology, with its conviction of sin, its self-despair, and its abandonment of salvation by works, is the deepest of possible

> examples, but we meet others in every walk of life. . . . How pleasant is the day when we give up striving to be young—or slender! Thank God! we say, *those* illusions are gone. Everything added to the self is a burden as well as a pride.

Something relevant to the points now under consideration may be found also in Sherrington's comment on reactions (or inlaid precautions) against unbearable pain or stress in the human organism:

> Again in life's final struggle the chemical delicacy of the brainnet can make distress lapse early because with the brain's disintegration the mind fades early—a rough world's mercy towards its dearest possession.

There are, it seems, many ways for this to occur without signs of any change that we yet have objective means to detect, chemically or microscopically. Such changes may occur under the stimulus of agents that do not have direct physical contact with the brain or with any part of the body.

Withdrawal, or limitation of one's quest in living, appears in many forms. The decision for taking such a step may be consciously voluntary, but it seems likely that many influences less clear and simple may also play a part. In the earliest years of human life a great deal of complicated shaping may occur, with adaptive changes to promote survival by an automatic refusal (inability) to risk one's feelings (response) in the greatest subjective adventures. In adult life such decisions sometimes emerge in clear deliberation.

The activity of the psychopath may seem in some respects to accomplish a kind of protracted and elaborate social and spiritual suicide. Perhaps the complex, sustained, and spectacular undoing of the self may be cherished by him. He seldom allows physical suicide to interrupt it. Be it noted that such a person retains high intelligence and nearly all the outer mechanisms for carrying on the complicated activities of positive life. It is to be expected, then, that his function in the opposite (regressive) emotional direction might be more subtle than those of a less highly developed biologic entity. The average rooster proceeds at once to leap on the nearest hen and have done with his simple erotic impulse. The complex human lover may pay suit for years to his love object, approaching her through many volumes of poetry, through the building up of financial security in his business, through manifold activities and operations of his personality functions, and with aims and emotions incomparably more complicated and more profound than that of the rooster. When complexly organized functions are devoted to aimless or inconsistent rebellion against the positive goals of life, perhaps they may enable the patient to woo failure and disintegration with similar elaborateness and subtlety. His conscious or outer functioning may at the same time maintain an imitation of life that is uniquely deceptive.

Perhaps the emptiness or superficiality of life without major goals or deep loyalties, or real love, would leave a person with high intelligence and other superior capacities so bored that he would eventually turn to hazardous, self-damaging, outlandish, antisocial, and even self-destructive exploits in order to find something fresh and stimulating in which to apply his relatively useless and unchallenged energies and talents.

Like so much of what is often called dynamic interpretation of psychiatric disorder and of human behavior, these thoughts are purely speculative and without the slightest support of evidence. They are offered with no pretense whatsoever of constituting a scientific explanation.

The more experience I have with psychopaths over the years, the less likely it seems to me that any dynamic or psychogenic theory is likely to be established by real evidence as the cause of their grave maladaptation. Increasingly I have come to believe that some subtle and profound defect in the human organism, probably inborn but not hereditary, plays the chief role in the psychopath's puzzling and spectacular failure to experience life normally and to carry on a career acceptable to society. This, too, is still a speculative concept and is not supported by demonstrable evidence.

SURMISE AND EVIDENCE

If, in the so-called psychopath, we have a patient profoundly limited in ability to participate seriously in the major aims of life, how, we might inquire, did he get that way? Reference has been made to the traditional viewpoint from which it was assumed that an inborn organic defect left these people "constitutionally inferior" or "moral imbeciles." Such a congenital defect, it must be readily admitted, may exist and may account for the failure to experience life normally and hence to react sanely.

During the earlier decades of the twentieth century this concept of the psychopath prevailed. It was widely believed that these patients, often called *constitutional inferiors,* came almost exclusively from families loaded with *stigmata of degeneration* and *signs of neuropathic taint.* As time passed, it was noted that typical psychopaths were also seen in families of very respectable, ethical, and successful people and were entirely free from all physical stigmata of degeneration. Many pointed out that some of the statistical studies giving evidence of hereditary factors are not as reliable as they were once thought. Even the famous studies of the Jukes and the Jonathan Edwards families have been severely criticized and called fallible by some.

As already mentioned, Healy long ago pointed out that antisocial behavior often seemed to occur as a response to unhappy life situations, and Alexander formulated such disorder in psychoanalytic terms as a purposive acting out of unconscious pathologic conflict.

The concept of acting out, in lightly disguised symbolic deeds, might be vividly illustrated in the case reported here in which a man responded to what is often spoken of as being in the doghouse by putting on his dog's collar and spectacularly caricaturing canine behavior.* Another response to a similar situation can be found in the patient who literally got into a kennel at the veterinarian's and so exhibited himself.† Although these incidents picturesquely illustrate Alexander's concept of acting out, they do not in themselves constitute evidence of an unconscious conflict, which he has assumed causes the behavior. Neither patient showed any reaction that would support belief in the presence of inner, unconscious feelings of guilt or of the type of conflict attributed to psychopaths in such interpretations. The assumption of such guilt in these two patients must be made purely on faith in the theory.

Many other psychiatrists have attempted to explain the psychopath in terms of psychogenic causation. The studies of Greenacre led her to conclude that the confusing

---

*Chapter 3, The psychopath as businessman.

†Chapter 3, The psychopath as scientist.

influence of a stern, authoritarian father and an indulgent or frivolous mother is common in the early background of the psychopath. It is plausible to feel that such an influence might contribute to rebellious reactions and to a defective development of conscience and of ordinary social and personal evaluation. Karpman, in his extensive work with character and behavior disorders, offers the opinion that in most cases a psychogenic etiology can be established if adequate investigation is made. A relatively small percentage of those we call psychopaths, he believes, are not so motivated. These, presumably disordered because of inborn or constitutional defect, he distinguishes from the majority and calls anethopaths.

Knight's studies of severe alcoholics, many of whom were considered psychopaths, led him to believe that they often had "a parental background characterized by inconsistency and lack of unanimity in parental discipline resulting in conflicting unstable identifications in the son." A weak, pampering mother in combination with a domineering father whose severity was fitful and inconsistent appeared frequently in the background of Knight's cases. He feels that important causal relations between this early situation and the subsequent disorder are likely. Knight says:

> Innumerable personality shadings and accents are possible from a son's reaction to such parental management, but one regular result seems to be the fostering of excessive passive demands and expectations in the son, such passive, childish, feminine wishes being in marked conflict with masculine strivings inculcated by the father and by the cultural ideology absorbed from schooling and from contacts with other males.

I have over many years looked hopefully for evidence of parental influences on my patients such as those discussed by Greenacre and Knight. I have not, however, been able to find regularly, or even very frequently, the environmental pattern in early life that impressed them as, perhaps, offering an explanation of the problems found in their patients. I have also seen many well-adjusted people, and also many with problems very unlike those of the psychopath, who come from homes similar to those described by Greenacre and by Knight.

Adelaide Johnson has expressed a strong conviction that the delinquency of a child or teenager is sometimes caused by the parents' own *unconscious* impulses toward antisocial conduct. The child or teenager, she tells us, is craftily used as a pawn and unconsciously encouraged in theft, arson, sexual promiscuity, violence, or sexual perversion in order to fulfill the parents' unconscious emotional needs to carry out such conduct themselves. According to this formulation, the child, even after he has become an adult, remains unconscious of the parents' adverse influence and of his real motives for antisocial conduct. Furthermore, Johnson reports that the parents are often unwilling to give up their vicarious criminal satisfactions and that they may actively block the psychiatrist's attempts at therapy. Such an explanation has been accepted as a common cause for the psychopath's disorder by a number of prominent psychiatrists.

Perhaps there are delinquents and psychopaths in whom such influences play an important part. Let us remember, however, that some methods of trying to determine what is in the unconscious may allow us unwittingly to project items from our theories into the assumed motivation of the patient and also of his parents. If persistent but unconscious antisocial impulses are really active in the parents, we might also ask ourselves if such tendencies might have been conveyed to the offspring by hereditary factors. I think it very unlikely that the parents of the patients presented here and of the others studied by me found satisfaction, unconsciously or otherwise, in the persistent misconduct of their sons and daughters.

Lindner devoted almost an entire volume, *Rebel Without a Cause,* to the detailed report of one psychopath studied by hypnoanalytic methods. He believed that through processes of preverbal memory he was able to obtain from the patient a true report of significant and traumatic experiences which he dated as occurring at 6 or 8 months of age. Lindner gives a detailed and ingenious explanation of how he believes these experiences caused the patient to develop seriously disturbed relations with his parents and eventually to adopt the typical role of the psychopath. Despite the strong convictions of Lindner, his excellent presentation, and the superb title of his book, there is much that makes me skeptical about the significance of experiences reported as having occurred at such an early age and about the validity of what may be recalled through preverbal memory or established chiefly by the interpretation of symbols and dreams.

One reason for my skepticism is derived from the implausible and sometimes fantastic events occasionally reported by my own patients as having occurred in early childhood or infancy. Sometimes this material has impressed me from the beginning as fabrication or fantasy confused with memory. When teaching young physicians in psychiatric residency training, I was often also impressed by the influence of the examiner's convictions on items of experience reported by such patients. I found that some of these patients could be led on in almost any direction to report almost any sort of infantile recollection one sought to produce.

This proclivity in some patients may play a significant part in explaining how conscientious therapists find confirmation for widely differing and sometimes contradictory theories during prolonged investigations of a patient's infantile experiences and unconscious attitudes. It has tended to make me increasingly cautious about accepting as necessarily true historical data even from much later periods of life from patients who seem to be of this type. It has often been noted that the psychopath will very convincingly report entirely false incidents and attitudes in others, particularly in parents, that tend to put responsibility for his difficulties upon them.

It is also true that experiences ordinarily withheld or deeply repressed in other people are often quickly and readily divulged by these patients. Disgraceful and extremely uninviting deeds are sometimes reported with a relish that suggests pride in them. Although shame and terrible conflict are sometimes claimed in such matters and superficial indications of such claims may be impressive, I am unable to find at any level evidence that such affects are major or even quite real. This is a factor deserving constant attention, for it can enter very subtly into material obtained from patients of this sort. The point most difficult to corroborate, in my own experience, is the actual or innermost personal reaction of these patients to the events they report. It is more difficult than with others to tell what the events mean to them.

Some comments made by Jenkins are pertinent, it seems to me, to the question of whether or not psychopaths are acting out a conflict based upon unconscious feelings of guilt:

> Effective challenge to a basic faith always causes pain and a reaction ridden with emotion in which the issues can easily become clouded. . . . This challenge has been

> felt by some of the defenders of the modern psychodynamic faith which, at least initially, tended to a narrow conception that functional mental disorders and maladjustments are always due to conflicts within the personality. To enlarge this concept with a realization that morbid conditions and gross maladjustments may be due primarily to a *lack* of conflict within the personality represents a readjustment of thinking which is apparently beyond the flexibility of many professional persons. There is of course, a semantic problem involved. It was not difficult for mankind to understand poisoning, for it is easy to grasp the proposition, "what he ate made him sick." The understanding of the vitamin deficiency diseases was more difficult because of the greater semantic difficulty of the proposition, "what he did not eat made him sick." Yet this second proposition is as true and as necessary to any adequate consideration of illness as is the first. In the same way many of our dynamically oriented colleagues have great difficulty with the proposition, "The conflict he does not have makes him a psychopath." This concept is true and necessary, but requires at least a flexible application of classical psychodynamic theory.
>
> Theories are advantageous when they stimulate some resourceful new attack on a problem. They are handicapping when they make it difficult for us to recognize important facts. . . .
>
> If indeed we must get into the area of theory—and this is not entirely avoidable—I should like to propose that psychopaths differ from psychoneurotics and indeed contrast with them in their most important characteristics. The typical psychopath and the typical psychoneurotic are, in some important regards, on opposite sides of the normal. Where the psychoneurotic suffers from excessive inner conflict, the psychopath makes others suffer from his lack of inner conflict. Only the person who does not come in contact with serious cases of this sort, or whose mind is literally imprisoned by his faith in a theory can brush aside this fundamental difference.

I have become increasingly convinced that some of the popular methods presumed to discover what is in the unconscious cannot be counted upon as reliable methods of obtaining evidence. They often involve the use of symbolism and analogy in such a way that the interpreter can find virtually anything that he is looking for. Freud, for instance, from a simple dream reported by a man in his middle twenties as having occurred at 4 years of age drew remarkable conclusions. The 4-year-old boy dreamed of seeing six or seven white wolves sitting in a tree. Freud interpreted the dream in such a way as to convince himself that the patient at 18 months of age had been shocked by seeing his parents have intercourse three times in succession and that this played a major part in the extreme fear of being castrated by his father which Freud ascribed to him at 4 years of age. No objective evidence was ever offered to support this conclusion. Nor was actual fear of castration ever made to emerge into the light of consciousness despite years of analysis.

Faithfully following Freud's method of establishing proof by analogy, a prominent psychiatrist in his well-known book *Beyond Laughter* has given us a remarkable interpretation of the drum majorette. Most of us are likely to think that the average man's pleasant reaction to these well-built, sparsely clad young ladies who prance happily and often somewhat sexily before the band at football games can be pretty well accounted for by tastes and impulses quite obvious in nearly anyone's consciousness. Such tastes and impulses, according to the interpretation in *Beyond Laughter,* must be considered as superficial or perhaps even as the result of reaction formation. The lissome girl, we are solemnly told, stands out before the grouped band just as an erect penis stands out before the larger mass of the body. This analogy is taken as evidence that interest and excitement about the provocative lass do not lie primarily in the fact that any ordinary man would find her attractive. In our unconscious she is said to be equated with the erect male organ, and it is maintained that men really feel toward her, as she stands projected before the group, as they *unconsciously* feel toward the penis of another male. Our positive reactions toward her, we are told, arise from our unrecognized and unaccepted homosexuality. No corroborative evidence is offered, nor any doubt expressed, about this interpretation. It is soberly offered as a fact, presumably discovered by science.

The Dutch psychiatrist Peerbolte uses a similar method of analogy to establish what he considers satisfactory evidence of emotional trauma during embryonic or fetal life. A patient dreams that she is in a church and that the figure of Christ with a wooden leg walks toward her. The interpreter concludes that this indicates that she was frightened and shaken up by her father's penis when her parents had intercourse while she was a fetus in her mother's uterus.

Distrust for such glib use of the popular methods of interpretation has been strongly expressed by a few prominent and well-qualified psychoanalysts. Masserman, in a delightful article, gives us an important lesson in his brilliant satire, "The Psychosomatic Profile of an Ingrown Toenail." Let us quote from this article:

> Consider, I said, the toenail. Anthropologists have pointed out that man's mind developed when his arms were freed of the task of locomotion so that he could walk about the earth in an upright position, manipulating its resources and thinking about the heavens. Moreover, osteologists tell us that all of this in turn depended upon the hallux and its toenail. But libidinally speaking, the nail represents even more than this. Actually, it is the most protuberant part of the body, hard and rounded; in locomotion it describes a most suggestive to-and-fro movement—obviously, then, it is a basic penile symbol displaced, for a change, downward. But let us also remember the anatomic origin of this important little phallus, namely the *nail-bed*—also a most significant term. This in turn consists of an invagination of vascular tissue into a zone called, with intuitive propriety, the *stratum germinativum* or *matrix*—a region consummately feminine in its conformation, physiology, and import. Here, then, we have a psychosomatically significant microcosm; a womb-equivalent ever generating a masculine imago which normally goes forth to meet, explore, and conquer the external world.
>
> But now consider what happens when this normal functioning is disrupted by frustration and conflict; when, specifically, the erect nail is stubbed and traumatized, or is too long opposed by unyielding reality in the form of a repressive shoe. Clinically and perhaps personally we know the effects all too well: the nail, particularly at the peripheral portions of its individuality (or more technically, its "ego boundaries") turns about and digs its way back into the flesh of its origin. To those properly indoctrinated with psychosomatic understanding, however, a much deeper significance can be discerned in this process. It will be obvious, indeed, that the counter-cathected ungual masculinity, blocked from its exteriorizing libidinal outlets, introverts upon itself and eventually even seeks final regression through the mechanism of re-encapsulation and vascularization—i.e., a return to uterine existence. This formula, derived as it is by analogic thinking enlightened by metapsychologic insight, could of course stand on its merits alone about as well as others derived from similar research endeavors; fortunately, however, it can be further validated by objective

> clinical observation. Thus, it can be demonstrated that analysands of both sexes with ingrown toenails actually do have masculine aspirations and intra-uterine fantasies, and the mere fact that analysands *without* ingrown toenails have the same unconscious dynamisms serves merely to emphasize once again how the study of the abnormal can reveal profound truths about all mankind.

The material just quoted is from a lecture that Masserman gave to point out, by a playful reduction to absurdity, some of the overenthusiastic and unreliable uses of dynamic methods in psychology and psychiatry. Let us quote also his comments on the audience's reaction to his lecture:

> Here I ended my Lecture on Psychosomatics, rewarded by what I was sure was an understanding gleam in the eye of some of my listeners and trusting that, though I lacked the ribaldry of a Rabelais or the subtlety of a Voltaire, I might still have aroused a healthy whimsy of doubt about some of the verbal gymnastics that pass for serious thinking and investigation in the field. Imagine my consternation, therefore, when on meeting some of the members of the audience days and weeks later I was actually congratulated on the clinical and analytic perspicacity with which I had derived the specific dynamic formula for the etiology and possible therapy of that hitherto unexplored psychosomatic disorder—onychocryptosis, or ingrown toenail!

In dwelling on the pitfalls and possibilities of error that we face in attempts to explain the psychopath's disorder on a psychogenic basis, I do not mean to discount sober efforts to accomplish this by realistic methods. Let us, however, be cautious and tentative and try always to distinguish surmise from evidence.

I have noted incidents in the early life of some psychopaths that might serve as factors likely to promote rebellion against society, distort the normal aims of life, interfere with the development of basic values, and go far, perhaps, toward accounting for much of the behavior so familiar to all who know them well. Some of these early experiences might indeed go far toward explaining their emotional status that has been so effectively and succintly summarized by William and Joan McCord in their excellent book. They say:

> The psychopath feels little, if any, guilt. He can commit the most appaling acts, yet view them without remorse. The psychopath has a warped capacity for love. His emotional relationships, when they exist, are meager, fleeting, and designed to satisfy his own desires. These last two traits, guiltlessness and lovelessness, conspicuously mark the psychopath as different from other men.

But similar experiences also can be demonstrated in the background of many well-adjusted, happy, and successful adults. In a few of the cases reported here an impressive account was given of incidents and reported reactions (with indications of emotion) that could theoretically be said to explain emotional withdrawal (despite maintenance of excellent rational contact) from the areas or levels of living in which severe hurt, deep joy, genuine pride, shame, dignity, and love are encountered and experienced. Protest reactions, loss of insight, an acting out of unconscious impulses, a behavioral caricature, or a diatribe against life and its (for the psychopath) subjective emptiness could be interpreted as major causal factors in the disorder we encounter clinically. Such interpretations may be correct, but usually there are more elements of assumption or speculation than of evidence in what is offered in support of the argument.

A very large percentage of the psychopaths I have studied show backgrounds that appear conducive to happy development and excellent adjustment. Whatever part psychogenic factors may play, I am inclined to believe that there may be an important relationship between the abstruse, paradoxically compounded, and ambivalent nature of the influences and the complex and deeply masked nature of the disorder such factors may shape. If such a relationship exists, it may to some degree explain the special difficulties we have encountered in obtaining from the psychopath convincing subjective information about what has happened and about how he was affected by it.

In the patients presented here, social service reports and all ordinary information usually indicated normal and helpful family attitudes and general environments. The families themselves often impressed the examiner as good, healthy, wise, and eminently well-adjusted people whose children were particularly fortunate because of what they could offer as parents. When opportunities arose, as they sometimes did, to learn more of matters inward, subtle, and deeply personal, the observer was occasionally led to suspect that even in these apparently superior parents there were attitudes, frustrations, emotional confusions, and deficiencies that might have played a masked but crucial adverse role in the infinite complexities and paradoxes of parent-child relationships.

This is not to say that the parents were wrongly judged as conscientious or as superior people or that in many important respects they were not well adjusted. Despite conscientiousness and a good deal of wisdom and success, characteristics might exist which could, perhaps, subtly distort the milieu of an infant or a child.

People may be fair, kind, and genial, may hold entirely normal or even admirable attitudes about all important matters and yet unknowingly lack a simple warmth, a capacity for true intimacy that seems to be essential for biologic soundness (substantiality) in some basic relationships. There are men and women of whom it might correctly be said that it is impossible for them ever to become really personal. This aspect (or ingredient) of human experience is difficult to describe or to signify accurately. We do not encounter it squarely in thinking but feel it in perceptive modes or at reactive levels not readily translatable into speech. Let us remember, however, that such qualities may be found in parents of those who are not psychopaths.

Some who show only superior qualities in all their activities as citizens, in their work, and in all definable responsibilities seem to feel little need for the sort of specific attachment and affective closeness that perhaps constitute the core of deep and genuine love. They also seem to have little perception of such a need in others. There are people who show in changeless formality, poise, and cool "sensible attitudes" outer indications of what is being discussed, but it is not they who concern us at present. In others, genial informality and manifestations of more than ordinary warmth may prevail in relatively superficial friendships and routine social contacts, in professional and business associations, at dinner parties, and at club meetings. Where intimacy is normally limited, they may be spontaneous and show cordiality as real as anything appropriate for such occasions. Their inner formality and remoteness is not encountered until the observer approaches areas of privacy, deep levels of personal affect that ordinarily are only reached in relations between mates, between parent and child, or in the few other very intimate and cherished friendships or sharings of personal understanding and feeling that man never achieves in wholesale measure. Parents of this sort may give an impression of affording each other and the child all that is ideal, and affording it in abundance. One such parent will, however, leave the other (if normal) so deprived in essential needs that the child may be turned to for the exclusive and possessive intimacy normal between mates but full of pathologic potentialities in the other relationship.

The observations reported by Kanner in his study of infantile autism illustrate some of the points that are being discussed here. In the brilliant and outstandingly successful parents of these seriously disabled infants a complex and profound emotional deficiency was regularly encountered. During all my years of experience with hundreds of psychopaths, however, no type of parent or of parental influence, overt or subtle, has been regularly demonstrable.

Both hereditary factors and influences of the frustrating, or antisocial, environment seem evident in the development of delinquency in many of the patients described long ago by Healy. In the background of the intelligent, charming psychopath who appears in a family of prominent, ethical, and successful citizens, it is often far more difficult to find convincing evidence to account for his disorder on either basis. If an inborn biologic defect exists and plays an important part in such a psychopath's disorder, it is not necessary to assume that the defect is hereditary. Perhaps it may be the result of a subtle failure in maturation, an agenesis of unknown etiology. A much simpler and more grossly manifested defect of this sort is familiar in the pathology of congenital cerebral palsy. It is well known that encephalitis may be followed by changes in behavior and personality that cause some who have suffered from it to become indistinguishable from the psychopaths we have been discussing and that these changes may occur without any physical signs of neurologic damage.

Many psychiatrists have continued to express the conviction that some organic injury or deficiency underlies the psychopath's dysfunction. Although no neurologic lesion has been regularly demonstrated in the typical psychopath, it is also true, as Thompson reminds us, that no satisfactory proof of psychogenic factors as the cause of his disorder has been established. Referring to formulations of the psychopathology in terms of environmental influences, he says:

> Here too much is missing that might give us a rational explanation which would be subject to scientific scrutiny, and which would meet the postulates of science necessary for validity.

Numerous observers have reported records of electroencephalographic abnormality in psychopaths. Others have failed to confirm these findings of a specific abnormality. Over the past two decades still other investigators have expressed the conviction that there are nonspecific but definitely abnormal electroencephalographic findings in a significant percentage of psychopaths. In his interesting and valuable study, *Psychopathy: Theory and Research,* Hare in 1970 makes this summarizing comment:

> In spite of their limitations, the EEG studies of psychopathy have produced rather consistent results. One finding, that the widespread slow-wave activity often found in psychopaths bears a certain resemblance to the EEG patterns usually found in children, has led to a *cortical immaturity* hypothesis of psychopathy. A second hypothesis, based on the presence of localized EEG abnormalities, is that psychopathy is associated with a defect or malfunction of certain brain mechanisms concerned with emotional activity and the regulation of behavior. Finally it has been suggested that psychopathy may be related to a lowered state of cortical excitability and to the attenuation of sensory input, particularly input that would have disturbing consequences. [pp. 35–36]

A number of observers during the last decade have been impressed with the influence of chromosomal abnormality on aggressive and antisocial activity in the male. At one time it was reported that Richard Speck, who was convicted of murdering eight student nurses in Chicago in 1967, was an example of this condition. This report was subsequently proved false. Some commentators have gone so far as to argue that men with the XYY chromosomal pattern should be freed of legal responsibility for crimes of violence. Hare's comment on this subject impresses me as pertinent and accurate:

> Recent findings show that the presence of an extra Y chromosome in males (for example, XYY instead of the normal XY) may be related to extremely aggressive behavior (see the very readable account by Montagu, 1968). Whereas XYY chromosome complements are very rare in the normal population, it appears that this chromosome abnormality is found in about 2 to 3 percent of males whose behavior is so violent and aggressively antisocial that incarceration or institutionalization is required. In most cases these XYY males are over six feet tall, and they are frequently of subnormal intelligence. Whether the XYY complement is related to extremely aggressive forms of psychopathy (as opposed to other forms of criminal, antisocial behavior) is as yet unknown. Even if it is, the relationship would not really provide evidence one way or the other on the role of hereditary factors in psychopathy, since the XYY complement is not inherited—it apparently reflects the failure of the sex chromosomes to separate properly during formation of the sperm. Finally, the rarity of the disorder means that it could account for only a very small proportion of criminal behavior in general and aggressive psychopathy in particular.

If a neurologic defect does exist in the psychopath, it is also quite possible that influences in the milieu may play an important part also in shaping his pattern of life. It seems to me likely that such a defect, if present, must be one that affects complex mechanisms of integration in a subtle and abstruse manner. Some of the superior capacities encountered so often in psychopaths suggest that their difficulties might arise not only from deficiencies but possibly, even if rarely, by misused assets.

It seems reasonable to believe that there are varying susceptibilities to failure or to psychiatric disorder. Such susceptibilities may not necessarily be defects or intrinsically negative qualities. Could not superior emotional responses contribute to a boy's developing maternal attachments that can prove crippling in the degree to which he has capacity for loyalty? May not the precociously brilliant child, because of his advancement, encounter deep personal and social problems earlier than the average? And, will he, perhaps, sustain trauma that he might have avoided with additional experience? Such experience may be available to the mediocre child who, in his slower progress, meets the confusing situation a little later. Those whose feelings are highly developed may be more susceptible to hurt than others. The goals of the superior person often demand of him complicated choices and sacrifices that the average person never has to face. Disillusion and suffering because of frustrations escaped by most of his fellows might, it seems reasonable to think, in the child of great talent and potentiality, stimulate attitudes of withdrawal and cynical rejection or other pathologic reactions. Exceptional talent or capacity seems almost regularly to call for exceptional achievement or fulfillment and to put the subject under extraordinary responsibility and into situations peculiarly complex. Courage and initiative lead man not only to take physical risks but sometimes also into subjective ventures of many sorts with many dangers.

What we value in some as steadfastness may arise from potentialities that, through different shaping, might emerge in others as incorrigibility, inelasticity, or perhaps as those elements which may make a psychiatric disorder irreversible. Granting the likelihood of great variation in the basic potentialities of the organism, let us not forget that in so complex a matter as personality maturation and social adjustment not only defects but talents also may contribute to conflict, to confusion, to distortion of the life pattern, and, perhaps, to serious clinical disorder.

If what is good or wise or sound comes, or appears to come, mixed, so to speak, with what is untrue or deleterious and is identified in a single concept, and designated by the same term, peculiar difficulties may be promoted. Such difficulties, it seems reasonable to think, might be especially disturbing to the superior child. Conscientious acceptance of what is most necessary for normal growth and development may, under these circumstances, sometimes necessitate commitments to what must later be rejected if the organism is to survive. The deeper the capacity for loyalty, the more profound may be the stress, confusion, and eventual disillusionment.

The psychopath's inner deviation from the normal impresses me as one subtly masked and abstruse. So, too, it has often seemed that interpersonal and environmental factors, if they contribute to the development of his disorder, are likely to be ones so disguised superficially as to appear of an opposite nature. Something pertinent to this concept may be conveyed in these words by Thompson:

> Everything spiritual and valuable has a gross and undesirable malady very similar to it and possessing the same name. Only the very wise can distinguish between them.

I do not believe that the cause of the psychopath's disorder has yet been discovered and demonstrated. Until we have more and better evidence than is at present available, let us admit the incompleteness of our knowledge and modestly pursue our inquiry.

chapter 8 · What can be done?

This disease is beyond my practice.
—THE DOCTOR IN MACBETH

ILLNESS AND MISCONDUCT

A good deal has already been said about the difficulties and disappointments arising in our efforts to treat these patients generally known as psychopaths. A few more points will be added presently to the opinions already expressed, but if we are to make any progress therapeutically, it seems first necessary to clarify some broader issues.

Aside from the intrinsic obdurateness of the disorder that we find in the patient himself, there exist surrounding difficulties and absurdities that have made it quite impossible even to approach the central problem in any way except one that axiomatically predetermines defeat. Challenged by what is perhaps the most difficult therapeutic task in psychiatry, the physician is denied ordinary access to the area in which the task must be accomplished. It is only in exceptional instances that the therapist can get his hands on the patient, and even then he has little more opportunity to take useful measures than would a surgeon called upon to remove the gallbladder of a jackrabbit in full flight. Our medical, legal, and social concepts are so formulated and our institutions so devised that it is usually impossible to bring the psychopath into the range of treatment. Nor is it usually possible for him to be brought under the control of any agency that can protect him or others from the damaging effects of his disorder. This point is emphasized by Thompson in a helpful study:

> The administrative officers of penal institutions attempt to have such individuals transferred to mental hospitals because they believe them to be mentally ill. Knowing how little they can do for them and what difficult problems they are, the superintendents of mental hospitals attempt to get rid of them as soon as possible and transfer them back to the prison as "not psychotic." Pushed from prison to hospital and back again, wanted in neither, the psychopathic delinquent is essentially the orphan of both penology and psychiatry.

Many observers have apparently been impressed by the remarkable facility people of this sort show in avoiding the control of prolonged confinement in prisons or hospitals and in evading other usual and expected penalties for persistent illegal conduct. Hare in 1970 makes this comment:

> The hedonistic and self-centered acts of many psychopaths often go relatively unpunished. Studies by Robins (1966) and Gibbens, Briscoe, and Dell (1968) have

> shown that a surprisingly large number of psychopathic persons somehow manage to avoid incarceration in spite of the fact that their behavior may be grossly antisocial. In many cases they are protected by family and friends who may themselves be their victims. In other cases they may be charming and intelligent enough to talk their way out of prosecution. In any event, their behavior may be relatively unchecked and unpunished; and therefore very rewarding, persistent, and firmly established.

The exceptional patients who commit very serious felonies and are convicted sometimes, it is true, come and may remain under the legal restraints of prison. Like the patient with traditionally recognized psychosis, the psychopath cannot be counted on to seek treatment and even less to submit voluntarily to protective measures.

Two crucial points confront us in any attempt to deal practically with the disorder that has engaged our attention: (1) the question of distinguishing between illness (true disability) and willful or culpable misbehavior and (2) the question of legal responsibility or competency. These two matters are deeply interwoven and bring us eventually to the same basic problem. It will be helpful, however, to approach that problem through these two channels. Let us take them in order.

It has already been pointed out that in earlier times many types of dangerous or bizarre conduct that today are regarded as illness were attributed to witchcraft, demon possession, or other supernatural agencies. Along with and subsequent to this interpretation we find the practice of attributing misfortune and ordinary physical and psychiatric diseases to sin or some other form of voluntary wrongdoing. Those conditions earliest recognized as having a medical aspect are the ones in which injury, symptoms (somatic or psychic), and other outward features are most obvious. The overtness rather than the real degree of seriousness seems to have been the chief clue in these determinations. The medical practitioner was called upon to help with the mangled leg or the carbuncle while exorcism and other mystic rites were still the only measures provided for the patient suffering from such obscure pathology as leukemia or Addison's disease. Even when ideas still prevailed that wrongdoing was the primary cause of disease, treatment by the physician was accepted as an appropriate step to take in dealing with some of these afflictions. The compound fracture that followed a fall was treated by the surgeon during times when the fall was regarded as the result of a sorcerer's spell. So, too, salvarsan was administered to the patient with syphilis even by those who regarded him as ill primarily because of his voluntary wrongdoing.

After overt and vividly macroscopic expressions of psychosis (running naked through the streets and wildly shouting out messages received from the dead, arguing that one's body lacks an anus or one's blood is pure pus) had for some time been accepted as illness, decades passed before the patient with masked or cryptic schizophrenia and the well-oriented, careful, and brilliantly reasoning paranoiac could count on so regular or so early medical attention as they receive today. We have not yet learned to distinguish such patients very readily, and they sometimes remain without treatment or any protective social measures until their disorder is far advanced. Murder or some other tragic consequence may be necessary to bring them to examination and eventually to what treatment is available for their condition.

Forms of expressions of illness are not necessarily less serious, less dangerous, or less genuine because the superficial appearance of the patient reveals less obvious signs of a disorder. One of the factors contributing to our present difficulty in distinguishing the aspect of illness in the psychopath is, I believe, not dependent on the degree of whatever disorder he shows but on its type or nature.

Few (sane) theologians, philosophers, or jurists would contend today that present concepts of disease and methods of dealing with it, whether manifested in a predominantly somatic aspect or otherwise, have damaged religion or made nonsense of moral values. When something can be done to help the situation in its medical aspect, this is done without waiting to reach agreement on nonmedical absolutes, however important these ultimate questions may be for each of us.

The patient with pneumonia might not have become ill if he had not suffered exposure while he was out in severe weather robbing the bank. Another patient's hemorrhoids may or may not be related to his lazy habits of sitting around all day or to his becoming constipated and then unwisely taking powerful laxatives advertised on television. Here we may find a patient whose anxiety seems to be, in part at least, caused by a (cowardly) fear of accepting the responsibilities (and opportunities) of a new job and also by an old pathologic (wrong) tendency to rely on his mother for support and protection.

A man in severe agitated depression may say all his viscera have rotted until the stench is lethal and that his neighbor's crops wither under his glance. His throat may show deep lacerations from his last desperate attempt at suicide. No one questions the plain fact that he is ill and gravely ill. Some psychopathologists believe that he is ill primarily (or largely) because of his unconscious hate for those he loves and his impulses to destroy them. Even those who hold this belief agree that therapy is appropriate. It is also agreed that he must be supervised and protected, if necessary against his own will and judgment.

Just who or what (in a final philosophic showdown) is to blame for these situations is difficult indeed for anyone to say. That they are pathologic conditions deserving every available measure for their correction is not as difficult to determine.

An important point to express and, if possible, to establish is this: medical attention or any other practical step to help or ameliorate misfortune or pain must not wait for a threshing out on philosophic, metaphysical, and religious planes of the ultimate whys and wherefores, the final determining of blame or responsibility. It is possible and practicable to meet these emergencies at another point.

Reasons have been expressed already for the opinion that the psychopath differs fundamentally from the ordinary criminal or rascal.*Whether or not this argument is valid, let us seek a remedy for what obviously demands attention. Not only a patient's welfare but that of the community must be given consideration in any step we decide to take.

Many types of behavior formerly regarded as voluntary wrongdoing or the just results of sin are now classed as disease. This does not prove that eventually all wrongdoing will be plainly revealed as disease and all conduct necessarily evaluated at a level at which good and bad are nonexistent. There are, however, indications that medical, legal, and social remedial steps are often useful in dealing with situations that we have not yet assayed and may never unanimously assay in final terms of ethics.

Let us remember, however, that there are good reasons to believe that this tendency

*Chapter 5, The ordinary criminal.

to reclassify wrongdoing as illness has in recent decades gone too far—perhaps in some instances to the point of absurdity. Some commentators use the term *sickness,* or *illness,* glibly in referring to the cause of any bank robbery, embezzlement, forgery, murder, income tax fraud, or violation of traffic laws. The assumptions that underlie this practice are not usually supported by any actual evidence from psychiatric investigation but depend entirely upon the arbitrary choice of a term to exonerate those who have perpetrated antisocial acts.

It has become exceedingly popular to say routinely that crime is not the fault of the criminal but of society. Many commentators also insist that there is no such thing as a bad child but only bad parents. All this tends logically to promote the feeling that a person can do no wrong and need take no responsibility for his own misconduct, however deplorable or harmful to himself or to others. Suppose I want to rob a bank. Well, why not? If I do, I am not to blame. The blame instead will be put on society, or on my parents, or perhaps on a teacher in the first grade who traumatized me by discipline and must now be responsible for my rebellious self-expression. If we need other scapegoats to exonerate all criminals of any possible guilt, we might blame the grandparents, who from this viewpoint must in turn have been responsible for the evil in the criminal's parents. Arguments approximately as glib and unrealistic as these are to be found today in scientific literature. In trying to understand or estimate the psychopath, let us avoid these gratuitous and so often far-fetched assumptions. Is it possible that we have sometimes gone to extremes during recent years in this direction to a degree comparable to the follies of witchcraft in another?

LEGAL COMPETENCY AND CRIMINAL RESPONSIBILITY

It has been mentioned that the psychopath does not often cooperate willingly in treatment over any considerable period of time and that he also seems to be remarkably free from the ordinary legal and penal restraints that prevent others from repeatedly carrying out antisocial activity. Questions of legal competency and criminal responsibility play a fundamental part in the efforts of society to cope with psychopaths. Let us consider these concepts more closely.

The term *competency* in connection with our present problem is pertinent to questions of legal commitment, which is a procedure by which the psychiatric patient can, when necessary, be placed under treatment and appropriate restrictions even if this has to be done against his will and, if necessary, by force. Responsibility seems in many respects to be another aspect of the same thing. The incompetent person has been legally pronounced unable to look after his own affairs or make his own decisions about crucial matters. If a person is held to be legally responsible by a court, he is then considered to be culpable for any crime or other misdeed he may have committed and hence subject to legal penalties. Many assumptions, some of them about matters on which few entirely agree, lurk in various degrees of disguise in the almost limitless implications of these terms.

Probably most laymen, and perhaps some physicians, think of both incompetency and a lack of legal responsibility as identical with psychosis or *insanity.* As so helpfully pointed out by Davidson, this is incorrect, or at least incomplete and sometimes misleading. According to the law, Uncle John's will may be entirely valid, although he insisted for years that he talked with his dead grandmother and was diagnosed as having schizophrenia. Every psychiatrist knows people who hallucinate and are delusional but who should not be deprived of their liberty and sent against their will to institutions. A good example is offered in a 50-year-old woman who for fifteen years has carefully listened to a voice from her stomach which she "knows" is real and which often directs her. Advice given by the voice has on the whole been quite sensible and practical—never irrational! She has for a decade come at intervals to the outpatient clinic. So far as can be ascertained, her life has been undisturbing to others, and she has, with fair competency, carried out her own affairs.

It is true, nevertheless, that nearly everywhere in the United States it is usually necessary for medical evidence to establish the presence of a psychosis and for the court to pronounce a patient insane before he can be committed or in any way handled therapeutically or prophylactically against his wishes. Mental deficiency, it is true, may also serve as a basis for such action, although it is sometimes the practice to say that the degree of deficiency is so great as to render the patient psychotic. There are those who will argue that nevertheless he does not have a psychosis.

The technicalities of procedure vary from state to state. Items redolent of necromancy, and in which the glow of witch fires is still reflected, are not uncommon in these doings. Until after publication of the first edition of this book, in my native state the patient was "charged with being a lunatic." Most physicians and jurists would perhaps agree that for practical purposes incompetency, in the sense of making legal commitment advisable, indicates a disability (disorder or deficit) of such degree that the patient cannot be counted on to make a (normally) correct appraisal of his condition and (therefore) to choose what treatment or protection he needs.

In considering the questions that arise concerning legal competency and responsibility, let us remember that the determination of competency, on which commitment depends, is usually carried out by a few selected experts—a lunacy commission. On the other hand, as Cumming so well emphasized, questions of responsibility on which terms of imprisonment or even the death penalty may depend are determined by a jury of twelve laymen. Usually when a person is legally adjudged incompetent, it is on the basis of his being psychotic. Sometimes, however, a person who is psychotic may be held legally responsible because he is considered as knowing the nature and quality of his criminal deed and that it is wrong.

A case referred to by Guttmacher is illustrative. Let us quote from his interesting discussion:

> Spencer married a woman who had been raped about six years before. The man was found guilty of rape and was given a sentence of five years. They usually give longer sentences in Maryland, but he got five years. Spencer's wife, a very frail person, died without medical attention while this man was serving his penitentiary sentence. The cause of death was not determined, but Spencer was sure that her death was the result of the rape, which had occurred six years before, about three years before he had married her. The idea possessed him that his wife was not going to be able to rest in her grave unless she was really avenged, and he decided that it was his mission in life to right this great wrong. A few months after this man had been released from the penitentiary, Spencer went up to him and asked him to take a walk.

> They started walking down the road together, and Spencer was overheard by some people who passed to say, "You have been responsible for my wife's death. I hear voices at times telling me that I must kill you. Her spirit will never rest unless I carry out this request. I know that I am likely to hang for it and it's the wrong thing for me to do, but there is nothing else left for me to do." Whereupon he killed him. He pleaded insanity and the court, upheld by the court of appeals, ruled that he was not insane. The court of appeals said it was clear that the witness heard Spencer say that he was doing what he knew to be wrong and that he would be punished. That was all that the court needed to know in order to satisfy itself that he was a responsible agent.

The patient discussed by Guttmacher, despite the hallucinations which would surely have caused most psychiatrists to call him psychotic, was regarded as responsible because of his own statement to the effect that it was wrong to commit murder. An important question must be asked. Just how much knowing of the quality and nature of the act, just how much and what sort of evaluation and emotional appreciation of it, is proved or indicated by such a statement from a man who is hallucinating?

It is not unusual to find patients with schizophrenia who can pronounce correct verbal judgments about matters they fail to evaluate sanely or react to normally. A man was examined who had almost succeeded in strangling his wife to death. He "knew" this act was wrong at the time, was not apparently angry with her, and was glad he had been prevented from killing her. He had felt influences "from within" which were more effective in determining his decisions and acts than the impulse to avoid murder and to have his wife remain alive. This patient, who also had hallucinations and was obviously psychotic and schizophrenic, apparently did not attempt murder because of deficiency in the "intellectual" concept of right and wrong but probably because his personality was so altered that appreciation, the emotional significance, of the act was (otherwise) diminished or disordered. Another patient with schizophrenia may recognize his child, say that he loves his child, express all the correct attitudes "intellectually" about the situation, and still be so disordered in his responses that he will let the child drown or burn to death without making ordinary efforts to save him.

In contrast with these, the psychotic paranoiac as he plans an assassination may be able to feel strong hate and destructiveness (to experience criminal intent) similar in degree and quality to that of the normal man.

In the case discussed by Guttmacher, definite evidence of irrationality was demonstrable. But the contrary evidence of a localized rationality at the crucial point of being able to express an opinion that to kill the man was wrong was accepted as proof that he knew the nature and quality of the act. It might be said that here we have a "lesion of the intellect" demonstrated, but the lesion was not demonstrated to be in such a place as to prevent the man from making the rational statement about his deed.

Though competency and responsibility often seem to be two aspects of the same question in legal matters, there may be good grounds for sometimes considering them separately. Early in my experience with psychopaths I was struck with the idea that much might be gained if they could be considered psychotic. With the first edition of this book I expressed this opinion. I was led into this position by repeatedly observing how little a fully developed psychopath succeeds in leading a normal or acceptable life, and how badly needed was some means to control his antisocial and self-defeating proclivities.

I was not really thinking about responsibility from the other point of view; that is to say, about whether or not the person should be regarded as guiltless of crimes and other antisocial activities. For many years I have consistently tried to emphasize my strong conviction that psychopaths should not be regarded as psychotic in the sense of being "innocent because of insanity" of the wrongs they do.

I still feel as strongly as ever that the psychopath's defect constitutes a major disability for normal participation in human affairs, but I am convinced that I made a great mistake in expressing myself in such a way as to give the impression I believed he should be regarded as blameless, or not legally responsible for his misconduct. Despite traditional concepts and confusions, can we not conceive of a defect that seriously incapacitates and calls for restraining measures, without assuming that this defect necessarily absolves the subject from culpability and penalties of the law? Whatever in the psychotic patient there is that may render him not responsible, or less than normally responsible, for crime, cannot, in my opinion, be found in the psychopath's defect.

Many psychiatrists and jurists have protested over many decades against the M'Naghten Rules and have insisted that judgment should be made not on cognition (knowing) alone but that other aspects of the personality should be considered. In response to this criticism, the concept of "irresistible impulse," an alleged abnormality of the will, was advocated years ago and was adopted as law in some parts of the United States.

This theory of irresistible impulse so often advanced by the defense in questions of criminal responsibility deserves a brief discussion. As traditionally interpreted, the M'Naghten Rules obviously center examination on an assumed intellectual faculty. The concept of a pathologic and genuinely irresistible impulse attempts to center it on another assumed and discrete faculty, a hypothetical will. Quoting again from Guttmacher:

> Seventeen of our states . . . [in 1948] recognize that it is not only a question of whether a man knows that what he is doing is wrong, but [also] whether his will power is sufficiently undermined by mental disorder that he cannot adhere to the right, in which case he is not considered a responsible agent.

Hall expressed the belief that even where the irresistible impulse test was recognized in theory, it was not often respected in practice.

Nothing could be more obvious than the follies that may arise when an attempt is made to localize illness in a hypothetical volition dismembered from the integrate of human functioning. Arguments as to whether an impulse is pathologically strong or whether what resists it is pathologically weak soon become little more practical or more enlightening than arguments about priority between the hen and the egg. As Hall points out, it has been said that if legal questions are determined on such a basis "you will soon make irresistible an impulse which now is resistible and resisted because of penal law." A prominent psychiatrist is quoted as saying:

> From a psychological point of view, the impulse could not have been resistible, since the act was carried out in accordance with the impulse. It is difficult for me to conceive of an impulse which is resistible but not resisted.

Attempts to apply the M'Naghten Rules to a concept of faculty psychology vividly illustrate the weaknesses of faculty psychology. Attempts, within the confining framework of its assumptions, to examine not only an *intellect* but also a *will* are unlikely to be helpful since in neither pursuit can we encounter a reality of experience but must continue to deal with only verbal abstractions.

Many psychiatrists over several decades have been extremely bitter in their criticism, and sometimes in their ridicule, of the M'Naghten Rules, which for over a hundred years constituted the chief legal guide in determining criminal responsibility. As given by Hall, the essential points of the M'Naghten Rules lie in this statement:

> To establish a defense on the grounds of insanity, it must be clearly proved that at the time of the committing of the act the party accused was labouring under such a defect of reason from disease of the mind as not to know the nature and quality of the act he was doing or, if he did know it, that he did not know he was doing what was wrong.

Some of this criticism of the traditional rules has apparently been based on the wish by expert witnesses to express the opinion in psychiatric terms rather than in those familiar to the law and to laymen. Violent denunciation of the rules has also apparently been related to the concept of psychic determinism so vigorously espoused by Freud and very popular among psychiatrists for several decades. This doctrine is regarded by many as one of Freud's most important discoveries and as a foundation stone of dynamic psychiatry. Although it is often assumed to be a fact established by psychoanalytic research, we may note that Freud and all his followers have produced no scientific evidence whatsoever to support it. It remains purely an assumption.

A truly logical conclusion from psychic determinism would, of course, abolish the concept of personal responsibility altogether and along with it the basis of law and all the value judgments that underlie ethical conduct and even rudimentary civilization. Let us bear in mind, however, that those who profess allegiance to the doctrine almost never follow it to the inevitable conclusions it logically demands. There are many, nevertheless, who respond to its influence sufficiently to arrive at peculiar and interesting assumptions. Some of these are now popularly regarded as the essence of a liberal and scientifically enlightened mind. Going part of the logical way, but not all the way, they conclude that when crimes are committed, it is never the fault (responsibility) of the criminal but, inevitably, the fault of society.

Zilboorg, one of those who vigorously criticized the law, and the M'Naghten Rules especially, had this to say:

> When they all individually and jointly [judges, lawyers, and jury] ask me whether the defendant in the dock is in my opinion insane, I must candidly state, if I am to remain true to my professional knowledge and faithful to my oath, first, that I do not understand the question, and, second, that since I don't understand the question, I do not know whether the defendant is insane or not. I admit the situation is embarrassing and puzzling to all concerned, but it is beyond my knowledge and power to remedy or alleviate it.

Continuing a discussion of what he considered to be the basic differences between medical man and jurist, Zilboorg goes on to say:

> We have reached a rather disquieting parting of the ways. This is undesirable from both your [the jurist's] point of view and mine. Your rules are unintelligible to me, and my inability to follow them is unintelligible to you.

It is a matter of no little importance that joint action be continued, that every effort at cooperation be made to fit our social instrumentalities to the needs of the patient. It is important that new knowledge and understanding be used in these efforts. It is doubtful, as Hall points out, that the substitution of psychiatric terminology for the legal phrases would be of much practical or immediate help. To quote from Hall again:

> Imagine that, instead of a judge's instructions in terms of prevailing rules he said "... essential to the psychopathic personality may be a defective organization of the autotely ... and unsatisfactory adjustment of the heterotely." ... If, instead of "knowledge" or "understanding," "control," or "act," the language of the law ran in terms of *id, ego,* and *super-ego,* the psychiatrists would understand, but would many lay persons be much enlightened even after they were informed that the *"id"* is the "true unconscious," that the *"ego"* is that part of the mind that is "regulated by the reality principle," and that the *"super-ego"* is a sort of inner monitor synonymous with conscience?

It seems likely that Hall's suggestions offer more hope for common understanding and for effective action. (The need for such action is particularly urgent and obvious so far as psychopaths are concerned.) He suggests that concepts generally agreed upon in psychiatry be utilized to "implement the M'Naghten Rules." It is doubtful if any psychiatrist today conceives of personality function only in the abstractions of faculty psychology. The human being as we know him is integrated. We do not find him "thinking" without also "feeling." We do not observe acts of volition altogether free of emotion. Continuing, Hall clarifies the very point on which he feels agreement may be reached and which intelligent action may follow:

> This view of the participation of the rational functions, including evaluation, does not imply any depreciation of the role of the instincts in normal conduct. For consistently with this theory, one asserts the fusion of various aspects of the self. This means that moral judgment ("knowledge of right and wrong") is not reified as an outside, icy spectator of a moving self; on the contrary, the corollary is that value judgments are permeated with the color and warmth of emotion, as is evidenced by the usual attitudes of approval that coalesce with right decisions. Indeed all action, especially that relevant to the penal law, involves a unified operation of the personality.... The M'Naghten Rules provide an analytical device for dissecting this action.

If these rules can be thus used by the jurist, it seems obvious that as psychiatrists we can venture honest and sensible opinions on whatever evidence of medical impairment we find that may alter such a "knowing." When no longer dismembered and falsified in two-dimensional aspect but considered in all that we sometimes imply by *appreciation, realization, normal evaluation, adequate feeling, significant and appropriate experiencing,* the term does not restrict us solely to a discussion of the patient's reasoning abilities in the abstract.

In very impressive and helpful studies over a period of many years, Hall has brought out from the viewpoint of our legal co-workers in this area facts, appraisals, and suggestions which I feel can enable us to deal honestly and more effectively with questions of legal responsibility and competency. He has also politely but convincingly demonstrated some of the confusion contributed by us as psychiatrists to important issues. Interestingly enough, Hall demonstrates in our own psychiatric writings examples of the very dogmatism, the archaic and unrealistic approaches, and the adherence to dubious theory at the expense of vital fact which we have so readily ascribed to the law and its interpreters and so vigorously denounced.

If the jurist and the psychiatrist would approach our problem from the viewpoint expressed by Hall, it seems to me that much nonsense and tragedy could be avoided. After referring to typical arguments between those who argue for "reason" as a criterion and those who in contradiction emphasize "will," he says:

> Opposed to these views and avoiding their particularistic fallacies is the theory of the integration of the self.... In terms of this theory any interaction with the environment is integrated in the sense that the various functions of personality coalesce and act as a unit. Although it is useful to distinguish the important "modes" or attributes of such action, the various functions are not actually separate. On the contrary, the affective, the cognitive, and the conative functions as well as all others interpenetrate one another. Thinking (knowing, understanding) e.g., fuses with tendencies to action and it is permeated also in varying degrees by the warmth of the emotions.... Hence it is arbitrary and formalistic to assert that the psychotic's rational functions, including his knowledge of right and wrong, are unimpaired. There is only a certain awareness, a bare calculation unsupported by the strong pillar of sensitivity that, in normal adults, effects identification with a prospective victim or stimulates a vivid imagining of other consequences of the intended behavior; in short, the psychotic's conduct is unaccompanied by actual understanding of the moral significance of his action.

Many of these quotations illustrating arguments over the M'Naghten Rules and claims made by some psychiatrists that we are in a position to bring truly scientific knowledge to bear on crucial problems, still dealt with by antiquated methods, are from articles published over the last fifteen to twenty-five years. They are retained in the current edition of this book because I believe they are still pertinent to problems that have not yet been satisfactorily settled.

Despite the excellent points made by Hall, vigorous criticism of the law and particularly of the M'Naghten Rules has continued over the decades, chiefly from psychiatrists but also from jurists. Many of those who have expressed such bitter dissatisfaction with the M'Naghten Rules welcomed the Durham Rule as a tremendous and triumphant step forward. This rule, pronounced by Judge Bazelon in 1954, is to the effect that a defendant must not be held criminally responsible "if his unlawful act was the product of mental disease or mental defect." Speaking of the Durham Rule, Fortas has said, "Its importance is that it is a charter—a Bill of Rights for psychiatry." Judge Bazelon received official honors and a certificate of commendation from the American Psychiatric Association. Along with many psychiatrists, prominent legal scholars have enthusiastically expressed the conviction that "science," "scientific facts," and "the latest knowledge of human behavior" have made the M'Naghten Rules obsolete. They apparently assume that all this alleged psychiatric enlightenment can now be freely applied to legal problems.

On the other hand, Hall and some other critics have expressed fear that the Durham Rule might lead to the destruction of our jury system in criminal trials and turn over questions of guilt and responsibility to narrow experts who, however adequately trained in their limited field, may not really qualify as all-knowing judges on such questions and all that they involve. Hall and Cumming express the fear that various unproved and widely differing theories might be utilized by psychiatric witnesses to make arbitrary and absolute judgments that would have little relation to scientific fact. They also develop arguments that illustrate the danger of leaving such complex value judgments on such imponderables as the judgment of criminal responsibility solely to any experts known today. Although it is maintained by some that psychiatrists now have a scientific method of arriving at such a decision, the points made by Hall and Cumming raise grave doubts about this assumption and suggest that this is an area not yet proved arriving accessible to methods that are genuinely scientific. Forcing the methods of science, or a caricature of these methods, into areas that science is not now equipped to deal with does not endow judgments in these areas with validity, whatever words we may use to state the case. This specious and misleading practice has sometimes been called *scientism.*

It is interesting to note that in 1907 Grasset brought forth under the term *physiological responsibility* a concept very similar to that embodied in the Durham Rule. Grasset advocated that the judgment of responsibility be made merely on whether or not the capability of the organism is impaired. In this old concept he avoids decisions about free will versus determinism. He also refuses to confine his inquiry to disparate conceptual abstractions such as "knowing," "feeling," or "will." Instead he keeps his attention on the integrated reality of human functioning.

It has been customary over the decades for lunacy commissions to pronounce psychopaths competent and for juries to pronounce them sane and responsible. It is in the concept of competency that we meet our primary problems when we attempt to provide any improvement in methods of dealing with the psychopath. It is difficult to examine the most important aspects of competency, however, without becoming entangled with essential implications of legal responsibility. If we attempt to make pronouncements about responsibility, we are likely, unless we take particular care to signify what we are talking about, to find ourselves submerged in metaphysics and attempting solutions of ultimate philosophic and religious problems. However important or transcendent these problems may be and however we may solve them for ourselves, we are not, as psychiatrists, qualified to solve them as experts. We are, let us say, not *competent* to serve in such a role, nor are we *responsible.*

In approaching questions of competency in the psychopath, it is plain that he shows no defect in theoretical reasoning and that he lacks all the outer or peripheral manifestations of psychosis and usually even of minor psychiatric disorder. If, however, we consider the record of his actual performance, we nearly always find ample evidence to say that he is socially incompetent in the sense that he cannot carry out a sane plan of life or avoid repeated antisocial acts and other acts seriously damaging to himself.

McDougall long ago expressed a succinct and practical opinion on the essential question of competency:

> In practice the criterion adopted is: Can the patient be trusted to look after his affairs without undue risk to himself and others? And there is no other criterion.

As the reader must, I believe, agree, this sensible criterion, although regularly applied to any patient who has ever shown a delusion or a hallucination, is not in practice applied to those who lack these and some other traditionally accepted signs of "a lesion of the intelligence." If this criterion should be applied to psychopaths, it would be much less difficult to commit them and keep them under satisfactory control.

Karl Menninger, also, in referring primarily to questions of liability for punishment, has made a point that should be helpful if we apply it to the commitment of patients who are not charged with crime. "The psychiatrist," he says, "asks not 'Is that man responsible?' but 'Of what is he capable or incapable?' "

Despite the cogency of this position, it is not the common practice of psychiatrists, if the patient is diagnosed as psychopathic personality, to ask themselves such a question. Or, if they ask it, they arrive at a strange answer, and by extraordinary methods.

In estimating competency in most matters, intelligence as manifested in verbal reasoning carries a good deal of weight, but few who survive as adults continue to make the estimate entirely on this basis. Judgment is often spoken of as a matter somewhat different from and far more complicated than intelligence and is in general regarded as better demonstrated in behavior than in talk. In the old Stanford-Binet psychometric test we find the question, "Is it better to judge a man by his actions or by his words?" The normal 10-year-old child is supposed to answer this correctly. What disturbing thoughts may arise from this apply, I believe, as accurately to us in our role as psychiatrists as to legal authorities.

Despite the widespread and sometimes bitter disagreement among psychiatrists and at times among legal scholars, most patients with psychosis who need treatment and who need restraint can be legally committed and controlled. Although many psychopaths are, in my opinion, far more disabled than a large proportion of committed psychotic patients and in far greater need of control, it is very difficult to have such a patient committed. Before any important step toward solving the problems created by psychopaths can be taken, some legal means of controlling their antisocial, heedless, self-damaging, and irresponsible behavior must be devised.

If the Durham Rule devised by Judge Bazelon is followed, the question of competency in the psychopath would depend chiefly on whether his abnormality is correctly defined as a "mental disease or mental defect." It has long been customary in psychiatry and law to distinguish sharply between this abnormality and all the conditions to which the terms *mental disease* and *mental defect* are applied. Few psychiatrists could doubt that crimes committed by a psychopath are the product of his aberration. The psychiatrist-witness's opinion would, inevitably it seems, depend on whether or not he classified this aberration as mental. This decision, it seems to me, would in turn substantially depend on whether or not this term is limited in its meaning to an assumed disparate faculty of cognition. Thus, as far as the psychopath is concerned, it would appear that the psychiatrist in court is faced with essentially the same decision, whether he testifies under the M'Naghten Rules or the Durham Rule. Either may be interpreted narrowly and confined to mere cognition or more broadly, as Jerome Hall suggests that the M'Naghten Rules be interpreted. Decisions based on the M'Naghten Rules depend on the interpretation of the word *know,* and with the Durham Rules on the interpretation of *mental disease or defect.* It is hardly conceivable to me that a psychiatrist would arrive at anything but the same conclusion by either test in his opinion about a psychopath.

Hopes at first were high that the Durham Rule would free psychiatrists from archaic legal restrictions and allow them to bring truly scientific knowledge to bear in court on questions of competency and responsibility. With the passage of time this enthusiasm has waned. The scientific knowledge to deal so well with these problems claimed so confidently by some psychiatrists seems not to have proved effective. In a 1974 issue of *The American Journal of Psychiatry* Judge Bazelon himself expresses, in an article with the interesting title "The Perils of Wizardry," what I believe is a disappointment similar to my own in the prospects of his widely acclaimed rule enabling psychiatrists to bring a new and scientific solution to the old problems. I fear that many psychiatrists overestimated what we have to offer. Let us quote:

> The experiment undertaken by my court in its 1954 decision in *Durham v. United States** is a real lesson in regard to the role of psychiatrists in insanity defense. That case involved the formulation of a new test of criminal responsibility. It held that an accused person is not criminally responsible if his unlawful act was the product of a mental disease or defect. The purpose of this decision was to grant the psychiatrist his 100-year-old request to be allowed to tell what he knows and, just as importantly, what he does not know about the phenomenon of human behavior rather than face demands for conclusion resting on ethical, moral, and legal considerations beyond his expertise.
>
> The purpose of the Durham decision was not fulfilled. Psychiatrists continued adamantly to cling to conclusory labels without explaining the origin, development, or manifestations of a disease in terms meaningful to a jury. The jury was confronted with a welter of confusing terms such as personality defect, sociopathy, and personality disorder. What became more and more apparent was that these terms did not rest on disciplined investigation based on facts and reasoning, as was required for the fulfillment of the Durham decision. I regret to say that they were largely used to cover up a lack of relevance, knowledge, and certainty in the practice of institutional psychiatry.
>
> I am frequently asked, "Why don't you talk about what's wrong with courts and lawyers?" I have written countless opinions and articles and have delivered several "Bazelon jeremiads" about the problems in the practice of law before lawyers and judges. But here I am concerned with the culpability of psychiatrists in the failure to achieve the purpose of the Durham decision.
>
> First of all, psychiatrists did not acknowledge the limits of their expertise. Secondly, they failed to confront honestly and openly the conflicts that impaired their competence even when their expertise was sufficient and relevant. . . . I warned behavioral scientists not to fall into the same trap as described in *The Wizard of Oz.* In that Frank Baum classic, Dorothy and her companions followed the yellow brick road to find the Wizard of Oz, who lived in the Emerald City. They believed the wizard could give the tinman a heart, the lion some courage, and the scarecrow a brain. When they finally arrived, they discovered that the wizard was without expertise, a fake. In 1970 I commended the behavioral scientists for caring about people in distress but warned them of the dangers in playing wizard to the problems of society for which they had no expertise. The issue was not whether the behavioral scientists were good, but what they were good at.

Despite some very important achievements in the last half-century, psychiatry does not today, in my opinion, possess newly discovered and well-established facts which afford a scientific answer to the ultimate questions that for so long have arisen and caused confusion in determining responsibility. Whatever rule is followed when efforts to control the antisocial and self-destructive activities of a psychopath are being made, the verdict will probably depend on whether the estimation of his legal competency is based on outer appearance and the peripheral mechanisms of function or on his amply demonstrated incapacity to lead an adequate or socially acceptable life because of the serious inner pathology that only emerges in his actual performance as a member of the social group.

---

*Durham v. United States, 214 F 2nd 862, D.C. Cir., 1954.

Many believe that the New Penal Code, which seems to have supplanted the Durham Rule in most jurisdictions, is a better rule than that of Durham or of M'Naghten. Even with this New Penal Code the interpretation of the terms *mental disease* and *mental defect* is likely to vary among psychiatrists and continue to cause difficulty in judgments about the psychopath.

TREATMENT OR CONTROL

Several decades ago, while preparing the first edition of this book, I was profoundly impressed by two difficulties that stood in the way of dealing effectively with the psychopath. One of these was his apparent immunity, or relative immunity, from control by law. The other was his lack of response to psychiatric treatment of any kind.

Today both of these difficulties exist and, it seems to me, with little alteration. Let us consider first the question of legal control, of the problems that arise when steps are taken to protect the community and the patient from his misconduct. It is only on very unusual occasions that a psychopath can be committed as legally incompetent, and even when this occurs it is not likely that he can be kept long under medical supervision. Let us consider an example:

After years of expensive, fruitless, heartbreaking, and faithful efforts to keep him out of disaster, the family of a young (and in most respects typical) psychopath succeeded in having him pronounced incompetent and sent to a state hospital. Unlike most psychopaths, this patient had shown strong indications that he might murder one or more members of his family. This and the prodigious obviousness of his disability and his danger to the community strangely enough overbalanced the customary psychiatric concepts in this isolated instance, and he was admitted to be socially incompetent. There is no denying that this procedure was incorrect according to clearly defined medical rules.

After a few weeks of study he was found not to show any of the technical signs of irrationality (none of which had ever been suspected), diagnosed as a "psychopathic personality," and sent home as "sane and competent."

One of the psychiatrists at the hospital who had participated in this procedure explained his attitude as follows. He believed that this particular patient, no matter what his proper diagnosis might be, was more seriously disabled than a great many of the patients who would spend the rest of their lives in the institution. He also believed that the discharged patient was more dangerous to the community and more difficult to care for at home than, perhaps, half of those in the state hospital. The members of the staff, he felt, were motivated in their action by several impulses, directed by several judgments.

First of all, it was not in accordance with official psychiatric concepts to call such a patient psychotic. It was also against the rules of the hospital to keep a nonpsychotic patient against his will. There was, in addition, in some members of the staff a tendency to resist efforts to slip in or palm off on the hospital these psychopaths who are considered technically not eligible for care. There was opinion expressed about how crowded the place was already and about the dangers of being overrun with psychopaths if an exception was made and this one kept. Some felt it would not serve the cause of justice if this man were admitted by the staff of the state hospital to have mental disability, because this appraisal might be utilized in the future dozens or hundreds of times to help him evade legal penalties for the antisocial acts these doctors, like everyone else, realized he would continue.

There are not a few among those in charge of our state hospitals who feel that, with conditions as they stand, it would be more fitting for persons of this sort, when segregation or supervision of some type is urgently necessary, to be placed not in our present psychiatric institutions but in reformatories or prisons. There are others who feel that psychiatric care and many of the services and facilities now available in our mental hospitals could and should be made available to severely maladjusted psychopaths.

As our evidence has shown, I hope, the psychopath notoriously avoids the petty and temporary restraints that might be legally imposed. Those imprisoned for serious crimes return at length no less prone to continue these crimes. Even when under life sentence, the psychopath tends more readily than others to obtain parole and become again a social menace. Not only can he (perhaps involuntarily) mimic sanity in superlative fashion but also moral rebirth, salvation, and absolute reform, or perhaps transformation into a supercitizen. Among many examples one patient stands out:

This brilliant and charming young man, when in his early twenties, murdered another without provocation. Despite a typical record of psychopathic behavior, he so impressed the authorities that parole was granted after a few years. That which, if properly understood, would have warned the parole board against the extreme danger of releasing this man was interpreted as a mitigating factor, as grounds for giving him another chance. It was argued that emotional handicaps and variations from the normal personality patterns had played a part in his unfortunate deed. This, they reasoned, made him less culpable and more deserving of leniency. Like nearly all of his kind, he now showed no superficial signs of nervous or mental disorder (as this is generally understood) but indications of great promise. He inspired trust and confidence and gave a convincingly (theoretical) demonstration of reform, self-control, trustworthiness, sound ethics, and high ideals. Shortly after his release he again committed murder, this time of a woman and again with no discernible motivation of any consequence.

In institutions where psychiatric treatment is given, the psychopath, I believe, is much more likely than others who have committed serious crimes to convince his psychotherapist that treatment has been effective, that it has brought true insight and profound changes that now make him no longer a danger to society. This may lead to his being presented as one who richly deserves parole or pardon. The daily papers report many cases of armed robbery, rape, and murder resulting from such confidently optimistic estimates of therapeutic success. It is my impression that many of the attitudes underlying permissiveness have also contributed to this. And I think a gross overestimation of the influence of psychiatric treatment on criminals, whether or not they are psychopaths, has played a major role in these tragic events.

Although some protection to society is afforded by dealing out sentences of varying length to psychopathic offenders on the assumption that they are normal and to be punished in accordance with the degree of blame their crimes are judged to deserve, such protection is not reliable. The assumption that they will thereby learn their lesson and become safe inhabitants of the community is an assumption at sharp variance with simple facts. Poorly adapted as our present methods are to prevent the repetition of crime, we find them rapidly approaching travesty and farce when we look for what security they offer against initial crimes of tragic magnitude. An example will make the point clear:

In big letters on the front page of newspapers all over the United States the "Bestial Sex Slaying" of an 11-year-old girl by a boy 17 years of age is proclaimed. Details of torture and dismemberment follow. The horrible impact of impulses perverted from the aims of Eros and fused with those of hate and brutality arouses disgust and vengefulness in millions upon millions. Additional articles point out that the murderer, now remarkably callous and undisturbed by his act, had, over a period of many years, shown gross maladjustment and indifference to social values, to ordinary aims, and to the rights of others. He had on several occasions been placed in a reform school and kept for various periods determined in accordance with the legally estimated seriousness of his antisocial acts and with the amount of punishment these were officially regarded as deserving.

Had this boy expressed a few delusions or reported even once that he heard an imaginary voice (like many people who are quite harmless), he could have been hospitalized as long as hospitalization was regarded by experts as advisable. Lacking these and the other accepted technicalities that are presumed to determine competency and sanity, he could not be held in any institution beyond the arbitrary term to which he had been sentenced. His conduct had so strongly indicated that he could not without danger to others be left unrestricted in the community that his parents protested to the authorities against his release from custody. They urged that he be kept in the institution and gave adequate reasons for their plea. The authorities had no means of heeding this warning—no legal grounds for an alternative to the technically correct procedure of dismissing the patient. The regrettable results reflected in newspaper headlines soon followed.

If such patients could be evaluated in terms of their behavior and committed, like other psychiatric patients, not to limited terms of confinement but for indeterminate periods, the community would obviously obtain far better protection. The patient could then be held until his condition, as appraised by experts, indicated that he could be released with safety to himself and others. Let us grant that even the best of experts is not likely to prove infallible in such an appraisal. Even the wisest and most experienced psychiatrist may be misled by the appearance of profound change in the true psychopath who will later show himself to be as dangerous as before.

Some practical help might be afforded in controlling the psychopath by the general application of laws designed to increase progressively the penalty and term of confinement for those who repeatedly demonstrate by antisocial acts that they have not learned through experience and that they are still dangerous to the community. Some of these principles are reported to be embodied in the Greenstein Act (Pennsylvania), which was so designed that the psychopath, as well as other disordered but generally neglected persons who commit legal offenses, can be dealt with by safer as well as more rational and humane methods. Perhaps there is a need for similar changes throughout the nation.

Persons who show evidence of schizophrenic illness or of almost any other psychiatric disorder (excepting that of the psychopath) can, through existing facilities, usually be reached and sensibly dealt with before any legal offense against others is committed. In addition to the valuable contribution offered through the Greenstein Act and similar legal measures, I believe there is also need for some means of committing psychopaths on the primary basis of their demonstrated disability and need. Perhaps all or nearly all of these patients will in the demonstration of their disorder eventually commit antisocial acts by which they might, through facilities such as those afforded by the Greenstein Act, be reached. It is nevertheless true that very serious disability or gross maladjustment may, as in other psychiatric patients, be obvious despite the relatively trivial nature of the offenses which usually bring the psychopath into court.

Relatives, long confused about the nature of this problem, often sacrifice themselves grievously to keep the patient out of court, to prevent his going to jail, to spare his reputation (and perhaps their own, also), and to give him every advantage in the vain hope he will soon change his ways. Effective and rational handling of many patients might be expedited if relatives could initiate legal action for commitment through the same courts and agencies set up to deal with other psychiatric patients, and in the same way, without having to wait for still another crime and another conviction of the patient for legal offense as an obligatory condition, a prerequisite, to such steps. If the same procedure followed in dealing with other serious psychiatric conditions could be utilized without what many relatives would regard as "branding him a criminal," many advantages in addition to those afforded by the Greenstein Act might result.

Would this jeopardize the liberties of the citizen? Would it enable unscrupulous relatives, psychiatrists, and jurists to deprive people of the right to make their own decisions concerning treatment and hospitalization without sufficient cause? Would just about anyone whose conduct did not suit his neighbors (or his spouse, or his old maid aunt) find himself in danger of being declared psychiatrically ill and put away indefinitely?

These are, indeed, important considerations. As pointed out so well by Hall and Cumming, among others, a basic safeguard of freedom provided by law exists in the right to trial by a lay jury. The law, with good reason it seems, is firmly resistant to encroachments upon the jury's responsibility. It looks with distrust upon movements that may tend to place into the hands of an expert or specialist final decisions that might deprive a citizen of his liberty or arbitrarily determine the length of his incarceration whether it be in prison or in a psychiatric institution. This is very probably one of the reasons why it has been so difficult to devise legal measures to bring psychopaths under better control. Urgent as the need is for better control of these patients, we must recognize the grave danger that the law must take pains to avoid and try to work patiently with our legal colleagues toward some better solution of a very subtle and complex problem.

Even the laws that are now in force anywhere in our nation, if applied regularly and promptly, might enable us to gain far better control over the psychopath and to curtail more effectively his trespasses against society and his persistence in a self-damaging career. If his parents, other relatives, and friends would no longer keep on coming to his aid and paying him out of his deliberately self-made troubles but instead would let him face the ordinary consequences and suffer the ordinary penalties, something important would be accomplished. Though one could not count on the true or typical psychopath learning adequately by his experience and achieving a cure, even he would, at least, be better controlled and not left free to continue without substantial interruptions his persistently destructive career. If the nature of his abnormality were better understood, it would not then be used as grounds for mitigating sentences or for granting early parole, but might warn even the most permissive authorities against the dangers involved.

Over a period of many years I have remained discouraged about the effect of treatment on the psychopath. Having regularly failed in my own efforts to help such patients alter their fundamental pattern of inadequacy and antisocial activity, I hoped for a while that treatment by others would be more successful. I have had the opportunity to see patients of this sort who were treated by psychoanalysis, by psychoanalytically oriented psychotherapy, by group and by milieu therapy, and by many other variations of dynamic method. I have seen some patients who were treated for years. I have also known cases in which not only the patient but various members of his family were given prolonged psychotherapy. None of these measures impressed me as achieving successful results. The psychopaths continued to behave as they had behaved in the past.

Among such patients I recall a young millionaire whose family was able to place him in an institution where every possible resource of psychiatry was available, including psychoanalysis by one of the best-qualified and best-known men in our country. Everyone was eager that the patient stay as long as advisable and that every means of therapy be utilized, however expensive, time-consuming, or protracted. Despite these apparent advantages, nothing of importance was accomplished. At first the patient expressed great determination to obtain help and to get well. Evidence of such a desire steadily diminished, and eventually it became apparent that he had no real interest in the goals he had set for himself and of which he spoke for a while so eloquently. After a long and tremendously expensive period of hospitalization he left, apparently without regret, discontinued all pretense of seeking treatment, and returned to his familiar ways of behavior.

I am impressed also with the recollection of another patient, a woman in her thirties, for whom almost limitless wealth and strong family cooperation provided every therapeutic advantage. I referred her, long ago, to a colleague outstanding as a leader not only in psychiatry but also in psychoanalysis. Everything conceivable that might be needed in the most ambitious plans for treatment was available. After a careful study of the patient, this able and honest physician advised against any prolonged therapeutic endeavor, since he felt that the chances for substantial benefit were not sufficient to justify the attempt.

The family of still another patient had been told that a distant and renowned psychiatric institution might find some way to alter a persistent pattern of antisocial and self-defeating behavior in their 34-year-old son. I believed that he was a psychopath and did not feel hopeful. Psychiatrists at the hospital, after studying him at length and in depth, concluded that his maladjustment was probably a result of complex influences in early childhood, that it could be accounted for in dynamic terms.

They concluded also that long-term psychoanalytic treatment offered a fairly good chance of success, especially if it could be undertaken with the patient living outside an institution in a large city where he could find employment but where his financial affairs could be strictly controlled, not by his analyst, but by another medical person. There were several other features to a complicated situation that was set up in the hope of maintaining control of the patient and keeping him under analytic treatment, for years if necessary. This plan called for the expenditure of funds available to few families. Despite all these efforts, no notable changes occurred in behavior or in outlook.

These failures are typical of many others I have observed over the years.

For a while I had hoped that long-term treatment might be more effective if the patient could be induced voluntarily or constrained by commitment procedures to remain with the therapist for enough time to give his methods a thorough and adequate trial. I am no longer hopeful that any methods available today would be successful with typical psychopaths. I have now, after more than three decades, had the opportunity to observe a considerable number of patients who, through commitment or the threat of losing their probation status or by other means, were kept under treatment not only for many months but for years. The therapeutic failure in all such patients observed leads me to feel that we do not at present have any kind of psychotherapy that can be relied upon to change the psychopath fundamentally.

Nor do I believe that any other method of psychiatric treatment has shown promise of solving the problem. Physical methods of therapy, including electric shock, have been attempted. Prefrontal lobotomy, topectomy, and transorbital lobotomy have been used in a few patients with severe disorder. Some encouragement was expressed by a few observers about the effects of these measures, but apparently they have not proved to be a real solution of the problem.

I wish I could be optimistic about the accomplishments of psychiatry in treating and curing the psychopath. Some spokesmen for mental hygiene movements and for greater extensions of psychiatric influence tend to credit us, I fear, with far more power and effectiveness than we have really attained. Hundreds of millions of dollars are being spent to promote mental hygiene and psychiatric care. Many seem to believe that if we only had enough psychiatrists, or enough dynamically oriented psychiatrists, all problems of mental health, crime, and delinquency could be solved. This claim is seldom made directly in such absolute terms, but the implication plainly underlies many eloquent appeals for more and more funds from the state and federal governments. Some of the more zealous spokesmen even seem to feel that psychiatry has recently made such profound discoveries and devised such effective methods of eliminating not only illness and crime but also prejudice, superstition, and human error that we can and should settle racial and international problems and even revise the basic standards of morality.

Despite these enthusiastic and at times embarrassing claims in our behalf, our actual achievements should encourage profound modesty. So far no statistical evidence has been obtained to support a belief that our most ambitious, protracted, dynamic, and reputedly scientific methods of psychotherapy have proved more effective even in the psychoneuroses than the warmhearted but unpretentious methods used over the years by kind and wise physicians in the general practice of medicine. There is, we must conclude, no evidence to demonstrate or to indicate that psychiatry has yet found a therapy that cures or profoundly changes the psychopath.

I find that I am still in thorough agreement with these opinions expressed in 1969 by Lothar Goldschmidt:

> Psychiatrists have participated in legal proceedings (actively on behalf of clients and passively on behalf of the court) on the assumption that treatment is superior to the penal system. What treatment consists of has rarely, if ever, been described. Is it psychoanalysis on the traditional couch five times a week? drug therapy? electroconvulsive therapy? Whatever the case, psychiatry has been subjected to much abuse and has become an object of legal manipulation.
>
> A more cautious approach is long overdue. Psychiatry cannot pretend omnipotence. Members of the profession are fully aware that at the present state of our knowledge, treatment (in any form) is not a feasible means of either cure, rehabilitation, or even improvement of a large number (if not the vast majority) of sociopaths, many other character disorders, and many patients with a chronic psychosis with or

> without criminal tendencies. Often, custodial care remains the only alternative to prevent a patient from acting in a way dangerous to himself or to society.
>
> Since psychiatrists are not keepers of public morality, they cannot be designated a role of either jailers or judges. Their function is frequently limited to that of consultant.
>
> There are many who believe that the relations between law and psychiatry have become increasingly unscientific and unmedical, at times with disastrous impact on our society. The time-honored system of reward and punishment, in spite of its known limitations, cannot be arbitrarily replaced with vague though beautiful sounding statements about "treatment" as long as there is no sound medical or scientific evidence showing better results with the newer concept. Utopia has not yet been reached.
>
> There seems to be an urgent need for the American Psychiatric Association and for state and local representatives of psychiatry to take a firmer stand to dissociate psychiatry from this abuse of psychiatry. Misinterpretations and distortions of mental hygiene principles should be exposed and prevented. No legislative decisions about treatment should be encouraged unless they are based on documented and scientifically proven results. Should the profession neglect to do so, it will be argued that psychiatry passively condones the release of dangerous criminals into society.

If we have not yet devised adequate legal methods of controlling these destructive people and do not at present have a therapy to offer that has been demonstrated as effective, what, then, can we do?

Let us try to promote a general understanding of the serious nature of the psychopath's abnormality and of its strong tendency to persist despite all efforts toward correction or treatment. Let us cooperate with our legal colleagues in efforts to devise a more effective means of keeping psychopaths under adequate control. The degree of control should, insofar as possible, be regulated by the need, that is, by the degree of disability that the patient continues to demonstrate. Let us recognize psychopaths as differing greatly from the psychotic and psychoneurotic patients for whom our present hospitals and clinics have been designed and our current methods of treatment or control established.

It is urgent and obvious that we devise some more effective means of restraining these people in their persistently destructive careers. Henderson says, "It is amazing and almost paralyzing to realize the extent to which some of these cases may go before any action can be taken legally or medically to exert adequate control."

If a proper general understanding could be reached that such people have a serious psychiatric abnormality and are not likely under prevailing conditions to become better, and if this fact could be disseminated, their families might be able to reconcile themselves better to a major problem and seek more realistic ways of dealing with it.

By systems of parole, probation, and supervision designed specifically for patients of this type and devised to meet the sort of problems they present, it is probable that reasonably effective guidance could be maintained after hospitalization and, when necessary, restraint be applied pertinently and effectively. We must remember that under present conditions nearly all psychopaths are entirely on their own in the community and that the few with whom society gets any opportunity at all to deal fall under one or the other of two methods. Neither of these methods was evolved with any cognizance of the psychopath, but each for quite a different sort of problem.

On one hand, the existing psychiatric hospitals, parole arrangements, and mental hygiene clinics are set up to meet situations that arise in dealing with (legally) psychotic and psychoneurotic patients. With patients in these two groups, our methods, imperfect as they may be, are relevant to the situation.

On the other hand, we have the penal system with its preordained terms of restraint graded arbitrarily in what, perhaps during the last century, was agreed upon as a proper dose of punishment for this or that misdeed. Such punishments were presumably considered as having corrective (and perhaps prophylactic) effect on antisocial tendencies. Whatever efficacy this method may show for dealing with citizens in general, it has demonstrated year after year its lack of success in controlling the grave problems that continually multiply about the psychopath. Largely inaccessible to ordinary social agencies, this type of patient capers, reels, or plunges along his disastrous course.

Without medicolegal apparatus to reach him, without social instrumentalities designed to cope with his problems or those he makes for others, and with no general recognition even of his presence, we find ourselves emulating the ostrich and its proverbial tactics of evasion. When the situation becomes too alarming or too monumentally fantastic for us to continue these tactics and when it cannot any longer be blandly ignored, we find ourselves fumbling between the only two methods available, neither of which, we find immediately, is applicable to the real issues we confront. Psychiatrists finding it impossible under existing circumstances to continue any long-range plans are hardly to be blamed if they tend to regard these people as birds of passage through their institutions, that is, as patients in name only who seek temporary refuge there from other legal restraints, create much confusion and disorder, then leave when it suits their whim or convenience, to continue in their former maladjustment.

Turning now to penal facilities, now to psychiatric institutions, relatives, friends, doctors, lawyers, or the community at large, all find themselves at a loss, somewhat as if they were trying to measure areas in kilowatts or color in inches. Since the fire extinguisher did not particularly help the child's fever, which has become alarming, we gravely decide to apply a plaster cast. There are no really appropriate remedies available.

Without restraint and without any effective treatment, the psychopath continues, progressively accumulating in his social wake woe, confusion, despair, farce, and disaster, beyond any measure of these things I can convey. Exonerations in courts on the grounds of insanity are followed by discharges from hospitals because no nervous or mental disease is found. Sometimes when incompetency cannot be medically or legally established, common sense attempts a compromise and, perhaps unofficially, shows recognition of an aberration through leniency of judgment or an assumption of mitigating circumstances with the practical result of reducing terms of confinement in proportion to the degree of dangerous abnormality evident. This all too frequently amounts to diminishing whatever protection is offered the public directly in proportion to the degree of menace indicated by the disorder.

When given long-term psychotherapy in either prison or hospital, the psychopath has more ability than any other type of patient to stimulate the changes of attitude that may convince even the most conscientious therapist that he has effected a cure and that his patient is now ready for release and no longer a source of danger to others. Often the psychopath is clever and convincing enough to make the therapist feel also that the cure was specifically effected through cherished items of the therapist's creed of psychiatric theory.

We must remind ourselves once more of the gross and tragic misunderstanding that determined legal and medical attitudes toward patients suffering from ordinary types of psychosis in past centuries before we can realize the monstrous inefficacy of our present methods of dealing with psychopaths. Pinel, who is so justly venerated by the world today, did not discover any cure or any satisfactory treatment for the psychotic patients whom he liberated from the chains and dungeons into which they were thrown by a society that apparently could not realize they were ill but assumed them merely evil and vicious. Indeed, a hundred or more years passed before any regular therapy even remotely effective became available for patients in most psychiatric institutions. Even if another hundred years should pass before we discover a truly effective method of treatment for psychopaths, or for other offenders who commit brutal crimes, we must make a beginning by reappraising them (as Pinel reappraised psychotic patients) and revising methods for their care. Such a step in understanding these other kinds of disordered people must be made before we can hope to progress far toward the solution of their problem. Let us without delay recognize them for what they are and begin more realistically to plan medical and social facilities through which they can be intelligently treated or, at the very least, through which they will not be mistreated or left without control to endanger the community.

In properly set-up hospital or detention units and through adequate outpatient control, efforts might be made to utilize the excellent abilities of these patients and to provide whatever degree of supervision is found necessary to keep them occupied and out of trouble. This supervision would, as with other socially disabled patients, vary widely with various persons.

Such institutions and other community facilities and the regular practice of committing suitable patients to their supervision would soon bring new viewpoints to countless parents who, in shame and grief, blush over what they take to be the deeds of wickedness and depravity of their children and who wreck their own lives and fortunes seeking to protect, to rehabilitate, and to reform them. Women might learn in time not to sacrifice so readily their fortunes, their life plans, their grief, and their energy in indefatigable and fruitless struggles to support and nurse and pamper maturity into husbands and lovers whose profound deficit makes such maturity (by such means) impossible.

In speaking of hospital units and other facilities for parole and supervision, I do not propose that vast and expensive institutions be built in addition to those designed for patients with the traditional problems of psychiatry. I suggest rather that psychopaths be recognized clearly as a separate group and dealt with by rules and methods specifically adapted to cope with their problems and their behavior. Units for their care and control might be maintained in our existing institutions. It seems possible that such a step might lead to substantial economies instead of an additional burden of expense to the public. Vast sums of money are now being disbursed daily by the state to bring psychopaths repeatedly through due processes of the law, and all to no avail. At great cost relatives hopefully send them for treatment in expensive hospitals, which they leave on personal whim or prankish impulse. Enormous sums are wasted in futile efforts to reestablish them in business and to compensate victims for their continual malfeasances and follies. It is doubtful that the cost of even a most elaborate setup of detention units and outpatient facilities, which I do not propose, would equal the financial loss they now inflict, in addition to their socially damaging effects upon the community.

Even if no really adequate therapeutic measure should become available in the foreseeable future, it seems reasonable to hope that with facilities specifically designed for the direction and control of the psychopathic group these people might be maintained at a better level of adjustment despite the continued need of support and restriction. Even if we cannot count on curing their disorder, the goal of bringing about improvement in control and adjustment is not to be despised.

Impressed by points of similarity between the psychopath and the spoiled child, some psychiatrists have maintained that promising therapeutic possibilities might lie in establishing a really effective control whereby the patient would regularly, promptly, and persistently experience the logical results of (1) socially acceptable conduct and (2) irresponsible and destructive conduct. Mangun long ago reported encouraging results from such a program, and Woolley also expressed hopefulness about this approach to the problem.

Subsequently Thorne emphasized similar measures. Hare in 1970 gives this interesting summary of Thorne's approach:

> On the assumption that the psychopath's behavior reflects a maladaptive *life style* that is maintained by reinforcement from family, friends, and associates, Thorne has outlined what he considers to be the requirements of successful therapy with psychopaths. These are summarized as follows.
>
> 1. The therapist must have complete control over the financial resources of the psychopath, usually by being made trustee of his accounts.
> 2. Relatives and other interested parties must agree not to bail the psychopath out of his difficulties; he must be required to face the consequences of his own behavior.
> 3. The therapist must be very persistent in gradually getting the psychopath to exert some limits and controls over his own behavior.
> 4. The therapist should not protect the psychopath from the legal and social consequences of his actions.
> 5. The therapist should make it clear to the psychopath that he understands him thoroughly, knows what to expect, and will be convinced of his good intentions only through actions and not words.
> 6. The psychopath must be shown repeatedly that his behavior is self-defeating.
> 7. The therapist should search for a leverage point to stimulate more socially acceptable behavior. As a last resort, the therapist may have to use money, which he controls, as an incentive.
>
> In addition to these points, Thorne suggested that a great deal of patience, time, and money are required; in several cases, an investment of $15,000 per year for as long as 10 years was needed to effect a satisfactory outcome. It is not surprising therefore that no controlled research using Thorne's methods has been carried out; the investment in time and money is far too great and, many would say, not worth the effort.

Is it not our responsibility as psychiatrists to agree, despite all our notable differences about etiology, terminology, and technicalities of method, that such patients as those discussed here need medical reappraisal?

My proposals and opinions may be in many respects incomplete, superficial, or erroneous. It is too much to ask that the viewpoint of any one observer in so complex and confusing a matter be generally accepted as final. The whole field of psychiatry, by its very nature, abounds in questions still unanswered and about which diverse opinions naturally exist and arguments inevitably arise. If we cannot agree that the psychopath has anything like a psychosis or even a mental disorder, can we not all agree that some means is urgently needed of dealing more realistically with whatever it is that may be the matter with him? If some practical means of controlling the psychopath can be devised, perhaps eventually we may find his disorder to be not altogether beyond our practice.